The Historical Reliability
of the Gospels

The Historical Reliability of the Gospels

Craig L. Blomberg

INTER-VARSITY PRESS

Inter-Varsity Press
38 De Montfort Street, Leicester LE1 7GP, England
P.O. Box 1400, Downers Grove, Illinois 60515, U.S.A.

InterVarsity Press, U.S.A., is the book-publishing division of InterVarsity Christian Fellowship, a student movement active on campus at hundreds of universities, colleges and schools of nursing. For information about local and regional activities, write Public Relations Dept., InterVarsity Christian Fellowship, 6400 Schroeder Rd., P.O. Box 7895, Madison, WI 53707-7895.

Inter-Varsity Press, England, is the publishing division of the Universities and Colleges Christian Fellowship (formerly the Inter-Varsity Fellowship), a student movement linking Christian Unions in universities and colleges throughout the United Kingdom and the Republic of Ireland, and a member movement of the International Fellowship of Evangelical Students. For information about local and national activities write to UCCF, 38 De Montfort Street, Leicester LE1 7GP.

Distributed in Canada through InterVarsity Press, 860 Denison St., Unit 3, Markham, Ontario L3R 4H1, Canada.

All Scripture, unless otherwise stated, are from the Bible are from the Holy Bible, New International Version. Copyrighted © 1973, 1978, International Bible Society. Used by permission of Zondervan Bible Publishers.

Printed in the United States of America

Library of Congress Cataloging in Publication Data

Blomberg, Craig
The historical reliability of the gospels

Includes bibliographical references
1. Bible. N.T. Gospels—Evidences, authority, etc.
2. Bible. N.T. Gospels—Criticism, interpretation, etc.
3. Jesus Christ—Historicity
I. Title
BS2555.2.B585   1987   226'.066   87-2946

ISBN 0-87784-992-7

British Library Cataloguing in Publication Data

Blomberg, Craig
The Historical Reliability of the Gospels
1. Bible. N.T. Gospels—Evidences, authority, etc.
I. Title
226'.01   BS2555.5

ISBN 0-85110-774-5

17	16	15	14	13	12	11	10	9	8	7	6	5	4	3	2
99	98	97	96	95	94	93	92	91	90	89	88				

Table of contents

Foreword

There is, I imagine, no body of literature in the world that has been exposed to the stringent analytical study that the four gospels have sustained for the past 200 years. This is not something to be regretted: it is something to be accepted with satisfaction. Scholars today who treat the gospels as credible historical documents do so in the full light of this analytical study, not by closing their minds to it.

A problem arises in this television age from the exposure of the public to a bewildering variety of opinions about the gospels in particular and the New Testament in general, including both the current scholarly consensus (if such a thing exists today) and every sort of way-out interpretation of the data, with little or no guidance being given about the criteria by which competing views are to be assessed and a reasonable conclusion reached. In this situation a work like Dr Blomberg's is really helpful.

Dr Blomberg is a member of a team of scholars which has been engaged for a number of years on a 'Gospels Project', designed to explore the main critical issues in the study of the gospels in our time. The findings of this team have been published in a series of six volumes entitled *Gospel Perspectives*. But these volumes are written by scholars for scholars. What Dr Blomberg has done is to digest their contents and present them, in the light of his own study and understanding of the subject, to a wider public. His book calls for careful thought on the part of its readers, but does not require technical knowledge. Here is an answer to the questions: Is it possible for intelligent people nowadays to approach the gospels as trustworthy accounts of the life and teaching of Jesus? Must they be read with scepticism until their detailed information is confirmed? Or can we, in the light of present knowledge, take it for granted that their authors intend to record things that really happened? The answer which Dr Blomberg gives to these questions is positive and satisfying, because he gives ample evidence of accurate and up-to-date acquaintance with the subject of his work and with the relevant literature. I am very happy to commend it warmly to readers who are interested in this question, and especially to theological students.

F. F. Bruce

Preface

From 1980 to 1986 a series of six volumes entitled *Gospel Perspectives* has appeared from Sheffield University's JSOT Press. All six address the question of the historical reliability of the gospels at a technical, scholarly level. Volumes 1 and 2 gather together a relatively unstructured collection of essays, while volumes 3, 5 and 6 present articles relating to more specifically delineated themes; setting the gospels against the background of the various types of Jewish history-writing of the day; discussing the evidence for the traditions about Jesus from sources other than Matthew, Mark, Luke and John; and grappling with the unique problems surrounding the miracles of Jesus. Volume 4 is the only one which is not a multi-author work. Here Dr David Wenham has provided an intensive study of Mark 13, Matthew 24–25, and related passages containing Jesus' teaching on the events associated with the end times.[1] The entire series is the product of the Gospels Research Project of Tyndale House, Cambridge, a residential library and centre for biblical research under the auspices of the Universities and Colleges Christian Fellowship. The series thus gathers together the fruit of the labour of an international team of scholars over a period of nearly ten years.

The present book was born out of the desire to disseminate the findings of *Gospel Perspectives* to a wider audience at a somewhat more popular level. It is geared especially for the new theological student and the educated lay person, but its wide-ranging survey may be of value to scholars and pastors as well. It is also an independent work in its own right. Although *Gospel Perspectives* gave it its impetus, it by no means gives each volume or article equal attention; a few articles are virtually relegated to the footnotes. At the same time

---

[1]Full bibliographic information for the six volumes is as follows: vol. 1– *Gospel Perspectives: Studies of History and Tradition in the Four Gospels*, ed. R. T. France and David Wenham (Sheffield: JSOT Press, 1980); vol. 2– *Gospel Perspectives: Studies of History and Tradition in the Four Gospels*, ed. R. T. France and David Wenham (Sheffield: JSOT Press, 1981); vol. 3– *Gospel Perspectives: Studies in Midrash and Historiography*, ed. R. T. France and David Wenham (Sheffield: JSOT Press, 1983); vol. 4– David Wenham, *The Rediscovery of Jesus' Eschatological Discourse* (Sheffield: JSOT Press, 1984); vol. 5– *Gospel Perspectives: The Jesus Tradition outside the Gospels*, ed. David Wenham (Sheffield: JSOT Press, 1985); vol. 6– *Gospel Perspectives: The Miracles of Jesus*, ed. David Wenham and Craig L. Blomberg (Sheffield: JSOT Press, 1986). Hereafter, in the footnotes, *Gospel Perspectives* will be abbreviated *GP*.

it draws freely from a breadth of recent research, discussing numerous topics which the Gospels Research Project did not. But one objective of this book remains the same as for the six-volume series: 'to provide answers to the questions of historicity which will stand up to serious academic scrutiny and will provide some help for those who are perplexed by scholarly disagreement'.[2] Thus the discussion often bypasses a detailed presentation of consensus views which call into question gospel historicity, since they are well defended elsewhere, but focuses instead on lesser known studies which challenge the consensus.

A few words about format are in order. Where I rely heavily on an article in the *Gospel Perspectives* series, further documentation of the topic at hand is invariably available in that article. Translations from ancient sources, including Scripture, and from modern foreign-language works are my own unless otherwise indicated. To avoid repetition, however, such notices appear only once per section for a given translation, usually in the footnotes. The first reference to a modern source in each chapter supplies full bibliographic information; subsequent references use a shortened form.

I am deeply grateful to the Tyndale House Council for its invitation to me to participate in this project and for their generous research fellowship which enabled my wife and me to live for a year in Tyndale House during the writing of the book and to make regular use of its excellent library facilities. I owe special thanks to the warden, Dr Murray J. Harris, and the librarian, Mr David G. Deboys, for their constant helpfulness. They have also read and commented on the entire manuscript, as have Professor I. Howard Marshall, Dr Donald Guthrie, Rev. J. W. Wenham, Mr Stanley E. Porter, Mr Philip E. Satterthwaite and Mr Paul F. Mueller. To each I am deeply grateful. Further thanks go to my father, Mr John W. Blomberg, and to Dr Ruth B. Edwards and Mr David L. Williams, who each read one or more chapters of earlier drafts. Above all, my wife, Fran, who also has reviewed all that I have written and helped in innumerable ways with my research, deserves my wholehearted appreciation for her love, support and flexibility throughout our year in Cambridge. It is to her that I dedicate this book.

Craig L. Blomberg

---

[2]R. T. France and David Wenham, 'Preface', *GP*,1, p.6.

Abbreviations

BeO	*Bibbia e oriente*
Bib	*Biblica*
BJRL	*Bulletin of the John Rylands University Library of Manchester*
BSac	*Bibliotheca Sacra*
BTB	*Biblical Theology Bulletin*
CBQ	*Catholic Biblical Quarterly*
EQ	*Evangelical Quarterly*
ETL	*Ephemerides theologicae lovanienses*
ExpT	*Expository Times*
GP	*Gospel Perspectives*
GTJ	*Grace Theological Journal*
Hist & Th	*History and Theory*
HTR	*Harvard Theological Review*
HUCA	*Hebrew Union College Annual*
IDB	*Interpreter's Dictionary of the Bible*
Int	*Interpretation*
ISBE	*International Standard Bible Encyclopedia*
JAAR	*Journal of the American Academy of Religion*
JBL	*Journal of Biblical Literature*
JETS	*Journal of the Evangelical Theological Society*
JR	*Journal of Religion*
JRH	*Journal of Religious History*
JRT	*Journal of Religious Thought*
JSNT	*Journal for the Study of the New Testament*
JSOT	*Journal for the Study of the Old Testament*
JTS	*Journal of Theological Studies*
NIDNTT	*New International Dictionary of New Testament Theology*
NovT	*Novum Testamentum*
NTS	*New Testament Studies*
RB	*Revue biblique*
RevQ	*Revue de Qumran*
RSR	*Recherches de science religieuse*

SBL	*Society for Biblical Literature*
SJT	*Scottish Journal of Theology*
SNTU	*Studien zum Neuen Testament und seiner Umwelt*
ST	*Studia Theologica*
TheolBeitr	*Theologische Beiträge*
TrinJ	*Trinity Journal*
TU	*Texte und Untersuchungen*
TynB	*Tyndale Bulletin*
TZ	*Theologische Zeitschrift*
VC	*Vigiliae christianae*
WTJ	*Westminster Theological Journal*
ZNW	*Zeitschrift für die neutestamentliche Wissenschaft*

Introduction

In a popular novel, recently made into a television film, Irving Wallace invents a plot which includes the attempts of a worldwide Christian conspiracy to keep secret the discovery of ancient documents that allegedly disprove the gospel accounts of Jesus' life.[1] The story is entirely fictitious, but it does reflect the fact that some spectacular archaeological finds have emerged from the Middle East in the last forty years. The Dead Sea Scrolls have supplied copies of major portions of the Hebrew texts of the Old Testament nearly 1,000 years older than any previously existing copies. Documents found at Nag Hammadi in Egypt, dating from perhaps as early as the mid-second century, include a 'fifth gospel', falsely ascribed to the apostle Thomas, which contains 114 alleged sayings of Jesus, some similar to those in the New Testament and some quite different. None of these finds has destroyed the credibility of Christianity, or of the biblical narratives, and in many ways they have enhanced it. But Wallace's novel, like real-life history and archaeology, demonstrates one incontrovertible fact: the only completely convincing way to confirm or deny historical testimony is by comparison with other historical testimony, which of course will also stand in need of confirmation or denial.[2]

When one applies this principle to the New Testament gospels, a curious result emerges. Two somewhat opposite problems confront historians. On the one hand, they discover much less independent testimony to the life of Jesus than they might have expected concerning one who founded such a major world religion. On the other hand, when they look just at Matthew, Mark, Luke and John, it seems as though there is too much testimony. Many of the details of Christ's life are repeated in two or more of the gospels, sometimes even with identical wording, while in other places apparent discrepancies and contradictions cast doubts on the trustworthiness of the information supplied.

---

[1]Irving Wallace, *The Word* (New York: Simon & Schuster; London: Cassell, 1972).
[2]T. A. Roberts, *History and Christian Apologetic* (London: SPCK, 1960), p.35.

When all the evidence is in, not a few scholars would endorse this commonly used textbook summary of all that can be known about Jesus from historical research:

He was baptized by John the Baptist, and the beginning of his ministry was in some way linked with that of the Baptist. In his own ministry Jesus was above all the one who proclaimed the Kingdom of God and who challenged his hearers to respond to the reality he was proclaiming. The authority and effectiveness of Jesus as proclaimer of the Kingdom of God was reinforced by an apparently deserved reputation as an exorcist. In a world that believed in gods, in powers of good and evil, and in demons, he was able, in the name of God and his Kingdom, to help those who believed themselves to be possessed by demons.

A fundamental concern of Jesus was to bring together into a unified group those who responded to his proclamation of the Kingdom of God irrespective of their sex, previous background or history. A central feature of the life of this group was eating together, sharing a common meal that celebrated their unity in the new relationship with God, which they enjoyed on the basis of their response to Jesus' proclamation of the Kingdom. In this concern for the unity of the group of those who responded to the proclamation, Jesus challenged the tendency of the Jewish community of his day to fragment itself and in the name of God to reject certain of its own members. This aroused a deep-rooted opposition to him, which reached a climax during a Passover celebration in Jerusalem when he was arrested, tried by the Jewish authorities on a charge of blasphemy and by the Romans on a charge of sedition, and crucified. During his lifetime he had chosen from among his followers a small group of disciples who had exhibited in their work in his name something of his power and authority.

That, or something very like it, is *all* that we can know; it is *enough*.[1]

---

[1]Norman Perrin, *The New Testament: An Introduction* (New York and London: Harcourt, Brace, Jovanovich, 1974), pp.287–288 (italics mine). Interestingly, in his revision of ibid. (1982), pp.411–412, while preserving Perrin's original wording intact, Dennis C. Duling adds six additional sentences dealing with Jesus' birth, family, upbringing, travels, charisma, and community of followers.

This summary accepts many of the broad contours of the gospel narratives and a few specific details. Yet scholars and laity alike would often deny that this is enough. If, they would argue, out of all of the wealth of information supplied by the four gospels, only this small percentage is reliable, then Christianity is not worth anyone's allegiance. Jesus has been reduced to a mere human teacher, and not such an extraordinary one at that, whose ministry and message the four evangelists have largely distorted.

In fact, the true nature of the evidence is not nearly so bleak. Much scepticism about the gospels' reliability stems from faulty methods used in analyzing the gospels or from faulty presuppositions on which those methods depend. The hard data actually yield very positive results. This study will begin, therefore, by examining the various methods of historical criticism[1] that have been applied to the gospels. Chapter one surveys the main approaches employed throughout the history of the church. Chapter two turns to the distinctive developments of the last half-century which are often equated with 'modern scholarship'. Chapter three addresses the unique problems associated with the study of the miracle stories in the gospels. While focusing primarily on the issues raised by the application of historical criticism to these narratives, it also briefly considers the scientific and philosophical questions surrounding the concept of the supernatural. The next three chapters turn to the two problems of too much and too little historical testimony. Chapters four and five consider some of the most significant apparent contradictions among the gospel parallels, first by looking at several of the seeming discrepancies among the three Synoptic[2] Gospels (Matthew, Mark and Luke), and then by examining the distinctive questions raised by the Gospel of John. Chapter six deals with the evidence for Jesus' life and teachings outside the gospel tradition: in the rest of the New Testament writings, in other early Christian literature, and in contemporary Jewish and Graeco-Roman sources. Finally, the question suggested by the title of this book is raised again – are the gospels reliable history? Chapter seven thus consolidates the find-

---

[1]Throughout this book, as in biblical scholarship more generally, the word 'criticism' is used as a synonym for academic 'analysis' (similarly, 'critical' approximates to 'analytical'; and 'critic' to 'analyst'). It need not imply, as it often does in popular language, any negative value judgments about the contents of Scripture.

[2]So-called because of their remarkable similarities, such that parallel accounts can easily be set alongside one another in a 'synopsis' (literally, a 'together-look').

ings of previous chapters and outlines a method for dealing with the details of the gospel tradition which have not been discussed.

In 1943, Professor F. F. Bruce, who is today one of the most widely respected evangelical biblical scholars, produced his first book-length work, entitled *The New Testament Documents: Are They Reliable?* This book has undergone five revisions, the most recent in 1960,[1] and has faithfully served a generation of students and interested lay people. In many ways the present study seeks to function as an expanded and more amply annotated supplement to Bruce's work, though limiting the focus of attention to the gospels. It is no coincidence that its title resembles Bruce's title but the word 'historical' has been added to make clear that it is the question of historical reliability and not just theological trustworthiness which is being investigated.[2]

A comparison of tables of contents discloses important similarities and differences between this work and Bruce's. Bruce devotes a chapter to the gospel miracles just as this study does. He uses three chapters to survey the evidence for the Jesus-tradition outside the gospels; here the topic has been condensed into one chapter. He dwells at some length on the archaeological evidence which confirms the accuracy of details in the New Testament and on the early dating of the documents, which brings them into relatively close proximity with the events they narrate. He also emphasizes the New Testament's abundant textual attestation, that is, the number and nature of ancient manuscripts which have been copied and preserved from the Greek originals. These issues have not been explored further here, because their relevance for the gospels is more limited than for some of the other sections of the New Testament. Most of the events of Jesus' life have left no physical traces for archaeologists to unearth. Even a conservative dating of the gospels places them about thirty years after Jesus'

---

[1](London and Downers Grove: IVP).

[2]The words 'history' and 'historical' can of course themselves mean several different things. For a helpful survey of the range of definitions, see I. Howard Marshall, *I Believe in the Historical Jesus* (London: Hodder & Stoughton; Grand Rapids: Eerdmans, 1977), pp.47–48. Many of these definitions overlap and this study will normally have several of them in mind: a historical narrative recounts that which actually happened; it is the opposite of fiction; it does not contain numerous errors. The approach to history which believes it is impossible to separate fact from fiction in a given narrative is self-defeating. See below pp.54–58; and *cf.* R. D. Baird, 'Factual Statements and the Possibility of Objectivity in History', JRT 26 (1969), pp.5–22; H. White, 'The Question of Narrative in Contemporary Historical Theory', *Hist & Th* 23 (1984), pp.1–33.

death, a sufficient period of time for errors and distortions to creep into their accounts, if other factors conducive to such changes were present. And almost no one denies that highly accurate texts of what the four evangelists originally wrote have been preserved; the controversy today centres on whether or not what they wrote was true, that is, a valid or faithful record of the events.

At the same time, new challenges to the gospels' trustworthiness have arisen which played little or no role in the scholarly debates of past generations. Biblical critics have begun to draw much more heavily on the insights of literary criticism, hence the survey of the 'new methods of gospel study' in chapter two. The distinctives of John lead virtually all commentators to treat him quite differently from the Synoptists, so his gospel has been given special consideration. Nevertheless, even though a wide range of topics has been surveyed, there are still gaps and omissions. Much of what has been chosen for discussion has been dictated by the direction of recent evangelical research in general and of the *Gospel Perspectives* series in particular (see preface).[1] For the most part this survey makes no attempt to break fresh ground, but instead seeks to make the terrain traversed by recent scholarship familiar to a wider audience.

Lack of space has clearly prohibited the kind of detailed treatment which each individual topic requires if it is properly to be substantiated. A non-technical work of this nature risks two pitfalls. On the one hand, theological students may complain that its discussion is too brief and simplistic. On the other hand, lay people who are unaccustomed to the complexities of modern scholarship may wish that the issues were less intricate. Nevertheless, the book reflects the sincere hope that it may find a welcoming readership among both groups of people, for it is intended for student and lay person alike. For those who require more detail, there are frequent footnotes and the works to which they refer. The abundance of in-depth, well-reasoned conservative scholarship produced in the last two decades deserves more serious attention than it has often received. For those who find the discussion complex, a careful checking of the scriptural references provided throughout should offer much illumination. The issues

---

[1]For some thoughts on the major omissions of the latter, see Craig L. Blomberg, 'Concluding Reflections on Miracles and *Gospel Perspectives*', in *GP*,6, pp.443–457.

are not simple, and simplistic summaries serve neither the cause of Christianity nor of scholarship.

The thrust of this volume should be compared and contrasted with two opposing perspectives, both of which have acquired much popular currency. On the one hand, many who have never studied the gospels in a scholarly context believe that biblical criticism has virtually disproved the existence of Jesus or that no one can take the gospels seriously as sources of reliable historical information without surrendering intellectual integrity. The London Weekend Television series, *Jesus: the Evidence,* reproduced in print in slightly less idiosyncratic form by Ian Wilson,[1] tended to promote such distortions of the scholarly consensus and has been ably criticized by Professor James Dunn.[2] For the most part, the present study has ignored the most outlandish claims of isolated scholars and responded instead to what is widely accepted in academe even if it is less well known elsewhere.

On the other hand, a very popular conservative apologetic for the deity of Christ stems from C. S. Lewis's famous 'trilemma': the person who did and said the types of things the gospels portray Jesus as doing and saying could be no merely human teacher or prophet, however enlightened or exalted. He must be either a liar, a lunatic or the Lord.[3] The problem with this argument is that it assumes what is regularly denied, namely, that the gospels give entirely accurate accounts of the actions and claims of Jesus. One can preserve Lewis's alliteration and introduce a fourth option – the stories about Jesus were legends. This option represents the most common current explanation of the more spectacular deeds and extravagant claims of Jesus in the gospels: they were the product of the early church's desire to glorify him, and so it exaggerated its portraits of him above and beyond what the facts permitted. Unless one can successfully dismiss this alternative, one cannot appeal to Lewis's apologetic. An examination of the gospels' historical reliability must therefore precede a credible assessment of who Jesus was.

---

[1](London: Weidenfeld & Nicolson, 1984).

[2]J. D. G. Dunn, *The Evidence for Jesus* (London: SCM; Philadelphia: Westminster, 1985).

[3]C. S. Lewis, *Mere Christianity* (London: Collins; New York: Macmillan, 1955), p.52. *Cf.* Josh McDowell, *Evidence that Demands a Verdict* (San Bernardino: Here's Life, 1979), pp.103–109.

Traditional approaches to the reliability of the gospels

From the earliest days of the church until the late eighteenth century, belief in the historical reliability of the gospels usually followed as a corollary from belief in Scripture as inspired and infallible.[1] Few took the time to investigate systematically the extent to which the gospels could be shown to be reliable apart from this belief. The problem of the gospel parallels, however, was obvious from the start; if the gospels were completely trustworthy, then the apparent contradictions between parallel accounts had to be explained. As a result, the dominant approach to the question of gospel historicity for the first seventeen centuries of Christian reflection centred on the task of harmonizing the various evangelists' testimony. In the last two hundred years all this has changed. From the late eighteenth until the early twentieth centuries, scholarly study of Scripture often focused more on the dissonance between its component parts than on the harmony. An important question underlying the analysis of gospel parallels from either perspective involves the literary relationship among them. Why, especially with the Synoptics, do the gospels often agree with each other word for word while elsewhere greatly diverging one from another? Did one or more of the evangelists know and use the work of his colleagues in any form? Although these questions continue to be debated vigorously, they have been around long enough to be distinguished from the newer questions of

---

[1]Recent attempts to deny that the beliefs of the Christian church during this period included a commitment to the inerrancy of Scripture on every matter which came under its purview (most notably Jack B. Rogers and Donald K. McKim, *The Authority and Interpretation of the Bible* [San Francisco: Harper & Row, 1979]) seem to misrepresent the evidence. See esp. John D. Woodbridge, *Biblical Authority: A Critique of the Rogers/McKim Proposal* (Grand Rapids: Zondervan, 1982). The problem with this type of debate is that virtually all students of the Bible have recognized various degrees of imprecision in the gospel records but they disagree on when that imprecision deserves the label of 'error'.

gospel study on which chapter two will concentrate, and to warrant brief consideration in this chapter under the heading of 'traditional approaches'.

1 Harmony in the gospels

The first known attempt to construct a gospel harmony,[1] in which all four gospels were combined into one consecutive narrative, came in the late second century from a Syrian Christian named Tatian. His *Diatessaron,* from the Greek phrase, 'through four [gospels]', roughly follows the outline of Matthew for most of Jesus' ministry, and of John for Jesus' final week, while inserting supplementary information from Mark and Luke at the places Tatian felt most appropriate.[2] Some of Tatian's solutions to the more noteworthy differences between parallels were regularly adopted from then on. For example, in dealing with Matthew's 'Sermon on the Mount' (Mt. 5–7) and Luke's 'sermon on the plain' (Lk. 6:17–49), Tatian arranges the introductory verses in the order, Matthew 5:1; Luke 6:13–17; Mark 3:14–15; Matthew 5:2ff., to underline the fact that Luke's Jesus was also in the mountains but then descended to speak to the crowds at a place sufficiently level to accommodate everyone comfortably. Tatian then proceeds to record Matthew's longer version of the sermon, omitting the passages in which Luke mostly duplicates Matthew but inserting verses where Luke adds unparalleled material.

In other cases, Tatian's solutions are highly improbable. For example, Tatian splits Luke's account of Jesus' preaching in Nazareth (Lk. 4:16–30) into two parts, separated by twelve sections of intervening material, in order to place part of the account at the beginning of Jesus' public ministry (as in Luke) and part of it as parallel to Mark's first mention of Jesus in Nazareth, which does not occur until his Galilean ministry is well under way (Mk. 6:1–6). In a few instances, Tatian anticipates an approach which has only

---

[1]The reader of this book will be greatly helped by consulting a modern gospel harmony or synopsis while proceeding. Perhaps the most helpful is Kurt Aland, *Synopsis of the Four Gospels* (New York: United Bible Societies, 1976 [Greek-English edition]; 1979 [English only]).

[2]Tatian originally wrote in Greek, but only translations in other languages survived. In English, *cf. The Earliest Life of Christ Ever Compiled from the Four Gospels Being the Diatessaron of Tatian,* trans. from Arabic by J. Hamlyn Hill (Edinburgh: T & T Clark, 1894).

really caught on in recent years – recognizing that many of the gospel passages are grouped together topically rather than chronologically. Thus, in contrast to subsequent harmonists who insisted that Jesus must have cleansed the temple twice, once at the beginning of his ministry (Jn. 2:14–22) and once during the last week of his life (Mt. 21:12–13 and Mk. 11:16), Tatian combines all twelve of these verses into one coherent narrative. He then appends the story of the widow's mite (Mk. 12:41–44) and the parable of the Pharisee and the publican (Lk. 18:9–14), presumably because they likewise deal with the issue of true worship in the temple. Mark's sequence is then resumed with the two parts of the story of Jesus cursing the fig tree (Mk. 11:12–14, 19–23), but having already used the story of the temple cleansing, Tatian inserts the story of Nicodemus in between these groups of verses, because of its proximity in John to the temple cleansing (Jn. 3:1–21).

The church fathers display a similar variety of approaches to the gospel data. In a famous passage, the late second-century bishop of Lyons, Irenaeus, accounts for the overall differences in perspective on theological grounds: John wrote of Jesus as the divine Word of God, Luke emphasized his priestly role, Matthew spoke of him as a human being, and Mark stressed the importance of prophecy.[1] Interestingly, only the first of these four characterizations would be accepted today as a major emphasis of that evangelist. In the early third century, Origen of Alexandria recognized that some of the proposed harmonizations were incredible and admitted that at the historical level certain contradictions did in fact exist. But Origen argued that many texts had an allegorical meaning as well as a literal meaning; if harmony could not be achieved at the latter level, it could at the former. The example of the two temple cleansings is just such a case. Origen solves the difficulty by assuming that John's more 'spiritual' account is not the description of a literal activity of Jesus in Jerusalem but a symbolic narrative about the need for Jesus' followers to put away unrighteousness from their midst and to stop exploiting those who like oxen and sheep are senseless or empty and unstable like doves![2]

Although Origen's orthodoxy was suspect on several counts, the

---

[1] *Against Heresies*, III. 9–11.
[2] *Commentary on John* X, 16. For more detail on the approaches of various early church fathers, see R. M. Grant, *The Earliest Lives of Jesus* (New York: Harper; London: SPCK, 1961).

allegorical approach to solving problems, and to interpreting Scripture more generally, would have a long history ahead of it. Not until the Reformation would it meet sustained opposition. Nevertheless more sober exegetes did arise from time to time. The great fourth-century preacher, John Chrysostom, displayed a healthy blend of the type of 'additive' harmonization emphasized by Tatian, that is, where divergent accounts are explained as different extracts from a much fuller body of information, and of the type of theological explanation encountered in Irenaeus, where the unique emphases of the individual gospels are taken into account. In addition, Chrysostom seemed to foreshadow those who would later limit the infallibility of Scripture to matters of faith and practice, rather than also including details of history and geography: 'But if there be anything touching times or places, which they have related differently, this nothing injures the truth of what they have said . . . [but those things] . . . which constitute our life and furnish out our doctrine, nowhere is any of them found to have disagreed, no not ever so little.'[1] St. Augustine's approach was somewhat more nuanced, emphasizing that the gospels often fail to give a clear indication of the location or sequence of the events they are reporting, and that one is to assume continuity of time and place only when it is explicitly mentioned in the text. He also emphasized that parallel passages may vary in wording yet still convey the same sense, whereas highly divergent 'parallels' may in fact represent similar events from separate occasions in Jesus' life.[2]

Helmut Merkel seems to be correct in concluding that 'the mediaeval and Reformation expositors could add nothing fundamentally new to the solutions developed in the early church. Under Augustine's influence harmonization remained for most the reasonable approach.'[3] Not every apparent contradiction among the gospels was resolved to everyone's satisfaction, but most were content to trust that future study would offer better solutions. One contribution to research from these centuries that must not be

---

[1]*Homilies on the Gospel of St. Matthew*, I. 6. Trans. George Prevost, rev. M. B. Riddle, in *The Nicene and Post-Nicene Fathers*, vol. 10, ed. Philip Schaff (Grand Rapids: Eerdmans, 1975 [orig. 1889]), p.3. *Cf.* further Jerome D. Quinn, 'Saint John Chrysostom on History in the Synoptics', *CBQ* 24 (1962), pp.140–147.

[2]*Harmony of the Gospels*, II. 21, 14 and 29, respectively.

[3]Helmut Merkel, *Die Pluralität der Evangelien als theologisches und exegetisches Problem in der Alten Kirche* (Bern: Peter Lang, 1978), xxvii.

overlooked was John Calvin's magnificent commentary on *A Harmony of the Gospels Matthew, Mark and Luke* (Latin orig. 1555). Although many of Calvin's comments on exegetical perplexities relied on previous commentary, his rejection of the predominantly allegorical approach of mediaeval Catholicism rescued biblical interpretation from a sea of arbitrariness. Calvin also adopted perspectives that are still debated by contemporary expositors. For example, after comparing the two versions of the Lord's prayer (Mt. 6:9–13; Lk. 11:2–4), he considered the suggestion that Matthew's Sermon on the Mount might in fact be a composite construction gathering together Jesus' teaching from several different occasions.[1] But Calvin nevertheless followed his predecessors in trying to fit all the gospel passages together into one orderly outline of the life of Christ, even if in many cases his exposition was more concerned with what the individual evangelists meant rather than with a close comparison of all the apparent discrepancies.

2 Dissonance in the gospels

With the dawn of the Enlightenment, harmonizations of the gospels became increasingly suspect.[2] The presupposition that all Scripture could be equated with God's inspired word was challenged and scholars began to consider more seriously the possibility that some of the problems between gospel parallels did not have plausible solutions. This was because they appeared to involve significant embellishments, distortions, or contradictions of historical fact. As parts of the Bible came to be treated more and more as merely human literature, it became easier to assume that they contained errors like those found in any other ancient history book. Two German scholars who wrote during the late eighteenth century are often credited with pioneering this approach: J. S. Semler and J. D. Michaelis.

The two key theses for Semler's study were: (a) the Word of

---

[1]Vol. 1, trans. A. W. Morrison, ed. David W. Torrance & Thomas F. Torrance (Edinburgh: St. Andrew; Grand Rapids: Eerdmans, 1972), pp.204–205.

[2]Harmonizations were and are still produced, however, in various forms. One of the most recent, which creates one continuous narrative of the gospels and incorporates every verse of all four accounts into it, however unwieldy or unnecessarily repetitive it becomes, is Baird W. Whitlock, *The Gospel: The Life of Jesus* (New York: Schocken, 1984).

God and Holy Scripture are not identical, and (b) the question of what belongs in the canon of Scripture is purely a historical and not an ecclesiastical one. In other words, as a Protestant who did not believe in the infallible authority of any church tradition to tell him what to believe, Semler argued that scholarship had the responsibility to reopen questions of what belongs in Scripture and what is to be considered as reliable and of 'permanent worth for further religious development'.[1] Semler himself found much in Scripture that he believed to be inspired and authoritative, and he considered himself to be as faithful a Christian as his more traditional colleagues. In fact the principal corollary of his two theses was that Christians ought to seek to understand the original meaning of the Greek and Hebrew texts in their original historical settings much more so than was the case in his day.

What Semler initiated in part and unsystematically, Michaelis expanded with rigour and comprehensiveness, writing the first full-scale critical New Testament introduction, *Einleitung in die göttlichen Schriften des Neues Bundes (Introduction to the Divine Scriptures of the New Covenant)* in 1750. He also refused to accept the church's definition of the canon as a starting-point for his research but sought instead 'in a purely historical way to demonstrate the trustworthiness of the writings'.[2] He believed that many of the apparent discrepancies among the gospels could be harmonized, but did not feel constrained to eradicate them all. Semler's and Michaelis' relative conservatism, however, would not prevail for long. Many scholars came to apply the philosophical position of G.E.Lessing, arguing that the universal truths of religion could not be dependent on historical evidence, since the study of history leads only to probable rather than to infallible conclusions.[3] As a result, harmonization of the gospels, or of any other seemingly conflicting portions of Scripture, was seen as both unnecessary and misguided.

---

[1]Werner G. Kümmel, *The New Testament: The History of the Investigation of Its Problems* (Nashville: Abingdon, 1972; London: SCM, 1973), p.63, referring primarily to Semler's *Abhandlung von freier Untersuchung des Canons,* 4 vols. (1771–75). *Cf.* Hans W. Frei, *The Eclipse of Biblical Narrative* (New Haven and London: Yale, 1974), pp.111–112.

[2]Kümmel, *New Testament*, p.72.

[3]Lessing's so-called 'ugly ditch' originally referred to the claim that 'the contingent truths of history can never serve as the demonstration of eternal truths of reason'. See Stephen Neill, *The Interpretation of the New Testament 1861–1961* (Oxford: University Press; New York: Oxford, 1964), p.280. Despite the dates in his title, Neill begins with a 32-page chapter concisely surveying the situation from the late eighteenth century on.

The history of the last two centuries of gospel criticism, therefore, has been dominated by hypotheses which presuppose that the four evangelists frequently do not narrate reliable history. D. F. Strauss's two-volume *Das Leben Jesu, kritisch bearbeitet (The Life of Jesus Critically Examined)* in 1835–36 rejected both orthodox belief in Jesus' miracles as supernatural events and rationalist attempts to explain them as misinterpreted natural events. Instead Strauss argued that the miracle stories were unhistorical myths composed by the first Christians to explain what Jesus meant to them in language intelligible to their contemporaries, a view which to a large extent still prevails in scholarly circles, with only modest alterations. In fact, Strauss believed that the presence of contradictions between parallel accounts was one possible indication of the presence of myth. To cite just one example, in Luke 5:1–11 Jesus calls Peter to follow him after leading him miraculously to catch a great shoal of fish. In Mark 1:16–20 (*cf.* Mt. 4:18–22) Jesus calls Peter without working any miracle, yet in 3:13–19 he seems to choose his twelve disciples all over again. John has parallels to neither of these stories but does describe a miraculous catch of fish, followed by a commissioning of Peter, in his stories of Jesus' resurrection appearances (Jn. 21:1–19). Strauss ridicules previous attempts to harmonize all these data and concludes that the stories were 'placed by tradition in different periods' of Jesus' life and invented to illustrate his calling his disciples to be 'fishers of men'.[1]

A second 'giant' in nineteenth-century New Testament criticism was F. C. Baur. Building on the dialectic philosophy of G. W. F. Hegel, Baur interpreted the first century and a half of Christianity as the antithesis and subsequent synthesis between a conservative Petrine theology and a liberal Pauline one. When this interpretation was applied to the gospels, Matthew was seen as the most Jewish, and therefore most authentic, of the Synoptics, Luke as the most Gentile or Pauline, and Mark as a second-century attempt to reconcile the two.[2] Baur's views have been largely

---

[1]Trans. George Eliot, ed. Peter C. Hodgson (Philadelphia: Fortress, 1972; London: SCM, 1973), p.318. For a thorough study of the man and his significance, see Horton Harris, *David Friedrich Strauss and His Theology* (Cambridge: University Press, 1973).

[2]Ferdinand Christian Baur, *The Church History of the First Three Centuries,* trans. from 3rd Gm. ed. Allan Menzies (London: Williams & Norgate, 1878), 1, pp.77–82, 147–152. For an overview of Baur's 'school' and its influence, see Horton Harris, *The Tübingen School* (Oxford: Clarendon, 1975).

rejected by twentieth-century scholarship but his general principle that contradictory theologies best account for the divergences of the gospels is a regular presupposition of current research.

These and other developments led to a proliferation of 'lives of Jesus' – books which sought to identify those features of the gospel narratives that could be accepted as true indicators of what Jesus was really like. In a landmark study at the turn of the century, however, Albert Schweitzer exposed the weakness of almost all these works: Jesus was being re-created in the image of their authors at the expense of objective scholarship. Rationalists and romantics, Marxists and mythologizers, all saw Jesus as justifying their particular philosophies, and they rejected as unhistorical anything in the gospels which contradicted their own ideologies. Unfortunately Schweitzer fell into the same trap as he reinterpreted the gospels in view of his own commitment to 'thoroughgoing eschatology' – the belief that Jesus thought that he would see the end of the age in his lifetime but died mistaken.[1]

3 Evaluating the debate

In today's academic world, any biblical scholar who sets out to harmonize the gospels risks severe criticism from his or her colleagues. Some of this criticism is justified; some is not. On the one hand, it cannot be stressed too strongly that seeking responsibly to reconcile seemingly discordant testimony is the task of every historian, whether dealing with the biblical literature or with any other work of purported history, ancient or modern. Although the traditional desire to harmonize the gospels stems from a belief in their uniquely sacred nature, secular historians also regularly fit together apparently conflicting testimony in a way which vindicates the integrity of all the witnesses involved. Gilbert Garraghan's standard historiography textbook emphasizes that 'almost any critical history that discusses the evidence for important statements will furnish examples of discrepant or contradictory accounts and the attempts which are made to reconcile

---

[1]Albert Schweitzer, *The Quest of the Historical Jesus* (London: A. & C. Black; New York: Macmillan, 1910). For a briefer survey of the nineteenth-century quest for the historical Jesus, see esp. Ben F. Meyer, *The Aims of Jesus* (London: SCM, 1979), pp.25–48.

them'.[1] In addition, more often than one might expect, the details of two different events will reveal striking similarities, such as when the main characters of separate stories have the same names. In other cases, varying testimony will reflect the fact that the evidence consists of fragmentary excerpts from a much fuller, self-consistent body of evidence. Of course, quite commonly, certain discrepancies will prove to be genuine, and certain witnesses will be shown to have erred in various, often peripheral, details. But as Murray Harris emphasizes, even then 'the presence of discrepancies in circumstantial detail is no proof that the central fact is unhistorical'.[2] On the other hand, some proposed reconstructions of the life of Christ are so improbable that they are quite rightly discarded. But rejecting one attempt to solve a problem does not mean that the problem should be regarded as insoluble; other solutions may prove more persuasive.[3]

Just as harmonization, in principle, is by no means limited to texts believed to be inspired by God, so also Michaelis' rejection of an *a priori* commitment to Scripture's inspiration is a valid approach even for commentators who believe in that doctrine. It is possible to defend the accuracy of much of Scripture on purely historical grounds. As the 'evidentialist' approach to Christian apologetics stresses, one can apply widely accepted historical criteria to demonstrate the general trustworthiness of the gospels. The competing school of thought known as 'presuppositionalism' maintains that one must first assume their reliability and then demonstrate that the data form a consistent whole, thereby confirming one's presupposition.[4] Surely there is a place for both

---

[1] Gilbert J. Garraghan, *A Guide to Historical Method* (Westport, CT and London: Greenwood, 1973 [orig. 1946]), p.314.

[2] Murray J. Harris, *Raised Immortal: Resurrection and Immortality in the New Testament* (London: Marshall, Morgan & Scott, 1983; Grand Rapids: Eerdmans, 1985) p.68. Harris gives a good illustration with the accounts of Polybius and Livy of Hannibal's crossing of the Alps.

[3] For more detail and numerous examples from both biblical and extra-biblical sources, see Craig L. Blomberg, 'The Legitimacy and Limits of Harmonization', in *Hermeneutics, Authority, and Canon*, ed. D. A. Carson and John D. Woodbridge (Grand Rapids: Zondervan; Leicester: IVP, 1986), pp.139–174. Brevard S. Childs, *The New Testament Canon: An Introduction* (Philadelphia: Fortress; London: SCM, 1984), pp.143–209, goes a long way toward rehabilitating harmonization of the gospels as a valid enterprise, but he limits himself to broad, theological themes. Unfortunately, he does not think that many of the historical, chronological, or geographical details which so often seem to come into conflict with one another can be harmonized. On the other hand, harmonies of the life of Christ which try to place all the gospel passages into a plausible chronological order go well beyond the data available.

[4] The classic proponents of each of these viewpoints are B. B. Warfield and Cornelius van Til, respectively. See esp. Warfield's *The Inspiration and Authority of Scripture* (Philadelphia:

approaches. Much of the rationale for a series like *Gospel Perspectives* (see preface) is that open-minded enquirers from many different theological perspectives share enough common ground to enable them to proceed toward plausible resolutions of the differences that still separate them. Even the presuppositionalist owes his critics an honest and considered reply rather than a terse dismissal of their views simply because they are based on different presuppositions; by definition his position gives him no grounds for rejecting someone who argues consistently from a different starting point.

At the same time, the cumulative evidence of earlier research need not be neglected every time the biblical historian begins to work on a fresh issue. If previously 'intractable' problems have consistently yielded to patient analysis, the commentator may become more and more confident that new challenges can be met with equal success and less and less willing naïvely to equate superficial divergence with genuine contradiction. And despite two centuries of sceptical onslaught, it is fair to say that all the alleged inconsistencies among the gospels have received at least plausible resolutions. Chapters four and five will look at some of the most perplexing examples in more detail.[1]

Above all, Lessing's absolute dichotomy between the truths of history and religion must be rejected. It is unfair to demand fail safe proof of religious doctrines before one will accept them, since there is no way to acquire such proof. Although Lessing's position remains widely influential today in many theological circles, its only consistent corollary is a thoroughgoing agnosticism. People may of course act inconsistently and choose to believe in God or Jesus 'in spite of' what seems inadequate historical evidence. But this is by definition irrational, and actually unchristian, since Christianity is based on the concept of God acting *in history*. Moreover, as A. J. Ayer stressed, unless a religious claim is verifiable or falsifiable, it is, quite literally, 'non-sensical'.[2] Yet

Presbyterian & Reformed, 1948); and van Til's *In Defense of the Faith* (Philadelphia: Presbyterian & Reformed, 1955).

[1]For a very balanced analysis of 'the implications of inspiration' and 'conservatism and scepticism' in the historical analysis of the gospels, see the sections so entitled in I. Howard Marshall, 'Historical Criticism', in *New Testament Interpretation,* ed. I. Howard Marshall (Exeter: Paternoster; Grand Rapids: Eerdmans, 1977), pp.132–135.

[2]A. J. Ayer, *Language, Truth and Logic* (Harmondsworth and Baltimore: Pelican, 1971 [orig. 1936]). Ayer and the school of 'logical positivism' attempted to extend this principle to all language and thereby landed in the self-defeating position of affirming a universal statement

despite the oft quoted verse, 'we walk by faith and not by sight' (2 Cor. 5:7), Christianity does not require a 'leap in the dark' or a sacrifice of the intellect. Paul is quoted entirely out of context when this verse is treated as a rationale for believing without evidence (*cf.* 1 Cor. 15:3–8). Biblical faith is fundamentally commitment to a God who has intervened in the history of humanity in a way that exposes his activity to historical study.[1] Christians may not be able to prove beyond a shadow of doubt that the gospels are historically accurate, but they must attempt to show that there is a strong likelihood of their historicity. Thus the approach of this study is always to argue in terms of probability rather than certainty, since this is the nature of historical hypotheses, including those which are accepted without question.[2] Graham Stanton clearly summarizes the significance of this enterprise:

at least some aspects of the portrait of Jesus are essential to faith, for if historical research were ever able to prove conclusively that the historical Jesus was quite unlike the Jesus of the gospels, then faith would certainly be eroded. The gospel is concerned with history: not in that it stands if its claims could be verified by the historian, but in that it falls if the main lines of the early church's portrait of Jesus of Nazareth were to be falsified by historical research.[3]

In fact, a good case can be made for accepting the details as well as the main contours of the gospels as reliable. But, as noted above, even if a few minor contradictions genuinely existed, this would not necessarily jeopardize the reliability of the rest or call into question the entire basis for belief. In sum, no Christian should shrink from interacting with any critique of traditional opinion. If the critique is valid, he or she should want to know about it and

---

which was itself neither verifiable nor falsifiable. But in its more limited application to 'God-talk' Ayer's logic seems valid.

[1] *Cf. e.g. God, History and Historians*, ed. C. T. McIntire (New York: Oxford University Press, 1977); Herbert Butterfield, *Christianity and History* (London: G. Bell, 1949; New York: Scribners, 1950).

[2] *Cf.* Jacques Barzun and Henry G. Graff, *The Modern Researcher* (New York and London: Harcourt, Brace, Jovanovich, 1977), p.92: 'The historian arrives at truth through probability' but 'this does not mean "a doubtful kind of truth" but a firm reliance on the likelihood that evidence which has been examined and found solid is veracious.'

[3] Graham N. Stanton, *Jesus of Nazareth in New Testament Preaching* (Cambridge: University Press, 1974), p.189.

reassess the tradition, however associated with orthodoxy it may be in his or her mind or community. If it is invalid, careful study and analysis should sooner or later reveal that fact, and faith ought to be strengthened for having been tested and refined.

4 The Synoptic problem

One central issue in the last two centuries of gospel scholarship has been passed over deliberately so that it might receive special attention here. Closely related to the question of whether or not the gospels contradict each other is the question of their literary relationship. Since they are so similar in many respects, the question naturally arises as to whether any of the gospel writers knew one or more of the other gospels and utilized that information as he wrote. Certainly Luke admits familiarity with previous, presumably written, accounts of the events of Jesus' life (Lk. 1:1–4), but it is impossible to know if he had in mind any of the other three gospels in finished form. The question becomes particularly acute for a study of the Synoptic Gospels since they are much more like each other than like John, and since there are so many other conceivable ways that details from Jesus' life could have been collected and narrated (Jn. 21:25). A competent teacher knows enough to suspect some type of collaboration if two or more students submit essays with identical wording recurring time and again; the situation is no different with the historian examining written testimony of past events. The specific question of the literary relationship of the Synoptics has been called the Synoptic problem and has elicited several different hypotheses by way of reply. Because later chapters will presuppose a particular solution to this problem, brief consideration must be given to it here.

Interestingly, just two decades ago Stephen Neill could write that the Synoptic problem was one of the few settled issues of New Testament scholarship.[1] Mark was viewed as the first gospel written. Matthew and Luke then copied from Mark in various places, as well as drawing on a second source for a large number of Jesus' sayings which they had in common but which were missing from Mark. This hypothetical document was designated Q after the

---

[1]Neill, *Interpretation*, p.339.

German word *Quelle* meaning 'source'. Diagrammatically, the relationship resembles figure one below:

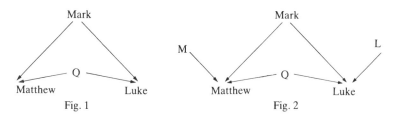

Fig. 1   Fig. 2

The virtual unanimity of support which this 'two-document hypothesis' commanded was due largely to the magisterial study from a previous generation by B. H. Streeter, *The Four Gospels: A Study of Origins*.[1] Streeter had in fact proposed an even more elaborate 'four-document hypothesis': in addition to depending on Mark and Q, Matthew and Luke had access to reliable, independent traditions peculiar to their respective gospels, designated M and L respectively (see figure two above).[2] Additionally, Streeter believed that Luke first wrote a shorter form of the gospel, which Streeter dubbed 'proto-Luke', that combined the information Luke had acquired from Q and L. Only later did Luke learn of Mark's Gospel, which then prompted him to revise and expand his first draft by incorporating Marcan elements into it.

All the pieces of evidence which led to the formation of these hypotheses and to the widespread acceptance of the less speculative 'two-document hypothesis' have been spelled out clearly elsewhere.[3] A sizeable majority of scholars still accepts this solution to the Synoptic problem, but this was not the case throughout most of the history of the church, and for the last twenty years a growing

[1](London: Macmillan, 1924; New York: Macmillan, 1925). Streeter of course built on the work of many before him, most notably the nineteenth-century scholars C. H. Weisse and H. J. Holtzmann. For a full history, though biased against this hypothesis, see H.-H. Stoldt, *History and Criticism of the Marcan Hypothesis* (Edinburgh: T & T Clark; Macon: Mercer University Press, 1980).

[2]Many would equate M and L with the distinctive oral traditions available to either Matthew or Luke rather than seeing them as written documents. Some would want to view Q in a similar light. These scholars will then speak of the 'two source' or 'four source' hypotheses rather than of two or four 'documents'.

[3]See esp. Donald Guthrie, *New Testament Introduction* (London: Tyndale; Downers Grove: IVP, 1970), pp.121–187; Joseph A. Fitzmyer, 'The Priority of Mark and the "Q" Source in Luke', in *Jesus and Man's Hope*, vol. 2, ed. D. Y. Hadidian (Pittsburgh: Pickwick, 1970), pp.131–170.

minority has also been advocating a different solution. Evidence from the early church fathers is ambiguous, but the second-century writer Papias was quoted as saying that Matthew first wrote down the 'sayings' of Jesus, seemingly something less than a full-scale gospel, in 'the Hebrew dialect' (possibly a reference to Aramaic).[1] Certainly from the time of Augustine on, it was regularly believed that the gospels were written in the order in which they appear in Scripture, and Mark was seen as a 'digest' of Matthew. Luke, in turn, drew on both previous gospels (see figure three below).

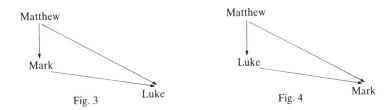

Fig. 3   Fig. 4

The priority of the Gospel of Matthew for Augustine, however, seems to have been based at least as much on its greater popularity in the church, which in turn stemmed from its fuller accounts of Jesus' teaching, than on any historical information he had about the order of writing. Today Streeter's greatest rival is J. J. Griesbach, a late eighteenth-century scholar, who believed that Mark stood third rather than first or second, as a summarizer of Luke as well as of Matthew. The material which Luke shares with Matthew is then attributed to his direct dependence on Matthew rather than to any hypothetical common source (see figure four above). The most ardent instigator of this revival of Griesbach's hypothesis has been William Farmer, who through his writing and organization of several international conferences on the topic has succeeded in winning to his position a number of notable figures.[2]

C. M. Tuckett has recently devoted an entire monograph to this revival, concluding that it is not as convincing as the 'two-

---

[1]Papias' writings have been lost; the quotation is preserved in Eusebius, *Ecclesiastical History*, III, 39.16.

[2]William R. Farmer, *The Synoptic Problem* (New York and London: Macmillan, 1964). A brief history of the various symposia appears in the collection of essays from the most recent one held in Cambridge in 1979, *New Synoptic Studies*, ed. William R. Farmer (Macon: Mercer University Press, 1983) vii–xlii. For a comparable anthology generally more critical of the Griesbachians, see *Synoptic Studies*, ed. C. M. Tuckett (Sheffield: JSOT Press, 1984).

document hypothesis'.[1] Three of his numerous arguments seem especially strong. First, Matthew and Luke only rarely deviate from Mark in the same way at the same time. This dissimilarity is precisely what one would expect if they were each utilizing Mark largely independently of one another; wider agreement with each other against Mark in passages where all three are 'parallel' would suggest some closer relationship between Matthew and Luke. The Griesbachians, on the other hand, have to assume that Mark, as he combined and condensed Matthew and Luke, was unwilling to deviate widely from information on which both his sources agreed. But this leaves them unable to explain why Mark omitted the large sections of Q material, which account for approximately 250 verses in Matthew and Luke. Second, despite valiant attempts to draw parallels with other conflations or abridgements from the ancient world,[2] Mark remains much more unlike any known summary or digest than like one. Finally, and perhaps most importantly, the explanations of the rationale behind each jump in Mark's hop-scotch alternation between Matthew and Luke have so far proved unconvincing, while the two-document hypothesis provides a basis for more credible outlines of the evangelists' editorial activity. It is also significant that studies of individual passages in the gospels, as opposed to more general works on the Synoptic problem overall, almost never utilize the Griesbach hypothesis in explaining the similarities and differences of content. It seems safest to retain Marcan priority as the most convincing solution to the Synoptic problem and to assume that Matthew and Luke also had access to a common tradition (Q), whether orally or in writing.[3]

On the other hand, Augustine's view based on the order of the gospels in the New Testament cannot be set aside altogether. Studies of individual portions of the gospels have frequently found plausible the idea that where their stories run parallel, Matthew preserves certain passages in forms which reproduce the original tradition more literally than Mark does. Volume 4 of *Gospel*

---

[1]C. M. Tuckett, *The Revival of the Griesbach Hypothesis* (Cambridge: University Press, 1983).

[2]As esp. with Thomas R. W. Longstaff, *Evidence of Conflation in Mark?* (Missoula: Scholars, 1977).

[3]A convenient summary of the evidence for and against the Q-hypothesis by one of its advocates appears in Howard Biggs, 'The Q Debate since 1955', *Themelios* 6.2 (1981), pp.18–28. The most thoroughgoing attempt to defend Luke's direct use of Matthew is Michael D. Goulder, *The Evangelists' Calendar* (London: SPCK, 1978), on which see below, pp.46–47.

Perspectives analyzes one such passage in great detail (see below, pp.142–143. The testimony of the church fathers cannot be dismissed as easily as some would like,[1] and a view which sees Matthew as revising and expanding a 'first draft' of his gospel in the light of Mark, similar to Streeter's approach to Luke, makes sense of much of the data. The more one is willing to accept the traditional claim that the Gospel of Matthew was written by the apostle himself, the more likely such a hypothesis becomes, since it is hard to imagine an apostle and eyewitness of most of Jesus' ministry so indebted to a non-apostolic writer like Mark, who at best only caught firsthand glimpses of isolated events in Jesus' life. Yet the fact that, according to early church history, Mark derived much of his information from Peter, who was the leader of the twelve and present for certain events (usually along with James and John) when the rest were not, does make it credible that Matthew would want to consult Mark for at least some information.[2] But the idea of Mark depending on Matthew's final product must almost certainly be rejected.

The rest of this study does not depend on Matthaean authorship of the gospel attributed to him or on any form of a 'proto-Matthew' hypothesis, however probable either may be. What is presupposed, however, is that whoever wrote this gospel had access to early traditions about Jesus in addition to Mark and Q.[3] The view that all Matthew's unparalleled material must be historically suspect flies in the face of Luke's claim to have had 'many' predecessors and does not tally with the evidence of second-century church fathers who still had access to orally transmitted teachings of Jesus not found in the four gospels (see below, pp.202–208).[4]

---

[1]In defence of its reliability, see C. S. Petrie, 'The Authorship of "The Gospel According to Matthew". A Reconsideration of the External Evidence', *NTS* 14 (1967–68), pp.15–32; R. Glover, 'Patristic Quotations and Gospel Sources', *NTS* 31 (1985), pp.234–251; A. C. Perumalil, 'Are Not Papias and Irenaeus Competent to Report on the Gospels?' *ExpT* 91 (1980), pp.332–337.

[2]A strong defence of Matthaean authorship is found in Robert H. Gundry, *Matthew: A Commentary on His Literary and Theological Art* (Grand Rapids: Eerdmans, 1982), pp.609–622, a defence that much more significant because of Gundry's much less traditional views on Matthaean manner of composition.

[3]Since the titles to the books of the Bible did not form part of the original manuscripts, all four gospels are, strictly speaking, anonymous. The names Matthew, Mark, Luke and John appear nowhere in the texts as their authors.

[4]*Cf.* Richard Bauckham, 'The Study of Gospel Traditions Outside the Canonical Gospels: Problems and Prospects', in *GP*, 5, p.377: 'Since the Apostolic Fathers knew non-Markan traditions in oral form, it is inconceivable that Matthew and Luke should not have done.

The same openness must be maintained toward Luke's unparalleled material. Admittedly, even the traditional claims concerning authorship place Luke, most probably a Gentile, one step further removed from the original events which he describes. He was probably never even in Palestine during the lifetime of Jesus. His information was therefore entirely second-hand, even if he believed it was nevertheless fully reliable (Lk. 1:1–4). Yet, whether or not all the details of Streeter's 'proto-Luke' hypothesis hold up, there is good evidence to support Luke's confidence in the accuracy of his narrative. The two primary portions of Luke which have no verbal parallelism with either Mark or Matthew are the infancy narratives (1–2) and the nearly twenty parables which comprise the bulk of his central section, often called the Peraean ministry (9:51 – 18:14). Here more than anywhere Luke has been suspected of giving free rein to a creative imagination rather than following reliable historical sources.[1] Stephen Farris, however, has shown that the Greek of Luke 1–2 is filled with grammatical and stylistic nuances which are not found with the same frequency elsewhere in Luke, or in a sizeable selection of other ancient Greek writings surveyed, but which make good sense as a very wooden, literal translation of Hebrew or Aramaic into Greek. Farris emphasizes that these features are not of the type that lends itself to conscious imitation by one who might want to give his writing a biblical (*i.e.* Old Testament) flavour, since they involve the frequency and usage of various prepositions, articles, adverbs and adjectives rather than more readily reproducible vocabulary or parts of speech.[2] Luke therefore most probably relied on earlier tradition for these chapters. As for the parables of Luke's central section, I have argued elsewhere that when one separates them from the surrounding teachings which

---

Christian literature outside the Synoptic Gospels provides so much evidence of independent, varying forms of Synoptic material that the *probability* is in favour of more, not fewer, Synoptic sources.' Bauckham goes on to argue for Matthew's widespread use of M as a trustworthy source.

[1]On the former, see esp. Raymond E. Brown, *The Birth of the Messiah* (Garden City: Doubleday; London: Geoffrey Chapman, 1977); on the latter, John Drury, *Tradition and Design in Luke's Gospel* (London: Darton, Longman & Todd, 1976).

[2]Stephen C. Farris, 'On Discerning Semitic Sources in Luke 1–2', in *GP*, 2, pp.201–237. *Cf.* his *The Hymns of Luke's Infancy Narratives* (Sheffield: JSOT Press, 1985), and my review of this book in a forthcoming issue of *EQ*. Farris's statistical method needs further testing before the validity of its results can be affirmed with confidence. But the arguments for a traditional origin of Luke 1–2 are not limited to this one kind of analysis; see esp. Rainer Riesner, *Jesus als Lehrer* (Tübingen: Mohr, 1981), pp.210–212.

Luke has attached to them, they line up in a remarkable pattern of inverted parallelism. Luke's outline seems to be a topical one, but he has preserved intact an arrangement of the parables that was widely used in the ancient world as a mnemonic device, suggesting that this unparalleled material also stemmed from a prior, faithfully transmitted source.[1]

There is ample reason therefore to believe that in all the major sections of their gospels, the three Synoptic writers depended on early sources for the information which they have recorded. The fears of certain Christians that 'source criticism' somehow requires a conclusion that the gospels cannot be trusted or were not Spirit-inspired are groundless. Source criticism cannot demonstrate that the first accounts of the various portions of Jesus' life were entirely trustworthy, but it can suggest that those accounts arose in a time and place in which many who had personally known Jesus still lived. The possibility of preserving reliable information was certainly present. Whether or not that possibility should be strengthened to a probability depends on other factors yet to be discussed.

---

[1] Craig L. Blomberg, 'Midrash, Chiasmus, and the Outline of Luke's Central Section', in *GP*, 3, pp.217–261.

CHAPTER TWO

New methods in gospel study

The last seventy years of biblical scholarship have produced a bewildering array of new theories about the composition and interpretation of the gospels. Not surprisingly, most have met with a fair amount of suspicion at first since cherished traditions die hard. From a theological perspective, many people understandably ask if God woud have left his people in the dark all these centuries and only revealed the truth to a group of twentieth-century scholars. If pushed too far, this type of reasoning leads to results which few Christians would want to accept. If truth is determined by what was believed for the longest period of time in church history, then Christians should revert to mediaeval Roman Catholic theology. This is a move which almost no branch of Christianity today would be prepared to take, including mainstream Roman Catholicism since its famous modernizations in the early 1960s stemming from the second Vatican Council. Of course what most Christians down through history have argued, whenever they have rejected the prevailing opinion on some matter of controversy, is that they are returning to a position held in *earlier* times which had been forgotten or distorted. The Protestant Reformation's emphasis on justification by grace through faith and on Scripture as the sole authority for establishing theology and ethics provides a classic illustration of a movement that believed it was returning to New Testament and first-century Christian tradition, while at the same time differing radically from the rest of Christendom in its day.

Most of the modern critical tools have been developed by Protestant scholars who see themselves as continuing in the spirit of the Reformation. Believing that many of the popular, traditional views about the Bible's formation still stem from inaccurate church tradition, they seek with more scientific and historical rigour to lay bare the true nature of the origins of Christian faith and its sacred Scriptures. How successful they have been, at least in the application of their methods to the study of the gospels, is the major focus of attention in this chapter. But at the outset it must be emphasized that this particular motive prompting modern criticism is a praiseworthy one. Of course other factors enter in. Movements which question traditional opinion on any facet of life are regularly seized and utilized by people whose objectives are more extreme than those of the movements' founders. Yet even the most conservative students of the New Testament today draw on findings and discoveries about the biblical world which have been unavailable to almost all their predecessors. Anyone who follows a translation more up to date than the Authorized Version, or consults a modern dictionary of New Testament Greek, or adopts the insights of any twentieth-century commentary, dictionary, or encyclopaedia on a given part of Scripture, or accepts the interpretations of a preacher who does any of the above, is heavily indebted to the textual, linguistic, and historical criticism of recent scholarship. And all three of these branches of criticism have discovered information about what the writers of Scripture at various points said and meant which subsequent generations failed to preserve.[1]

The methods of studying the gospels surveyed below are similarly valuable, and they should be approached in a positive spirit. At the same time, every tool of criticism can be abused. Conclusions can be drawn which the data do not warrant. What for many people separates these 'newer' methods from other approaches is that they have been most commonly employed to challenge the historical reliability of the gospels. But such a use of these new tools is unjustified; when handled properly each of them can actually help to corroborate the reliability of the gospels in various places.

1 Form criticism

A The classic approach

Rudolf Bultmann was probably the most dominant figure in twentieth-century New Testament scholarship. Following closely

---

[1]For good introductions to these disciplines, see, respectively, Bruce M. Metzger, *The Text of the New Testament: Its Transmission, Corruption, and Restoration* (New York and Oxford:

on the heels of his German colleagues K. L. Schmidt and Martin Dibelius, Bultmann helped to pioneer for gospel study in the 1920s a method already used in German Old Testament criticism – *Formgeschichte,* literally 'form history'.[1] This method has been widely recognized to involve three major components.[2]

(1) The various passages and stories in the gospels about what Jesus said and did are categorized according to 'form'. Some are parables, some miracle stories, some proverbial sayings of wisdom. Some stories serve only to lead to a climactic saying of Jesus and have thus been called 'pronouncement stories' (*e.g.* Mk. 2:15–17 or 3:31–35).[3] A few are termed 'legends', and are often, though not always, regarded as unhistorical accounts of Jesus or the disciples, designed to illustrate some virtue or vice (*e.g.* Lk. 2:41–49 or Mt. 27:3–8). Several other categories have also been suggested though not always agreed upon. As in the case of the 'legend', some of the forms seem to be classified according to their contents more than their structure.

(2) Each form is assigned to a context in the life of the first-century church in which it would have most likely been used. The presupposition employed here is that the different kinds of passages circulated independently of one another in the early church. Pronouncement stories, for example, could have provided effective illustrations for popular preaching. Miracle stories certainly aided early Christian apologetic against Greek and Roman religions which deified their heroes. Legends are said to reflect the sincere but over-enthusiastic attempts of popular story-tellers to dramatize and glorify a genuine attribute of one of the gospel characters.

(3) The history of the oral transmission of each form is pos-

---

University Press, 1968); Moisés Silva, *Biblical Words and Their Meaning* (Grand Rapids: Zondervan, 1983); F. F. Bruce, *New Testament History* (London: Thomas Nelson, 1969; Garden City: Doubleday, 1972).

[1]Rudolf Bultmann, *The History of the Synoptic Tradition* (Oxford: Blackwell; New York: Harper & Row, 1963 [German orig. 1921]); Martin Dibelius, *From Tradition to Gospel* (Cambridge: James Clarke, 1934; New York: Scribner's Sons, 1965 [German orig. 1919]); K. L. Schmidt, *Der Rahmen der Geschichte Jesu* (Darmstadt: Wissenschaftliche Buchgesellschaft, 1969 [orig. 1919]).

[2]For a more detailed presentation, see E. V. McKnight, *What Is Form Criticism?* (Philadelphia: Fortress, 1969).

[3]This term comes from the first of the English form critics, Vincent Taylor, *The Formation of the Gospel Tradition* (London: Macmillan, 1933), p.30. Bultmann had called them apophthegms; and Dibelius, paradigms. More recently, the term 'controversy story' has become popular for those passages in which the pronouncements arose out of some conflict which Jesus had with the Jewish leaders and in which he adopted a radical stance.

21

tulated for the period of time before it was first written down in one of the gospels or in one of their source documents. Parables, it is said, were relatively well-preserved because of their distinctive character and structure, but the beginnings and endings of them were often altered, especially as they were applied to new contexts. The 'pronouncement' in a pronouncement story was likely to have been better preserved than the material preceding it, much like the punch line of a joke which can be led up to in several ways. In fact, form critics developed detailed 'laws' describing the transmission of oral tradition based on analogies from apocryphal Christian tradition and from other ancient non-Christian oral traditions. Thus they concluded that the information which the gospel writers finally collected and wrote down was a fairly unstable mixture of fact and fiction, history and legend, sober narrative and fanciful embellishment.[1] At the same time, many of the early form critics were reacting against an almost thoroughgoing agnosticism about the ability of historical research to substantiate the information in the gospels, so that in one sense their movement represented a swing in a slightly more conservative direction.

As the oldest of the 'new' methods which this chapter surveys, form criticism has lost much of the appeal it once had even among its greatest devotees. It is appropriate, therefore, to begin a critique with a recognition of its positive value. By far the most significant of its three endeavours was the first. To recognize what for a longer work of literature would be called its 'genre' is necessary for valid interpretation. Parables, for example, must not be interpreted like straightforward history; although they are very lifelike in many ways, Jesus may have included some details in them simply to make the stories lively and interesting. One of the most misinterpreted of Jesus' parables is the story of the rich man and Lazarus (Lk. 16:19–31), which has been used repeatedly to provide in great detail a realistic depiction of life after death. In fact, the picture of the rich man in Sheol and Lazarus in Abraham's bosom separated by a chasm but able to call to each other across it is paralleled by popular Jewish and Egyptian folk-tales.

---

[1]Step (3) has sometimes come to be separated from (1) and (2) and labelled 'tradition criticism' or 'tradition history'; here it is being treated as part of 'form criticism' to which it is historically and organically connected. In the study of the New Testament, 'the gospel tradition' usually refers to the body of information about Jesus' teaching and ministry which was passed along from one person to the next before the four gospels were written.

Jesus may have simply adopted well-known imagery but then adapted it in a new and surprising way to warn the godless wealthy about their need for repentance in this life before their fate is sealed (verses 27–31 are less paralleled in their counterparts).[1] The objection that Luke does not specifically call this passage a 'parable' is most decisively countered by form criticism; approximately half the stories in the gospels which are commonly called parables are not specifically labelled as such, but they are recognized by the common form and structure which they share with passages specifically termed parables. In the case of Luke 16:19–31, the introduction alone offers important cues. The parable begins, 'A certain man was . . .' This is the exact formula which Jesus employed in the two preceding parables of the prodigal son (15:11–32) and the unjust steward (16:1–13) and seems to correspond to the modern 'Once upon a time . . .' Just as people today recognize such a phrase as the opening of a fairy-tale, so Jesus' audience would have been prepared by the start of a parable to recognize it as a fictitious narrative.[2]

Not only can form criticism help us to analyze the form properly and therefore correctly interpret the meaning of an individual passage, but it can also illuminate larger sections of the gospels. The gospels' outlines of the life and teachings of Christ are often non-chronological; the order of passages is simply too different from one gospel to the next to argue otherwise. Form criticism, however, rules out the idea that these stories were arranged in arbitrary sequence, since many times the rationale for juxtaposing passages seems to be their similarity in form. Thus Mark 2:1 – 3:6 (*cf.* Mt. 9:1–17; 12:1 – 14; Lk. 5:17 – 6:11) collects together a group of pronouncement or controversy stories and Mark 4:35 – 6:6a (*cf.* Mt. 8:23–34; 9:18–26; 13:53–58; Lk. 8:22–56; 4:16–30) a group of miracle stories. Matthew and Luke follow Mark's sequence in certain places and radically depart from it in others, as shown by the parenthetical references above to the parallels. They in turn offer their own collections of forms – a concentration of healing stories in Matthew 8–9 and of parables in Luke 14–16, to

---

[1]See Joachim Jeremias, *The Parables of Jesus* (London: SCM; Philadelphia: Westminster, 1972), pp.182–186. Jeremias' work is by far the most masterful example of both the strengths and weaknesses of form criticism as applied to the parables.

[2]For more detail on this and similar examples of the form criticism of the parables, see Craig L. Blomberg, *Interpreting the Parables* (forthcoming) ch. two.

cite two of the more noteworthy examples.

The second item on the form-critic's agenda proves more speculative. It is very difficult to recover clear-cut evidence as to how the various gospel stories were used in the early church prior to their being written down. Although the hypothesis of the use of pronouncement stories in popular preaching seems plausible enough, it is striking that the rest of the New Testament and other early Christian literature supplies no concrete example of that actually happening. The legend may be an inappropriate form to apply to the gospel traditions because of Christianity's unique concern for earthing God's actions in history. On the other hand, second-century evidence makes it quite likely that the miracle stories were used apologetically as the form critics claimed (see below, p.86). In this case recognizing how the early church used a particular portion of the gospel tradition may then suggest ways in which the church today can do likewise.[1]

The biggest problems with form criticism arise when one takes the third and final step, *i.e.*, writing the history of the traditions. Several considerations challenge the notion that stories of what Jesus did and said would have been significantly distorted as they were passed along by word of mouth.[2] (1) The short period of time between the actual events described (*c.* AD 27–30) and the time in which Mark wrote (*c.* AD 70–75 at the latest, and probably pre-70) distinguishes the formation of the gospels from most other allegedly parallel processes of oral transmission in antiquity, which generally span several centuries. Eyewitnesses of Jesus' ministry, including hostile ones, could easily have refuted and discredited the Christian claims during this period if they were in any way mistaken. (2) This relatively short span of time was probably even shorter than the forty year maximum just noted, since Q (see pp.12–13) probably dates from the 50s. Additionally, as with the disciples of the ancient Jewish rabbis, Jesus' followers may well have privately kept written notes while passing along the tradition

---

[1]Very helpful in this respect is Eric Franklin, *How the Critics Can Help* (London: SCM, 1982), pp.11–23.

[2]For elaboration, see *e.g.* Graham N. Stanton, 'Form Criticism Revisited', in *What about the New Testament?* ed. Morna Hooker and Colin Hickling (London: SCM, 1975), pp.13–27; E. E. Ellis, 'New Directions in Form Criticism', in *Jesus Christus in Historie und Theologie*, ed. G. Strecker (Tübingen: Mohr, 1975), pp.299–315; Stephen H. Travis, 'Form Criticism', in *New Testament Interpretation*, ed. I. H. Marshall (Exeter: Paternoster; Grand Rapids: Eerdmans, 1977), pp.153–164.

orally in public. There is no reason why Jesus' disciples could not have begun such note-taking even while he was still alive, since Jesus sent them out on their own on at least two missions to preach the gospel. After the ascension this practice would have become even more likely.[1] (3) The so-called laws of the transmission of the tradition are anything but 'laws'. E. P. Sanders, in one of the earliest studies to use computer technology to gather data relevant to biblical studies, analyzed in detail the gospel traditions which have been preserved in textual variants, the early church fathers and New Testament apocrypha, and demonstrated that no consistent trends exist concerning the lengthening or shortening, preservation or distortion of the tradition.[2] If anything, other shorter studies have demonstrated a slight tendency for detailed material to become abbreviated, condensed, more stereotyped and less vivid as the stories of Jesus were continually retold in the Gentile world, all precisely the opposite of what the first form critics alleged! Certainly this is the trend that is observable if one compares parallel passages in Mark and Luke, and to a lesser extent in Mark and Matthew.[3] These phenomena led a group of Scandinavian scholars to propose a very different approach to the history of the oral tradition behind the gospels.

B Memorizing the tradition?

In 1959 Professor Harald Riesenfeld of Uppsala published a seminal article, 'The Gospel Tradition and its Beginnings'.[4] In it he argued that the appropriate analogy for understanding the history of the oral tradition behind the gospels was not the relatively fluid process of transmitting popular folk-tales, as the form critics had assumed, but the much more rigid patterns of memorization and paraphrase dominant in rabbinic circles in the centuries immedi-

---

[1]These points were emphasized in a ground-breaking article, unfortunately never translated into English, by Heinz Schürmann, 'Die vorösterlichen Anfänge der Logientradition', in *Der historische Jesus und der kerygmatische Christus*, ed. H. Ristow and K. Matthiae (Berlin: Evangelische Verlagsanstalt, 1960), pp.342–370. A good summary, however, appears in René Latourelle, *Finding Jesus through the Gospels* (New York: Alba, 1979), pp.157–168.

[2]E. P. Sanders, *The Tendencies of the Synoptic Tradition* (Cambridge: University Press, 1969).

[3]*Cf. e.g.* Leslie R. Keylock, 'Bultmann's Law of Increasing Distinctness', in *Current Issues in Biblical and Patristic Interpretation*, ed. Gerald F. Hawthorne (Grand Rapids: Eerdmans, 1975), pp.193–210; Craig L. Blomberg, 'Tradition and Redaction in the Parables of the Gospel of Thomas', in *GP*,5, pp.177–205.

[4]*TU* 73, pp.43–65. The article was reprinted in the more accessible collection of Riesenfeld's essays, *The Gospel Tradition* (Philadelphia: Fortress, 1970), pp.1–29.

ately following the birth of Christianity. According to Riesenfeld, Jesus probably had his disciples memorize his most significant teachings and perhaps even certain narratives about what he did. Thus there is every reason to believe that they were reliably preserved. Riesenfeld's student, Birger Gerhardsson, developed these ideas into a full-length technical monograph, *Memory and Manuscript: Oral Tradition and Written Transmission in Rabbinic Judaism and Early Christianity*.[1] In addition to documenting how widespread and prodigious the practice of memorization was in ancient rabbinic circles (many rabbis had the entire Old Testament and much of the oral law committed to memory!), Gerhardsson also developed the idea that Jesus' twelve disciples formed an authoritative circle of leadership which carefully safeguarded the traditions and prevented them from the inevitable distortion to which indiscriminate use would have led. Paul especially points to the existence of such a circle when he speaks of 'delivering' and 'receiving' tradition handed down to him (*e.g.* 1 Cor. 11:23; 15:3), employing language also used by the rabbis to refer to the transmission of their teachings.[2]

Reaction to Riesenfeld and Gerhardsson was largely negative, as reaction to wholesale challenges to the status quo often is. But their critics had some legitimate questions. Was not Jesus sufficiently different from other Jewish teachers so as to make any hypothesis based on the assumption that he taught just like any other rabbi rather dubious? Were not the practices of second- and third-century rabbis, almost exclusively the product of the Pharisaic branch of Judaism, more uniform after the destruction of the temple and of rival Jewish sects in AD 70 than before? Is not the evidence in the gospels and Acts of Jesus' disciples' memorizing teaching and passing it on in fixed form so scant as to call into question massive inferences based on a few comments by Paul? Most crucially, does not the sheer diversity of language and detail between Synoptic parallels almost entirely undermine a hypothesis of memorization, which would require the gospels to be even more similar to each other than they are?

---

[1] (Lund: Gleerup, 1961).
[2] For a more detailed summary of the positions of the 'Scandinavian school', see Peter H. Davids, 'The Gospels and Jewish Tradition: Twenty Years after Gerhardsson', in *GP*,1, pp.75–99. Davids also offers a balanced critique which underlies the comments in the next paragraph.

Gerhardsson has remained undaunted in the face of his critics and has explained and refined his position further.[1] But it is a German scholar, Rainer Riesner, in his recent doctoral dissertation at Tübingen, who has advanced the discussion initiated in Uppsala to a promising new level.[2] Rather than focusing exclusively on rabbinic practices which Jesus might not have adopted, Riesner comprehensively surveys the educational methods common to ancient Israel and her neighbours. He concludes that at least six good reasons exist why Jesus' followers would have carefully preserved accurate information about him without necessarily memorizing it word for word. (1) Jesus followed the practice of Old Testament prophets by proclaiming the Word of the Lord with the kind of authority that would have commanded respect and concern to safeguard that which was perceived as revelation from God. Just as many parts of Old Testament prophecy are considered by even fairly sceptical scholars to have been quite well preserved, so Jesus' words should be considered in the same light. (2) The fact that Jesus presented himself as Messiah, even if in a sometimes veiled way, would reinforce his followers' concern to preserve his words, since one fairly consistent feature in an otherwise diverse body of first-century expectations was that the Messiah would be a teacher of wisdom. (3) The gospels depict Jesus as just such a teacher of wisdom and phrase over 90% of his sayings in forms which would have been easy to remember, using figures and styles of speech much like those found in Hebrew poetry.[3] (4) There is widespread evidence in the gospels of Jesus commanding the twelve to 'learn' specific lessons and to transmit what they learn to others, even before the end of his earthly ministry. In addition to the obvious missions of Mark 6:7–13 and parallels (in this book abbreviated 'pars.') and Luke 10:1–17, subtler hints appear in Mark 13:28; Luke 11:1; Mark 9:10 and Acts 2:42.[4]

---

[1]Birger Gerhardsson, *Tradition and Transmission in Early Christianity* (Lund: Gleerup, 1964); see also his *The Origins of the Gospel Tradition* (London: SCM; Philadelphia: Fortress, 1979).

[2]Rainer Riesner, *Jesus als Lehrer* (Tübingen: Mohr, 1981). An English translation of this work is forthcoming. The direction of Riesner's discussion was anticipated in his 'Jüdische Elementarbildung und Evangelienüberlieferung', in *GP*, 1, pp.209–223.

[3]Robert H. Stein, *The Method and Message of Jesus' Teaching* (Philadelphia: Westminster, 1978), pp.1–33, provides an excellent sampling of these forms.

[4]It has often been argued that Matthew and Luke have added an emphasis concerning Jesus as teacher which was not important to earlier stages of the tradition. Yet despite the longer sermons of Matthew and the additional parables in Luke, Mark actually refers to Jesus as a teacher and to his teaching activity proportionately more often than either Matthew or Luke.

(5) Elementary education for boys until at least the age of twelve was widely practised in Israel in Jesus' day, so texts like Acts 4:13 cannot mean that the disciples had no competence in reading, writing and memorization. (6) Almost all teachers in the Jewish and Graeco-Roman worlds gathered disciples around them in order to perpetuate their teachings and lifestyle, so however different Jesus was from the rabbis in other ways, he probably resembled them in this respect. If he envisaged his disciples as in some sense continuing his ministry for any length of time (see pp.33–35), then he certainly would have been concerned that they preserve his message and mission intact.

Riesner's conclusions have been strengthened by two other German theses which discuss the general conservatism of tradition in the early church and the role of Christian 'teachers' in preserving that tradition.[1] The only problem which Riesner does not cover in detail is the question of the differences among the Synoptics as they now stand. However much may have been memorized, clearly at some stage of the tradition the early church felt free to paraphrase, rearrange, explain, and abbreviate the information which it had acquired. On this issue illumination is offered by a different source – what has been called a modern revolution in the study of ancient folklore and its oral transmission.[2]

C Flexible transmission within fixed limits

Studies by anthropologists such as A. B. Lord on Eastern Europe and J. Vansina on Africa have enabled scholars to observe twentieth-century examples of oral folklore and sacred history being preserved by specially designated members of very traditional communities uninfluenced by the development of literacy or technology.[3] Their discoveries demonstrate the viability of a mediating view between the classic form-critical and memorization

---

For this and other reasons R. T. France, 'Mark and the Teaching of Jesus', *GP*, 1, pp.101–136, demonstrates that Mark is also very much interested in portraying Jesus as an authoritative teacher.

[1]P.-G. Müller, *Der Traditionsprozess im Neuen Testament* (Freiburg: Herder, 1982); and A. F. Zimmermann, *Die urchristlichen Lehrer* (Tübingen: Mohr, 1984), respectively.

[2]The first person to apply this information directly to a critique of form criticism was Erhardt Güttgemanns, *Candid Questions concerning Gospel Form Criticism* (Pittsburgh: Pickwick, 1979). In its place, however, Güttgemanns advocates a type of structuralism (see below, pp.58–62) that is even more radical than the form criticism he rejects.

[3]Albert B. Lord, *The Singer of Tales* (Cambridge, MA: Harvard, 1960); Jan Vansina, *Oral Tradition: A Study in Historical Methodology* (London: Routledge & Kegan Paul; Chicago: Aldine, 1965).

hypotheses, although it is a view that turns out to be much closer to the latter than to the former. Lord, for example, studied certain Yugoslavian folk-singers who had 'memorized' epic stories of up to 100,000 words in length. The plot, the characters, all the main events, and the vast majority of the details stayed the same every time the stories were retold or sung. Members of the community were sufficiently familiar with them to correct the singer if he erred in any significant way. Yet anywhere from 10% to 40% of the precise wording could vary from one performance to the next, quite like the variation found in the Synoptic gospels. Lord itemizes the types of changes as (a) 'saying the same thing in fewer or more lines', (b) 'expansion of ornamentation, adding details of description', (c) 'changes of order in a sequence', (d) 'addition of material . . . found in texts of other singers', (e) 'omission of material' and (f) 'substitution of one theme for another, in a story held together by inner tensions'.[1] The similarity between this list and a list of changes describing the differences among the Synoptics is striking indeed.[2] When one recalls that ancient Jews regularly sang, or chanted, their traditions, not the least as a help to the memory, one recognizes the presence of a helpful analogy.

A second important contribution of studies like those of Lord is an emphasis on the fundamental difference between the process of transmitting oral tradition and that of editing written documents. In the former instance, there is no single identifiable, stereotyped 'original form' of the tradition. Each time the folk-singer recreates the story, it is slightly different and no version is significantly closer to or further from the historical events being narrated. Once a community fixes its traditions in writing, all this can change suddenly. Now there is a fixed, authoritative document which serves as the standard by which to judge all further narrations of the events in question. This has led a few scholars to reject the applicability of the oral model to the gospels as they now exist, since the evangelists apparently drew on written sources for at least part of their information.[3] But this overlooks the fact that

[1]Lord, *Singer*, p.123.
[2]For one such list, see Latourelle, *Jesus*, pp.207–211. For Lord's own application of his findings to gospel criticism, see his 'The Gospels as Oral Traditional Literature', in *The Relationships among the Gospels*, ed. William O. Walker, Jr. (San Antonio: Trinity University, 1978), pp.33–91; and *cf.* the responses to his paper by C. H. Talbert and Leander E. Keck (pp.93–122).
[3]See esp. Werner Kelber, *The Oral and the Written Gospel* (Philadelphia: Fortress, 1983).

oral traditions often continued and remained highly authoritative even after written accounts of them were produced; many ancient writers comment on the greater trustworthiness of the former over the latter. To cite Lord once again, 'The use of writing in setting down oral texts does not *per se* have any effect on oral tradition.' It is only when a community accepts the idea of a fixed text that the situation changes. 'This means death to oral tradition and the rise of a generation of "singers" who are reproducers rather than re-creators'.[1] By the mid-second century, a similar phenomenon was occurring in Christianity, but it is obvious that in the earlier years in which the evangelists were writing their gospels they did not see their sources as dictating the only way in which the life of Jesus could be told.

Very similar conclusions arise from a study of the oldest targums, the Aramaic paraphrases of biblical books, used in the ancient Jewish synagogues, which interspersed occasional commentary into the text itself. Bruce Chilton, for example, has compared the differences among the three Synoptic accounts of Jesus' temptation in the wilderness with three of the targumic renderings of Exodus 12:42, which insert at this point 'the poem of the four nights', a reflection on four key occasions of God's self-revelation: creation, the covenant with Abraham, the original Passover night and the end of the age. Chilton shows how the types of similarities and differences among both sets of parallels resemble each other remarkably and might be due to similar characteristics of oral tradition. Chilton has since repeated the experiment with one other test case.[2] Apparently, however, no one has accepted the challenge to apply his approach to further examples, so how widely his method would work remains uncertain. At the very least he has confirmed in the above two instances what the previous studies surveyed in this section have been suggesting as a working hypothesis for the entire Synoptic tradition: there is every reason to believe that many of the sayings and actions of Jesus would have been very carefully safeguarded in the first decades of the church's history, not so slavishly as to hamper freedom to

---

[1]Lord, *Singer*, pp.128, 137.

[2]Bruce D. Chilton, 'Targumic Transmission and Dominical Tradition', in *GP*,1, pp.21–45. *Cf.* his 'A Comparative Study of Synoptic Development: The Dispute between Cain and Abel in the Palestinian Targums and the Beelzebul Controversy in the Gospels', *JBL* 101 (1982), pp.553–562.

paraphrase, explain, abbreviate and rearrange, but faithfully enough to produce reliable accounts of those facets of Christ's ministry selected for preservation.

Two issues not inherently bound up with form criticism have nevertheless regularly prevented scholars who have studied the oral history behind the gospels from adopting as conservative a conclusion as this.

D Christian prophecy

The first issue involves the claim that when early Christians exercised the gift of prophecy they regularly spoke what they believed were messages revealed by the risen and ascended Lord which were not always distinguished from the words of the earthly Jesus. Many of the sayings in the gospels attributed to Jesus would therefore be creations of the early church attempting to apply the Word of God to pressing concerns in local fellowships. Sometimes these prophets would have been entirely faithful to the spirit of Jesus, but, allowing for human error, sometimes they probably were not.

Despite acceptance of this theory by many scholars, there is scant evidence to support it.[1] The closest parallels come from the practices of certain Graeco-Roman prophets speaking in the name of mythological gods, especially at oracles or temples of healing. The only New Testament example which records words of the ascended Lord spoken directly to his people appears in the book of Revelation in the letters to the seven churches in Asia (Rev. 2:1 – 3:22). Yet even here it is clear that John is not claiming that these sayings of Jesus came from his earthly life. The examples of Christian prophecy in Acts are clearer still. Here Luke gives the name of the prophet speaking – Agabus (Acts 11:28; 21:10–11) – so that no one could confuse his words with those of his Lord. And even if such confusion did occur elsewhere, it seems unlikely that the church would ever have accepted any purported message from Jesus noticeably unlike the things he taught during his earthly life. Paul clearly stressed that all alleged prophecy had to be evaluated (1 Cor. 14:29), and the fundamental biblical criterion for evaluating prophecy was that it must conform to the previously

---

[1]See esp. David Hill, *New Testament Prophecy* (London: Marshall, Morgan & Scott; Richmond: John Knox, 1979), pp.160–185.

revealed word of God.[1] Further, if the gospel writers felt so free to include prophetic messages as words of the earthly Jesus, it is astonishing that there are no 'sayings' of Jesus addressing some of the most divisive controversies in the early church, for example the role of circumcision or speaking in tongues.

Two very recent works have sought to advance this debate further. M. E. Boring avoids some of the objections to previous hypotheses of creative prophecy by limiting his analysis to first-century Christian texts, by emphasizing that the prophets probably would have reworked authentic sayings of Jesus or else invented material largely consistent with those sayings, and by showing how expressions like 'the word of the Lord' or 'the Lord said' in the New Testament are often ambiguous – they can introduce Old Testament quotations, sayings of Jesus, or inspired utterances of later Christian speakers and writers.[2] What Boring fails to demonstrate, however, is that the phrase 'Jesus said' was similarly ambiguous or that it was ever attached to a Christian prophet's creation in a way which made it indistinguishable from Jesus' earthly teachings. Boring goes to great lengths to establish detailed criteria by which these prophets' teachings may be identified in the gospels, but one of these criteria requires the teaching to be suspect already on other grounds. One cannot thus postulate the widespread influence of Christian prophecy as a reason for believing much of the Jesus tradition to be inauthentic. One can only appeal to this theory to help explain why the tradition was accepted as authoritative, given other reasons for rejecting its historical reliability. David Aune, in the most detailed analysis of *Prophecy in Early Christianity and the Ancient Mediterranean World* so far produced, explains further and concludes that

> scholars, it appears, have seized the hypothesis of the creative role of Christian prophets because it both accounts for the additions to the sayings tradition and absolves the early Christians from any culpability in the forging of inauthentic words of Jesus. In spite of the theological attractiveness of the theory, however, the historical evidence in support of the theory lies

---

[1]See esp. J. D. G. Dunn, 'Prophetic "I"-Sayings and the Jesus Tradition: The Importance of Testing Prophetic Utterances within Early Christianity', *NTS* 24 (1978), pp.175–198.

[2]M. Eugene Boring, *Sayings of the Risen Jesus* (Cambridge: University Press, 1982).

largely in the creative imagination of scholars.[1]

E The delay of Christ's return

The second issue which many sceptics raise in questioning the reliability of the oral tradition which preceded the writing of the gospels deals with the length of time which Jesus and his followers thought would elapse before the end of the world. Several of Jesus' very solemn pronouncements sound as though he believed that he would return within the lifetime of at least some of his disciples: 'Truly I say to you that certain people are standing here who will surely not taste death until they see the kingdom of God having come in power' (Mk. 9:1); 'Truly I say to you that this generation will surely not pass away until all these things happen' (Mk. 13:30); 'Truly I say to you, you will surely not complete the cities of Israel before the Son of man comes' (Mt. 10:23). As time went by and Jesus did not come back, so this view affirms, Christians' hope for his imminent return began to recede and they recognized the need to preserve the story of Jesus for future generations. But not having anticipated this need, they had not preserved entirely reliable traditions on which to draw.

The hypothesis about the 'delay' of Christ's return influences the interpretation of the New Testament in a number of significant ways. But at least three key observations weigh against it. (1) None of the verses cited above should be taken to mean that Jesus mistakenly believed that he would return to earth in the first century. In fact, each has several alternative interpretations that are more likely. Perhaps the best are that in Mark 9:1 Jesus was referring to his subsequent transfiguration as an important foreshadowing of his final coming 'in power',[2] that in Mark 13:30 the 'all things' do not include his return but only the signs leading up to his return,[3] and that in Matthew 10:23 he is predicting the con-

---

[1](Grand Rapids: Eerdmans, 1983), p.245.

[2]See *e.g.* C. E. B. Cranfield, *The Gospel according to St. Mark* (Cambridge: University Press, 1977), pp. 285–288. Others argue that an emphatic proclamation that some would not die before an event only a week away makes no sense. Against this, see his 'Thoughts on New Testament Eschatology', *SJT* 35 (1982), p. 503: 'I would assume that the point of the solemn language about not tasting death is that the persons referred to would have the privilege of seeing in the course of their natural life what others would only see at the final judgment.'

[3]Cranfield, *Mark*, pp. 407–409. Elsewhere Cranfield persuasively characterizes the whole of New Testament eschatology in terms of this tension between the signs being fulfilled and the Parousia (return) of Christ delayed; see his 'The Parable of the Unjust Judge and the Eschatology of Luke-Acts', *SJT* 16 (1963), pp. 300–301: 'the Parousia is near . . . not in the sense that it

tinually incomplete mission of preaching the gospel to all the Jews.[1] (2) A large percentage of Jesus' teaching, including that which even more radical scholarship accepts as authentic, presupposes the continuing existence of Jesus' followers as an organized community teaching others about him. For example, Jesus takes ethical stands on such issues as marriage and divorce, payment of taxes and submission to the government, and perhaps most important of all, the application of the Old Testament commandments to everyday life, as epitomized in the Sermon on the Mount. (3) Even if the disciples had interpreted Jesus' teaching to mean that he would return in their generation, they would not have been the first Jews to have believed that the end of the age would come quite soon. Ever since the days of the writing prophets of the Old Testament, Israel had been hearing the message that the Day of the Lord was at hand (*e.g.* Joel 2:1; Ob. 15; Hab. 2:3). Yet this seldom deflected her from her course of carrying on with the ritual of the Law and living as though she had centuries ahead of her. May one expect any less from Jesus' followers? The behaviour of those Thessalonians who stopped working because they believed that Christ's return was imminent (2 Thes. 3:6–15) seems to have been an exception; at least Paul certainly discouraged it. 2 Peter 3:8–9 suggests that most Christians did not change their theology or invent alleged teaching of Jesus to mask his original claims when the delay in his return became apparent; rather they simply underlined the vast chasm between God's and man's perspectives on time: 'A day with the Lord is as a thousand years . . . The Lord is not slow as some count slowness . . .' Moreover, this interpretation of God's delay, based on Psalm 90:4, had already been applied by Jews in pre-Christian times to *their* questions concerning God's 'tardiness'.[2] The idea that the early church must have

---

must necessarily occur within a few months or years, but in the sense that it may occur at any moment and in the sense that, since *the* decisive event of history has already taken place in the ministry, death, resurrection and ascension of Christ, all subsequent history is a kind of epilogue, an interval inserted by God's mercy in order to allow men time for repentance, and, as such an epilogue, necessarily in a real sense short, even though it may last a very long time.'

[1] F. F. Bruce, *The Hard Sayings of Jesus* (London: Hodder & Stoughton; Downers Grove: IVP, 1983), p.109. *Cf.* Robert H. Gundry, *Matthew: A Commentary on His Literary and Theological Art* (Grand Rapids: Eerdmans, 1982), pp.194–195, although his conclusion that the saying is inauthentic is highly improbable in the light of its enigmatic nature.

[2] Richard Bauckham, 'The Delay of the Parousia', *TynB* 31 (1980), pp.3–36. The most thorough study of the tension between the imminence and delay of Christ's return in the New Testament is A. L. Moore, *The Parousia in the New Testament* (Leiden: Brill, 1966), who

drastically altered her approach to the Jesus tradition when it dawned on her that his return might not be so immediate seems very poorly founded.

To sum up, form criticism has rightly focused attention on the period in which information about Jesus' life circulated primarily by word of mouth. No matter how trustworthy and competent the gospel writers may have been, if the tradition on which they relied was faulty then the gospels which they composed would be defective. But, far from undermining one's confidence in the church's ability and desire to preserve such information intact, the understanding of the oral stage of the gospel tradition presented here only serves to corroborate the claim made explicit by Luke that his gospel enables enquirers into Christianity to know the certainty of the things about which they have been taught (Lk. 1:4).

2 Redaction criticism

A The method

Although much of the variation between gospel parallels undoubtedly stems from the period of oral tradition, not all of it does. The four evangelists by their own admission have different perspectives on the life of Christ which they wish to emphasize (see esp. John 20:31). The early church's decision to include four gospels rather than just one, or rather than a harmony like Tatian's, reflects the recognition that Matthew, Mark, Luke and John each had distinctive emphases which should not be abandoned or blurred. Form criticism too easily tended to view the gospel writers as mere compilers of tradition, splicing together various snippets of information into a somewhat disjointed whole. It was only natural, then, that the pendulum should eventually swing away from this extreme and move in the direction which has come to be known as redaction criticism (in German, *Redaktionsgeschichte*). This discipline recognizes the evangelists as full-fledged redactors, that is, editors, in selecting, arranging, and rewording their sources to highlight particular theological and stylistic emphases. In the words of Richard Soulen's *Handbook of Biblical Criticism*, redac-

concludes that the end for Jesus 'was *in some sense* near' but that 'evidence is lacking that he held to a delimited hope' (p.190).

tional study 'seeks to lay bare the theological perspectives of a Biblical writer by analysing the editorial (redactional) and compositional techniques and interpretations employed by him in shaping and framing the written and/or oral traditions at hand (see Luke 1:1–4)'.[1]

The three scholars who are regularly credited with the development of modern redaction criticism are Günther Bornkamm, Willi Marxsen, and Hans Conzelmann, with their impressive studies of the theologies of Matthew, Mark and Luke, respectively.[2] To cite just one conclusion from each, Bornkamm argued that Matthew consistently portrayed Jesus' disciples in a more positive light than did his sources in order that he might encourage the fledgling faith of the young Christians to whom he was writing. Marxsen maintained that Mark focused more on Jesus' ministry in Galilee and on teaching about his second coming because he was writing to a church in that region who believed in Christ's imminent return. Conzelmann claimed that Luke was the first to envision an ongoing church age and so inserted features into his gospel which pointed to a delay in Christ's return.

B Critique

In many ways, redaction criticism has proved a healthy corrective to form criticism, not least because it focuses on the gospel texts as they now stand rather than on their uncertain pre-history. One can defend only the probability of Christians accurately preserving the details of Jesus' teaching as they passed it on by word of mouth, because there is no ancient testimony which specifically describes how they did this. But one can look at the four gospels and see how they vary. In other words, granted that the early church *could* have handed down reliable information about Jesus, do the differences even just among the Synoptics permit one to maintain that it *did* do so? As chapter one demonstrated, the varying theological perspectives of the evangelists have been recognized since antiquity. Redaction criticism in this sense is scarcely a new

---

[1](Guildford: Lutterworth; Richmond: John Knox, 1977), pp.142–143. A few writers want to separate these two tasks and speak of 'redaction criticism' and 'composition criticism', but the majority keep them together.

[2]G. Bornkamm, G. Barth, and H.-J. Held, *Tradition and Interpretation in Matthew* (London: SCM; Philadelphia: Westminster, 1963); Willi Marxsen, *Mark the Evangelist* (Nashville: Abingdon, 1969); Hans Conzelmann, *The Theology of St. Luke* (New York: Harper & Row; London: Faber & Faber, 1960).

method; only its name is. But only with the recent, widespread acceptance of the two-document hypothesis as the solution to the Synoptic problem could the method be refined and the question specifically phrased: how drastically have Luke and Matthew altered the passages which they acquired from Mark and Q?[1]

All redaction critics, therefore, have at least this much in common: by analyzing the various ways in which the gospel writers have edited their sources, they seek to identify the distinctive theology of each, which is so easily lost sight of in a harmonistic study of the life of Christ. No one who respects the fact that Scripture contains four distinct gospels should object to this endeavour. Those who argue that redaction criticism is inherently destructive because it focuses on the apparent contradictions between gospel parallels cannot make those discrepancies disappear merely by ignoring them![2] But many redaction critics bring unwarranted presuppositions with them to their work which has tended to give the method a bad name in certain quarters. Eight of the most serious of these follow.[3]

(1) Some have assumed that an author's perspective emerges only from a study of how he has edited his sources. But most authors regularly cite information from various authorities precisely because they agree with it and do not need to modify it in any way. The theological emphases of the different gospel writers must therefore be determined on the basis of what is stressed where they leave their sources unchanged as well as where they make alterations. Bornkamm, for example, fails to take adequate notice of all the instances where Matthew echoes Mark's criticism of the disciples' lack of faith. The need to consider a whole gospel as a unity becomes that much more urgent in the cases of Mark and John, where any written sources on which they may have relied no longer exist and can be reconstructed only with great

---

[1]Two introductions to redaction criticism which stress this point are Norman Perrin, *What Is Redaction Criticism?* (Philadelphia: Fortress, 1969; London: SPCK, 1970); and Robert H. Stein, 'What is Redaktionsgeschichte?' *JBL* 88 (1969), pp.45–56.

[2]North American evangelicals, for example, have heatedly disputed this question; the debate is well-chronicled in D. L. Turner, 'Evangelicals, Redaction Criticism and the Current Inerrancy Crisis', *GTJ* 4 (1983), pp.263–288; and, by the same author, 'Evangelicals, Redaction Criticism and Inerrancy: The Debate Continues', *GTJ* 5 (1984), pp.37–45.

[3]For a more comprehensive list of problems, with elaboration, see D. A. Carson, 'Redaction Criticism: On the Legitimacy and Illegitimacy of a Literary Tool', in *Scripture and Truth*, ed. D. A. Carson and John D. Woodbridge (Grand Rapids: Zondervan; Leicester: IVP, 1983), pp.123–128. Also helpful is the brief introduction of Stephen S. Smalley, 'Redaction Criticism', in Marshall, *Interpretation*, pp.181–195.

speculation and margin for error. This point is increasingly being recognized by redaction critics of all stripes and is not as much of a problem as it once was.

(2) Some treat virtually every pair of passages with any similarity as variants of one original saying or event in Jesus' life. Yet most good teachers or preachers regularly repeat themselves, so it is highly unlikely that Jesus did not do the same. The contexts of alleged parallels must be carefully examined to make sure that they are referring to the same event, especially if the details make it seem as if two or more evangelists have contradicted each other. Jesus almost certainly used many of his short, proverbial sayings in several different contexts, and probably some of the parables which seem very similar and yet very different can be explained in this way as well (see below, p.148). On the other hand, one cannot resolve all the apparent discrepancies among the gospels this way. Jesus, for example, celebrated only one Last Supper with his disciples, so it will not work to explain the differences between the Synoptic accounts of that meal as coming from different occasions in his ministry!

(3) Drawing conclusions about the nature of the communities which the gospel writers were addressing is a much more subjective process than many critics admit. It is one thing to note characteristic differences between two gospels; it is another entirely to infer from these the precise situations in the early church which led to these emphases. And not every passage in the gospels was included simply because it addressed a relevant need in the church; some stem from historical or biographical interest in the person of Jesus as well.[1] Thus although Bornkamm's hypothesis of a group of young Christians needing encouragement is a plausible explanation for Matthew's apparent playing down of the disciples' failures, it is just as plausible that Matthew merely felt Mark's account too susceptible to misunderstanding or one-sided in its presentation and chose to paint a more balanced picture.

(4) Many redaction-critical studies build on the unjustified assumptions of more radical form criticism. Redaction criticism by itself is inherently more reassuring than form criticism. It gives one greater confidence in the gospel writers to realize that the differen-

---

[1]Defending this point at length, in view of widespread insistence to the contrary, is Graham N. Stanton, *Jesus of Nazareth in New Testament Preaching* (Cambridge: University Press, 1974).

ces among them were deliberately introduced for rational, identifiable reasons- to stress one facet of Jesus' character and ministry instead of another- rather than being simply the unfortunate end-product of an oral tradition that inevitably made mistakes in transmission. But that greater confidence evaporates if the redaction critic accepts the theory of an unreliable tradition and then assumes that the four evangelists introduced further changes. Like the example of the man who found himself possessed by eight demons instead of one, the last state becomes worse than the first (Lk. 11:24–26).

(5) Some less sceptical scholars have attempted to alleviate this problem by arguing that the question of how a given story about Jesus was passed along by the tradition and then edited by the evangelists is irrelevant to the question of its normativeness for Christians today. Put another way, an alleged saying of Jesus need not be authentic for it to be authoritative. Since Christians traditionally have believed that God's Spirit inspired only the gospel writers and not all those who may have preceded them in handing down Jesus' teaching, all that counts is the final form of the gospels.[1] Nevertheless, though well intentioned, this approach makes Christian belief unfalsifiable and therefore unjustifiable (*cf.* above, pp.10–12). Had the first Christians adopted it, they would have had no rationale for excluding the apocryphal gospels from the canon; the very notion of a canon implies belief in the ability to separate truth from error. Christians do believe that the evangelists are the inspired interpreters of the Jesus tradition, but if their interpretations should distort or misrepresent what he did and said then they must be rejected as not inspired after all rather than clung to as authoritative without any proper basis for such respect.

(6) Minor grammatical and syntactical differences between parallels are sometimes invested with deep theological significance. More balanced redaction criticism, however, explains many of these differences in the light of the distinctive styles of each author. Luke, probably a native Greek, writes much more art-

---

[1]Proponents of this view have come to refer to their approach as canon criticism. The method is associated especially with Brevard S. Childs's massive *Introduction to the Old Testament as Scripture* (Philadelphia: Fortress; London: SCM, 1979); see now also his *The New Testament Canon: An Introduction* (Philadelphia: Fortress; London: SCM, 1984). For an evangelical endorsement of this approach, see Robert H. Stein, 'The "Criteria" for Authenticity', in *GP*,1, p.229.

istically and fluently than Mark, whose prose is more awkward and more Semitic. Matthew's and John's styles fall somewhere in between, leading to inconclusive debates as to whether or not they reflect the type of writing which could be attributed to Jewish apostles of Christ. In any event, all four gospels often alter their sources simply to clarify potentially ambiguous wording.

(7) Closely related to this is the problem of distinctive vocabulary. Some redaction critics believe that a careful analysis of how often a given word or expression occurs in each of the gospels can enable one to separate an evangelist's diction from that of the tradition he inherited. On this basis they confidently assign virtually every word in every verse to either redaction or tradition. To be sure, a limited amount of this dissection seems possible. Luke, for example, concludes his quotation of Mark 2:17b, 'I have come not to call the righteous, but sinners,' by adding the words 'to repentance' (Lk. 5:32). Since the Greek words for 'repent' and 'repentance' occur fourteen times in Luke's gospel and only three times in Mark, it is reasonable to assume that this is an important topic for Luke and that he has added the reference in 5:32 to explain more precisely what kind of call Jesus was extending to 'sinners'. This type of explanatory paraphrase accounts for a large portion of the minor differences between gospel parallels, and to recognize particular words and themes as favourites of a given author can suggest that certain paraphrases were carefully planned. But many examples are not so clear-cut. How often must a word or topic occur in a given gospel and how rare must it be in that gospel's sources for one to assign it with confidence to the evangelist's redaction? Most studies of this nature drastically exaggerate the amount of material that can be so identified.[1]

(8) Finally, and most significantly, redaction critics have regularly assumed that the material which the evangelists have added or the changes they have made to their sources cannot rest on historical tradition. The various redactional emphases of each evangelist are then usually exaggerated by these scholars so that distinctives turn into contradictions, while plausible harmoniz-

---

[1]More conservative scholars are not exempt from this over-confidence; two works which succumb are Gundry, *Matthew*; and, to a lesser extent, Bruce D. Chilton, 'An evangelical and critical approach to the sayings of Jesus', *Themelios* 3 (1978), pp.78–85. For a statistically sound approach to more cautious judgments, see Lloyd Gaston, *Horae Synopticae Electronicae* (Missoula: SBL, 1973).

ations are seldom considered. This abuse of redaction criticism ignores several facts. (i) Despite frequent claims to the contrary, the evidence remains strong that the gospels were written by the authors to whom they are traditionally ascribed – apostles or close associates of apostles.[1] These men could therefore supplement the sources on which they drew with information from their own experiences and memories. Material occurring in only one gospel is therefore not automatically without historical basis. (ii) A free paraphrase of a saying of Jesus can often reproduce its original meaning as faithfully as a literal translation.[2] (iii) John claims that Jesus promised that the Spirit would teach his disciples 'all things', help them to remember what he had said to them (Jn. 14:26), and 'guide them into all truth' (Jn. 16:13). This sugggests that the gospel writers believed they could acquire accurate historical information even apart from human sources. (iv) Above all, theology and history are not opposites. A historian can hold strong views about the significance of certain events and still write reliable history. In fact, partisan proponents of a given point of view are sometimes even more accurate than detached observers; consider, for example, the first impassioned accounts from Jewish sources of the Nazi holocaust which turned out to be more accurate than the reports of 'objective' news media.

In spite of these eight excesses, redaction criticism remains a valuable tool. Its abuse can be avoided, and, when stripped of the excess baggage it tends to attract, it offers insights into the emphases of the evangelists which make the differences among the gospels understandable. Chapter four will note several specific applications of redaction criticism that actually help to clear up some of the more notorious discrepancies between parallels. Here a few general principles for discovering the key distinctives of Matthew, Mark, Luke and John may prove helpful. (1) Focus especially on transitional sentences or paragraphs that connect one section to the next. (2) Look for statements that summarize previous material, pointing out crucial concepts that are being

---

[1]The defence of the traditional claims for authorship in Donald Guthrie, *New Testament Introduction* (London: Tyndale; Downers Grove: IVP, 1970), pp.33–34, 69–72, 98–109, 241–271, remains persuasive.

[2]The philosophy behind the production of modern Bible paraphrases, and to a more limited extent, a translation like the *Good News Bible* (*Today's English Version*), takes it as axiomatic that a freer rendering of the text is designed to *preserve* the original meaning since it is more clearly understood. The form is changed but the content remains the same.

stressed. (3) Note editorial asides and explanatory comments. (4) Examine changes to source material where they can be identified – what has been added or omitted, highlighted or played down. (5) Keep track of themes, language, and vocabulary that are repeated frequently or which appear in climactic positions in the narrative. (6) Above all, search for clues as to why the stories have been arranged in the order they have, looking not just for chronological connections but also for topical groupings and collections of similar forms.[1]

The results of such study pay rich dividends. Not only do the long observed differences in perspective on Jesus become clearer – Matthew's Son of David, Mark's suffering servant, Luke's compassionate teacher and John's Word incarnate – but subtler differences emerge too. Luke is the gospel most concerned with the salvation of the outcasts of society, John with portraying Christ's death as exaltation, and Mark with delicately balancing Christ's human and divine natures.[2] Eric Franklin's little book, *How the Critics Can Help,* offers a stirring account of the spiritual benefit of such an exercise: 'We approach the evangelists as preachers; we sit at their feet to hear their proclamation. And we approach them as pastors as we listen into, as we overhear their concerns for their contemporaries.' Again, 'the first questions we should be asking are, What is the evangelist seeking to proclaim to his contemporaries through his use of this episode in the life of Jesus? How is he seeking to strengthen faith by way of it? What insights into belief in the Lord Jesus does it give?'[3] Although Franklin fails to implement his approach to redaction criticism consistently, his objectives merit praise. Such goals can only help and not harm those who seek to interpret the gospels as they were originally meant to be understood. But as a tool for calling into question the

---

[1]For these and other similar criteria see Robert H. Stein, 'The "Redaktionsgeschichtlich" Investigation of a Markan Seam (Mc 1,2lf)', *ZNW* 61 (1970), pp.71–83; and Grant R. Osborne, 'The Evangelical and Redaction Criticism: Critique and Methodology', *JETS* 22 (1979), pp.316–321.

[2]These statements reflect just a few of the issues discussed in three of the best redaction-critical studies available, all carried out under the restrictions we have noted above, pp.41–42. See, respectively, I. H. Marshall, *Luke: Historian and Theologian* (Exeter: Paternoster; Grand Rapids: Zondervan, 1970); Stephen Smalley, *John: Evangelist and Interpreter* (Exeter: Paternoster; Grand Rapids: Zondervan, 1978); Ralph P. Martin, *Mark: Evangelist and Theologian* (Exeter: Paternoster; Grand Rapids: Zondervan, 1972). Keith F. Nickle, *The Synoptic Gospels: An Introduction* (Atlanta: John Knox, 1981; London: SCM, 1982), is also very good in summarizing recent studies.

[3]p.33.

historical reliability of the gospels, redaction criticism fails badly. For when one considers the number of different ways the story of Jesus might have been told, the striking feature that a careful comparison of the Synoptic Gospels discloses is how similar the three actually are. There are apparent inconsistencies, but the similarities far outweigh the differences. And of the differences which do appear, many simply reflect varying theological interpretations of the same historical events without calling into question the fundamental historicity of the events themselves.

3 The gospels as midrash

If form criticism deals primarily with the gospel traditions before they were written down, while redaction criticism analyzes the evangelists' own contributions to the tradition, midrash criticism cuts across both disciplines. Midrash criticism considers the relationship of the gospels to various Old Testament passages to which they may refer.

A Uses of the term

Broadly speaking, the Hebrew word 'midrash' means 'interpretation'. Most of its uses fall under one of two headings: either the nature or genre of an entire piece of writing or the exegetical or interpretative methods used within a given work.[1] As a genre, the term midrash is used to refer to types of exposition of the Hebrew Scriptures. Examples under this heading in turn subdivide into three major categories: (a) the targums, (see above, p.30); (b) more elaborate 'rewritten Scriptures', like the late first-century Jewish historian Josephus' *Jewish Antiquities* or the *Biblical Antiquities* of approximately the same date mistakenly ascribed to Philo, which expand and embellish portions of Old Testament history with imaginary dialogue and legendary creations much like a historical novel; and (c) the earliest Jewish biblical com-

---

[1]For a brief survey of 'Varieties and Tendencies of Midrash', see the article so entitled by Bruce Chilton (subtitled 'Rabbinic Interpretations of Isaiah 24.23') in *GP*, 3, pp.9–32. For a more comprehensive overview, see Gary G. Porton, 'Midrash: Palestinian Jews and the Hebrew Bible in the Greco-Roman Period', in *Aufstieg und Niedergang der römischen Welt*, II. 19.2, ed. W. Haase (Berlin and New York: de Gruyter, 1979), pp.103–138; or Renée Bloch, 'Midrash', in *Approaches to Ancient Judaism: Theory and Practice*, ed. William S. Green (Missoula: Scholars, 1978), pp.29–50.

mentaries, which proceed through a text explaining its meaning, suggesting applications, or discussing related Scriptures or teachings and stories of the rabbis which it calls to mind.

When midrash refers to methods of interpreting Scripture, one or more of the ancient lists of rules handed down by the rabbis is usually in mind. The slightly older contemporary of Jesus, Hillel, is credited with formulating seven main rules, but by the middle of the second century these had been expanded into thirty-two. Many of the principles follow logic which would be readily accepted today: reasoning from what applies in a less important case to what will apply in a more important case, interpreting Scripture with Scripture, especially where common language or imagery appears, establishing a general principle on the basis of specific examples (or vice-versa), or consulting the context of a passage for insight into its meaning. Other items are highly arbitrary: rearranging the letters in a word to make it say something different, drawing conclusions on the basis of the numerical value of the letters in a word (since in Hebrew letters were used for numbers), or allegorizing a passage to make its details stand for something other than what the text is obviously describing. In between are a number of ambiguous rules which could lead to seemingly unjustified interpretations but need not always do so: interpreting an earlier passage of Scripture by a later one, seeing a double meaning in a passage due to a play on words or pun, or viewing a prophecy which seemed to have a previous fulfilment as being fulfilled again in the present due to a striking recurrence of a pattern of religiously significant events.[1]

B Applications to the gospels

The applicability of the term midrash to the gospels will clearly vary, therefore, depending on which definition is involved.

1 Midrash as a genre

In no sense are the gospels as a whole paraphrases, elaborations,

---

[1]For an introduction to 'Jewish Hermeneutics in the First Century', see the chapter so entitled in Richard N. Longenecker, *Biblical Exegesis in the Apostolic Period* (Grand Rapids: Eerdmans, 1975), pp.19–50. For a full list of the various compilations of rules, see Hermann L. Strack, *Introduction to the Talmud and Midrash* (Philadelphia: Jewish Publication Society of America, 1931), pp.93–98. For a similar threefold division of these rules into: (a) close reading of the text, (b) speculative discourse, and (c) a combination of (a) and (b), with extensive

or interpretations of the Old Testament. They are not concerned to narrate the sacred history of the Jews but to tell the story of contemporary events associated with the life of Jesus. In the process, however, they do refer to Scripture both explicitly and implicitly, so if their overall genre is not midrashic perhaps certain portions are. Two sections replete with scriptural quotations and allusions are the stories of Jesus' infancy and his passion, especially in Matthew (chs. 1–2 and 21–27), and the teaching of Jesus, most notably his parables, in Luke 9:51 – 18:14. Not surprisingly, much of the material in these sections has repeatedly been equated with midrash, and the question has been raised whether the Old Testament passages might not have given birth to the narratives and teachings associated with them. In other words, the gospel writers would not be recording actual historical events but imaginatively involving Jesus in fictitious narratives and teachings inspired by Old Testament texts. Perhaps, for instance, Matthew did not know where Jesus was born (Mt. 2:6), but since he knew that Micah had prophesied that the coming shepherd of Israel would come from Bethlehem (Mi. 5:2), he created a story to make Jesus' history match up with prophecy. Similarly, if Jesus and his family never really had to flee into Egypt (Mt. 2:14–15), the idea for inventing such a story could have arisen from Hosea 11:1 – 'Out of Egypt I called my son.'[1] Or to take an example from the other end of Jesus' life, perhaps the figure of thirty silver pieces as the price for Judas' betrayal of Christ (Mt. 27:9) was not based on historical fact but was inspired by the reference to the same sum of money paid as a wage in Zechariah 11:12–13. Since each of these examples creates certain historical difficulties when taken as factual, one can understand why an approach which views them as a type of midrash appeals to many.[2]

The fundamental flaw with this position emerges from a paradoxical observation. When ancient Jewish authors invented unhis-

---

examples from the rabbinic literature, see Jacob Neusner, *Midrash in Context* (Philadelphia: Fortress, 1983).

[1]For a detailed discussion of various types of midrash seen by some in the infancy narratives of both Matthew and Luke, see Raymond E. Brown, *The Birth of the Messiah* (New York: Macmillan; London: Geoffrey Chapman, 1977). Brown rejects the notion of midrash as genre in these narratives but nevertheless views them as a complex mixture of fact and fiction.

[2]For more detail on these specific passages and a critique of this view, see, respectively, R. T. France, 'Scripture, Tradition, and History in the Infancy Narratives of Matthew', in *GP*,2, pp.239–266; and Douglas J. Moo, 'Tradition and Old Testament in Matt.27:3–10', in *GP*,3, pp.157–175, from which several comments in the next paragraph are also drawn.

torical narratives inspired by Old Testament texts, they generally quoted and interpreted Scripture quite literally. Since they were composing fiction they were free to tailor their creations to the texts which generated them. Precisely the opposite is the case for most of the gospel passages in question. In many cases the Old Testament references are reworded or reapplied in ways that make it much more likely that the gospel writers were trying to show how the Old Testament fitted the events of Jesus' life and not the other way around. Hosea 11:1, for example, is not a prophecy in its Old Testament context but a reference to the Exodus. And although thirty pieces of silver are mentioned by Zechariah, Matthew attributes the quotation to Jeremiah, presumably because the bulk of Matthew 27:9–10 is a composite of allusions to that earlier prophet (suggestions include Je. 18:2–3; 32:7–9, and perhaps most plausibly 19:1–13). As R. T. France concludes, 'if the history were being created out of the text, there would be no need to adapt the text to fit the history.'[1] This of course raises the separate question of whether or not the gospels have cited Scripture fairly, which will be taken up in a moment.

The case of the central chapters of Luke's gospel is more subtle. Here there are few overt citations of the Old Testament, but several writers have argued that Luke's outline is dictated by Scripture. In a nutshell, they believe that the seemingly haphazard sequence of teachings in chapters 9–18 actually parallels a sequence of references in Deuteronomy.[2] A few of these parallels prove suggestive. The excuses offered for not attending the feast in the great banquet parable of Luke 14:16–24 resemble the exemptions from serving in Israel's army in Deuteronomy 20:5–8. Was the parable meant to emphasize that reasons for not going to war in Old Testament times were invalid when used to reject God's call to enlist with his 'kingdom troops'? Similarly, Deuteronomy 21:15–21 prescribes legislation for the inheritance due a firstborn son and the capital punishment deserved by a rebellious one, while Luke 15:11–32 virtually inverts these principles with the parable of the prodigal. Most of the alleged parallels, however, are much

---

[1]R. T. France, 'Jewish Historiography, Midrash, and the Gospels', in *GP*,3, p.109.

[2]Thus originally C. F. Evans, 'The Central Section of St. Luke's Gospel', in *Studies in the Gospels*, ed. D. E. Nineham (Oxford: Blackwell, 1955), pp.37–53; and recently elaborated in John Drury, *Tradition and Design in Luke's Gospel* (London: Darton, Longman & Todd, 1976); and M. D. Goulder, *The Evangelists' Calendar* (London: SPCK, 1978).

more vague and less plausible. But even if this structure did underlie Luke's writing it would not prove that he invented the teachings of Jesus to mirror the Old Testament sequence, merely that he arranged them to fit it.[1]

Michael Goulder has gone one step further and hypothesized that the outlines of all three of the Synoptics were inspired by the Old Testament, specifically by the various sequences of passages selected for weekly reading in the Jewish synagogues.[2] The probability that so many details from Jesus' life just happened to match all manner of Old Testament passages, most of them non-prophetic, is minuscule, so Goulder concludes that many of the gospel stories were 'midrashically' invented. But this type of 'lectionary' hypothesis, previously proposed for parts of the gospels and generally rejected, is extremely improbable for a number of reasons.[3] The two most important are that the parallels Goulder proposes are usually quite subtle and imprecise and that he consistently has to admit exceptions to the patterns he has postulated, thus undermining whatever credibility shorter sequences of parallels might begin to build up.

In fact, all the studies which equate the genre of parts of the gospels with midrash and thereby conclude that they are not historical overestimate the amount of creative activity not only of the four evangelists but also of the Jewish midrashists with whom they are being compared. The earliest targums only rarely insert any large-scale invention not found in Scripture, while the ancient commentaries arouse curiosity with the way they interpret and apply Scripture, not with the way they alter it. The only clear cases of significant embellishment of Old Testament history come from the 'rewritten Scriptures'. Yet even here the rewriting is not as drastic as some scholars allege. F. G. Downing's careful study of *Jewish Antiquities* concludes that Josephus rarely if ever invented his material outright; even the few narratives wholly unparalleled in the Old Testament canon probably stemmed from oral (though

---

[1] For further critique of these and other outlines of Luke's 'travel narrative', and for an alternative approach, see Craig L. Blomberg, 'Midrash, Chiasmus, and the Outline of Luke's Central Section', in *GP*, 3, pp.217–261.

[2] Goulder, *Calendar; cf.* his earlier *Midrash and Lection in Matthew* (London: SPCK, 1974).

[3] See the excellent critique by Leon Morris, 'The Gospels and the Jewish Lectionaries', in *GP*, 3, pp.129–156. More briefly, on Goulder's misuse of the concept of midrash, see Philip S. Alexander, 'Midrash and the Gospels', in *Synoptic Studies*, ed. C. M. Tuckett (Sheffield: JSOT Press, 1984), pp.1–18.

not necessarily historical) tradition.[1] Richard Bauckham's survey of the little-known work of 'pseudo-Philo' makes much the same point: an analysis of *Biblical Antiquities* 'obliges us to recognise that writing "midrash" means using traditions', and 'it reopens the door to the possibility that an Evangelist's traditions, however "midrashic" his procedure in using them may be, could be historical in origin.'[2]

One final hypothesis which sees midrash as the appropriate genre by which to identify at least one gospel stands apart from all the rest, because its author wants at the same time to defend the complete infallibility of the Scriptures. The author is an American evangelical, Robert Gundry, whose commentary on Matthew elaborates this hypothesis at great length.[3] Gundry identifies the genre of Matthew as midrash, not as a commentary of any kind on the Old Testament but as a commentary on Mark and Q. In other words, he believes that Matthew has treated these two sources in the same way that midrashic texts, especially the 'rewritten Scriptures', treated the Old Testament. Gundry argues that this genre of writing was well-known in the first century, so that Matthew's readers would have understood what he was doing and recognized his gospel as something much like what today would be called a historical novel. Gundry also believes they would have known Mark and Q, or at least the oral traditions underlying them, so that they could readily pick out anything which Matthew had added or altered. They would accept the traditional material as factual history and Matthew's additions and alterations as edifying embellishment, just as the Jews separated pious legend from Old Testament history in their midrashic works. In short, this theory affirms that everything which Matthew intended to present as factual was accurate history; what was not factual was never meant to be taken as such, and so his narrative may still be called infallible.

To Gundry's credit he has devised an ingenious synthesis of positions usually believed to be incompatible with each other. He has rightly stressed that history and fiction are often formally indistinguishable apart from subtle clues which are not always

---

[1]F. Gerald Downing, 'Redaction Criticism: Josephus' *Antiquities* and the Synoptic Gospels (I)', *JSNT* 8 (1980), pp.46–65.

[2]Richard Bauckham, 'The Liber Antiquitatum Biblicarum of Pseudo-Philo and the Gospels as "Midrash" ', in *GP*,3, p.67.

[3]Gundry, *Matthew*. Cf. his defence and clarification of his views in his four short articles in *JETS* 26 (1983), pp.41–56, 71–86, 95–100, 109–115.

noticed.[1] And he has correctly insisted that one interpret the gospels in the light of the attitudes toward narrating history which prevailed in first-century Judaism rather than in the twentieth-century western world. Nevertheless, his hypothesis remains largely unpersuasive.[2] Gundry offers no solid evidence to support his claim that Matthew's church would have known the traditions behind Mark and Q sufficiently well and in a sufficiently fixed form to enable them to pick out his unhistorical additions. Indeed, the closer on the heels of Mark that Matthew was writing (and Gundry wants to date both at least as early as the mid-60s), the less time Matthew's church would have had to learn about Mark and to become as familiar with it as with the Old Testament.[3] More seriously, all the examples of midrashic rewriting of Scripture deal with what was already ancient, canonical history by the time of the first century. There is very little evidence that Jewish authors embellished *contemporary* history in the same way. For example, in the commentaries on Old Testament prophecy found among the Dead Sea Scrolls, as F. F. Bruce stresses, the 'one thing these commentators did not do was to try to "create" recent history out of the biblical texts. Recent events and the current situation provided them with their data.' If these did not exactly match what Scripture seemed to prophesy, it was the biblical text 'that was adapted, not the data which formed the raw material of the interpretation'.[4]

2 Midrash as a method of interpretation

Many of the methods of citing and explaining Scripture which the gospel writers shared with the early rabbis are widely accepted today as legitimate. For instance, Jesus regularly appealed to

---

[1]On this topic, see *e.g.* Thomas J. Roberts, *When Is Something Fiction?* (Carbondale: Southern Illinois University; London: Feffer & Simons, 1972), who rightly stresses that 'if I tell someone something I know is factually untrue but I do not warn him of this, I am lying to him' (p.21), but who goes on to note that such warnings may be limited to a prefatory remark, a type of title, the context in which the work is set, or certain 'fantastic' details in the narrative.

[2]For article-length reviews, see D. A. Carson, 'Gundry on Matthew: A Critical Review', *Trin J* n.s. 3 (1982), pp.71–91; Philip B. Payne, 'Midrash and History in the Gospels with Special Reference to R. H. Gundry's *Matthew*', in *GP*, 3, pp.177–215; Douglas J. Moo, 'Matthew and Midrash: An Evaluation of Robert H. Gundry's Approach', *JETS* 26 (1983), pp.31–39, with a rejoinder to Gundry's reply in pp.57–70.

[3]Gundry insists (see esp. his 'On Interpreting Matthew's Editorial Comments', *WTJ* 47 [1985], pp.319–328) that his position does not depend on Matthew's community knowing other forms of the gospel tradition, although he thinks it likely they did. But to relinquish this supporting argument is to abandon the one aspect of his position which could make it somewhat plausible.

[4]F. F. Bruce, 'Biblical Exposition at Qumran', in *GP*, 3, p.87.

arguments 'from the lesser to the greater', and not just when he was quoting Scripture (*e.g.* Mt. 7:11 – 'if you therefore being evil know how to give good gifts to your children, how much more will your father in heaven give good things to those who ask him'). Again, recognizing a kind of midrash known in rabbinic circles as the *proem* (a brief homily) behind certain gospel passages can actually strengthen the case for seeing them as authentic unities rather than composite collections of tradition and redaction. Luke 10:25–37 aptly illustrates one type of proem, called *yelammedenu rabbenu* ('let our master teach us'), which involves a dialogue including a question and quotation(s) from Scripture (verses 25–27; *cf*. Dt. 6:5; Lv. 19:18), a second Scriptural quotation (verse 28; *cf*. Lv. 18:5), exposition often by means of a parable linked to the initial texts by catchwords (verses 29–36 with verbal links via 'neighbour' and 'do'), and a concluding allusion to the second quotation (verse 37).[1]

Texts in which the evangelists (or Jesus) do not seem to be 'playing fair' with the Old Testament create greater problems. Several factors besides simple paraphrase may account for seemingly inaccurate quotations of scriptures. The Hebrew manuscripts used for most modern translations of the Old Testament represent a remarkably accurate transcript of what was originally written. Portions of the Hebrew Bible found among the Dead Sea Scrolls, about a thousand years older than previously known manuscripts (*c*. 100 BC versus *c*. AD 900), have substantially confirmed the quality of the traditional Hebrew text. Yet at the same time they have revealed variant readings in some instances which support the accuracy of the ancient Greek and Aramaic versions (the Septuagint and the targums) in places where they were formerly thought to have rendered the original Hebrew unfairly.[2] It is likely that on a few occasions a New Testament writer's quotation reflects an accurate translation of just such a variant Hebrew text. In many cases, however, a New Testament writer may simply quote a current, popular version of the Old Testament like the Septuagint or a targum when the point he is making does not

---

[1]E. E. Ellis, 'How the New Testament Uses the Old', in Marshall, *Interpretation*, pp.205–206, *contra* most critics who find any or all of verses 25–29 and 36–37 as secondary additions.

[2]For a clear summary of the various possibilities, with examples, see Moisés Silva, 'The New Testament Use of the Old Testament: Text Form and Authority', in Carson & Woodbridge, *Scripture and Truth*, pp.147–165.

depend on the distinctive form of that popular version or when that version gives a valid interpretation of the original.[1]

Perhaps the most perplexing of all are those passages which accurately cite Scripture but do not seem to interpret it properly. Matthew's use of Hosea 11:1 – 'Out of Egypt I called my son' – which seems to turn a straightforward historical statement about the Exodus into a prophecy of Jesus' flight from Herod has already been noted. Is this simply a midrashic pun on the word 'son', arbitrarily reading a meaning which the word can have elsewhere in the Old Testament (*i.e.* Messiah) into Hosea's passage where it clearly refers to Israel? Similar problems recur throughout the New Testament.[2]

Traditionally Christians have divided the New Testament passages involving the prophetic interpretation of Old Testament texts into two categories – literal and 'typological' fulfilment. Typology comes from the Greek word for 'type' or 'pattern' and was a recognized means of analyzing current events in both Jewish and Graeco-Roman circles prior to the dawn of Christianity. France's definition is representative:

> there is a consistency in God's dealings with men. Thus his acts in the Old Testament will present a pattern which can be seen to be repeated in the New Testament events; these may therefore be interpreted by reference to the pattern displayed in the Old Testament. New Testament typology is thus essentially the tracing of the constant principles of God's working in history, revealing 'a recurring rhythm in past history which is taken up more fully and perfectly in the Gospel events'.[3]

---

[1]Luke seems frequently to have taken this tack in his use of the Septuagint. See Darrell L. Bock, *Proclamation from Prophecy and Pattern: Lucan Old Testament Christology* (Sheffield: JSOT Press, forthcoming). On agreements between the gospels and the Isaiah targum, supporting the authenticity of Jesus' distinctive use of that portion of the Old Testament, see Bruce Chilton, *A Galilean Rabbi and His Bible* (London: SPCK; Wilmington: Glazier, 1984), although this material comprises only a minuscule portion of Jesus' teaching.

[2]Darrell L. Bock, 'Evangelicals and the Use of the Old Testament in the New', *BSac* 142 (1985), pp.209–223, 306–319, helpfully discusses a number of these and categorizes evangelical attempts to deal with them. A remarkably comprehensive catalogue of allegedly midrashic uses of the Old Testament in the New appears in Alejandro Diez-Macho, 'Derás y exégesis del Nuevo Testamento', *Sefarad* 35 (1975), pp.37–89.

[3]R. T. France, *Jesus and the Old Testament* (London: Tyndale, 1971; Grand Rapids: Baker, 1982), p.39; quoting in the last sentence G. W. H. Lampe, *Essays on Typology*, p.27. *Cf.* Douglas J. Moo, *The Old Testament in the Gospel Passion Narratives* (Sheffield: Almond, 1983), p.31. See Richard M. Davidson, *Typology in Scripture* (Berrien Springs, MI: Andrews University, 1981), for a thorough survey of the historical and exegetical meanings of this term.

When the gospel writers use typology, then, they are often not claiming to be interpreting the meaning of the Old Testament passages cited but rather showing how contemporary events are falling into a pattern so reminiscent of what God did in the past that they can only explain the present in terms of God acting again.

Thus when Matthew says that Hosea 11:1 was fulfilled by the holy family's sojourn in Egypt, he is calling attention to the striking coincidence that just as Israel had to be protected and delivered from Egypt in Moses' day, so now God's Messiah had to be sheltered in that foreign land until he could return safely to his home. In Walter Kaiser's words, 'both Israel and the infant Jesus were the objects of God's love and deliverance in the face of an oppressor.'[1] Such a parallel seems hardly coincidental; it must point to something religiously significant. If someone objects that this approach does not describe a true 'fulfilment' of Scripture, the proper reply is that the Hebrew and Greek words for 'fulfil' had a broader range of meanings than their modern English counterpart. Brevard Childs offers this definition: 'A word is fulfilled when it is filled full to form a whole.'[2] Or as Colin Brown explains, 'the OT passages are not treated as mere predictions but as anticipations.' A passage will anticipate 'an event of a similar kind but ultimately more significant in God's purposes for the salvation of mankind'.[3] In one sense all the Old Testament is self-consciously incomplete, looking forward to the time when God would save his people once and for all. Thus Jesus can speak of his fulfilling all Scripture (Mt. 5:17; Lk. 24:27), as a whole, without implying that every individual sentence in the Old Testament was meant to describe some facet of the Messiah's ministry.

Contemporary study of midrash does not seem to offer any more adequate explanation for the difficult interpretations of the Old Testament by the New than this more traditional appeal to typology, and it may actually cover up the fact that the kind of

---

[1] Walter C. Kaiser, Jr., *The Uses of the Old Testament in the New* (Chicago: Moody, 1985), pp.51–52. Kaiser, however, rejects the notion of typology which is not grounded in the Old Testament author's intention because he does not see how it could have had any apologetic value. But to the Jewish mind of the first century, arguing for the presence of God's saving activity on the basis of recurring patterns in history would have proved very persuasive, and there is no good reason why modern exegetes should not accept such an approach as well.

[2] Brevard S. Childs, 'Prophecy and Fulfillment', *Int* 12 (1958), p.267.

[3] Editor's note to R. Schippers, 'πληρόω', in *NIDNTT*, 1, p.737.

biblical interpretation found in the gospels is relatively rare in other ancient Jewish literature[1]. Moreover, appeals to midrash too readily offer an 'easy way out' by shortcircuiting detailed Old Testament exegesis. Many passages which at first glance seem to be treating the Hebrew Scriptures unfairly turn out after closer scrutiny to be appealing to the larger context in which the specific Old Testament quotation appears or to terms which could refer to more than one character or event at the same time – Israel's 'shepherd', the 'suffering servant' or Abraham's promised 'seed'. And while it is important to tackle the difficult passages, one must not lose sight of the fact that almost all the use of Scripture in the gospels is quite straightforward and intelligible.[2]

Are the gospels midrash? Do they contain or employ midrash? Clearly the answer that must emerge from this study is that it depends on how one defines the term. No entire gospel is a commentary on any portion of earlier Scripture, but small sections seem to be. No gospel very closely resembles the ancient Jewish works specifically called midrash, but midrashic methods of interpretation seem to appear from time to time within the evangelists' narratives. More commonly, what some have explained by appealing to midrash is better understood in terms of typology. A more helpful question is whether or not the gospels' use of the Old Testament, or their use of sources like Mark and Q, in any way damages their credibility as reliable history. When phrased in this fashion, one can answer with confidence that they have emerged unscathed.

4 Recent hermeneutical developments

Unlike form, redaction and midrash criticism, a number of the newest methods for studying the gospels claim to be interested not in questions about historical reliability but only in questions involving interpretation. Yet careful analysis reveals that challenges to the historicity of the gospels do emerge even if they are not necessarily central to the concerns of the critics using these

---

[1]Leonhard Goppelt, *Typos* (Grand Rapids: Eerdmans, 1982), p.200.
[2]On both of these points see esp. Longenecker, *Exegesis*, esp. pp.51–78, 133–157, and, in a much more persuasive work than his more recent commentary, Robert H. Gundry, *The Use of the Old Testament in St. Matthew's Gospel* (Leiden: Brill, 1967), esp. pp.205–234.

methods. These historical questions are the only aspects of the recent hermeneutical developments which can be discussed in any detail here.

A The new hermeneutic

Flourishing first in the 1960s and associated with such names as Ernst Fuchs, Gerhard Ebeling, Hans-Georg Gadamer, and Eberhard Jüngel, the 'new hermeneutic' came to refer to a movement which emphasizes the subjectivity of the process of interpreting biblical texts.[1] Rather than underlining the ability of an interpreter to arrive at the objective meaning of a given text, this school of thought highlights the fact that all interpreters come to the text with certain presuppositions about what it must be saying. If they are to avoid reading their own thoughts and prejudices into Scripture they must learn to let the text 'interpret' them, challenging their preconceptions about what it means, and creating what has come to be called a 'language-event' whereby they hear the Word of God afresh with new insight.

Thus far the new hermeneutic's emphasis offers a humbling and necessary corrective to those readers of the Bible who think that their interpretations, usually coinciding with the theological tradition or denomination to which they belong, encapsulate all the truth all the time! But sometimes this emphasis has led to the more extreme claim that one can *never* be confident that his or her interpretations are valid with any high degree of probability. If no objective meaning is recoverable, then no reliable history is recoverable, because readers can never be sure whether or not they have misunderstood the gospels by thinking that they were supplying historical information when in fact they were not.[2]

This full-blown scepticism or relativism has from time to time cropped up in the writings of both philosophers and secular historians too, but it is no longer widely held in those circles because of

[1]Much of the literature on the subject is dated; two of the better, more recent introductions are William G. Doty, *Contemporary New Testament Interpretation* (Englewood Cliffs, N.J.: Prentice-Hall, 1972), pp.28–51; and A. C. Thiselton, 'The New Hermeneutic', in Marshall, *Interpretation*, pp.308–333. For a fuller treatment, Robert W. Funk, *Language, Hermeneutic and Word of God* (New York and London: Harper & Row, 1966) is still valuable.

[2]Two continental writers who have been bolder in this assertion than most of their English-speaking counterparts are Franz Hesse, *Abschied von der Heilsgeschichte* (Zürich: Theologischer Verlag, 1971), pp.59–60; and Günter Klein, *Rekonstruktion und Interpretation* (München: Kaiser, 1969), pp.237–261. Hesse and Klein combine interests of the new hermeneutic with an older, more Bultmannian, existentialism.

a number of obvious flaws in its logic: (1) It confuses the way knowledge is acquired, which is subjective, with the validity of that knowledge, which is objective. (2) It assumes that incomplete knowledge implies false knowledge. (3) It overlooks the similarities between scientific and historical method which allow both to achieve a degree of objectivity. (4) It asks for exemption for its own work. To be consistent, the person claiming that no attempt to write history can ever be fully reliable must admit that he or she has made a statement about history that cannot be fully reliable. (5) It uses 'subjectivity' as a meaningless term since without the existence of objective truth there is nothing to which subjective claims can be subject.[1] To condense these five flaws into one, complete relativism confuses facts with their interpretations. Maurice Mandelbaum's classic philosophical discussion of this issue concludes: 'the truth of a historical work consists in the truth of its statements, not in the fact that the author judged as he did.'[2] No matter how much statements and judgments overlap, they must be kept separate, since without any statements of fact there is nothing to be judged.[3]

A less extreme and much more common position than complete historical scepticism is the claim that, as narratives, the gospels cannot be translated into any other form of language. Stories are not the same as histories; the former have plots, themes, major and minor characters; the latter, if in pure form, provide merely an uninterpreted chronicle or list of events. The more a chronicle reads like a narrative, the less one is able to distinguish fact from interpretation even if both are present. The more a history-book reads like a story-book, the more likely it is that it was written not just to tell 'what happened' but rather to 'do something' to its readers, for example, to entertain, encourage, warn, or promote a certain ideology. And it is clear that the gospels are much more than unconnected lists of facts but full-fledged stories with all the literary characteristics just enumerated. To put it another way, if

---

[1]These five points are concisely set out in David Fischer, *Historians' Fallacies* (New York: Harper & Row, 1970; London: Routledge & Kegan Paul, 1971), pp.42–43, n.4.

[2]Maurice Mandelbaum, *The Problem of Historical Knowledge* (New York: Harper Torchbooks, 1967 [orig. 1938]), p.183. *Cf*. his more recent *The Anatomy of Historical Knowledge* (Baltimore and London: Johns Hopkins, 1977), pp.145–194.

[3]*Cf*. also G. J. Renier, *History: Its Purpose and Method* (London: George Allen & Unwin, 1950), p.50; Arthur C. Danto, *Analytic Philosophy of History* (Cambridge: University Press, 1965), pp.27–111; Morton White, *Foundations of Historical Knowledge* (New York: Harper & Row, 1965), pp.3–4.

the extreme practitioners of the new hermenuetic argue that one ought never to label *any* piece of writing as reliable history, many more of its devotees claim that the similarities between the gospels and novels (which are usually at least in part fictitious) show that one should never claim that *the gospels* are reliable history. By their own admission, they were written for purposes altogether different from those of historians – to persuade people to become Christians or to deepen already existing faith in Jesus.[1]

At first glance, it seems strange to think that anyone could carefully read the gospels and seriously believe that they were not purporting to recount some historical events. One might wish to argue that they had not always succeeded and that errors of fact had crept in, but to treat the gospels as wholly fictitious seems even harder to accept than the midrashic view which saw them as a mixture of fact and fiction. But in actuality Jesus himself regularly employed a form of teaching – the parable – in which fictitious narratives teach theological truth in historical garb. And it is by generalizing from the case of the parables that the new hermeneutic has developed the theory of an entire gospel's narrative as metaphor. No one ever bothers to argue about whether there ever was a man who hired labourers for his vineyard at all times of the day and then paid those who had worked only one hour as much as those who had worked twelve (Mt. 20:1–16); in fact it is highly improbable that any Jewish landowners in Jesus' day would have done so. Rather it is recognized that the point of the parable is not to describe something that happened but symbolically to demonstrate characteristics of the kingdom of God. In philosophical language, it is not a proposition – a statement that can be labelled true or false – but a performative – an utterance which performs an action such as promising, warning, giving, or demanding.[2] In this parable, Ernst Fuchs explains, Jesus is *pledging* that 'there will be no disappointment for those who, in face of a cry of "guilty", nevertheless found their hope on an act of God's kindness' and *determining* that he will 'give up everything else for this

---

[1]This paragraph is a composite of the views of a number of authors linked to the new hermeneutic in varying ways. But *cf.* esp. Paul Ricoeur, 'Biblical Hermeneutics', *Semeia* 4 (1975), pp.27–148; Hans Frei, *The Identity of Jesus Christ* (Philadelphia: Fortress, 1975); James Barr, *The Bible in the Modern World* (London: SCM; New York: Harper & Row, 1973), pp.53–74, although these scholars differ from each other in important ways as well.

[2]The term 'performative' is especially well known through the work of J. L. Austin, *How To Do Things with Words* (Cambridge, MA: Harvard; Oxford: Clarendon, 1962).

faith'.[1] Is it not at least conceivable, then, that an entire gospel is in some sense 'parabolic', revealing the presence of the kingdom of God by means of a powerful story which communicates God's intentions for human relationships, completely apart from the question of whether or not the events in that story really occurred?

The fairest reply to this question would seem to be to agree that it is conceivable but highly improbable. On the one hand, the new hermeneutic's analysis of parables is at best one-sided. It requires that all the interpretations of the parables in the gospels, including those ascribed to Jesus, be rejected as inauthentic since parables cannot be interpreted in propositional terms. It neglects the fact that while performative utterances are more than propositions they are not less.[2] To pledge oneself to act compassionately toward society's undeserving must presuppose certain beliefs about them, for example that God loves them in spite of their sinfulness. And although it is irrelevant for the meaning of the parable whether or not such a landowner ever existed, the question of historical reliability returns when one asks if Jesus ever really told this particular parable. The parables may have revealed aspects of God's kingdom by means of fictitious stories, but they require that Jesus was a historical person claiming to be inaugurating the kingdom of God on earth by means of his teaching and ministry. The original language-events require a speaker to create them and to invest them with the meaning which the new hermeneutic ascribes to the parables.

On the other hand, even if one were to grant the new hermeneutic's view of parables, it would not be clear that a similar approach could apply to the gospels in their entirety. Most who view the gospels as fiction nevertheless see them as functioning in a way which requires that the basic facts about the life, death and resurrection of Jesus be historically accurate. If the gospels are promising or offering new possibilities for human relationships, then something must have happened in history to make those new possibilities available.[3] The history of human attempts to reform

---

[1]Ernst Fuchs, *Studies of the Historical Jesus* (London: SCM; Naperville: Allenson, 1964), p.37.

[2]Thiselton, 'New Hermeneutic', p.326. *Cf.* his *The Two Horizons: New Testament Hermeneutics and Philosophical Description* (Exeter: Paternoster; Grand Rapids: Eerdmans, 1980), p.443.

[3]*Cf.* esp. Kevin J. Vanhoozer, *A Passion for the Possible: The Gospel Narratives and Paul Ricoeur's Hermeneutic Philosophy* (Cambridge: University Press, forthcoming).

the world and eradicate evil is a history of failures; visions of Utopia do not create it. Unless the gospels narrate events which really happened and which offer one the opportunity to experience a quality of existence available in no other way, then there is no rational explanation for the formation of the early church and for the nature of its preaching. For the one thing that the New Testament or other early Christian literature never provides is an account of Jesus' followers recounting the teachings of their master in the hopes of creating a life-changing 'language-event' for their audiences. Rather they reveal a consistent preoccupation with just a handful of the details of Jesus' life, especially those surrounding his crucifixion and resurrection, confirming that their faith was based on the reality and significance of certain events in recent *history*. This in no way implies that the sole or even primary reason for the composition of the four gospels was an interest in preserving details about Jesus' life for the sake of future historians. It does imply, however, that what they did record for the sake of encouraging their audiences to believe had to be historical for it to be effective.

B Structuralism

Completely apart from the issue of the historicity of the gospels, the new hermeneutic suffered severe abuse at the hands of those who recognized that its idea of a 'language-event' had personified the spoken word, giving it an unwarranted, quasi-mystical power, surpassing that of any human speaker. Those who could no longer believe in a transcendent God believed that they could at least accept a transcendent Word.[1] The method which has in certain circles eclipsed the new hermeneutic in popularity and influence strictly limits its analysis to written texts. That method is known as structuralism. But unlike traditional literary analysis, structuralism focuses not so much on the 'surface structure' of a text – for example, the plot, themes, or motifs of an individual story – as on the 'deep structure' – the underlying and more fundamental features which form the basis of all narratives, for example, the functions, motives, and interaction between the main characters and objects in a narrative, and, most notably, the types of opposi-

---

[1]*Cf.* A. C. Thiselton, 'The Supposed Power of Words in the Biblical Writings', *JTS* 25 (1974), pp.283–299.

tions and their resolutions that develop as the text unfolds. Like all the methods surveyed in this chapter, structuralism means different things to different people. Most helpful is a threefold classification: structuralism as (a) an ideology putting itself forward as the only valid method of analyzing literature, (b) a method of studying certain structures underlying a piece of literature neglected by but compatible with other more traditional methods, and (c) a method of studying certain surface features of the text which suggest connections between various details which might otherwise be overlooked.[1]

As an ideology, structuralism is inherently bound up with a dialectic philosophy, determinism and atheism.[2] In other words, structuralism as an ideology claims that language determines thought rather than vice-versa. It is unconcerned to examine the historical context of a piece of writing, concentrating instead exclusively on the details within that work which reveal its meaning. It looks especially for characters and themes which oppose each other and for how, if at all, they are reconciled, in keeping with a dialectic view of the world which sees all history and narrative as the product of conflict and as attempts to synthesize contrary positions. As a result, it believes that there is no true personal freedom and therefore no transcendent God. Not surprisingly, the three countries out of which this type of structuralism largely emerged are Russia, Czechoslovakia, and France. As a philosophy which claims to exclude all others, and which would therefore allege that preoccupation with historical questions was inappropriate, it contradicts itself, since it uses its own *ahistorical* examination of literature to support Marxist theories about the nature of *history* as class conflict.

In the English-speaking world, relatively few have embraced structuralism as their overall world-view, but many have found value in it as one method among many, when divorced from its

---

[1]None of the book-length introductions to structuralism in biblical studies is as lucid as one might wish; the best is perhaps Daniel Patte, *What Is Structural Exegesis?* (Philadelphia: Fortress, 1976). Much clearer but almost too brief to be of much help are Carl Armerding, 'Structural Analysis', *Themelios* 4 (1979), pp.96–104; and A. C. Thiselton, 'Structuralism and Biblical Studies: Method or Ideology?' *ExpT* 89 (1978), pp.329–335.

[2]Robert Detweiler, 'After the New Criticism: Contemporary Methods of Literary Interpretation', in *Orientation by Disorientation,* ed. Richard A. Spencer (Pittsburgh: Pickwick, 1980), p.13; Vern Poythress, 'Philosophical Roots of Phenomenological and Structuralist Literary Criticism', *WTJ* 41 (1978), p.166.

philosophical presuppositions.[1] The method is still largely irrelevant to concerns about the historicity of a text, but not always. Several studies of the parables found only in Matthew or Luke, for example, have argued that their deep structures differ significantly enough from those of the parables common to two or three of the Synoptics so as to call into question their authenticity. Gerhard Sellin, for one, argues that most of the parables found only in Luke have three main characters – a king/father/master figure with two subordinates (sons/servants), of whom one is a good example and one a bad. In most cases the protagonist or hero of the story is the good subordinate, although 'good' may be defined in ways shocking to the Pharisees in Jesus' audience – consider the prodigal son (Lk. 15:11–32), the repentant tax collector (18:9–14), or the beggar named Lazarus (16:19–31). In the other gospels, however, this triadic structure is less frequent, and when it does appear the main character seems to be the authority figure – the king who gave the marriage feast for his son (Mt. 22:1–10) or the vineyard owner who destroyed his wicked tenants (Mk. 12:1–9 pars.).[2] But this type of argument cuts two ways. If it can be argued that an author always creates consistent types of relationships and connections among his stories' characters, then it is equally valid to argue that the presence of such patterns in texts which superficially seem quite different indicates a common author. Thus Dan Via has stood Sellin's analysis on its head, showing that he has evaluated the evidence selectively and misleadingly, and that in fact Jesus' parables throughout the Synoptics disclose 'deep structures' which are much more similar to than different from each other.[3] Nevertheless, the application of such structural analysis either to prove or to refute the authenticity of a given text seems highly dubious, since structuralism as an ideology argues that many of the deep

---

[1]Raymond F. Collins, *Introduction to the New Testament* (Garden City: Doubleday; London: SCM, 1983), pp.231–271, has taken the bold step of giving it as much treatment and weight as he does form and redaction criticism. *Cf.* the similar assessments of Elizabeth S. Malbon, 'Structuralism, Hermeneutics, and Contextual Meaning', *JAAR* 51 (1983), pp.207–230, and Brian Kovacs, ed., 'A Joint Paper by the Members of the Structuralism and Exegesis SBL Seminar', in *SBL 1982 Seminar Papers,* ed. Kent H. Richards (Chico: Scholars, 1982), pp.251–270.

[2]Gerhard Sellin, 'Lukas als Gleichniserzähler: die Erzählung vom barmherzigen Samariter (Lk 10, 25–37)', *ZNW* 65 (1974), pp.166–189; 66 (1975), pp.19–60; also his 'Gleichnisstrukturen', *Linguistica Biblica* 31 (1974), pp.89–115. *Cf.* Michael D. Goulder, 'Characteristics of the Parables in the Several Gospels', *JTS* 19 (1968), pp.51–69.

[3]Dan O. Via, 'Parable and Example Story: A Literary-Structuralist Approach', *Semeia* 1 (1974), pp.105–133.

structures it analyses are common to *all* narrative.

The same is not necessarily the case with studies of the 'surface structure' of a text.[1] When form and redaction critics became preoccupied with dissecting the gospel stories into bits and pieces pertaining to different stages of the tradition, they often overlooked various textual features which suggested the passages were more tightly woven unities. Different types of parallelism balancing the various sections of a passage can often suggest that it was a carefully composed whole from its outset. Of course one can argue that the gospel writers imposed this structure by inventing an entire story and attributing it to Jesus. Yet where there is reason to believe, using form and redaction criticism, that at least *part* of the story is authentic, then analysis of surface structures can lead to the conclusion that *all* of the story is authentic, by showing that the entire story hangs together as a coherent whole with features not readily open to manufacture by a 'scissors-and-paste' editor. To cite an example from the parables again, many scholars have argued that the second section of the story of the prodigal son (Lk. 15:25–32, about the older brother) could not be part of what Jesus originally spoke since it complicates the plot and distracts our attention from the main point, already complete with verse 24, about God's love for sinners. On the other hand, Mary Tolbert has demonstrated that verses 11–24 and verses 25–32 are actually quite similar in structure with each 'half' dividing into four subsections alternating between narrated and direct speech, with verbal and conceptual parallels pairing each subsection. Thus she concludes: 'this kind of structural analysis clearly shows the authenticity of the elder son episode: It is neither an interpolation nor an awkward addendum. It is a necessary and important part of the total configuration of the parable.'[2] Unfortunately, little of this kind of structural analysis has been applied to large portions of the gospels to enable one to assess its overall worth. In principle, however, it could prove highly valuable, for it is both fairer and more logical to try to look for characteristics which explain a text as a totality rather than immediately assuming at the slightest sign of an

---

[1]Since so much of structuralism is concerned to delve beneath the surface of a text, some scholars have proposed different terms altogether for this type of structural analysis. 'Rhetorical criticism' and 'stylistics' are two of the most frequent alternatives, though each of these subsumes broader questions as well.

[2]Mary A. Tolbert, *Perspectives on the Parables* (Philadelphia: Fortress, 1979), p.101.

apparent inconsistency that it is a combination of authentic tradition and unhistorical redaction.

C Post-structuralism

The 'radical' late sixties and early seventies not only provided wide publicity first for the new hermeneutic and then for structuralism, but they also spawned a number of other avant-garde movements in literary criticism. These have been appropriated in biblical studies only by a few and for the most part only within the last decade. At least two of these took shape as conscious reactions against structuralism; hence the term 'post-structuralism'.[1] These are generally referred to as 'deconstruction' and 'reader-response criticism'.

By far the most bizarre movement in the literary world of recent years, deconstruction is most closely associated with a French philosopher and proponent of Nietzsche, Jacques Derrida. It is almost impossible to define in a sentence, but T. K. Seung makes a commendable attempt: the process of 'generating conflicting meanings from the same text, and playing those meanings against each other'.[2] Dominic Crossan illustrates a kind of deconstruction applied to the gospels when he argues that, although they highlight Jesus' teaching in parables about God, they advocate belief in Jesus as 'the Parable of God' – God's own self-communication. The texts actually undermine the perspectives they assert.[3] Or again, with the parable of the prodigal son, Crossan discovers an allegory about interpretations of the world. The father stands for reality, the older brother for realism in interpretation, and the prodigal for the one who abandons the search for realism. Thus the inversion of the two sons' roles at the end of the parable proves that 'he who finds the meaning loses it, and he who loses it finds it'![4]

---

[1]*Cf.* D. S. Greenwood, 'Poststructuralism and Biblical Studies: Frank Kermode's, *The Genesis of Secrecy*', in *GP*,3, pp.263–288.

[2]T. K. Seung, *Structuralism and Hermeneutics* (New York: Columbia University Press, 1982), p.271. As with structuralism, simple introductions are hard to find, and the nature of the movements being described has much to do with this. But two valiant attempts are Jonathan Culler, *On Deconstruction: Theory and Criticism after Structuralism* (Ithaca: Cornell, 1982; London: Routledge & Kegan Paul, 1983); and Christopher Norris, *Deconstruction: Theory and Practice* (London and New York: Methuen, 1982).

[3]See, among others, J. D. Crossan, *The Dark Interval* (Niles, IL and Harlow: Argus Communications, 1975).

[4]J. D. Crossan, *Cliffs of Fall: Paradox and Polyvalence in the Parables of Jesus* (New York: Seabury, 1980), p.101. For a survey and critique of Crossan's works, see Frank B. Brown and

Reader-response criticism refers to a loosely structured move-ment especially indebted to the American literary critic, Stanley Fish. Most of its advocates reject authorial intention as the key to interpretation and assert that 'meaning is a product of the inter-action between text and reader'.[1] This is similar to the emphasis of the new hermeneutic except that it is concerned with the written text rather than the spoken word. Reader-response criticism also tends to emphasize the autonomy of the interpreter of the Word, whereas the new hermeneutic stresses the demands the Word imposes on the interpreter. Both deconstruction and reader-response criticism are post-structuralist in that they agree with structuralism that a text is not to be interpreted in terms of its historical context, while denying structuralism's claim that objec-tive meaning can be found *in* the text even at some 'deep' level. But if interpretation does not involve trying to find out either what an original author intended or what his written text means, then the only thing left is the subjective impression created in the mind of the person who reads the text. The constraints on this subjec-tivity stem primarily from 'interpretive communities', that is, groups of readers who share traditional methods, conventions and value judgments in analyzing certain texts, and not from any unalterable message which the text fossilizes. If the new her-meneutic argues that an interpretation of the gospels as historical misunderstands their authors' intentions, and if structuralism argues that such an interpretation is simply irrelevant since mean-ing is found in a text rather than in its author's intentions, then post-structuralism views such an interpretation as wrong in assuming that objective meaning is recoverable at all.

Consistent post-structuralists of course fall into the same self-defeating trap which ensnares thoroughgoing relativism (the view that no interpretations are more or less valid than any other). Whoever adopts this view must likewise admit that his or her own views are unworthy of any special attention. Not surprisingly, therefore, most post-structuralists are inconsistent and simply emphasize that one has to take more seriously than is customary

Elizabeth S. Malbon, 'Parables as a *Via Negativa*: A Critical Review of the Work of John Dominic Crossan', *JR* 64 (1984), pp.530–538.

[1] James L. Resseguie, 'Reader-Response Criticism and the Synoptic Gospels', *JAAR* 52 (1984), p.322. *Cf.* Stanley Fish, *Is There a Text in This Class?* (Cambridge, MA and London: Harvard, 1980), p.3 *et passim*.

the fact that different readers see different things in the same texts even when they are well informed about the texts' historical and literary contexts. Rather than suppressing this observation, the interpreter should revel in it, according to the post-structuralist. Frank Kermode, for example, interprets all of Mark in the light of Jesus' statement about parables in Mark 4:11–12; the gospel both reveals and conceals it meaning. Thus Kermode can in one breath indulge both in traditional grammatical-historical criticism, finding out what this or that Greek word could have meant to a first-century speaker, and in a sort of 'free-association', interpreting details in Mark in the light of such literature as James Joyce's *Ulysses* and justifying his approach by appealing to the type of allegorizing already found in Mark 4![1] But this is to confuse the meaning of a text, which cannot change once the text is complete, with its significance, which varies from one reader to the next.[2]

Reader-response criticism, however, properly points out that an author's intention in writing something may often be either irrecoverable or unachieved. Less radical practitioners suggest a more holistic model by which meaning resides in a text, and interpretation seeks to appropriate textual clues to the intentions of the author with respect to a given audience.[3] In this case certain constraints are placed upon interpreters as they go about their work. Robert Fowler, for example, suggests that Mark has created the story of the feeding of the 5,000 (Mk. 6:30–44) on the model of the feeding of the 4,000 (Mk. 8:1–10) and arranged the two accounts in his gospel into a sequence which would highlight the irony of the disciples' failure to understand how Jesus could provide food for the multitudes (Mk. 8:4).[4] Though this is probably not the best solution to the question of why Mark has two separate narratives about strikingly similar feeding miracles (see below, pp.147–148), it does reveal careful attention to possible meanings

---

[1]Frank Kermode, *The Genesis of Secrecy* (Cambridge, MA and London: Harvard, 1979). The Gospel of Mark has so far proved most conducive to reader-response criticism, with its abrupt transitions, apparent doublets, and uncertain ending.

[2]P. D. Juhl, *Interpretation* (Princeton: University Press, 1980), pp.12–14, notes that this is one of the most valuable contributions of E. D. Hirsch (*Validity in Interpretation* [New Haven and London: Yale, 1967]), even though other aspects of Hirsch's theory have been successfully challenged.

[3]Thus *e.g.* Norman R. Petersen, 'The Reader in the Gospel', *Neotestamentica* 18 (1984), pp.38–51. *Cf.* Steven Mailloux, *Interpretive Conventions: The Reader in the Study of American Fiction* (Ithaca and London: Cornell, 1982), pp.93–125.

[4]Robert M. Fowler, *Loaves and Fishes* (Chico: Scholars, 1980).

inherent within the text itself and not just in the minds of its interpreters. With this type of reader-response criticism, historians need not fear unemployment; while the appropriation of literary methods has raised important questions about the interpretation of texts, questions about their historical reliability and intentions still may play a significant role in gospel criticism.

D Social-scientific methods

The final category in this survey of the latest hermeneutical developments deals with methods borrowed from the social sciences. A number of biblical scholars have begun to apply psychological, anthropological, and especially sociological procedures to the study of the Scriptures and their environment.[1] As with the new hermeneutic, structuralism, and post-structuralism, when applied to the gospels these are primarily employed as aids to interpretation rather than as methods for defending or challenging historical accuracy. But exceptions creep in. Thus Gerd Theissen, who has done as much as anyone to promote the social-scientific study of New Testament Christianity, can boast that 'a sociology of the Jesus movement transcends the dispute of both "conservative" and "critical" exegetes over the authenticity and historicity of the tradition'. Yet immediately he adds that 'indeed, it does make a contribution toward solving these problems. For it suggests that we should assume a continuity between Jesus and the Jesus movement and in so doing opens up the possibility of transferring insights into the Jesus movement to Jesus himself.'[2] In other words, a sociological study of Jesus' environment may make perplexing elements of his ministry more understandable and therefore believable. For example, some of his more stringent requirements for discipleship (*e.g.* Mt. 8:20 or Mk. 6:8–11 pars.) may make better sense when they are seen as applying only to those who literally left their homes and families to join his itinerant ministry. In a different vein, Howard Kee returns to an argument reminis-

---

[1]See, respectively, Northrop Frye, *The Great Code: The Bible and Literature* (New York: Harcourt, Brace, Jovanovich, 1981; London: Routledge & Kegan Paul, 1982); Bruce J. Malina, *The New Testament World: Insights from Cultural Anthropology* (Atlanta: John Knox, 1981; London: SCM, 1983); and Derek Tidball, *An Introduction to the Sociology of the New Testament* (Exeter: Paternoster; Greenwood, SC: Attic, 1983). The last of these is a survey of a large number of recent studies. On these and related issues, see more briefly, R. J. Banks, 'Setting "The Quest for the Historical Jesus" in a Broader Framework', *GP*,2, pp.61–82.
[2]Gerd Theissen, *The First Followers of Jesus* (London: SCM [= *Sociology of Early Palestinian Christianity* (Philadelphia: Fortress)], 1978), p.4.

cent of the new hermeneutic when he uses sociological analysis to contend that ancient miracle stories, including those in the gospels, may never have been intended to report historical fact but only to depict in symbol a belief in God's power to heal sickness, bring order out of chaos, defeat evil powers, or become one with his people.[1] But then the type of reply given to the new hermeneutic would seem to apply here as well (*cf.* pp.57–58).

5 Conclusion and case study

Three of the methods surveyed – form, redaction and midrash criticism – regularly claim that the gospels are a mixture of fact and fiction, of reliable history and imaginative embellishment. In each this claim is unjustified, but the methods offer valuable exegetical insights when stripped of their negative presuppositions about the historical unreliability of the gospel tradition. The fourth main section of this chapter surveyed methods used primarily in interpreting the meaning of the gospels rather than in assessing their historical accuracy. Each of these, however, has at times impinged on questions of historicity, since it can be argued that the meaning of part or all of the gospels is that they are not to be taken as history. It is undeniable that this argument applies in at least one case, that of the parables, but it is not likely to apply elsewhere. At the very least the main outline of the events of Jesus' life, death and resurrection must be historical or the claims of Christianity become incomprehensible. The very distinctiveness of the Judaeo-Christian tradition over against its pagan counterparts lay in its belief in one omnipotent God acting in observable events in history, and the distinctiveness of Christianity over against Judaism centred around the belief that such divine action came to a decisive climax with the person and work of Jesus. Sceptics down through the ages argued that those beliefs were not true, but seldom did they maintain that those beliefs were not what Scripture was claiming. That the latter notion has proliferated in recent times may be due to the uneasy conscience of modern scholars who have broken with their traditional Christian heritage but who hope to

---

[1] Howard C. Kee, *Miracle in the Early Christian World* (New Haven and London: Yale, 1983). In still other cases, social-scientific approaches unjustifiably rule out from the start the possibility of the supernatural.

Matthew 21:33–46	Mark 12:1–12	Luke 20:9–19[1]
'Hear another parable. There was a householder who planted a vineyard, and set a hedge around it, and dug a wine press in it, and built a tower, and let it out to tenants, and went into another country. When the season of fruit drew near, he sent his servants to the tenants, to get his fruit; and the tenants took his servants and beat one, killed another, and stoned another. Again he sent other servants, more than the first; and they did the same to them. Afterward he sent his son to them, saying, ''They will respect my son.'' But when the tenants saw the son, they said to themselves, ''This is the heir; come, let us kill him and have his inheritance.'' And they took him and cast him out of the vineyard, and killed him. When therefore the owner of the vineyard comes, what will he do to those tenants?' They said to him, 'He will put those wretches to a miserable death, and let out the vineyard to other tenants who will give him the fruits in their seasons.' Jesus said to them, 'Have you never read in the scriptures: ''The very stone which the builders rejected has become the head of the corner; this was the Lord's doing, and it is marvelous in our eyes''? Therefore I tell you, the kingdom of God will be taken away from you and given to a nation producing the fruits of it. [And he who falls on this stone will be broken to pieces; but when it falls on any one, it will crush him.]' When the chief priests and the Pharisees heard his parables, they perceived that he was speaking about them. But when they tried to arrest him, they feared the multitudes, because they held him to be a prophet.	And he began to speak to them in parables. 'A man planted a vineyard, and set a hedge around it, and dug a pit for the wine press, and built a tower, and let it out to tenants, and went into another country. When the time came, he sent a servant to the tenants, to get from them some of the fruit of the vineyard. And they took him and beat him, and sent him away empty-handed. Again he sent to them another servant, and they wounded him in the head, and treated him shamefully. And he sent another, and him they killed; and so with many others, some they beat and some they killed. He had still one other, a beloved son; finally he sent him to them, saying, ''They will respect my son.'' But those tenants said to one another, ''This is the heir; come, let us kill him, and the inheritance will be ours.'' And they took him and killed him, and cast him out of the vineyard. What will the owner of the vineyard do? He will come and destroy the tenants, and give the vineyard to others. Have you not read this scripture: ''The very stone which the builders rejected has become the head of the corner; this was the Lord's doing, and it is marvelous in our eyes''?' And they tried to arrest him, but feared the multitude, for they perceived that he had told the parable against them; so they left him and went away.	And he began to tell the people this parable: 'A man planted a vineyard, and let it out to tenants, and went into another country for a long while. When the time came, he sent a servant to the tenants, that they should give him some of the fruit of the vineyard; but the tenants beat him, and sent him away empty-handed. And he sent another servant; him also they beat and treated shamefully, and sent him away empty-handed. And he sent yet a third; this one they wounded and cast out. Then the owner of the vineyard said, ''What shall I do? I will send my beloved son; it may be that they will respect him.'' But when the tenants saw him, they said to themselves, ''This is the heir; let us kill him, that the inheritance may be ours.'' And they cast him out of the vineyard and killed him. What then will the owner of the vineyard do to them? He will come and destroy those tenants, and give the vineyard to others.' When they heard this, they said, 'God forbid!' But he looked at them and said, 'What then is this that is written: ''The very stone which the builders rejected has become the head of the corner''? Every one who falls on that stone will be broken to pieces; but when it falls on any one it will crush him'. The scribes and the chief priests tried to lay hands on him at that very hour, but they feared the people; for they perceived that he had told this parable against them.

---

[1]The texts are taken from the RSV. The bracketed portion of Matthew's version is not found in some ancient manuscripts.

salvage something of it which scholars from other backgrounds might accept. However well-intentioned, it seems likely that such 'mediation' is doomed to failure through lack of sufficient evidence and logic.

Each of the new methods for gospel study does help at times to explain why the gospel parallels differ in the ways that they do. The parable of the wicked tenants, which appears in all three Synoptics, conveniently illustrates some of the ways each of these methods can be employed to defend the historical accuracy of the gospel accounts rather than to attack it (see p.67).

There can be no doubt that Matthew, Mark and Luke are recounting the identical parable here, even though there are significant differences between their versions of it. In each of the three gospels this passage occurs as part of Jesus' teaching in the temple during the final week before his crucifixion. In each gospel Jesus has just finished responding to the question about his authority to cleanse the temple and in each he goes on to address the question about paying taxes, although Matthew adds an additional parable both before and after this one. Many of the differences among the parallels are insignificant; the gospels do not claim to supply a highly literal translation of Jesus' words. Besides having been translated into Greek, Jesus' teachings have been freely paraphrased throughout the gospels, as a glance at any synopsis reveals. Nor is it hard to see in this instance that the essence of the parable has been retained intact in each version; few of the differences qualify as 'apparent contradictions'. Those that do so have plausible explanations, but a mere harmonization of the data does not explain why the parable was told so differently in each case. The new methods for gospel study suggest some possible explanations which point to rational reasons for the divergences; the variation is not arbitrary. Of course some suggestions can only be tentative, and often quite different explanations are also conceivable.[1]

Two features of Luke's text make good sense in the light of form criticism. First, his version at the outset excises all description of the vineyard. This is probably due to the tendency of oral tradition

---

[1]The best detailed study of this parable in its three versions (as well as an interesting parallel in the so-called Gnostic Gospel of Thomas) is Klyne Snodgrass, *The Parable of the Wicked Tenants* (Tübingen: Mohr, 1983).

to omit unnecessary or incidental details.[1] Second, his account streamlines and organizes the sending of the various servants so that only three appear, the fate of each is clearly described, and they form a sequence of increasing severity, capped by the murder of the son. This pattern clearly reflects the tendencies of popular storytelling to use groups of three characters or episodes which build to a climax.[2]

Balancing these contributions of the oral tradition are a number of features most probably due to the evangelists; here redaction criticism enters in. Luke introduces an element of uncertainty into Mark's version of the landlord's decision; instead of an unqualified 'they will respect my son', he writes, 'it may be they will respect him.' Luke was no doubt trying to avoid a possible misunderstanding of Mark's version since the tenants did not respect the landlord's son. Because the landlord's relationship with his tenants resembles God's behaviour toward his people, Luke wanted to make sure that no one misinterpreted the parable by thinking that God did not realize what would happen when he sent *his* son.[3] After Jesus' closing quotation from Scripture, Matthew introduced an even more obvious theologically motivated addition with his unparalleled statement about the kingdom of God being given to a new people. Unless one improperly assumes that Matthew had no access to any other information about the teaching of Jesus besides Mark's gospel, there is no reason to doubt the authenticity of this addition. But why did only Matthew include it? A reasonable explanation would be that, as the evangelist most interested in the offer of the gospel to the Jews, he was most concerned to stress the need for Israel's leaders to repent lest they fall from God's favour entirely.[4] This motivation probably also explains why only Matthew preserved the self-indicting response of the crowd after Jesus asked what they thought the landlord would do to the wicked tenants. One can easily harmonize this response with Mark's version which has Jesus answer his own question and with Luke's

---

[1] H.-J. Klauck, *Allegorie und Allegorese in synoptischen Gleichnistexten* (Münster: Aschendorff, 1978), p.292.

[2] Kelber, *Gospel*, p.59.

[3] Charles E. Carlston, *The Parables of the Triple Tradition* (Philadelphia: Fortress, 1975), p.79.

[4] David Hill, *The Gospel of Matthew* (London: Oliphants, 1972; Grand Rapids: Eerdmans, 1981), p.301.

which has the crowd respond to Jesus' answer with a shocked, 'God forbid!' It is absurd to imagine everyone in the crowd replying in unison with the identical words, like a trained choir, and completely realistic to suppose Jesus should then state the response he endorsed, no doubt shouted out by one of his supporters and in turn eliciting cries of reproof from his opponents[1]. But the reason why none of the Synoptists chose to tell the whole story becomes clear only by studying their varying theological emphases.

The references to Scripture in the opening and closing of this passage alert one to the possible presence of midrash. The description of the vineyard comes from Isaiah 5:1–2 and the saying about the cornerstone cites Psalm 118:22. The parable elaborates Isaiah's equation of the vineyard with Israel (5:7) and links up with the final quotation by a play on words – the Hebrew and Aramaic for 'stone' and 'son' are very similar. The parable and its context therefore comprise a *proem* midrash,[2] making it unlikely that the reference to the psalm was a later addition, as is often alleged. In this case the appearance of midrash does not resolve an apparent contradiction between parallels but supports the authenticity of a feature of the passage common to all versions, by challenging the popular argument that the final verses were not integrally linked with the parable.

The new hermeneutic's emphasis on the parables as performatives is vindicated by the concluding observation that Jesus' opponents recognized that the parable was attacking them. This was no innocuous illustration of insignificant doctrine but a life-threatening proclamation! Further, their hostile response to Jesus' teaching explains some of the puzzling sayings elsewhere and enhances the case for their authenticity. Most notably, it makes sense of Jesus' claim that by speaking in parables he was actually driving some in his audiences further away from the kingdom (*e.g.*

---

[1]*Cf.* John Calvin, *A Harmony of the Gospels Matthew, Mark and Luke,* vol. 3, trans. A. W. Morrison, ed. David W. Torrance and Thomas F. Torrance (Edinburgh: St. Andrew; Grand Rapids: Eerdmans, 1972 [Latin orig. 1555]), p.18: 'There is no contradiction if we examine the sense more closely. There is no doubt that they [the Jewish leaders] would have agreed with Christ over the penalty which fell to such wicked servants, but when they saw that the charge and sentence were laid against themselves, they cried "God forbid".' *Cf.* the similar approach of J. Alexander Findlay, *Jesus and His Parables* (London: Epworth, 1950), p.54, to the divergent textual forms of the parable of the two sons (Mt. 21:28–32).

[2]Ellis, 'Form Criticism', pp.313–314.

Mk. 4:11–12 pars.) – not that they failed to catch his meaning but that it was so direct and confrontational that they were forced either to accept it and be welcomed or to reject it and be repelled.[1]

Structuralist analyses of the parables do not always agree with each other, and a passage as complex as this makes agreement that much more difficult.[2] Sellin's observations about the triadic structure of parables, though, may prove helpful. Despite the attention given to the servants and the son, the three main characters who represent the authority figure and his contrasting subordinates are the landlord, the wicked tenants and the new tenants who will replace them. These in some sense stand for God, the unrepentant Israelites and his faithful but dispossessed followers.[3] This analysis relegates the servants and the son to a lesser role; the main thrust of the parable would be unchanged had the landlord appeared in person to collect his rent and received rebuff. Although Christians can scarcely read this story without relating the murder of the son to Christ's crucifixion, it is not clear that everyone in Jesus' original audience would have made that equation. Thus, rather than rejecting the episode about the son as a later addition to the parable by Christians who were recalling the cross, one can remain confident that it was there from the beginning, since its significance for how Jesus understood his own mission is at best implicit. This is precisely how most of Jesus' references to himself in the Synoptics appear.

Finally, the post-structuralist emphasis on the varying responses of different readers dovetails nicely with the harmonization of the divergent reactions of the crowd to Jesus' parable. Everyone does not react in the same way to a well-told story and it is unrealistic to label the gospels as contradictory because they report different reactions. As for social-scientific perspectives, it is interesting to note that the type of social customs and interaction presupposed throughout the parable closely mirror the contractual arrangements of the day. The behaviour of the master, quite strange by

---

[1]*Cf.* William L. Lane, *The Gospel according to Mark* (Grand Rapids: Eerdmans, 1974; London: Marshall, Morgan, & Scott, 1975), p.159, n. 35; Klauck, *Allegorie*, p.251.

[2]Two quite different structuralist approaches to this parable are found in Pheme Perkins, *The Parables of Jesus* (New York: Paulist, 1981), p.190; and Robert W. Funk, *Parables and Presence* (Philadelphia: Fortress, 1982), pp.53–54.

[3]Most commentators can agree on this point regardless of whether or not they admit some element of allegory in the parables. There is, however, no good reason for denying the presence of allegory; see Blomberg, *Parables*, ch. one and ch. six.

modern standards in permitting and indulging in so much violence, actually coincides with the ruthless behaviour of many wealthy landowners in first-century Palestine.[1] The sociology of the day illuminates the psychology of the individual. This realism makes the parable more intelligible and more believable as an authentic teaching of Jesus.

The thrust of this survey of new methods for gospel study is clear. The challenges they have posed to the historical reliability of the gospels all fail to overthrow the traditional confidence in that reliability which older commentators more consistently displayed. In fact, all the methods can be used, though sometimes in quite modified form, to strengthen that confidence. If the debate about the historicity of the gospels is to advance any further, it must be not on the basis of new methods of study but on the actual details of the texts themselves. This is the issue which chapters four and five take up. But first there is one other question of method which must be addressed.

---

[1]Snodgrass, *Tenants*, pp.31–40.

Miracles

Six large jars of water suddenly appear filled with wine. A man walks across a lake, apparently defying the law of gravity. Five thousand men, plus an unknown number of women and children, satisfy their hunger from a quantity of food originally numbering five loaves of bread and two fish and finish with enough leftovers to fill twelve baskets full. This is part of the world of the miracles of Jesus described in the New Testament gospels, to say nothing of numerous healings, exorcisms and even resurrection from death. Who today can believe in such stories? Even if the survey of gospel criticism in previous chapters has uncovered no convincing reasons for rejecting the reliability of the narratives of the life of Jesus, surely, many would argue, the line must be drawn here. There is an intuitive sense with which even the most devout believer must share the tension that the sceptic feels when it comes to the credibility of miracle stories. Moreover, even the person open to the possibility of miracles does not believe every strange tale of the supernatural. Thus an examination of the problem of identifying genuine miracles must follow a discussion of their credibility.

1 The problem of credibility

The reasons for rejecting the gospel miracles ultimately revolve around three issues. Broadly speaking, these may be called the scientific, the philosophical and the historical objections.

A The scientific objection

Although Rudolf Bultmann was a theologian, many of his scientific colleagues would have agreed with his famous pronouncements of a generation ago that 'man's knowledge and mastery of the world have advanced to such an extent through science and technology that it is no longer possible for anyone seriously to hold the New Testament view of the world'. Instead, 'the modern conception of human nature as a self-subsistent unity immune from the interference of supernatural powers' must take its place.[1] In short, the scientific objection to the credibility of miracles is that the discovery of the natural, physical laws by which the universe operates has proved them impossible. Those who hold this view sometimes go on to explain that people used to believe in miracles because they had only a primitive scientific understanding. The Christian doctrines of the virgin birth and resurrection, for example, could spring from just such a pre-scientific milieu. Only a moment's thought is required, however, to realize that people of every age have known that two human parents are needed for conception and that death is irreversible. Others argue, more plausibly, that while people in New Testament times knew full well that the types of miracles described in the gospels were highly extraordinary, their openness to the supernatural led them to believe in what science has now proved impossible.

Interestingly enough, many scientists today would not feel the force of this objection as strongly as they might have earlier in this century. Physical science has undergone a revolution of massive proportions in which belief in the inviolability of the laws of Newtonian mechanics has given way to quantum theory, in which physical 'laws' are recognized as only 'provisional descriptions of observed regularities in nature'.[2] Heisenberg's 'principle of indeterminacy' illustrates the radical nature of this scientific upheaval. Physicists are unable to know at the same time both the position and momentum of a sub-atomic particle, making it impossible to rule out a given configuration of particles. Any physical occurrence could thus theoretically happen at some time by sheer chance, however slim the probability of that occurrence. When first presented with this revolution in physics, some Christians rushed to point out that the scientific door was once again open for the biblical miracles. But the unpredictable combinations of sub-

---

[1]Rudolf Bultmann, 'New Testament and Mythology', in *Kerygma and Myth,* ed. H.-W. Bartsch (London: SPCK, 1953), pp.4, 7.

[2]Ernest Lucas, 'Miracles and Natural Laws', *Christian Arena* 38.3 (1985), p.9. On the varying degrees of uncertainty attaching to all scientific paradigms, see esp. Thomas S. Kuhn, *The Structure of Scientific Revolutions* (Chicago: University of Chicago, 1970).

atomic activity have not overthrown the principles of how the larger objects function which these particles make up. Gravity, for example, still prevents a person from walking on water![1]

Most defenders of miracles today, therefore, do not deny the validity of the regularities of nature. Instead they deny that a miracle must be a *violation* of such 'laws'. Despite all the marvellous advances of physics, no one has yet proved, if God as traditionally conceived by Jews and Christians exists, why he might not occasionally suspend or transcend the otherwise fixed regularities of nature. No physical principles need be violated if a new causal agent is introduced. Norman Geisler, a leading American Christian apologist, puts it this way: 'belief in miracles does not destroy the *integrity* of scientific methodology, only its *sovereignty*. It says in effect that science does not have sovereign claim to explain all events as natural, but only those that are regular, repeatable, and/or predictable'[2]. There is an important analogy here with human behaviour, since persons, even with their finite powers, by freely choosing to start or end various actions, regularly bring about new events which otherwise would not have occurred by natural forces alone. If persons can change the physical world, how much more ought God to be able to do so!

This approach however presupposes that some kind of omnipotent personal agent exists. Miracles follow logically if theism is true but not if deism or atheism is. Traditionally believers have argued for God's existence by means of various philosophical 'proofs', but many today, theologians included, believe that all such logic has been shown to be faulty.[3] Some feel that to try to prove that God exists is to deny faith its proper place as the foundation of religion, though it is not obvious why anyone should continue to believe a given doctrine if all the evidence contradicted it. This is not the place to digress into a discussion of the debate, except to note that not everyone has abandoned hope of formulating more compelling versions of some of the traditional arguments for God's existence.

---

[1]For a clear discussion of the revolution in modern physics and its implications for Christianity, see Colin A. Russell, *Cross-currents: Interactions Between Science and Faith* (Leicester: IVP; Grand Rapids: Eerdmans, 1985), pp.198–224.

[2]Norman L. Geisler, *Miracles and Modern Thought* (Grand Rapids: Zondervan; Exeter: Paternoster, 1982), p.58.

[3]Representative of evangelical thought are K. E. Yandell, *Christianity and Philosophy* (Leicester: IVP; Grand Rapids: Eerdmans, 1984), pp.48–94, who believes that the 'proofs' demonstrate only the coherence of theism; and C. S. Evans, *Philosophy of Religion* (Leicester and Downers Grove: IVP, 1985), pp.45–76, who affirms that they also show its reasonableness.

A promising approach is the one taken by William Craig, who expresses his argument quite simply: (1) Everything that begins to exist has a cause of its existence, (2) the universe began to exist, therefore (3) the universe has a cause of its existence, which can also be shown to be personal since it must be the result of someone's free choice to create. Of the two premises, the controversial one is the second; perhaps the universe has always existed? But Craig draws on the work of ancient Arabic philosophers and mathematicians to argue that this would imply an actual infinite succession of moments in time past, which is empirically, though not theoretically, impossible. More simply, time by definition must have had a beginning; it is logically nonsensical to say that it always existed. Less abstractly, Craig also notes the widespread agreement among scientists today that the universe in fact has been both expanding and moving towards maximum entropy (running down or decaying) ever since it came into being with a 'big bang' billions of years ago. This is a concept that could be harmonized with belief in God as the creator.[1]

In fact, physical science today seems more open to the possibility of God than it has been for generations, although old prejudices die hard. The agnostic astronomer Robert Jastrow concludes that in the study of the origins of the universe 'the scientist's pursuit of the past ends in the moment of creation' and that 'this is an exceedingly strange development, unexpected by all but the theologians'.[2] In some circles physicists are even more willing to believe in miracles than biblical scholars are![3] As P. Medawar's celebrated work, *The Limits of Science,* demonstrates, the notion that science has proved the supernatural impossible must be abandoned.[4]

B The philosophical objection

To admit the possibility of miracles like those found in the gospels is a far cry from acknowledging their probability. The classic

---

[1]William L. Craig, *The Kalam Cosmological Argument* (London: Macmillan, 1979); popularized in his *The Existence of God and the Beginning of the Universe* (San Bernardino: Here's Life, 1979). For a rational justification of God's attributes, see Stephen T. Davis, *Logic and the Nature of God* (London: Macmillan, 1983; Grand Rapids: Eerdmans, 1984).

[2]Robert Jastrow, *God and the Astronomers* (New York and London: Norton, 1978), p.115.

[3]Stephen T. Davis, 'The Miracle at Cana: A Philosopher's Perspective', in *GP*,6, pp.425–426. *Cf.* Werner Schaafs, *Theology, Physics, and Miracles* (Washington, DC: Canon, 1974).

[4](San Francisco: Harper & Row, 1984; Oxford: University Press, 1985). Medawar still denies God's existence, not on scientific grounds, but due to the problem of evil.

philosophical objection to miracles stems from the eighteenth-century Scotsman, David Hume, in his *Enquiry concerning Human Understanding,* section 10.[1] Hume claimed that the probability will always be greater for a natural than for a supernatural explanation of some apparently miraculous event. To substantiate this claim, he gave four main reasons: (1) No alleged miracle has ever been supported with the testimony of a sufficiently large number of witnesses who could not have been either deceived or deceivers. (2) People in general crave the miraculous and believe fables more readily than they ought. (3) 'Miracles' only occur among barbarous peoples. (4) Miracle stories occur in all religions and thereby cancel each other out since they support irreconcilable doctrines.[2]

Hume's arguments have found critics and supporters ever since they were published. The most convincing responses from the defenders of miracles include the following: Claim (1), even if true, does not prove that *no* alleged miracle will ever have adequate testimony, and in fact a good case can be made for affirming that the witnesses of the gospel miracles do offer adequate testimony. Claim (2) probably is true, but all it means is that testimony about miracles must be examined with extra caution and suspicion before it is accepted. Claims (3) and (4) are demonstrably false in the absolute form in which Hume has stated them. Many highly educated Westerners today believe in miracles, and no religion stands or falls with a claim about the resurrection of its founder in the way that Christianity does.[3]

Hume, however, went further. Even if all four of his arguments should prove false, Hume alleged that the weight of probability would still favour a non-miraculous explanation of every extraordinary phenomenon, simply because that is how the vast majority of events in the world, both ordinary and extraordinary, are explained. In short, the uniform testimony of human experience is against admitting a miraculous explanation for some won-

---

[1]A convenient edition is that of L. A. Selby-Bigge and P. H. Nidditch (Oxford: Clarendon; New York: Oxford, 1975). This volume also contains Hume's *Enquiry concerning the Principles of Morals.*

[2]For this summary and the response to Hume below, see esp. William L. Craig, 'The Problem of Miracles: A Historical and Philosophical Perspective', in *GP,*6, pp.17–19, 22–27, 37–43. *Cf.* also Davis, 'Miracle at Cana', pp.430–436; and Richard Swinburne, *The Concept of Miracle* (London: Macmillan; New York: St. Martin's, 1970).

[3]On this latter point, see esp. Sir Norman Anderson, *Christianity and World Religions* (Leicester and Downers Grove: IVP, 1984).

drous occurrence. For example, one should never accept the claim that Jesus raised Lazarus from his tomb after his death four days earlier, because if x stands for the number of people that have died in the history of the world *without being* raised (a very large number!), then the odds are x to 1 (very poor odds!) against Lazarus having died and *being* raised.

This line of reasoning, however, proves too much. If historians applied it consistently to their examination of human testimony, they would rule out everything unique or unusual that ever occurred, including things generally held to be non-miraculous. This was recognized at least as long ago as 1819, when Richard Whately, in his *Historical Doubts Relative to Napoleon Buonaparte,* applied Hume's method to a study of the life of Napoleon, a unique individual in many ways. Whately demonstrated by it that one has no reason to believe that most of the accounts of his life are true, a conclusion which is patently absurd. It is possible to avoid much of this absurdity by applying Hume's principles only to allegedly miraculous events, and not to all unusual events. This is the approach most of his modern defenders have adopted. But current debate tends to focus more on the historical objection than on the philosophical objection.

C The historical objection

The rise of the so-called 'historical-critical method' of studying the Scriptures (see chapters one and two) pre-dated the work of the late nineteenth-century German historian, Ernst Troeltsch, by more than a century, but it was he who gave the method its most objective criteria. Most relevant for a study of the miracles is his principle of analogy. In essence, Troeltsch declared that the historian has no right to accept as historical fact the account of a past event for which he has no analogy in the present. For example, one would not believe an ancient story about warfare in which an army massacres thousands of opposing soldiers in battle without suffering a single casualty, because one knows from modern experience that wars inevitably inflict substantial losses on both sides. So too the historian who has never experienced miracles of the kind attributed to Jesus, or who after thorough investigation of the world as it exists in his age has no knowledge of such events ever occurring, may not accept that such miracles could ever have happened.[1]

There are at least two possible ways of replying to Troeltsch (and to Hume, to the extent that he anticipated Troeltsch here). One is to deny the validity of his principle; the other is to deny that no one today experiences miracles. Probably both approaches are valid. To begin with the second, it is difficult to claim that miracles only occurred in 'Bible times'.[2] This question will arise again (see below, pp.94–95), but for now it is worth simply noting that there is a growing awareness that much in our world today is 'paranormal' – uncanny events that cannot be explained by natural causes so far discovered.[3] And, as in the Bible, not all the supernatural involves good actions; much supports the notion of a demonic realm as well. But even if all contemporary 'miracles' could be explained on other grounds, Troeltsch's first point seems equally questionable. Using a frequently cited illustration, how could a 'historian' from ancient days who had lived all his life in the tropics, and who had no knowledge of anyone who had travelled to more temperate climates, ever come to believe in the existence of ice?[4] To paraphrase the German theologian Wolfhart Pannenberg, who has led a movement in his homeland back to at least a limited acceptance of the miraculous, it is not the lack of analogy that suggests something is unhistorical but only the presence of an

---

[1]Many of Troeltsch's key works have never been translated into English, but for a convenient summary of his thought, see his 'Historiography', in *Encyclopaedia of Religion and Ethics,* ed. James Hastings, vol. 6 (New York: Chas. Scribner's Sons; Edinburgh: T & T Clark, 1913), pp.716–723.

[2]John A. Witmer, 'The Doctrine of Miracles', *BSac* 130 (1973), pp.126–134, represents one line of Christian thought which holds to this idea by linking miracles with the formation of the canon of Scripture. But the only reason Witmer can offer is that 'the gift of miracles provided by God for the apostolic church (1 Cor. 12:28, 29) is undoubtedly among those temporary gifts of the Holy Spirit that passed away with the apostles' (p.133). This last clause probably refers to 1 Cor. 13:10, but it is highly unlikely that when Paul wrote of certain gifts passing away 'when the perfect comes' he was referring to the time of the completion of the Bible. Nowhere else does Paul use 'perfect' in that sense (it refers much more naturally to the end of this age and the return of Christ), nor does he even show any realization that he was writing letters that would be included by Christians in a collection of books set apart as a 'New Testament'.

[3]See *e.g.* the remarkable collection of apparently true stories of non-religious 'miracles' in Geoffrey Ashe, *Miracle* (London: Routledge & Kegan Paul, 1978).

[4]For one of the most balanced and penetrating critiques of Troeltsch to date, see William Abraham, *Divine Revelation and the Limits of Historical Criticism* (New York and Oxford: University Press, 1982), pp.92–115. Hume himself anticipated this objection and tried to deal with it by arguing that the person who had never seen water freeze could not rule out the possibility of ice, since he had never been in a place with the conditions necessary to obtain it (*Enquiries*, p.114, n. 1). But the same argument can apply to miracles; one who has never been in a position to experience God's direct intervention into the affairs of the world cannot rule out the possibility that he might so intervene.

analogy to something already known to be unhistorical.[1] For example, the reason many people, including Christians who believe in the biblical miracles, dismiss most U.F.O. sightings out of hand is not because U.F.O.'s have been proven not to exist, but because the sightings usually resemble other ones which have turned out to be air-balloons, the 'northern lights', shooting stars, or the like. The same logic should be applied to the gospel miracles.

Thus neither the scientific, nor the philosophical, nor even the historical obstacles to miracles prevent one from believing at least some miracle stories.[2] But why then, the sceptic often asks, do believers not accept every story of an alleged miracle that someone claims to have experienced? And if the answer comes back, as in the example just discussed, that many miracle stories resemble demonstrably fictitious narratives, then the sceptic looks for parallels to the *gospel* miracles in other writings which are not accepted as recounting historical fact. In short, if the upshot of this section has been to show that miracles may be credible, the next question must be to decide if they are identifiable. More specifically, can one identify the miracles in the gospels as genuine, especially in the light of similar stories told about other revered men of old?

2 The problem of identification

Christians have traditionally believed that the miracle stories in the Bible relate supernatural events that really happened, while at the same time they reject most or all of the similar stories told in other religious literature from the ancient world. To see if this attitude can be justified as far as the gospels are concerned, at least two separate sets of questions need to be examined. First, what are the 'parallels' to the miracles of Jesus in the Mediterranean world of his day, and how significant are they? Second, what is the evidence for the reliability of the gospel miracles stories, apart from the problem of alleged parallels, and how strong is that evidence?

---

[1]Wolfhart Pannenberg, *Basic Questions in Theology,* vol. 1 (London: SCM; Philadelphia: Fortress, 1970), pp.48–49.

[2]For further discussion, see the comprehensive study of Colin Brown, *Miracles and the Critical Mind* (Exeter: Paternoster; Grand Rapids: Eerdmans, 1984). In more popular form, *cf.* his *That You May Believe: Miracles and Faith Then and Now* (Exeter: Paternoster; Grand Rapids: Eerdmans, 1985).

A The question of parallels

Sceptics who believe Jesus worked few or no miracles must explain how he soon came to be portrayed as a spectacular miracle worker. Their explanations usually assume that the early church clothed Jesus in the garb of other religious figures and movements of the day in order to exalt him and commend him to others. Four main types of parallels are identified. (1) Some point to the apocryphal gospels and acts, which contain many incredible stories about Jesus and his followers not found in the New Testament. They assume that the processes which led to the creation of these later legends already began during the formation of the New Testament. (2) Others find closer parallels in Greek religion and mythology, in which ancient heroes over time became transformed into 'divine men', complete with a repertoire of miraculous deeds to authenticate them. (3) Still others identify the first-century world of magic and sorcery, not too different from what today might be called the occult, as the place to find an explanation for the traditions about Jesus. (4) Finally, in what seems to be the latest fashion, some see parallels among the legends of the rabbis and other Jewish leaders of Jesus' day, a few of which involve some remarkable miracles. Each of these approaches therefore deserves closer scrutiny.

1 The miracles in the New Testament apocrypha

These are the 'parallels' least often cited. In the second and third centuries, numerous legends grew up around the infancy and childhood of Jesus, his crucifixion and resurrection, and the subsequent ministries of the apostles. Often these involved bizarre events – the child Jesus miraculously lengthening a leg of an imbalanced bed which Joseph is building for a customer (Infancy Gospel of Thomas 13), all the Roman statues bowing down to Christ during his trial before Pilate (Acts of Pilate 5–6), or John effectively commanding the bedbugs to sleep peacefully in a corner of his room so that he might rest at ease (Acts of John 60–61)! Many similar prodigies abound in this literature. None of these legends can be proved early enough to have influenced the four evangelists, but some would argue that the gospel miracle stories developed from the same type of legends of an earlier date.

The character of most of the apocryphal miracles, and indeed of the apocrypha more generally (see pp.215–219), differs so markedly from that of the canonical gospels that it is hard to believe the same processes led to the formation of both. The apocrypha seem to reflect belief in a God who works miracles 'on demand', thereby compelling people to believe in Christianity. They often tell of wonders worked for vengeful, trivial, or heretical reasons, in a fashion hard to reconcile with the spirit of the gospels. Most important of all, they almost exclusively deal with the 'gaps' in the New Testament record. They imaginatively fill the undocumented portions of the ministries of Jesus and his followers with spectacular deeds, but for the most part avoid rewriting the canonical accounts. When one considers the *carte blanche* provided by John 20:30 and 21:25, which point out the vast number of unrecorded events in Jesus' adult ministry, the silence of the apocrypha speaks volumes.[1] Their failure to narrate further miracles from this period in Jesus' life suggests that their authors recognized the inviolability of the scriptural accounts, and perhaps that many of the apocrypha were not even intended to be read as serious history.

The major exception is the so-called Gospel of Peter (see pp.217–218). Much of this narrative is understated and frequently parallels the canonical gospels. Nevertheless, it seems to have stemmed from a heretical branch of Christianity known as docetism. Docetism (from the Greek word *dokeō* for 'seem') believed that although Jesus was fully God, he only seemed to be human, in contrast with the New Testament gospels in which Jesus' human nature is undeniable. David Wright very carefully sifts the evidence for and against this assessment and concludes that the testimony of the Gospel of Peter must be rejected as largely unreliable. Its description of the resurrection (see p.105) forces one who would argue for its authenticity 'to champion a case burdened by improbability'.[2]

2 Greek heroes

Ancient Greek mythology overflows with stories which tell of gods and men performing wonders quite similar to those found in the

---

[1] For several of the above points, *cf.* Paul J. Achtemeier, 'Jesus and the Disciples as Miracle Workers in the Apocryphal New Testament', in *Aspects of Religious Propaganda in Judaism and Early Christianity,* ed. Elisabeth S. Fiorenza (Notre Dame, IN: University Press, 1976), pp.149–186.

[2] David F. Wright, 'Apologetic and Apocalyptic: The Miraculous in the *Gospel of Peter*', in *GP,* 6, p.415.

New Testament.[1] Four of the most famous examples may be considered. Alexander the Great is said to have been born of a virgin and later in his life to have accepted accolades as a god (*e.g.* Plutarch, *Life of Alexander* 2:3–6, 27:8–11). The patron 'saint' of physicians, Asclepius, accomplished miraculous healings of many kinds and even raised the dead (*e.g.* Ovid, *Fasti* 6:743–762). The god Dionysus once a year for the festival in his honour at his temple in the province of Elis caused wine to appear in empty water cauldrons (Pausanius, *Description of Greece* 6:26.1–2). Most striking of all, a wandering first-century philosopher named Apollonius, from Tyana in Cappadocia, showed great wisdom as a child, performed healings as an adult, correctly predicted the future, exorcised demons, appeared to his followers after he died, and ascended bodily into heaven. Or at least so says his biographer, Philostratus, writing in the early part cf the third century. One of the most striking parallels to a miracle from the life of Jesus is found in *The Life of Apollonius of Tyana* 4:45 (*cf*. Lk. 7:11–17):

A girl had died just in the hour of her marriage, and the bridegroom was following her bier lamenting as was natural his marriage left unfulfilled, and the whole of Rome was mourning with him, for the maiden belonged to a consular family. Apollonius then witnessing their grief, said: 'Put down the bier, for I will stay the tears that you are shedding for this maiden.' And withal he asked what was her name. The crowd accordingly thought that he was about to deliver such an oration as is commonly delivered as much to grace the funeral as to stir up lamentation; but he did nothing of the kind, but merely touching her and whispering in secret some spell over her, at once woke up the maiden from her seeming death; and the girl spoke out loud, and returned to her father's house. . .[2]

Of course virtually nobody believes that Apollonius really did this and other prodigies attributed to him. Instead he is seen as a wise philosopher who may have been able to bring about a few remark-

---

[1]For a list and discussion of some of the more obscure parallels, see Barry L. Blackburn, ' "Miracle-Working ΘΕΙΟΙ ΑΝΔΡΕΣ" in Hellenism (and Hellenistic Judaism)', in *GP*,6, pp.185–218.

[2]Trans. by F. C. Conybeare (London: Heinemann; Cambridge, MA: Harvard, 1912 [Loeb Classical Library, vol. 1]), pp.457–459.

able healings but for the most part has been the 'victim' of his followers, who sought to turn him into a god. It is little wonder that many accuse Christianity of treating Jesus in the same way!

On the other hand, the majority of the miracles in Greek religion bear no resemblance to those of Jesus: men talking with the animals and birds, and even transforming themselves into other creatures, charming rocks and trees with their music, appearing and disappearing, or appearing in two places at the same time, travelling the world without eating, or sending their souls on journeys while their bodies remained at home. Nevertheless there are enough stories which resemble the gospel miracles in some way to convince many that the first Christians turned Jesus into a god much in the same way as the Greeks created divine men out of ancient heroes.[1]

The evidence looks impressive when it is all lumped together, but taken piece by piece a different picture emerges. The life of Alexander the Great was elaborated and embellished for a period of more than 1,000 years; the earliest sources portray him as quite different from the mythological figure into which later legends transformed him. Alexander's most reliable ancient (second-century) biographer, Arrian of Nicomedia, says nothing of his 'virgin birth', so-called because his father Philip supposedly saw a snake curled up next to his wife the night before Alexander's conception and was warned in a dream to 'seal her womb' because a child was to be miraculously born.[2] In the gospels, however, there is no source or layer (*cf.* pp.12–18) which is free from claims of Jesus being involved with the miraculous.

In the case of Asclepius, there is much debate as to whether he even existed as a real man. If he did, he was almost certainly a primitive physician and not just a miraculous healer, since his temple 'priests' later combined both medicine and superstition in their treatment of patients. Where miracles did occur, they might

---

[1]Many of the most important works adopting this point of view have never been translated from German, but two exceptions offering convenient summaries are H.-D. Betz, 'Jesus as Divine Man', in *Jesus and the Historian,* ed. F. T. Trotter (Philadelphia: Westminster, 1968), pp. 114–133 (supporting the view); and Gerd Theissen, *Miracle Stories of the Early Christian Tradition* (Edinburgh: T & T Clark; Philadelphia: Fortress, 1983), pp.265–276 (giving a critique of the view).

[2]Plutarch also lived and wrote in the first two centuries of the Christian era, but he relates this legend with some scepticism, an attitude not retained in the later tradition. A good introduction to the development of legends about Alexander is found in Robin L. Fox, *The Search for Alexander* (Boston: Little, Brown, & Co.; London: Allen Lane, 1980), pp.33–46.

often be accounted for by what today would be called psycho-somatic processes.[1] As for Dionysus, he was almost certainly an imported god of Eastern mythology from the very beginning of his appearance in Greece. In the instance of the fountains flowing with wine, even some ancient writers questioned the truth of the claim, while others explained it by believing that the priests secretly entered the temple by night to substitute liquids and deceive the masses.[2]

The parallels with Apollonius cannot be dismissed as quickly. But unlike the previous examples, the story that Philostratus relates arose only after Jesus' life. If anyone modeled their 'biography' after someone else's, it would have to be Philostratus who imitated the gospel writers and not vice-versa. Few accept this theory, though, leaving the most likely conclusion that the two are entirely independent of each other.[3] In the case of the resurrection story quoted above, even its author was never quite sure if the girl was entirely dead or just comatose. The beginning of the quotation above is more literally translated, 'A girl had seemed to die' (*tethnanai edokei*; *cf.* the phrase 'seeming death' later in the passage), and Philostratus goes on in the same paragraph to write of Apollonius that

> whether he detected some spark of life in her, which those who were nursing her had not noticed, – for it was said that although it was raining at the time, a vapour went up from her face – or whether life was really extinct, and he restored it by the warmth of his touch, is a mysterious problem which neither I myself nor those who were present could decide.

Murray Harris believes that Philostratus has portrayed Apollonius 'as a beneficent exorcist driving out an evil spirit by whispering into the victim's ear or over the victim's body a magical spell that

---

[1]See *e.g.* W. K. C. Guthrie, *The Greeks and Their Gods* (Boston: Beacon; London: Methuen, 1950), pp.247–253.

[2]The most recent of a whole series of studies, mostly in German, debating the relationship between the Dionysus myths and the Cana miracle is Ingo Broer, 'Noch einmal: Zur religionsgeschichtlichen "Ableitung" von Jo 2, 1–11', *SNTU* 8 (1983), pp.103–123. The most thoroughgoing refutation of the alleged connections between the gospels and the Dionysiac myths is Heinz Noetzel, *Christus und Dionysos* (Stuttgart: Calwer Verlag, 1960).

[3]For a brief, readable and convincing summary of what the true Apollonius was most probably like, see B. F. Harris, 'Apollonius of Tyana: Fact and Fiction', *JRH* 5 (1969), pp.189–199.

included her name'. Harris adds that the differences between Luke and Philostratus 'are so numerous and substantial . . . that any theory of their interdependence or their dependence on a common tradition may be discounted'.[1]

To sum up, the evidence from several recent studies suggests that no clear stereotype of a 'divine man' predated the second century AD.[2] Among those called divine men during the time of or before the writing of the gospels, no consistent pattern of miracle-working activity emerges, and close parallels with specific events in Jesus' life are rare. When the patterns become more consistent and the parallels closer, several generations have already elapsed since the life of Christ, so that the evangelists cannot be accused of moulding their stories to fit a stereotyped form of Greek 'diviniz-ation'.[3] It is likely, however, that many of the Graeco-Roman heroes were involved in some genuinely extraordinary events – probably a combination of what today could be explained scientif-ically with a few truly paranormal phenomena, and probably a little fraud or deception as well. What is more, similarities between Jesus and others in his day do not always mean that the supernatural in the gospels can be dismissed, since there may have been genuine supernatural activity elsewhere. Significantly, this is the approach consistently taken by Christian apologists in the first centuries of the church's history.[4]

3 Magic and exorcism

In the last century, over a thousand 'magical papyri' have come to light, which contain instructions for spells and incantations used in the Greek-speaking communities of pre-Christian Egypt. Not sur-prisingly, certain scholars would conclude that Jesus' miracles, and especially his exorcisms, had some connection with the ancient practices of magic. Of course, this is hardly a new allegation. Mark

[1]Murray J. Harris, ' "The Dead Are Restored to Life": Miracles of Revivification in the Gospels', *GP*,6, p.303.
[2]In addition to Blackburn, see esp. David Tiede, *The Charismatic Figure as Miracle Worker* (Missoula: Scholars, 1972); and Carl Holladay, *Theios Anēr in Hellenistic Judaism* (Missoula: Scholars, 1977). Holladay points out that, contrary to what one might expect, the influence of Greek thought in the Jewish world actually made Jews less rather than more open to any attempt to turn the heroes of their past (*e.g.* Abraham, Moses, David, Solomon) into god-like figures.
[3]*Cf.* J. D. Kingsbury, 'The "Divine Man" as the Key to Mark's Christology – The End of an Era?' *Int* 35 (1981), pp.243–257.
[4]Harold Remus, *Pagan-Christian Conflict over Miracle in the Second Century* (Cambridge, MA: Philadelphia Patristic Foundation, 1983).

3:20–30 illustrates how some of the Jewish leaders attributed Jesus' power to cast out demons to an alliance with the prince of the demons, Beelzebul. And in the first centuries of church history, the predominant non-Christian explanation of Jesus' unusual powers accused him of some kind of sorcery.[1]

Modern scholarship is usually not quite this blunt. John Hull, for example, sees Jesus as employing magical techniques, in which 'superhuman, supernatural entities are linked by invisible bonds of sympathy to visible and material things'. This linkage enables the skilful magician 'to swing the enormous forces of the universe in the desired direction'.[2] Hull goes on to link this use of intermediate means most closely with exorcism: 'There does not seem to be a single reference in pre-Christian or first century literature to the expulsion of demons troubling the mind or causing disease which is not associated with magic . . . This then was the sort of figure the demon-mastering Christ would appear to be.'[3] Morton Smith goes even further and, like the ancient pagans who interpreted 'eating flesh' and 'drinking blood' as meaning that Christians practised cannibalism, links the Lord's Supper with some occultic ritual whose true meaning has been largely suppressed. Smith also believes in the authenticity of a recently discovered eighteenth-century manuscript purporting to be the work of the first-century Christian, Clement, which hints at secret, nightly, and possibly homosexual relationships between Jesus and Mark.[4] Finally, Otto Böcher, who, like Hull, links exorcism with magic, proceeds to interpret virtually all the biblical miracles as exorcisms. Thus he notes how the gospels use the same word 'rebuke' for describing Jesus casting out a demon (Mk. 1:25), healing a fever (Lk. 4:39) and stilling a storm (Mk. 4:39). Böcher believes that Jesus' contemporaries attributed virtually all sickness and natural calamity to demonic influence.[5]

---

[1]The Jews gave this as a rationale for his execution (see the Babylonian Talmud tractate, Sanhedrin 43a), while a second-century theologian, Origen, had to defend Christianity against a similar charge by the pagan philosopher, Celsus (*Contra Celsum* 1:38).

[2]John M. Hull, *Hellenistic Magic and the Synoptic Tradition* (London: SCM; Naperville: Allenson, 1974), pp.37–38.

[3]Ibid., pp.63–64.

[4]Morton Smith, *The Secret Gospel* (New York: Harper & Row, 1973; Wellingborough: Aquarian, 1985); also his *Jesus the Magician* (New York: Harper & Row; London: Victor Gollancz, 1978).

[5]Otto Böcher, *Das Neue Testament und die dämonischen Mächte* (Stuttgart: Katholisches Bibelwerk, 1972).

Few scholars have fully endorsed the extreme positions of Smith and Böcher. Smith himself, in order to defend his hypothesis has to argue that the present form of the gospels represents an attempt to 'cover up' the truth about Jesus, and yet he believes that fragments of a book he discovered, which he calls the Secret Gospel of Mark and which has far less evidence in support of its reliability, have better preserved the truth![1] Edwin Yamauchi convincingly refutes Böcher's equation of all diseases with the demonic by showing that throughout the ancient Middle East illnesses were attributed to many different causes and were often dealt with in surprisingly advanced, 'scientific' ways.[2] In the gospels the clearest example that would seem to support Böcher is the story of the epileptic (Mt. 17:15)[3] who is viewed as demon-possessed and is therefore exorcised. Yet this is the only place in the gospels where references to disease and demon possession appear in the same passage, so it is more probable that in this solitary instance the possession was causing the sickness. This of course raises the larger question of how one should interpret the exorcism stories and their apparent link with magic which Hull pointed out.

For most Westerners today, with the exception of some charismatic Christians, the danger is not that they see all sickness as demonic but that they see none of it that way. For them, the scientific, philosophical, and historical objections to belief in miracles, treated earlier in this chapter, apply equally strongly to belief in Satan and his demons. But in addition to the responses to those objections given above, it is important to add here that contemporary experience is making it more and more difficult to deny the reality of demon possession in Western society today. Anyone who has not studied a serious, factual account of the frightening resurgence of the practice and results of occult and Satanic rituals in many corners of today's otherwise highly rationalistic and technologized culture should do so before trying

---

[1]Reviews of Smith have been sharply critical even by many who are also sceptical of the gospel miracle stories. See esp. Howard C. Kee, *Miracle in the Early Christian World* (New Haven and London: Yale, 1983), pp.211–212, n. 69.

[2]Edwin M. Yamauchi, 'Magic or Miracle? Diseases, Demons and Exorcisms', in *GP*,6, pp.89–183.

[3]*Contra* AV and Phillips translation, which call him a 'lunatic'. The symptoms described closely parallel those of a grand mal seizure: premonition, unconsciousness, muscular rigidity, jerking, limpness and recovery. *Cf.* ibid., pp.129–130.

to dismiss demons as the outmoded invention of primitive people.[1]

Some of the parallels between Jesus' exorcisms and healings and those of others in his day are admittedly noteworthy (*e.g.* Philostratus, *Life of Apollonius* 4:20; b. Pesaḥim 112b; Josephus, *Antiquities* 8:46–49). Features found elsewhere in ancient accounts of exorcism which are also apparent in the gospels include: (a) the attempt to discover the demon's name in order to gain mastery over him (Mk. 5:9), (b) the use of touch or the laying on of hands (Mt. 9:29; Mk. 6:5; Lk. 4:40), and (c) the application of spittle (Mk. 7:33; 8:23; Jn. 9:6). On the other hand the differences far outweigh the similarities. Point (a) occurs only once in the four main exorcisms that Mark recounts, while (b) and (c) *never* occur in exorcisms but only in healings and were often practised as legitimate, therapeutic treatment.[2] When Jesus does touch people as part of the healing process, or more dramatically when they reach out to him as if a mere touch of his clothing could cure them (*e.g.* Mk. 5:28–30), he makes it clear that it is the people's faith and not any magical methods which saves them (*cf.* Mk. 5:34). Furthermore, certain common exorcistic practices never occur in the gospel accounts of either sick or demon-possessed people. Jesus uses none of the elaborate spells or incantations, often involving the careful repetition of nonsense syllables, so prevalent in his day. He does not alter the tone of his voice, he does not appeal to any authority outside himself (even Christian exorcism differed in this respect in that it specifically invoked the name of Jesus), and he does not even pray to God before commanding the demons to come out. Finally, no magical objects appear, in sharp contrast to the array of paraphernalia listed by Graham Twelftree for Jewish and Greek 'parallels': incense, rings, a bowl of water, amulets, palm tree prickles, wood chips, ashes, pitch, cummin, dog's hair, thread, trumpets, olive branches, and marjoram![3] And not only are the New Testament exorcisms different from other accounts of Jesus' contemporaries, they also vary among themselves in subtle ways which suggest that they are not wholesale inventions

---

[1]One of the best works of this nature, written by an Anglican priest who began his study as a sceptic, is John Richards, *But Deliver Us From Evil* (London: Darton, Longman & Todd; New York: Seabury, 1974). *Cf.* Dom Robert Petitpierre, *Exorcising Devils* (London: Robert Hale, 1976); and for a symposium of American evangelical thought, *Demon Possession*, ed. John W. Montgomery (Minneapolis: Bethany, 1976).

[2]Yamauchi, 'Magic or Miracle?' pp.135–140.

[3]Graham H. Twelftree, 'ΕΙΔΕ. . .ΕΓΩ ΕΚΒΑΛΛΩ ΤΑ ΔΑΙΜΟΝΙΑ. . .' in *GP*,6, p.383.

of later Christians.[1] Jesus was most certainly an exorcist, but not, in any meaningful sense of the term, a magician.[2]

4 Charismatic Judaism

As a resurgence of interest in Jesus' Jewish roots sweeps over New Testament studies as a whole, it is only natural that the search for parallels to Jesus' miracle-working activity should shift from the pagan to the Jewish world. Of course, the apocryphal gospels, stories of divine men, and accounts of magic and exorcism had Jewish counterparts, and not a few scholars apply more than one of the three categories to Jesus' miracles. But most of the 'parallels' examined so far appeared in circles dominated by Greek thought, more prevalent outside the land of Israel than inside. Today there is a growing recognition that valid parallels to Jesus' life and ministry, if they are to be found at all, will more likely come from a Palestinian environment, so that the lives of key first-century Judaean and Galilean leaders are being examined with greater care.

The Jewish scholar, Geza Vermes, perhaps more than anyone else, has propounded the view that Jesus can be likened to what he calls 'charismatic' Jewish teachers of the first century. These were figures who, like Jesus, wandered about gathering followers, relatively independent of the more established sects of the Pharisees, Sadducees, Essenes and Zealots. Two who are especially linked with miracle-working are Honi the Rain-Maker and Rabbi Hanina ben-Dosa. The former was said to have been able to pray for rain and receive it after the fashion of Elijah in the Old Testament.[3] The latter has a whole series of miracles attributed to him: surviving a poisonous snake-bite unharmed, healing the sick from a distance simply by the fluency of his prayer to God, having bread appear in his wife's oven when they had run out, enabling a lamp

---

[1]See *e.g.* Bruce Chilton's study, 'Exorcism and History: Mark 1:21–28', in *GP*,6, pp.253–271. *Cf.* J. Ramsey Michaels, 'Jesus and the Unclean Spirits', in *Demon Possession*, pp.41–57.

[2]Some definitions of magic are so broad as to make Jesus a magician, but they risk rendering him indistinguishable from, say, an eccentric business executive! Thus David Aune, 'Magic in Early Christianity', in *Aufstieg und Niedergang der römischen Welt,* ed. H. Temporini and W. Haase, II, 23.2 (Berlin and New York: de Gruyter, 1980), p.1539, defines magical wonders as those which 'occur within a context of social deviance in which widely accepted but generally unattainable goals highly valued . . . are thought to be accomplished for particular individuals through the application of generally successful management techniques'.

[3]For complete details, see William S. Green, 'Palestinian Holy Men: Charismatic Leadership and Rabbinic Tradition', in *Aufstieg*, II, 19.2 (1979), pp.619–647.

to burn on vinegar rather than oil when his daughter accidentally poured in the wrong liquid, and miraculously extending the beams on a neighbour's house when they turned out to be too short to support it adequately![1]

On the one hand, it is refreshing to see scholars, especially Jewish ones, appreciating once again the distinctively Jewish milieu out of which Jesus emerged. The more correspondences that occur between the gospel portrait of Jesus and the known facts of first-century Palestinian Judaism, the more convincingly it can be argued that the gospels are accurate. On the other hand, it is doubtful, at least in the case of the miracles, that the parallels are any closer here than with the previous cases examined. A. E. Harvey's analysis, from his 1980 Bampton Lectures in Oxford, is so incisive and carefully worded that it deserves extended citation:

> The most common miracle attributed to holy men of his [Jesus'] time and culture was that of procuring rainfall – an important and welcome feat in a country absolutely dependent on seasonal rain. But this is something never credited to Jesus. Again Jewish miracle-workers certainly succeeded in curing diseases, but there is a notable absence of reports of the curing of any kind of lameness or paralysis . . . Above all, Jesus is credited with three instances of a very notable miracle indeed: that of raising a dead person to life. The frequently alleged parallels to this are highly questionable. The Jewish tradition knows of no actual instances of such a feat: it merely suggests that a rabbi of exceptional holiness might in theory be capable of it . . . Stories of miraculous deeds are mainly confined to a small group of men whom it has been customary to call 'charismatics' and whom the rabbinic sources themselves call, significantly, 'men of deed'. These men – Honi the Rain-maker and Hanina ben Dosa are the only two of whom we have any detailed knowledge – have a very clear frame of reference for their miraculous feats. They were men of prayer, and the degree of intimacy which they gained with their heavenly father afforded them an almost physical guarantee that their prayers would be answered . . . There is a notable humorousness – almost a flippancy – about the way they were narrated

---

[1] Geza Vermes, *Jesus the Jew* (London: Collins; Philadelphia: Fortress, 1973), pp.69–78; also his *Jesus and the World of Judaism* (London: SCM, 1983; Philadelphia: Fortress, 1984), pp.7–9. *Cf.* also the Babylonian Talmud, tractate Ta'anith 24b–25a.

which suggests that these 'deeds' were by no means regarded as the most significant thing about them.[1]

This picture differs markedly from that of the gospels, which usually depict Jesus relying entirely on his own authority, without praying to God before working a miracle. The audible prayer before the raising of Lazarus includes the explanation that it is only for the benefit of the crowd (Jn. 11:42). The gospels also place the miracles in the centre and not at the periphery of his ministry, and they describe his wonderful deeds as signs of the kingdom of God which was arriving. It seems fair to accept Harvey's conclusions about the apparent parallels between Jesus' miracles and those of his contemporaries: 'The style of the "Charismatic" is not the one chosen by Jesus . . . We have come to the remarkable conclusion that the miraculous activity of Jesus conforms to no known pattern.'[2] The fact that these observations come from a scholar who is still sceptical of the accuracy of at least certain parts of the gospels makes those observations all the more impressive.

B The question of reliability

1 *General considerations*

The uniqueness of Jesus' miracles is itself an argument for their authenticity, by the criterion of dissimilarity (see p.247). This uniqueness extends in the majority of cases to the simplicity and directness of Jesus' style, the immediacy with which his power takes effect, and the restrained nature of the narratives which understate the sensational. All these features fit well with the motives attributed to Jesus' miracle-working activity. Jesus is concerned both to reward and to stimulate faith, but more often than not he is also moved by sheer compassion for people's needs.

Even more significant, though, is the relationship between his miracles and his teachings. When Jesus came to the synagogue in his hometown, Nazareth, at the start of his Galilean ministry, he astounded his friends and family by his exposition of Isaiah 61:1 – 'The Spirit of the Lord is upon me, because he has anointed me to preach good news to the poor. He has sent me to proclaim

---

[1]A. E. Harvey, *Jesus and the Constraints of History* (London: Duckworth; Philadelphia: Westminster, 1982), pp.100, 104.

[2]Ibid., pp.107, 113.

release for the captives and recovery of sight for the blind'. What stunned the congregation was Jesus' declaration: 'Today this Scripture has been fulfilled in your hearing' (Lk. 4:18, 21).[1] In the light of this claim that Jesus himself was fulfilling Isaiah's prophecy, it is easy to lose sight of a secondary but very important feature of the quotation – Jesus' preaching and healing are bound up inseparably with each other. The same combination recurs when the imprisoned John the Baptist sends disciples to Jesus to see if he really is the promised Messiah. Jesus replies, 'Go announce to John what you hear and see: the blind see again and the lame walk, lepers are cleansed and the deaf hear, and the dead are raised up, and the poor receive good news' (Mt. 11:4b–5). Jesus' marvellous deeds are thus more than acts of mercy, and more than pointers to his divine origin, for as already noted, his enemies could allege that the supernatural source of his power was the devil rather than God. Instead they are primarily signs and indications of the fact that the Messianic age for which the Jews had so long been waiting, the time of the new covenant and the era of the kingdom of God inaugurated on earth, had now arrived in the person and ministry of Jesus. Signs and indications, however, do not add up to proof. Just as Jesus' teaching could remain obscure to those who were not given the secrets of the kingdom, so also even his own disciples could witness the feedings of 5,000 and 4,000 and still complain shortly afterwards that they had no bread. Jesus responds (Mk. 8:17–18) by quoting the same prophecy (Is. 6:9) that he did when they failed to grasp his parables (Mk. 4:11–12).

In all these ways, then, the accounts of Jesus' miracles differ from the other miracle stories of the ancient world. Moreover, if one accepts Jesus' teaching about his ushering in the kingdom of God, then one ought to accept the reality of his miracles. The two go hand in hand, since Jesus uses the miracles to authenticate his teaching. And it is fair to say that modern scholarship, even of the most sceptical variety, has agreed that if anything in the gospels is reliable it is the teaching of Jesus about the kingdom of God.[2] It is

---

[1] On the authenticity of these verses, see Bruce Chilton, 'Announcement in *Nazara:* An Analysis of Luke 4:16–21', in *GP*,2, pp.147–172. For the most detailed study of their significance, see R. B. Sloan, *The Favorable Year of the Lord* (Austin: Schola, 1977).

[2] The literature on this topic is vast; the most comprehensive recent study is G. R. Beasley-Murray, *Jesus and the Kingdom of God* (Exeter: Paternoster; Grand Rapids: Eerdmans, 1986). *Cf.* also George E. Ladd, *The Presence of the Future* (Grand Rapids: Eerdmans, 1974; London:

also important to recall that in the gospels no section of any size is free from the miraculous. It is impossible, despite the optimism of nineteenth-century liberalism, to strip away layers of tradition and lay bare an account of a Jesus who never worked miracles. Not only are the miracles found in all four gospels and all four 'sources' (Mark, Q, M and L), but they are also referred to in other sections of the New Testament (*cf. e.g.* Acts 10:38; 1 Cor. 15:4–8; Heb. 2:4; 2 Pet. 1:17–18), the testimony of the first-century Jewish historian Josephus, and the compilation of Jewish oral traditions known as the Talmud.[1]

Evidence for the general reliability of the gospel portrait of Jesus as a miracle-worker does not, however, prove the authenticity of every individual miracle. The form of the miracle stories varies, so further analysis requires differentiation of various categories of miracles. The healings and exorcisms need little additional treatment; the latter have already been discussed, and the former are now seldom questioned even by fairly sceptical scholars. Too many medical miracles continue today among religious people who believe that God rewards their faith for even the most die-hard secularist to dismiss all of them as fraudulent, though contrary to some Christians' expectations God does not work miracles 'on demand' as an automatic reward for faith (*cf.* 2 Cor. 12:7–10). But if gospel criticism less frequently challenges the authenticity of the healing and exorcism narratives, it still debates their interpretation. Some will attribute unexplained healings to the power of suggestion, which science and medicine may one day better understand and control. Similarly, demon possession is often redefined along the line of 'any altered state of consciousness indigenously interpreted in terms of the influence of an alien spirit',[2] without necessarily accepting that people who think

SPCK, 1980); and Bruce Chilton, *God in Strength: Jesus' Announcement of the Kingdom* (Freistadt: F. Plöchl, 1979).

[1]On Josephus, see *Antiquities* 18:3.3 (and *cf.* pp.200–201). Parts of this famous passage about Jesus have often been suspected as coming from later Christian scribes but the reference to his alleged ability to work miracles is usually not one of them. Graham Twelftree, 'Jesus in Jewish Traditions', in *GP*,5, p.304, finds this portion authentic but cautions against a simple equation of Josephus' term 'surprising feats' or 'paradoxes' with 'miracles'. On the Talmud see above, p.87, n.1. Other possible, but by no means certain, references to Jesus' miracles in ancient and mediaeval Jewish history are discussed in H. van der Loos, *The Miracles of Jesus* (Leiden: Brill, 1965), pp.160–170. Van der Loos's study is the most comprehensive treatment of the gospel miracles in recent years and is generally favourable to their authenticity.

[2]Vincent Crapanzano, 'Introduction', in *Case Studies in Spirit Possession,* ed. Vincent Crapanzano and Vivian Garrison (New York and Chichester: Wiley, 1977), p.7.

they are demon-possessed really are. But whatever the explanation, the facts remain. People are cured of sickness and freed by exorcism of what they believe is spirit possession, apart from any demonstrable, natural causes. To assume that Jesus, or any other religious leader past or present, had similar power does not defy reason in the least. The presence of such power does not by itself determine the nature of its source; Christians have consistently affirmed the existence of both the divine and the demonic. One must examine the purpose of the 'miracles' in question and the types of religious claims made by the people involved.[1]

2 Nature miracles

The growing willingness of many scholars to accept at least some of Jesus' miracles seldom extends to the stories in which he demonstrates his power over forces in the natural world.[2] Here there seem to be no modern counterparts to which one can appeal. Yet there is also a growing recognition that, when secondary emphases of the gospel writers are laid to one side, the main point of these miracles in every instance involves the powerful arrival of the kingdom of God.[3] The miracles are dramatic demonstrations of God's reign, with imagery often very similar to that found in the parables. By the same principle that applies to the stories of Jesus' healings, one ought logically to accept that any accounts which fit in so well with the undeniably authentic portion of his teaching stand a good chance of being reliable history themselves. A few illustrations may clarify.

At first glance, the story of Jesus' cursing the fig tree (Mk. 11:12–14, 20–25) seems more worthy of the apocrypha than of Scripture, especially when Mark specifically states that it was not the season for figs (verse 14). When one realizes, however, that Jesus' action derives from his belief that the kingdom of God was in the process of arriving, then the passage makes more sense. The fig tree was a well-known symbol for Israel in the Old Testament

---

[1]Everett Ferguson, *Demonology of the Early Christian World* (Toronto: Edwin Mellen, 1984), p.114. Many modern religions and sects offer initiates 'scientific' methods for developing the power of mind over matter for positive ends. The potentially destructive long-term physical effects, like their more overtly religious claims, are kept well-hidden.

[2]For conclusive documentation of this fact, see Gerhard Maier's survey, 'Zur neutestamentlichen Wunderexegese im 19. und 20. Jahrhundert', in *GP*,6, pp.49–87.

[3]For more detail on this and the rest of this section, see Craig L. Blomberg, 'The Miracles as Parables', in *GP*,6, pp.327–359.

(*cf. e.g.* Je. 24:1–10; Mi. 7:1–6; Ho. 9:10), and Jesus had already told a parable about a fig tree in danger of being cut down, clearly symbolizing the peril in which the Jewish nation placed herself by rejecting her Messiah. Jesus, like many of the Old Testament prophets before him, was dramatizing his message with an object lesson or 'enacted parable'. Just as he withered a fig tree which bore no fruit, so also God would take away the privileges of Israel if she did not repent and turn to her appointed Saviour.

A similar symbolic explanation makes sense of the water turned into wine. In a story otherwise bereft of explanatory detail, John's reference to the six stone jars 'for the purification rites of the Jews' (Jn. 2:6) stands out. When one recalls the parable of Jesus which compares his teaching and ministry to new wine and wineskins (Mk. 2:22), this reference no longer seems as puzzling. The water represents the old ways of Judaism; the wine, the new covenant relationship established by Christ, a relationship he would make explicit in the Last Supper when he identified the cup of wine with his blood soon to be shed.

It is not clear what amount of the symbolism in these two incidents was obvious to those who first witnessed the miracles, but awareness of it clearly predated the evangelists' redaction, since their emphases lie elsewhere: faith in the context of prayer and forgiveness more generally (Mk. 11:24–25); and Jesus' glory, the disciples' belief, and Mary's relationship with her son (Jn. 2:4–5, 11). As with the parables, some of what Jesus originally intended by his miracles may have remained obscure to his disciples until after they reflected on them further (*cf.* Mk. 4:11–12 with 8:17–18).

Similar symbolism can be found, to one extent or another, in the stilling of the storm, the feedings of the multitudes, the walking on the water, and the miraculous catches of fish. Jesus provides food in abundance and masters the wind and the waves since God's kingdom was to bring an overflowing harvest and complete protection from danger. This symbolism has led some scholars to suppose that the nature miracles were invented by someone in the early church on the basis of the parallels with the parables, or with similar stories in Old Testament or extra-biblical sources. But a detailed examination of each alleged parallel renders this assumption unfounded. The closest parallels are with some of the Old Testament miracles associated with Elijah and Elisha (1 Ki. 17–2 Ki. 8).

And unless it is doubted that those miracles occurred, such parallelism can only enhance the case for the truth of the gospel stories. Unfortunately, current Old Testament critics tend to be even more sceptical about the supernatural than their New Testament counterparts. The critical problem with the miracles of Elijah and Elisha has traditionally centred around their apparently arbitrary and frivolous nature; the classic example is Elisha making a sunken axe-head float on the river! Leah Bronner, though, has shown that all these miracles could have originated in conscious opposition to similar claims by the worshippers of the Canaanite god Baal. Thus in the case of the floating axe-head, Elisha is demonstrating his power over the river, as he does elsewhere in parting the waters of the Jordan, and showing that it is Yahweh and not Baal who rules the waves.[1]

A similar problem occurs in connection with one apparent miracle so far unmentioned. In Matthew 17:27, after explaining to Peter that the sons of the king are exempt from paying tax, Jesus concludes, 'But so as not to offend them, go to the sea and cast a hook, and take the first fish that comes up, and after you open its mouth you will find a shekel; take that and give it to them on behalf of me and you.' This apparent miracle differs from the others in the gospels in several ways. It is the only one Jesus works, at least in part, to benefit himself. It is the only one in which he is not relieving some acute, human need. The next closest example would be the miracle at Cana, but running out of wine at a wedding was at least an acute social embarrassment. Richard Bauckham diminishes the force of these observations by arguing that the miracle is designed to teach the lesson 'that God does not exact taxation from his people', but provides for them, 'as a father provides for his children'.[2] Bauckham also speculates that Jesus and his followers at this particular time might have been almost penniless. Moreover, as F. F. Bruce stresses, the fish known as the *musht* was apparently attracted to foreign objects in the Sea of Galilee, so that the miracle would not have consisted of Peter's finding the coin in the fish's mouth

---

[1]Leah Bronner, *The Stories of Elijah and Elisha* (Leiden: Brill, 1968). Bronner does not believe all the stories to be authentic, for other reasons, but her work has dealt with the most serious problem involved.

[2]Richard Bauckham, 'The Coin in the Fish's Mouth', *GP*,6, p.224.

but in Jesus' knowing in advance that it would be there.[1]

Another distinctive of Matthew 17:27, however, might prove even more important in helping to understand what Jesus meant. Unlike all the other miracles in the gospels, this one is never *narrated*. In other words, Matthew never says that Jesus actually did anything unusual; all he describes is a somewhat cryptic command. He may mean to imply that Peter went and did as he was told and found the coin in the fish's mouth, but he never actually says this. In view of Peter's consistent tendency to misunderstand Jesus, one should be cautious about assuming too much. In verses 25–26, Jesus has just been speaking to Peter in a metaphor about a king and his sons, so it would be quite natural if Jesus did not intend verse 27 to be taken literally either. Perhaps he is using a dramatic figure of speech to make the point that Bauckham says he is making, without actually expecting Peter to act upon it. Something very similar happens in Luke 22:35–38: Jesus asks the disciples a 'yes-no' question (*cf*. Mt. 17:25), follows it up with a command (regarding preparation for battle), and they misunderstand by interpreting it literally.[2] Peter persists in this misunderstanding when he cuts off Malchus' ear in the Garden of Gethsemane (Jn. 18:10). But whether it be literal or figurative, Bauckham's work has at least shown that it need not be seen as out of step with what Jesus teaches elsewhere.

3 Reanimations[3]

Just as some would equate apparently miraculous healings with the power of mind over matter and apparent demon-possession with psychological malaise, so one might suggest a natural explanation for the reanimation narratives in the gospels. For example, one could cite numerous incidents in modern hospitals in which people have been resuscitated a considerable time after their vital signs

---

[1]F. F. Bruce, *The New Testament Documents: Are They Reliable?* (London and Downers Grove: IVP, 1960), p.73.

[2]Assuming the correctness of the view that takes Jesus' concluding 'It is enough' as an outburst of exasperation. For more on the possibly metaphorical nature of Mt. 17:27, see Craig L. Blomberg, 'New Testament Miracles and Higher Criticism: Climbing Up the Slippery Slope', *JETS* 27 (1984), pp.425–438. *Cf.*, more briefly, R. T. France, *The Gospel according to Matthew* (Leicester: IVP; Grand Rapids: Eerdmans, 1985), pp.268–269.

[3]The term 'resurrection' will be reserved for an awakening to a life that does *not* involve subsequent death. 'Reanimation' will be used interchangeably with 'resuscitation' and 'revivification' for the revival of a corpse when there is no reason to assume the person did not die again later.

ceased. Such 'parallels' might just explain a gospel reanimation account like that of Jairus' daughter (Mk. 5:21–24, 35–43), who had died only moments before Jesus' arrival, but they afford no help in making credible the story of Lazarus' revivification after four days in the grave (Jn. 11:17). Not surprisingly, most scholars seek instead to explain these stories as some kind of fiction.

More helpful is the study by Murray Harris, who points out a number of often overlooked details which would not have likely appeared in a fictitious narrative. In the case of the reanimation of the widow of Nain's son (Lk. 7:11–17), it is interesting that Jesus speaks to the mother before approaching the bier. This corresponds exactly to the custom in Galilee (the province in which Nain is located), at least as attested in the Talmud (b. Shabbat 153a).[1] There the women in Galilean funeral processions are said to have walked in front of the casket, while in the better known province of Judaea, they walked behind it. It would have been quite easy for the foreigner, Luke, to have erred on this detail unless he was relying on accurate historical sources. Similarly, a writer inventing this story might well have depicted joy rather than awe as the initial reaction to the miracle, would probably have chosen a more significant city than Nain for its occurrence, and could easily have given more details about what happened to the young man after his life was restored. Harris concludes, 'As an account of the instantaneous reanimation of a corpse, the pericope is remarkably restrained and unadorned; sensational detail is conspicuously absent. Such extraordinary sobriety of diction points to its authenticity.'[2] The same kind of detail coupled with restraint characterizes even as spectacular a story as the raising of Lazarus; there are really no separate objections to the historicity of this passage apart from those characteristic of all parts of John's gospel (ch. five). Rudolf Schnackenburg, for example, whose three-volume commentary on John is one of the most comprehensive and sanest critical works on the Fourth Gospel, admits that John's account must be based on a historical core of material about 'an extraordinary event in Bethany'.[3]

---

[1]A distinction between Galilean and Judaean custom of this nature has a *prima facie* probability of dating back to the first century, since from early in the second century and onwards the Jews were largely dispersed from Palestine.

[2]Harris, 'Revivification', p.299.

[3]Rudolf Schnackenburg, *The Gospel according to St. John,* vol. 2 (London: Burns & Oates; New York: Seabury, 1980), p.345.

Ultimately, though, one's view of the trustworthiness of the reanimation narratives will almost always hinge on one's view of the accounts of the resurrection of Jesus himself. If his resurrection is believable, then the reanimations pose no problem. If his resurrection is not believable, then there is probably not enough positive evidence to support the authenticity of the reanimation stories on their own. This leads to a discussion of the last major topic of this chapter, the resurrection of Jesus.

C The resurrection

As might be expected, the amount of scholarly discussion of the resurrection of Jesus far surpasses the quantity devoted to any other miracle in the Bible. George Ladd provided one of the clearest discussions of its historicity and significance in his book of a decade ago, *I Believe in the Resurrection of Jesus*.[1] In the present study attention will focus primarily on more recent developments in the debate within the academic world, while also summarizing some of the age-old arguments for the resurrection's credibility which still seem valid.

1 The testimony of the gospels

Today very few scholars opt for the alternatives to belief in the resurrection that have been most commonly offered down through the ages, and which still surface from time to time in popular literature. These include the swoon theory, according to which Jesus did not quite die on the cross, but revived in the tomb, managed to escape, and appeared to his disciples before expiring shortly thereafter;[2] the original counter-claim of the Jewish authorities that Jesus' disciples stole the body (Mt. 28:13); the notion that Jesus' followers went to the wrong tomb and thus found it empty; and the idea that all the witnesses of the resurrection experienced some kind of mass hallucination. Such 'explanations' require more faith for one to believe in them than does the supernatural explanation that Jesus did in fact rise bodily from the

---

[1](London: Hodder & Stoughton; Grand Rapids: Eerdmans, 1975).
[2]A notable exception is J. D. M. Derrett, *The Anastasis of Jesus: The Resurrection of Jesus as an Historical Event* (Shipston-on-Stour: P. Drinkwater, 1982). Derrett's hypothesis succeeds, however, only by accepting the extreme higher-critical scepticism regarding many of the details of the gospel accounts when it supports his theory and yet rejecting the same critics' conclusions when they contradict his theory.

grave.[1]

Instead, the most common approach today to the gospel accounts of Christ's resurrection is to treat them as at least partially legendary. The three main reasons for this assessment have been: (1) The accounts resemble the myths in other ancient religions about gods who died and rose again – often on an annual basis in conjunction with the coming of winter and spring, respectively, but also in the Gnostic writings where a heavenly redeemer comes to earth to save humanity. (2) If Mark was the earliest of the gospels to be written then it is striking that he has by far the shortest account of all four (Mk. 16:1–8). Verses 9–20 as printed in some English translations do not appear in the oldest manuscripts now available, thus leaving in the original text no mention of Jesus' appearing to anyone. Matthew, Luke and John can then be seen as imaginative expansions of what was originally a very brief and enigmatic narrative about some women's Easter morning confusion. (3) Even if one wants to take everything in the gospels at face value, the different writers simply contradict each other too often to be believable. Mark speaks of a young man who greeted the women at the tomb, Luke of two men, Matthew of an angel, and John of two angels. Mark's and Matthew's Jesus appears only in Galilee; Luke's, only in Jerusalem. No two gospels' lists of the women who went to the tomb are the same, nor do they agree on whether it was still dark or already after dawn. Other less glaring differences also appear.

All three of these reasons for scholarly scepticism have often been addressed by defenders of the resurrection's historicity. In the case of the alleged mythical parallels, on the one hand the evidence suggests that the Gnostic redeemer myth does not predate the writing of the gospels and that other alleged parallels are not that close or numerous.[2] On the other hand, the entire New Testament sets itself against any view which equates God and nature or sees the need for annual or repeated atonement (see esp. Heb. 9:26).[3] Pheme Perkins, who by no means supports the auth-

---

[1]See *e.g.* Ladd's summary of a refutation of each in *Resurrection*, pp.132–142.

[2]E. M. Yamauchi, *Pre-Christian Gnosticism* (London: Tyndale, 1973; Grand Rapids: Baker, 1983). Veselin Kesich, *The First Day of the New Creation* (Crestwood, NY: St. Vladimir's Seminary Press, 1982), pp.38–47, highlights the distinctives of Jesus' resurrection over against those of the so-called mystery religions.

[3]C. S. Lewis's simplified discussion in *Miracles* (London: Geoffrey Bles; New York: Macmillan, 1947), pp.136–140, remains quite helpful on this point.

enticity of all the gospel data, nevertheless stresses that 'given the marginal status of resurrection and immortality in Judaism as well as paganism . . . it may well be that Christianity has created a hope and expectation rather than responded to a widely held pattern of belief or practice'.[1] As for Mark's very abbreviated version of the climax of the gospel, redaction critics have repeatedly argued that Mark's emphasis on the fear of God and the misunderstanding of the disciples probably explains his decision to end the story where he does, rather than any lack of knowledge about the later details of the resurrection. Finally, it is remarkable to observe how often the alleged contradictions among the gospels are cited without a discussion of the many proposed solutions which can fit them together in a very plausible and natural manner. John Wenham has quite recently devoted an entire book to a harmonization of the accounts and few of his proposals are entirely new.[2] There is scarcely room to summarize all his main points, but in the case of the sample 'contradictions' mentioned above, one can offer the following brief replies: (a) angels generally appear in Scripture as men, and if one of the two were the primary spokesman, it would not be surprising if sometimes only he were mentioned; (b) it is likely that Jesus appeared to the eleven in Jerusalem, then later in Galilee when they had gone home after the Passover, and then once again in Jerusalem upon their return in preparation for the feast of Pentecost;[3] (c) if Salome is both the 'mother of James and John' and the sister of Mary, Jesus' mother, there is no irreconcilable problem with the lists of women; and (d) it is not unfair to describe the world as still rather dark at the first glimpse of morning daylight. The apparent discord among the gospels can be alleviated, but it must be admitted that any reconstruction of the events is speculative. At the same time, the very presence of limited divergence in otherwise parallel narratives can itself testify to their reliability. Hans Stier, a German classical historian, seems more judicious than many of his biblical colleagues, even if one

---

[1]Pheme Perkins, *Resurrection* (Garden City: Doubleday, 1984; London: Geoffrey Chapman, 1985), pp.62–63.

[2]John Wenham, *Easter Enigma: Do the Resurrection Stories Contradict One Another?* (Exeter: Paternoster; Grand Rapids: Zondervan, 1984); *cf.* more briefly, Ladd, *Resurrection*, pp.91–93; Murray J. Harris, *Raised Immortal: Resurrection and Immortality in the New Testament* (London: Marshall, Morgan & Scott, 1983; Grand Rapids: Eerdmans, 1985), pp.69–71.

[3]C. F. D. Moule, 'The Post-Resurrection Appearances in the Light of Festival Pilgrimages', *NTS* 4 (1957–58), pp.58–61.

might prefer to modify his two references to 'contradictions' with the word 'apparent'.

> the sources for the resurrection of Jesus, with their relatively big contradictions over details, present for the historian for this very reason a criterion of extraordinary credibility. For if that were the fabrication of a congregation or of a similar group of people, then the tale would be consistently and obviously complete. For that reason every historian is especially sceptical at that moment when an extraordinary happening is only reported in accounts which are completely free of contradictions.[1]

In short, it simply will not do to ascribe the majority of the resurrection narratives to the pious imagination of the early church. In fact, a growing number of scholars today recognize this, and current debate has largely shifted to the question of what the early church *meant* by its accounts of the resurrection. Even if one argues that the stories are largely reliable in what they recount, the question remains of how they should be understood. How literal an interpretation is appropriate? Must the imagery imply a bodily resurrection or does it merely depict dramatically what took place on an invisible, spiritual plane?

Today the most common views of the resurrection which attempt to answer these questions can be grouped together into four categories. (1) Some follow in the footsteps of the first 'demythologizers' (those form critics who sought to identify and reinterpret 'mythical' elements in Scripture) and reduce the resurrection stories to nothing more than graphic presentations of the conviction in the hearts of Jesus' followers that his cause did not die with him on the cross. Willi Marxsen, for example, one of Bultmann's most famous students, views the resurrection as the way to describe how 'someone discovers in a miraculous way that Jesus evokes faith even after his death'.[2] But if this were so, it would be hard to see why the disciples came to refer to this event

---

[1]Hans E. Stier, in *Moderne Exegese und historische Wissenschaft*, p.152, cited by Hugo Staudinger, *The Trustworthiness of the Gospels* (Edinburgh: Handsel, 1981), p.77. Grant R. Osborne, *The Resurrection Narratives: A Redactional Study* (Grand Rapids: Baker, 1984), illustrates how the theological diversity of the gospel parallels can be fully appreciated even when one believes that all the historical data can be harmonized.

[2]Willi Marxsen, *The Resurrection of Jesus of Nazareth* (London: SCM; Philadelphia: Fortress, 1970), p.138.

as a resurrection at all; they could simply have referred to Jesus being exalted or glorified, as the rest of the New Testament does, without using language which more naturally implies an empty tomb and a living body.[1]

(2) A slightly less sceptical approach suggests that the disciples must have had some extraordinary experience but views it as entirely subjective – not an event which an impartial observer could have experienced as well. One recent proponent of this position, Rudolf Pesch, takes a surprisingly positive stance on the reliability of the gospels concerning how Jesus prepared his disciples for his death. After all, Jesus repeatedly predicted his crucifixion and resurrection, so a vision of some kind confirming his followers' hope that he would return to life is exactly that for which they had been psychologically prepared.[2] But although it may be true that the disciples ought to have been expecting Christ's resurrection, the gospels tell us that in fact they were not. Far from it, John describes them crouching behind locked doors, defeated in spirit, and fearful that their lives would be the next in jeopardy (Jn. 20:19), an embarrassing admission not likely invented by the later church. Furthermore, the impact of a crucifixion on a group of devout Jews was not quickly overcome; according to the Old Testament, one who died such a death was cursed by God (Dt. 21:23). The sceptical reaction of all who first heard the women's report and the fact that the appearances were spread out over a period of forty days pose further problems for one who would explain these stories as subjective visions in the minds of those psychologically prepared to receive them.[3]

Neither of these first two approaches requires that Jesus' tomb ever really was found empty, and they emphasize the fact that the gospels never stress the claim that it was. But a rapidly growing number of scholars recognizes that the evidence for Jesus' tomb

---

[1] A point not often noticed but rightly stressed by the excellent Greek Orthodox study of Kesich, *Creation*, p.81.

[2] A detailed discussion and critique of Pesch's hypothesis, which has been developed in stages in several, sometimes inaccessible, German sources, appears in Hans-Willi Winden, *Wie kam und wie kommt es zum Osterglauben?* (Frankfurt: Peter Lang, 1982).

[3] It is refreshing to see these points stressed in the excellent little study of Heinzpeter Hempelmann, *Die Auferstehung Jesu Christi – eine historische Tatsache?* (Wuppertal: Brockhaus, 1982), pp.16–17, since so little evangelical, academic literature has been published in Germany in recent years. Another work of the same nature is Werner Freudenberg, *Ist er wirklich auferstanden?* (Wuppertal: Brockhaus, 1977). In English see esp. Harris, *Raised*, pp.38–40, 57–65.

being empty is virtually irrefutable. Much of this evidence has been concisely summarized by William Craig in a series of studies;[1] only a few of the highlights may be touched on here. To begin with, the gospels never actually describe the resurrection itself, a surprising omission if the story of the empty tomb were being fabricated. The apocryphal Gospel of Peter (paragraphs 9–10, lines 35–42) provides by stark contrast an example of how early Christian fiction reads, as it tells how the guards at the tomb saw two angels, whose heads touched the clouds, descend from heaven, enter the tomb, and emerge supporting a third man whose head rose above the clouds, while the vision of a cross followed them and a voice spoke from heaven! Second, the part of Mark 16 that does describe the discovery that Jesus' body was missing, however brief, would not likely have been a fictitious invention since its main characters are women, in a rather bewildered state no less, whose testimony in the ancient world was considered largely unreliable. Third, the Jewish authorities, who had every reason to want to refute Christianity, could never produce the body of Jesus inside *or* outside a tomb.

In spite of this evidence, there are still at least two options left. (3) On the one hand, many will admit that some kind of objective resurrection occurred – Jesus really did come back to life and leave the tomb – but they will assert that it defied description and would not necessarily have been recordable had, say, videotaping equipment been available. It was in some way linked inseparably with the faith of those who already believed in Jesus. Explanations of this position, however, are seldom entirely clear. Eduard Schweizer, for example, typifies this ambiguity at the end of an otherwise lucid article on 'Resurrection – Fact or Illusion?' Having earlier affirmed that the empty tomb is 'one of the most reliable pieces of information about the historical course of events that we possess', he concludes that the 'resurrection is certainly no illusion'. Yet immediately he adds, 'it is no fact either in the sense of an event which could be proved objectively without our getting involved. It is a living reality which starts at the moment in which God's

---

[1]William L. Craig, 'The Bodily Resurrection of Jesus', in *GP*,1, pp.47–74; also his 'The Empty Tomb of Jesus', in *GP*,2, pp.173–200 (a slightly expanded version of which appears as 'The Historicity of the Empty Tomb of Jesus', *NTS* 31 [1985] pp.39–67); and, 'The Guard at the Tomb', *NTS* 30 (1984), pp.273–281. *Cf.* also his *The Historical Argument for the Resurrection of Jesus* (Toronto: Edwin Mellen, 1986 [not accessible to me]).

life-power enters the life of mortals.'[1] Clearly Schweizer wants to distance himself from those who see the event as all in the disciples' minds but he seems to imply that an unbeliever present would not have seen and heard what the disciples did. In the New Testament, however, Jesus did not just appear to those who already believed in him, and who might have wanted to mistake a vision, however objective and non-self-induced, for something more tangible, as is often argued. Even if one brackets the example of Paul, to whom Jesus appeared only after the ascension, there is still the case of Jesus' brother James, who apparently did not become a believer during Christ's earthly ministry and yet led the church in Jerusalem not many years after his death (*cf*. Jn. 7:5 with Acts 15:13). What triggered his conversion unless it was his experience of the risen Lord to which Paul refers in 1 Cor. 15:7? And if one replies by assuming that James was psychologically *en route* to becoming a disciple, there is the counter-example of Thomas, already a disciple, who would not believe until he had received empirical proof of the resurrection (Jn. 20:25).

(4) A final position, therefore, remains the most adequate, and it is the one which most Christians throughout the church's history have affirmed in their creeds and confessions of faith as fundamental doctrine. Jesus rose bodily from the grave in a way which anyone present for his appearances could have perceived, even if that perception could not be described in comprehensive detail. The fact that he appeared only to those whom God chose for witnesses and not to all the people (Acts 10:41) does not contradict this. Rather, it suggests that Jesus was selective about when and where he would reveal himself, not that different people present when he did appear experienced contradictory sensations.[2] Jesus went out of his way to demonstrate that his resurrected body was tangible (Lk. 24:39; Jn. 20:27). Harris argues that Jesus' resurrected state was essentially 'one of invisibility and therefore immateriality',[3] but it is hard to see why the latter necessarily

---

[1]*Horizons in Biblical Theology* 1 (1979), pp.148, 157. *Cf*. the similar ambiguity in Perkins, *Resurrection*, p.393: 'Certainly the removal of a body from the world might be considered an event . . . that is in principle open to public witness. But . . . the identity of the body of Jesus with the crucified in the New Testament narratives performs a different function from that of providing information about Jesus' physical remains.' Surely this is a false dichotomy.

[2]*Cf*. Harris, *Raised*, pp.46–50. Paul's own experience on the Damascus road does not necessarily prove what the pre-ascension appearances were like (ibid., pp.55–56).

[3]Ibid., p.53.

follows from the former. Scripture simply does not describe the nature of Christ's body prior to his ascension while he was not with the disciples.

The Shroud of Turin, allegedly one of the graveclothes of Jesus, for so long hidden by Roman Catholic authorities from examination, seems now to provide even further, tangible corroboration of Jesus' crucifixion and resurrection. In 1978 the shroud was subjected to a battery of scientific experiments, and none of the investigators has yet offered a convincing explanation for how the image of a man crucified in virtually every way like Jesus was formed on this linen cloth, with traces of pollen grains from first-century Palestine, unless it is the genuine imprint of a dead man, scourged, beaten, bloodied, pierced in the side and pricked around the head, who somehow disappeared from his wrappings without defacing the grotesque markings that had been left. Naturalistic hypotheses have not accounted for the absence of signs of decomposition and of the body being unwrapped, or for a probable light or heat scorch from a dead body in a state of *rigor mortis*. Of course some scientists prefer to suspend judgment and wait in the hope of new evidence or hypotheses which will prove the shroud to be something other than Jesus' burial cloth. Since the case for the resurrection does not depend on their findings this attitude poses no threat to belief.[1]

The strongest argument for this fourth view of Jesus' resurrection is that it fits best with the Jewish pictures of the general resurrection of the dead at the end of the age, which consistently involve real bodies. If anything, they are sometimes even more 'physical' than in the gospel stories, undoubtedly due to the graphic vision in Ezekiel 37 of flesh and sinews re-attaching themselves to dry, lifeless bones. L. Oberlinner's argument that these parallels do not support the historicity of the gospel accounts, since they involve the resurrection of corpses without the creation of entirely new bodies, overlooks just how 'earthy' Christ's resurrection body was, with the scars of his suffering still visible (Jn. 20:27).[2] To be sure, it was more than the reanimation of his former

---

[1]The best detailed presentation of the current state of shroud research and its implications is Kenneth E. Stevenson and Gary R. Habermas, *Verdict on the Shroud* (Ann Arbor: Servant, 1981; London: Robert Hale, 1982). More concise and less positive is Raymond E. Brown, 'Brief Observations on the Shroud of Turin', *BTB* 14 (1984), pp.145–148.

[2]*Cf. e.g.* Lorenz Oberlinner, 'Die Verkündigung der Auferweckung Jesu im geöffneten und leeren Grab', *ZNW* 73 (1982), pp.159–182.

body, but it was not less.

2 The testimony of Paul

For the other miracles of Jesus, only the testimony of the four gospels is available for consultation, but a study of the resurrection must also consider what Paul writes in 1 Corinthians 15. Here one is on much firmer historical ground, according to the critical consensus. Almost no one doubts that Paul wrote this letter or that he was telling the truth when he 'delivered' to the Corinthians the list of witnesses of the resurrection in verses 3–7 as one which he had 'received' from Christians who preceded him. The Greek words for 'deliver' (*paradidōmi*) and 'receive' (*paralambanomai*) in this context are often used as fairly technical terms for the transmission of tradition. Almost certainly such information would have been related to Paul by the disciples in Damascus (*c.* AD 33) or in Jerusalem during his first visit there after becoming a Christian (*c.* AD 35). Regardless of one's attitude towards the gospels' testimony, therefore, it is extremely difficult to deny that here at least is accurate information. The question then becomes not, 'Is Paul recounting reliable history?' but 'What exactly does he mean?' The problem is complicated by the rest of 1 Corinthians 15, Paul's own reflections on the certainty and significance both of Jesus' resurrection and of the coming resurrection of all the dead.

Critical scholarship on Paul's understanding of the resurrection has tended in the last quarter-century to follow the proposals of Hans Grass. Grass admits that Paul speaks here of a bodily resurrection but he denies that it was a physical body.[1] After all, Paul explicitly states in 1 Corinthians 15:44 that one's life in this world is in a 'physical body', whereas at the resurrection it will be in a 'spiritual body'. As a result, Grass adopts the subjective vision hypothesis; as Craig explains, 'because the body is spiritual, the appearances of Christ were in the form of heavenly visions caused by God in the minds of those chosen to receive them.'[2] 'Physical', however, is not the best or usual way of translating the Greek word found in verse 44 (*psychikos*); for Paul it regularly means 'natural', that is, simply pertaining to this world, though often

---

[1]Hans Grass, *Ostergeschehen und Osterberichte* (Göttingen: Vandenhoeck & Ruprecht, 1961).

[2]Craig, 'Resurrection', p.47. The next three paragraphs are also heavily indebted to Craig's discussion in his various articles.

implying 'unregenerate' (see esp. 1 Cor. 2:14). When Paul contrasts the bodies of this life with those to come, he is most probably using the word 'spiritual' (*pneumatikos*) to mean 'supernatural', or even 'regenerated' in the sense of 'made new', rather than denying them some kind of objective, tangible existence.

Grass, and those who have followed him, offer two other main reasons for rejecting a physical resurrection body. First, Paul goes on in 1 Corinthians 15:50 to proclaim: 'flesh and blood cannot inherit the kingdom of God'. Second, by adding his own experience of the risen Christ to the list of appearances back in 15:8, Paul suggests that he had the same type of experience as did the others who saw Jesus alive again. Yet Acts 9:7 makes it clear that Paul's companions did not see the vision that Paul did, although they heard a noise, so Paul's experience was not entirely objective. Neither of these objections proves very weighty. To begin with, 'flesh and blood' was a standard Semitic idiom for 'frail, mortal existence'; if Paul were denying the physical nature of the resurrection body he would more probably have used the common idiom 'flesh and bones'. Second, simply listing those people to whom Jesus appeared does not imply an identical experience on the part of everyone on the list. The gospels themselves prove that it is hard to group all of Jesus' appearances into one uniform category; at times he could eat, drink and be touched, while at other times he seemed to be able to vanish and materialize again without explanation. What is more significant is that when Paul has an entirely subjective experience, or one about the nature of which he is uncertain, he indicates precisely that (*cf.* 2 Cor. 12:1–4, describing his visit to the 'third heaven'; and Acts 16:9; 18:9; 22:17, in which he receives visions from the Lord regarding his travel itinerary).[1]

Not only does Grass's approach to 1 Corinthians 15 thus fail, but two additional details in verse 4 point positively to an objective, bodily resurrection of Jesus. The first detail is the reference to Christ's burial. When this occurs in a sequence of co-ordinate clauses all beginning with the word 'that' ('that [he] died, . . . that he was buried, that he was raised, . . . that he appeared') with no other details given as to why it should be mentioned at all, the natural implication is that just as a burial requires a physical body

---

[1]*Cf.* Harris, *Raised*, p.48.

so also the resurrection that follows involves a physical body (*cf.* Rom. 6:4 and Col. 2:13). The discovery of an empty tomb does not prove what happened to its occupant, but if he is then seen elsewhere the presumption is that it is his body and not just his spirit that has risen. So also a reference to a resurrection appearance does not by itself determine how objective that experience was, but if it is preceded by reference to a burial the presumption is that a body has been involved both inside and outside the grave.

The second detail is the phrase 'on the third day'. Since no one saw Jesus leave the tomb, why did his followers claim that this happened on Sunday morning unless something objective had convinced them that only at this time was the tomb really empty? As Wenham explains, 'if Paul was thinking of spiritual survival in spite of bodily death . . . Jesus could be said to have survived death from the moment of expiry.'[1] Many have tried to argue that this phrase is not to be interpreted literally but stands rather as a figurative way of saying 'at God's appointed time'. Theologically significant events frequently happen 'on the third day' in Scripture, for example, Abraham's would-be offering of Isaac (Gn. 22:4), God's giving of the Law (Ex. 19:16), Hezekiah's miraculous healing (2 Ki. 20:8), and most significantly the prophecy of Israel's restoration (Ho. 6:2). Yet if the significance of this phrase is only theological and not also chronological, one is left without an explanation as to why Christians began to gather to worship together on the first day of the week (the 'third day' after Friday, by inclusive reckoning) in honour of the resurrection, despite all the inconvenience and misunderstanding this caused, rather than continuing their customary practice as Jews of celebrating the Sabbath on the seventh day of the week.

3 Conclusion

If the resurrection of Jesus really happened, then none of the gospel miracles is in principle incredible. This is not because God can do anything supernatural, no matter how eccentric or arbitrary. Christian belief in God's omnipotence does not include ascribing to him the power to do that which is logically contradict-

[1]Wenham, *Easter Enigma*, p.53.

ory (*e.g.* making the legendary stone so big that he can't move it!) or that which is against his nature (*e.g.* doing evil). But it is precisely in this way that the gospel miracles differ from so many of their counterparts in other religious and philosophical traditions – they all fit together in a consistent pattern, revealing Jesus as sent by his Father to usher in the kingdom of God and make known God's will and ways on earth. This revelation in turn meshes with the main details of the rest of Christ's teaching and ministry.

The major concern in this chapter, once the possibility of miracle was established in the first place, has been to show the reasonableness of believing not in all alleged miracles past or present but in the particular miracles recorded in the gospels. The significance of those miracles has been dealt with only as it bore on the question of their historicity. Despite a long tradition in Christian apologetics of arguing from the miracles to the existence of God, it seems rather that God's existence needs to be either demonstrated or presupposed before the miracles can be believed. In somewhat parallel fashion, neither do the miracles of Jesus by themselves prove his deity. Scripture teaches that Elijah and Elisha worked strikingly similar miracles, but the Jews never came to believe in either of them as God. A remarkable, contemporary testimony to this logic appears in the work of an orthodox Jewish scholar, Pinchas Lapide, who believes in the physical, bodily resurrection of Jesus but sees him not as the Messiah but as a divinely ordained prophet preparing the way for the Messiah, much as Christians view John the Baptist. Lapide adopts this stance because not all the Old Testament prophecies associated with the Messianic age were fulfilled in Jesus' lifetime, most noticeably the promises about world peace and prosperity.[1] Clearly one has to examine all the testimony of the gospels about what Jesus did before one can decide for oneself who he was. But that does not make the miracles any less important. They may not prove all the claims of Christianity, but if they did not occur the way the gospels say they did, then many of Christianity's claims could be disproved. In C. S. Lewis's well-chosen words, 'the accounts of the "miracles" in first-century Palestine are either lies, or legends, or history. And if all, or the most important of them

---

[1]Pinchas Lapide, *The Resurrection of Jesus* (Minneapolis: Augsburg, 1983; London: SPCK, 1984).

are lies or legends then the claim which Christianity has been making for the last two thousand years is simply false'.[1] Much recent scholarship, however, has served to strengthen the view that the miracles are historical and that the Christian claim is true.

---

[1]Lewis, *Miracles*, p.97.

Contradictions among the Synoptics?

The conditions under which the Synoptic Gospels were formed may well have been very conducive to the careful preservation of reliable information about Jesus. But historians make mistakes even under the best of conditions. For many scholars what counts most is neither the general climate in which the gospel traditions circulated, nor any theoretical debate about the possibility of miracles, but the actual data of the gospels themselves. If the different versions of Jesus' life which Matthew, Mark and Luke present are irreconcilably at odds with each other, then at least one of them cannot be considered an accurate account, regardless of the circumstances which led to its composition.

Because the New Testament has been scrutinized with more intensity than any other work of literature in the history of the world, it is not surprising to discover that virtually every passage in the gospels has been seen as conflicting with some other passage by someone or other at some time in history. One short chapter can scarcely begin to respond to all the charges of error or contradiction. But most of the charges have been answered adequately many times over by those who have written in defence of the gospels' trustworthiness. The vast majority of readers of the Synoptic Gospels in all ages have been struck not by the differences among them but by their remarkable similarity. Even those who distinguish between the main themes of different New Testament authors such as Paul or John have often grouped the testimony of the first three gospel writers together, not seeing the theological differences among them as noteworthy enough to merit individual treatment.[1]

---

[1]This is true especially from a survey of New Testament theologies of both conservative and liberal persuasion. *Cf. e.g.* the chapter divisions in Rudolf Bultmann, *Theology of the New Testament,* 2 vols. (New York: Scribner; London: SCM, 1951–55); and W. G. Kümmel, *The*

Nevertheless certain differences of historical detail between parallel passages and between the overall outlines of the gospels lead many modern critics to conclude that the Synoptics cannot be viewed as particularly reliable in the information they present. This chapter will note some of the most commonly cited examples of these divergences but it will argue that the apparent discrepancies are just that – apparent and not genuine – and that they do not call into question the reliability of the gospel witness. If anything, the minor variations that do occur, when coupled with the much greater amount of close agreement in detail, actually strengthen confidence in the evangelists' trustworthiness. Verbatim parallelism, on the other hand, where it occurs, only proves that one writer has copied from another and offers no independent corroboration of his testimony. And the variations which appear in most of the parallels are no greater, and often much more trivial, than those which characterize any two independent historical accounts of the same events – a different selection of details, themes, and phraseology, which periodically brings one account into apparent tension with the other because each reflects a unique perspective and neither tells the whole story.[1] The most obvious examples of the seeming discrepancies in the gospels may be surveyed under seven major headings.

1 Conflicting theology?

Only since the rise of redaction criticism has this category become a significant one. Many redaction critics synthesize the teaching of one of the three Synoptics on a given topic in such a way as to pit it over against the teaching of one of the others. Usually these syntheses result from one of the eight misuses of redaction criticism enumerated in chapter two (pp.37–41). The evangelists very rarely present specific statements in parallel passages which make opposing theological points; rather it is the overall impression created by the gospel writers on a particular topic which leads

---

Theology of the New Testament (Nashville: Abingdon, 1973; London: SCM, 1974); with George E. Ladd, *A Theology of the New Testament* (Grand Rapids: Eerdmans, 1974; Guildford: Lutterworth, 1975); and Donald Guthrie, *New Testament Theology* (Leicester and Downers Grove: IVP, 1981).

[1]*Cf. e.g.* Hugo Staudinger, *The Trustworthiness of the Gospels* (Edinburgh: Handsel, 1981), pp.17–23.

scholars to assess their theological positions as contradictory rather than complementary. Thus it has already been noted how the so-called delay of the Parousia supposedly altered the perspective of the later New Testament writers (above, pp.33–35); when applied to the gospels this belief leads to the conclusion that Luke's portrait of Jesus' teaching about the last days contradicts Mark's. Luke allows for a long interval of time before Christ's return (*e.g.* Lk. 19:11; 20:9), while Mark still thinks it will happen immediately (Mk. 9:1; 13:30).[1] This view, though, neglects the evidence both in Luke's gospel for Jesus' teaching on the imminence of the end (*e.g.* Lk. 12:35–40; 21:24) and in Mark's gospel for an interval preceding the end (most strikingly Mk. 13:10, which Luke omits).[2] This is not an example of an apparent contradiction between parallel passages, but only a contradiction between certain scholars' inadequate summaries of the overall teaching of the evangelists. Examples of the same phenomenon could be multiplied but they are largely irrelevant to the task at hand.

In a few instances, however, an apparent contradiction between parallels has provided the impetus for hypotheses of conflicting theologies. Günther Bornkamm, for example, used the differences between Matthew's and Mark's accounts of the stilling of the storm (Mk. 4:35–41; Mt. 8:23–27) to develop his view about how Matthew rejected Mark's perspective on the disciples, transforming them from faithless failures into paradigms of obedience. Whereas Mark has Jesus awaken to the disciples' cries for help, immediately rebuke the wind, and then berate the twelve for their lack of faith, Matthew describes Jesus' criticizing the disciples only before he works the miracle, and even then gives them credit for having some faith ('men of little faith'). After the miracle, the implication, according to Bornkamm, is that the disciples no longer disbelieve at all.[3] Robert Gundry finds this divergence an unambiguous example of the type of variation between Matthew and his sources which compels him to view the gospels as con-

---

[1]So esp. Hans Conzelmann, *The Theology of St. Luke* (New York: Harper & Row; London: Faber & Faber, 1960), pp.95–131.

[2]*Cf.* E. E. Ellis, 'Present and Future Eschatology in Luke', *NTS* 12 (1965–66), pp.27–41; C. E. B. Cranfield, *The Gospel according to St. Mark* (Cambridge: University Press, 1977), pp.388–389.

[3]G. Bornkamm, G. Barth, and H.-J. Held, *Tradition and Interpretation in Matthew* (London: SCM; Philadelphia: Westminster, 1963), pp.52–57.

tradictory. He then adds:

> To pretend they are not – by suggesting, say, that no faith means not enough faith or that different kinds of faith are in view – is to open the door to somersaulting exegesis which could with equal legitimacy deny the clarity of scriptural statements expressing primary doctrines.[1]

In other words, the contradiction between 'little faith' and 'no faith' is so clear to Gundry that to deny it would be to reject the plain meaning of the text in favour of special pleading.

Such a claim is puzzling, to say the least. There are examples that will be discussed later for which a reaction such as Gundry's is more understandable (*e.g.* the question of whether or not Christ permitted the disciples to take a 'staff' with them on their first missionary journey – see pp.145–146), but this example hardly falls into such a category. Regardless of the timing of the rebuke, it is extremely difficult to turn Jesus' words in Matthew 8:26 ('Why are you afraid, men of little faith?'), however gently spoken, into a compliment! 'Little' faith remains just that – not very much faith. Granted, Matthew has softened the force of Mark's wording somewhat, and he does on the whole paint the disciples in a slightly more positive light than Mark. But this hardly produces an irreconcilable contradiction, as if Matthew had made Jesus praise the disciples' great faith. What appear are different perspectives on the disciples' ever-wavering response to Jesus throughout his earthly ministry, with Matthew choosing to highlight the positive side as a model for the fainthearted among his readers and Mark underlining the more negative side *for precisely the same reason* – to encourage those in his audience who felt inadequate that they too could grow in their Christian lives, just as the twelve matured despite such a rocky start.[2] The same redactional tendencies reappear in the conclusions to the accounts of Jesus' walking on the water. In Matthew the disciples confess Jesus as the Son of God

---

[1]Robert H. Gundry, *Matthew: A Commentary on His Literary and Theological Art* (Grand Rapids: Eerdmans, 1982), p.626.

[2]On Matthew, *cf.* Gerd Theissen, *The Miracle Stories of the Early Christian Tradition* (Edinburgh: T & T Clark; Philadelphia: Fortress, 1983), pp.137–138; P. F. Feiler, 'The Stilling of the Storm in Matthew: A Response to Günther Bornkamm', *JETS* 26 (1983), pp.399–406; on Mark, on the theme of the disciples' misunderstanding more generally, *cf.* Ernest Best, *Mark: The Gospel as Story* (Edinburgh: T & T Clark, 1983), pp.93–95.

(Mt. 14:33); in Mark they maintain a fearful silence (Mk. 6:51). Here John Heil persuasively argues that Mark has deliberately withheld the reference to 'the Son of God', saving it for its climactic appearance in Mark 15:39.[1] It is also less appropriate since he has not narrated the episode of Peter walking on the water (Mt. 14:28–31).[2] As with the accounts of the stilling of the storm, the theological perspectives are not identical, but they are complementary rather than contradictory.

Less radical redaction criticism that avoids the errors noted in chapter two has reinforced this conclusion time and again concerning the theological distinctives of the Synoptists.[3] The apparent contradictions that are usually discussed when assessing the gospels' historical value do not normally fall under this heading of conflicting theology. The same is true of form criticism's dissection of an individual passage or section *within* one of the gospels, as for example, when a parable or pronouncement story is said not to fit its introduction or conclusion. Whatever tension might seem to exist, it obviously did not prevent the evangelist from compiling the passage as it now stands, so for him at least the 'inconsistencies' must not have been irreconcilable.[4] The six remaining categories therefore focus on the more traditional types of apparent contradictions between gospels which scholars regularly debate.

2 The practice of paraphrase

By far the most common kind of difference between gospel parallels involves simple variation in language. No one expects two different writers to retell a particular story with the identical

---

[1]John P. Heil, *Jesus Walking on the Sea* (Rome: PBI, 1981), p.75.

[2]Robert H. Mounce, *Matthew* (San Francisco: Harper & Row, 1985), p.146.

[3]In addition to the studies noted on p.42, n.2, *cf.* the commentaries of D. A. Carson, 'Matthew', in *The Expositor's Bible Commentary,* ed. F. E. Gaebelein, vol. 8 (Grand Rapids: Zondervan, 1984), pp.1–599; William L. Lane, *The Gospel according to Mark* (Grand Rapids: Eerdmans, 1974; London: Marshall, Morgan & Scott, 1975); I. H. Marshall, *The Gospel of Luke* (Exeter: Paternoster; Grand Rapids: Eerdmans, 1978); and from a less conservative perspective the excellent, brief survey of J. D. Kingsbury, *Jesus Christ in Matthew, Mark, and Luke* (Philadelphia: Fortress, 1981).

[4]For a refutation of the notion that certain tendencies of the tradition's transmission require a rejection of any portion of the parables or their contexts as inauthentic, see Craig L. Blomberg, *Interpreting the Parables* (forthcoming), chap. two. The arguments used there in fact apply to numerous other forms of the Synoptic tradition as well.

words, but modern concerns for accurate quotation make many uneasy with certain examples of free paraphrases of others' speech. The ancient world, however, had fewer such qualms. Greek and Hebrew had no symbols for quotation marks, and a historian or biographer referring to what some person said did not necessarily try to cite his exact wording. So long as what he wrote was faithful to the meaning of the original utterance, the author was free to phrase his report however he liked, and no one would accuse him of misquoting his source or producing an unreliable narrative.[1] Even defenders of Scripture's infallibility freely admit that the evangelists usually record only Jesus' *ipsissima vox* (actual voice) rather than his *ipsissima verba* (actual words).[2] Thus when Mark and Luke report that the voice from heaven at Jesus' baptism declared, 'You are my beloved son with whom I am well pleased' (Mk. 1:11; Lk. 3:22), while Matthew's account has 'This is my beloved son with whom I am well pleased' (Mt. 3:17), Matthew has probably just reworded Mark in order to highlight the fact that the heavenly voice spoke not only for Jesus' benefit but also for the benefit of the crowd (and so as well for those who hear about the story later). The harmonization in the ancient, heretical Gospel of the Ebionites, which made the heavenly voice speak twice, once as in Matthew and once as in Mark,[3] is both misguided and unnecessary. It illustrates how not to approach the vast majority of gospel parallels (but see p.148).

This type of minor variation in wording occurs with virtually every pair of gospel parallels but does not call into question their historical reliability.[4] Occasionally, however, the changes are substantial enough that the two versions could be taken as contradictory, but in each case they need not be. At least five categories of these more substantial changes may be discerned.

---

[1]On historical reporting in the ancient world in general, which is appealed to here and elsewhere in this chapter, see *e.g.* A. W. Mosley, 'Historical Reporting in the Ancient World', *NTS* 12 (1965–66), pp.10–26; and W. C. van Unnik, 'Luke's Second Book and the Rules of Hellenistic Historiography', in *Les Actes des Apôtres: Traditions, rédaction, théologie*, ed. Jacob Kremer (Gembloux: Duculot; Leuven: University Press, 1979), pp.37–60.

[2]See esp. Paul D. Feinberg, 'The Meaning of Inerrancy', in *Inerrancy*, ed. Norman L. Geisler (Grand Rapids: Zondervan, 1979), p.301.

[3]Cited by Epiphanius, *Heresies*, 30:13.7–8.

[4]*Cf.* Robert H. Stein, *Difficult Passages in the Gospels* (Grand Rapids: Baker, 1984), pp.18–20, who notes this conclusion already in the work of St. Augustine.

A Summaries introducing new terminology

Toward the beginning of their gospels, both Matthew and Mark epitomize Jesus' message as the preaching of repentance in light of the arrival of the kingdom of God (Mk. 1:14–15; Mt. 4:17). Surprisingly, however, only Mark refers to this message here as 'the gospel'. In fact, Mark uses this noun eight times, Matthew only four, and Luke and John in their gospels never, leading some scholars to speculate that Mark was the first person to apply this Greek term for 'good news' (*euangelion*) to Jesus' message.[1] This suggestion cannot be proved, but there is nothing in principle improbable with it. If it is correct, then Mark has simply appropriated an apt Greek expression which perfectly characterizes the nature of Jesus' preaching, even if Jesus never used an exact Aramaic equivalent to the expression. In other words, Mark has condensed or summarized Jesus' much more detailed teaching into a formula which expresses the heart of his message – 'repent and believe in the gospel'. Whether or not Jesus himself used these exact words on any particular occasion in his ministry is then irrelevant (and impossible to determine).

A second possible example of this process is more controversial. In Matthew's account of the 'Great Commission', Jesus commands the twelve to make disciples and to baptize them 'in the name of the Father, Son, and Holy Spirit' (Mt. 28:19), whereas when Luke depicts the disciples' first carrying out this command, they baptize 'in the name of Jesus Christ' (Acts 2:38; *cf.* 8:16; 10:48; 19:5). Many scholars believe that Jesus could not have said anything as explicitly Trinitarian as Matthew suggests, because the Trinity was a later development in Christian theology, but this belief rests on unfounded presuppositions about the nature of New Testament Christology.[2] The fact that Peter did not literally reproduce the baptismal formula of the Great Commission after his sermon at Pentecost may suggest, however, that Matthew has distilled the essence of Jesus' more detailed parting instructions for the twelve into concise language using the terminology developed later in the

---

[1]Ralph P. Martin, *New Testament Foundations*, vol. 1 (Grand Rapids: Eerdmans, 1975), pp.23–29. *Cf.* Leander Keck, *A Future for the Historical Jesus* (Nashville: Abingdon, 1971; London: SCM, 1972), p.32, on Mark 1:14–15: 'This is almost universally acknowledged to be at the same time a formulation by the church and an accurate summary of what Jesus had to say.'

[2]See esp. *Christ the Lord*, ed. H. H. Rowdon (Leicester: IVP, 1982), for evidence of 'high' Christology from the earliest stages of the Christian church.

early church's baptismal services. Matthew would then have recognized that Jesus' self-understanding included the idea of unity with the Father (on which see pp.251–252) and the Spirit (*cf*. Mt. 12:28–32 pars.), whether or not Jesus ever encapsulated that concept in an explicit Trinitarian formula.[1] Or as R. E. O. White puts it, 'if Jesus commanded the making of disciples and the baptising of them "in My name", and Matt. expressed Christ's fullest meaning (for disciples "of all nations") by using the fuller description current in his own day, who shall say that he seriously misrepresented our Lord's intention?' After all, 'the Commission's thought and phrasing are such as might admirably summarise much that Jesus had said.'[2] On the other hand, Robert Mounce suggests that it would have been 'quite natural' for Jesus to have gathered together into summary form his own references to the Father, the Son, and the Holy Spirit.[3] In that event, the formulas in Acts may be abbreviations pointing to the theological significance of baptism as 'a transference of the rights of possession' to Jesus.[4]

B Theological clarification

Many examples could be listed under this heading. Chapter two already noted Luke's amplification of Jesus' call to tax collectors and sinners, explaining that it was a call 'to repentance', as well as Luke's addition of 'perhaps' to the words of the landlord in the parable of the wicked tenants – 'perhaps they will respect him [my son]' – avoiding the impression that God was taken by surprise when the Jewish leaders rejected *his* son (see above, pp.40, 69). Similar concern for theological clarity has no doubt motivated Matthew to qualify the beatitude 'blessed are the poor' (Lk. 6:20) with the phrase 'in spirit' (Mt. 5:3). He has not distorted a promise originally made to all the materially poor regardless of their spiritual condition. Rather he has recognized the close equation between poverty and piety in certain first-century circles and

---

[1]*Cf*. Grant R. Osborne, 'The Evangelical and Redaction Criticism', *JETS* 22 (1979), p.311; R. T. France, 'The Authenticity of the Sayings of Jesus', in *History, Criticism and Faith,* ed. Colin Brown (Leicester and Downers Grove: IVP, 1976), pp.130–131.

[2]R. E. O. White, *The Biblical Doctrine of Initiation* (London: Hodder & Stoughton; Grand Rapids: Eerdmans, 1960), pp.343–344.

[3]Mounce, *Matthew*, p.277.

[4]Murray J. Harris, 'Baptism and the Lord's Supper', in *In God's Community: The Church and Its Ministry,* ed. D. J. Ellis and W. W. Gasque (London: Pickering & Inglis, 1978), p.19.

phrased the words of Jesus in a way which clarifies that when he blessed the poor he was thinking of 'those who stand without pretense before God as their only hope'.[1] Similarly, Matthew has Jesus enjoin his followers to be 'perfect' as their heavenly Father is, where the Lucan parallel employs the word 'merciful' (Mt. 5:48; Lk. 6:36). It is possible that the Aramaic word which Jesus could have used (*sh^elim*) implied both concepts in its original context. The two versions have simply highlighted different nuances of the concept. As F. F. Bruce explains, Jesus was declaring that 'you must be perfect (that is, all-embracing, without any restriction) in your acts of mercy or kindness, for that is what God is like'.[2]

Two of the most striking examples of this type of divergence appear in Jesus' teaching to his disciples about relationships with their families and to the rich young ruler about his view of Jesus. In the former instance, Luke reports that Jesus warned: 'If someone comes to me and does not hate his father and mother and wife and children he cannot be my disciple' (Lk. 14:26). At first sight Matthew appears drastically to tone down his version: 'He who loves father or mother more than me is not worthy of me, and he who loves son or daughter more than me is not worthy of me' (Mt. 10:37). But Matthew's paraphrase is a fair interpretation of what Jesus' harsher sounding statement in Luke meant; in semitic language and thought, 'hate' had a broader range of meanings than it does in English, including the sense of 'leaving aside', 'renunciation' or 'abandonment'.[3] Moreover, as G. B. Caird explains, 'the semitic way of saying "I prefer this to that" is "I like this and hate that" (*cf.* Gn. 29:30–31; Dt. 21:15–17). Thus for the followers of Jesus to hate their families meant giving the family second place in their affections.'[4]

In the latter case, Mark and Luke describe Jesus beginning his

---

[1]Robert A. Guelich, *The Sermon on the Mount* (Waco: Word, 1982), p.75. *Cf.* Neil J. McEleney, 'The Beatitudes of the Sermon on the Mount/Plain', *CBQ* 43 (1981), pp.5, 10.

[2]F. F. Bruce, *The Hard Sayings of Jesus* (London: Hodder & Stoughton; Downers Grove: IVP, 1983), p.76. *Cf.* W. C. Allen, *A Critical and Exegetical Commentary on the Gospel according to St. Matthew* (Edinburgh: T & T Clark, 1907), pp.55–56. The two accounts of Jesus' great sermon diverge enough to make it difficult to ascribe all the differences to the evangelists' redaction. Probably 'Q' was passed down in more than one form. See esp. Marshall, *Luke*, p.245.

[3]Bruce, *Hard Sayings*, p.592.

[4]G. B. Caird, *The Gospel of St. Luke* (Harmondsworth and Baltimore: Penguin, 1963), pp.178–179.

reply to the rich young ruler's question, 'Good teacher, what must I do to inherit eternal life?' with the words, 'Why do you call me good? No one is good but God' (Mk. 10:17–18; Lk. 18:18–19). Matthew, however, rephrases both question and answer to read, 'Teacher, what good must I do to have eternal life?' and 'Why do you ask me about the good? There is one who is good' (Mt. 19:16–17). Most likely, Matthew wishes to avoid the potential misunderstanding of the previous version which would take Jesus to be denying his own goodness. In the Jewish milieu which emphasized good works as central to righteousness, Matthew has surely captured the point of the young man's question, recorded more literally in Mark and Luke. As for Jesus' counterquestion, Matthew could hardly have intended to change the true point of Mark's version since he concludes with the identical affirmation of God alone as good.[1] But it is only when one understands Matthew's theological concerns that the rationale for his alterations becomes intelligible.

C Representational changes

In at least three clear cases, as he writes for the least Jewish audience of all the gospels and with the most fluent Greek style of the four, Luke changes the imagery of his narrative from something distinctively Palestinian to its Graeco-Roman counterpart. The parable of the two builders is the most developed example of this process of 'representational change'[2] (Mt. 7:24–27; Lk. 6:47–49). Luke adds that the wise man who built his house on the rock 'dug deep and laid a foundation', a practice much more common outside Palestine than within, and turns the description of the raging torrent, appropriate for the small, dry Israeli desert river-beds suddenly swollen with rain, into a calmer flood, more characteristic of a larger river such as the Syrian Orontes slowly

---

[1]For details of a possible harmonization, see D. A. Carson, 'Redaction Criticism: On the Legitimacy and Illegitimacy of a Literary Tool', in *Scripture and Truth,* ed. D. A. Carson and John D. Woodbridge (Leicester: IVP; Grand Rapids: Zondervan, 1983), pp.135–137. Carson's disclaimer that his harmonization need not be the correct one does not mean he finds it indefensible but that he believes there are other, perhaps equally defensible, alternatives. For a solution on text-critical grounds, see J. W. Wenham, 'Why Do You Ask Me About the Good? A Study of the Relation Between Text and Source Criticism', *NTS* 28 (1982), pp.116–125.
[2]The term comes from Joachim Jeremias, *The Parables of Jesus* (London: SCM; Philadelphia: Westminster, 1972), pp.26–27, who notes these and other examples.

overflowing its banks.[1] So too only Luke's version of the parable of the mustard seed has the plant growing in a garden rather than a field (Lk. 13:19, *cf.* Mk. 4:31; Mt. 13:31). Jewish purity laws forbade the planting of a mustard seed in a garden, but in the Graeco-Roman world this was a common practice. And Luke's account of the lowering of the paralytic through the roof of the house where Jesus was teaching removes Mark's reference to 'digging', which would have been necessary with the typical thatched roofs of Palestine, and replaces it with a description of the removal of 'tiles', more common atop buildings elsewhere in the Roman empire (Mk. 2:4; Lk. 5:19). All these changes simply help a non-Jewish audience to picture the scenes more vividly and comprehensibly in their minds, even if the actual details of the imagery have changed. Modern Bible paraphrases often do much the same; the Living Bible, for example, changes David's lamp to a 'flashlight' and Paul's command to greet the brethren with a holy kiss to the injunction, 'shake hands warmly' (Ps. 119:105; Rom. 16:16).[2] So it should not cause distress to discover that the original writers of Scripture did much the same. The meaning of the overall passage in each case remains unaltered; in fact it is precisely in order to preserve its intelligibility for a foreign audience that the details of the picture are changed.

D Synecdoche

A common figure of speech of both literature and conversation is the use of a part of an object for the whole. The poet speaks of 'three sails' when he means three ships, and the captain cries, 'All hands on deck', when he means 'all sailors'. Two seeming discrepancies between gospel parallels which have been explained in several different ways may perhaps be best understood as instances of this type of metaphorical expression called synecdoche. The first involves Jesus' promise, 'If you therefore being evil give good gifts to your children, how much more will your heavenly father give good things to those who ask him.' This is how Matthew words it (Mt. 7:11), and Luke follows him almost exactly except for the

---

[1]J. Alexander Findlay, *Jesus and His Parables* (London: Epworth, 1950), pp.95–96; Simon Kistemaker, *The Parables of Jesus* (Grand Rapids: Baker, 1980), pp.7–8.

[2]Of course not all modern readers are happy with these particular modifications. For the complexities of translating the imagery of Scripture and the necessity of substituting cultural equivalents, see John Beekman and John Callow, *Translating the Word of God* (Grand Rapids: Zondervan, 1974), esp. pp.24–25, 124–150, 201–211.

striking substitution of 'Holy Spirit' for 'good things' in the final clause (Lk. 11:13). Because the Holy Spirit is one of his favourite themes, it is quite likely that Luke made the change and that Matthew renders Jesus' words more literally. But since the Holy Spirit is the preeminent example of the type of 'good thing' which is a heavenly gift (*cf.* Mk. 13:11 pars.; Jn. 14:16–17; Acts 1:8), and thus the most important part of the whole, the change is quite justifiable.[1]

A similar example of very close parallelism in wording with a sudden, striking change in terminology occurs at the end of Jesus' parable of the children in the market-place. Is wisdom justified by her 'deeds' (Mt. 11:19) or her 'children' (Lk. 7:35)? Part of the problem here stems from the fact that both statements are somewhat enigmatic. Most likely their point is that even though the Jewish leaders have rejected both John the Baptist and Jesus, just as the children in the parable refused their playmates' invitation to play both 'funeral' and 'wedding', the wisdom of God's plan of salvation for his people will be shown to be true and righteous by the message and ministry of his emissaries. Luke perhaps preserves the more original wording; wisdom's 'children' are preeminently John and Jesus but ultimately all who form part of God's people. Matthew, in keeping with his emphasis on the mighty acts of God in Christ, uses synecdoche to refer to the key element which demonstrates the righteousness of God's children – their actions. Or, with the slightly different nuances which Harald Sahlin proposes:

> wisdom retains its claim to righteousness as much through 'her works', that is through the course of events in the history of salvation, as also through 'all her children', that is through the prophets and messengers of God who have conducted the affairs of God for justice and salvation.[2]

---

[1]Similarly Eduard Schweizer, *The Good News according to Luke* (London: SPCK; Atlanta: John Knox, 1984), p.192: 'Luke mentions the Holy Spirit (vs. 13) because for him the Spirit represents the embodiment of all that is good . . . and because he knows how ambiguous all "good things" are.' *Cf.* Guelich, *Sermon on Mount*, p.359. For a different explanation of this divergence on text-critical grounds, see Craig L. Blomberg, 'The Legitimacy and Limits of Harmonization', in *Hermeneutics, Authority, and Canon*, ed. D. A. Carson and John D. Woodbridge (Grand Rapids: Zondervan; Leicester: IVP, 1986), pp.145–146.

[2]H. Sahlin, 'Traditionskritische Bemerkungen zu zwei Evangelienperikopen', *ST* 33 (1979), p.84.

There is no contradiction between Matthew and Luke, only complementary perspectives on the same concept.

E Partial reports of longer sayings

The approach of some commentators of previous generations, who assumed that every variation in the wording of someone's speech from one gospel to the next meant that the same thing must have been said more than once in different ways, can lead to some absurd reconstructions. A recent, often cited example is the notion that Peter actually denied Jesus six times due to the minor variations between the gospel accounts of his remarks.[1] Such a harmonization flies in the face of Jesus' own prophecy, on which all four gospels agree, that Peter would deny Jesus three times and then the cock would crow. But it is equally inappropriate to reject all attempts to harmonize varying accounts by means of this approach; it would be quite natural for one writer to record one part of a narrative and for another to focus on a different part. The use of paraphrase combined with variation in the selection of wording can account for still further differences.

Thus when one asks what the high priest and Jesus actually said to each other during his interrogation by the Sanhedrin on the night of his arrest, it is quite possible that Luke has preserved the most detailed record of the dialogue (Lk. 22:67–70), since he seems to be dependent on a special source for much of his passion narrative.[2] Matthew and Mark would then have condensed into one the two questions, 'Are you the Christ?' and 'Are you the Son of God (the Blessed)?', which did not mean the same thing to most first-century Jews, and would have only recorded part of Jesus' reply (Mt. 26:63–64; Mk. 14:61–62). Alternatively, Luke may have rewritten Mark to distinguish more clearly the issues at stake in the interrogation. Either way, Jesus' fateful answer is probably preserved more literally in Matthew and Luke ('you say so'/'you say that I am'), since all three Synoptics agree that later that

---

[1]Harold Lindsell, *Battle for the Bible* (Grand Rapids: Zondervan, 1976), pp.174–176; *cf.* Johnston M. Cheney, *The Life of Christ in Stereo* (Portland: Western Baptist Seminary Press, 1969), pp.218–220. In fact the real problem lies not in what Peter said but in who accused him; it is quite likely that more than three people accused him of being a disciple of Jesus (completely apart from any attempt to harmonize the parallels, note the references to 'the bystanders' in Mark 14:70 and to 'they' in John 18:25), but it is entirely unnecessary to assume that he replied with more than three denials (the evangelists have merely paraphrased these in different ways).

[2]David R. Catchpole, *The Trial of Jesus* (Leiden: Brill, 1971), pp. 153–203.

morning Jesus replied to Pilate in a similarly cryptic fashion (Mk. 15:2; Mt. 27:11; Lk. 23:3). Mark, however, abbreviates Jesus' response to the high priest with the simple, forthright declaration, 'I am' (Mk. 14:62), to clarify that Jesus' answer was affirmative, even if he was implying by his more veiled manner of speech that he preferred another form of self-reference.[1] Instead of Messiah or Son of God, roles which for his contemporaries did not always include the suffering which he understood his mission to embrace, Jesus preferred the title 'Son of man' (see further, pp.249–251). On this all three Synoptists agree, as they describe Jesus explaining his confession to the Sanhedrin: 'you will see the Son of man seated at the right hand of Power.'

The question of the centurion's outcry following the crucifixion resembles the problem of the wording of Jesus' confession. Mark and Matthew have him declare Jesus to be God's Son, while Luke offers a much tamer admission: 'certainly this man was righteous' (Mk. 15:39; Mt. 27:54; Lk. 23:47). Both versions reflect the redactional emphases of the gospels in which they are found. Mark and Matthew highlight Jesus as God's Son much more so than does Luke, whereas Luke, in both his gospel and Acts, stresses the fact that Jesus and the early Christians were innocent of any crime against Israel or Rome. But why could not the centurion have spoken with more detail than any one of the gospels records, something which gave rise to both versions? This was the suggestion of Alfred Plummer nearly a century ago, and endorsed much more recently by Leon Morris: 'the sense in which a Roman would have used the term [Son of God] is better given in Luke's words. Plummer paraphrases, "He was a good man, and quite right in calling God his Father".'[2] The centurion could easily have deduced Jesus' character from his exemplary behaviour on the cross and might well have heard something about the claims of Jesus from all the public stir of that week. Each evangelist has then selected the emphasis most consonant with his distinctive themes.

As with each of the previous examples considered, the freedom

---

[1]Some have argued that Jesus really denied the titles ascribed to him; others have denied that the affirmative was qualified, despite Jesus' apparently indirect manner of speaking. But see D. R. Catchpole, 'The Answer of Jesus to Caiaphas (Matt. xxvi. 64)', *NTS* 17 (1970–71), pp.213–226.

[2]Leon Morris, *The Gospel according to St. Luke* (London: IVP; Grand Rapids: Eerdmans, 1974), p.330; Alfred Plummer, *A Critical and Exegetical Commentary on the Gospel according to St. Luke* (Edinburgh: T & T Clark, 1896), p.539.

to paraphrase which the evangelists exhibit may not be consistent with modern preoccupations with word-for-word citation but it certainly does not distort the truth of the gospel narratives. Even today in informal conversation substantial paraphrases of another's speech are accepted as faithful to its original meaning, so there is no reason to object to the fact that the ancient world permitted a similar flexibility with more formal reports. At any rate the overall historicity of the gospel events is hardly called into question by these minor variations in wording.

3 Chronological problems

A major reason why some critics lightly esteem the historical value of the gospels is that many of the accounts of incidents from Christ's life do not occur in the same order or location in one gospel as they do in the next. But from at least as long ago as the time of St. Augustine, it has been recognized that the gospels did not set out to supply a detailed itinerary of Jesus' ministry with every event in its proper chronological sequence, but frequently arrange passages in topical or thematic order instead (*cf.* the examples on pp.23–24).[1] Scholars of a more traditional mould have often tried to reconstruct comprehensive 'lives of Christ', but their outlines can only be hypothetical. Apart from the infancy and passion/resurrection narratives,[2] the gospels simply do not provide enough information about the time and place of the incidents recorded to enable them to be fitted together with confidence into a chronologically precise harmony. Modern redaction criticism, moreover, can usually supply a plausible rationale for why a given evangelist chose to change the order of his sources. But if one applies the principle of assuming a chronological connection between two portions of the Synoptics only when the text explicitly presents one, then the apparent contradictions of sequence vanish. This is especially true when one realizes that the Greek words sometimes translated as 'now' or 'then' in English (*e.g. kai* or *de*)

---

[1]As emphasized by John D. Woodbridge, *Biblical Authority* (Grand Rapids: Zondervan, 1982), p.42.

[2]Here harmonizations can be achieved up to a point. See *e.g.* Robert H. Gundry, *Survey of the New Testament* (Exeter: Paternoster; Grand Rapids: Zondervan, 1970), pp.119–123, 179–205. On the resurrection stories, see also above, p.102.

often need only mean 'and', without implying that one event happened after the one previously narrated.

Many examples are widely accepted even by conservative commentators. Luke, for example, moves his notice of John the Baptist's imprisonment from its place in the middle of Jesus' Galilean ministry (Mk. 6:14–29) to its beginning in order that it may form the natural conclusion of his section on John the Baptist's mission (Lk. 3:1–20). He also brings forward the account of the sermon in Nazareth (Mk. 6:1–6; Lk. 4:16–30) as a keynote summary of Jesus' teaching and rejection in order to introduce his activity in Galilee. On the other hand, Luke places the account of the call of Peter, John and James later in his narrative and combines it with his distinctive story of the miraculous catch of fish (Lk. 5:1–11; *cf.* Mk. 1:16–20), perhaps to avoid giving the impression which Mark's sequence might create, that these disciples' decision to join Jesus was more spontaneous and unmotivated than it actually was (*cf.* p.174, on Jn. 1:35–51).[1]

A less clear-cut example comes with the story of Jesus' healing blind Bartimaeus and his companion (Mk. 10:46–52; Mt. 20:29–34; Lk. 18:35–43). Mark, followed by Matthew, claims that the miracle occurred as Jesus and his entourage were leaving Jericho, while Luke seems to think it happened as they were 'drawing near'. Because archaeology has demonstrated that there were two places in New Testament times called Jericho – the Old Testament city for the most part desolate and the rebuilt Herodian resort-town a few miles away – a popular harmonization has envisaged Jesus as on the road in between the old and new sites. Yet no one reading Mark or Matthew by itself would ever guess that the old city was implied; unless he were told otherwise a first-century reader would automatically assume that the city called Jericho, where throngs of people flocked to Jesus, was the new, plentifully inhabited site. Probably Luke has just abbreviated Mark, as he does consistently elsewhere, leaving out the reference to the departure from Jericho. Mark after all begins his passage in agreement with Luke, by reporting that Jesus first came *to* Jericho, but

---

[1]Joseph A. Fitzmyer, *The Gospel according to Luke I–IX* (Garden City: Doubleday, 1981), p.560. S. O. Abogunrin, 'The Three Variant Accounts of Peter's Call: A Critical and Theological Examination of the Texts', *NTS* 31 (1985), p.592, also suggests that Mark may have omitted the miracle of the fish-catch to avoid an overemphasis on the person of Peter, in keeping with his redactional tendencies elsewhere.

his style is somewhat inelegant in stating that 'they came to Jericho and as he is going out of Jericho . . .' (Mk. 10:46). Luke therefore improves the style by excising the latter clause, so that one must not press him to mean that the miracle narrated in 18:36–43 occurred immediately after the action of verse 35. Luke simply records Jesus' arrival, Mark presupposes his entrance into and exit from the town, which Luke omits, and then both describe the healing as Jesus was on his way out. The blind man would have sat by the roadside, as beggars customarily did, all the while (18:35), but would only have realized the significance of the passing visitor when crowds were accompanying him upon his departure (18:36).[1] The type of gap which must be presupposed between verses 35 and 36 is hinted at by Luke's omission of any mention of crowds as Jesus was entering, and is consistent with the type of literary abridgement which occurs throughout the gospels (*cf.* secs. 2 E and 4).

A possible objection to this reconstruction surfaces in Luke 19:1, when Luke reports his next story, the conversion of Zacchaeus, as occurring while 'they were going through Jericho'. But Luke does not say this occurred 'after' the previous miracle, so there is no contradiction. Luke regularly introduces passages with no clear temporal connection with what precedes; here the only link is the word 'and' (*kai*). The aorist participle, 'having entered' (*eiselthōn*) modifies the main verb, 'was going through' (*diērchéto*) but need not imply action consequent to 18:43 (*cf.* the introductory aorist participle in 12:1, 17:20 and 18:31). Rather Luke seems to have relocated this passage topically so that it can form the middle of a climactic sequence of three passages about Jesus upending traditional Jewish expectation.[2] Each successive scene causes severer shockwaves – healing the blind, who were often thought to be sinful and thus punished by their incapacity, fraternizing with a tax collector, who had demonstrably betrayed his nation in the eyes of the Pharisees by working for Rome, and telling a parable about the destruction of a nobleman's servants and enemies who clearly stood for the Jewish leaders. Theological considerations explain Luke's outline, while claims of contradic-

---

[1]Interestingly, John Calvin, *A Harmony of the Gospels Matthew, Mark and Luke*, vol. 2, trans. T. H. L. Parker, ed. David W. Torrance and Thomas F. Torrance (Edinburgh: St. Andrew; Grand Rapids: Eerdmans), p.278, anticipated this solution long before the advent of modern redaction criticism.

[2]*Cf.* Walter L. Liefeld, 'Luke', in *Expositor's Bible Commentary*, VIII, p.1006; Marshall, *Luke*, p.692; Calvin, *Harmony*, II, p.281.

tions with Mark can be sustained only when the gospels are read in a way which they were never intended to be.

As a final illustration of this process, one might point to a famous example of variation in order *within* a given passage. In Q's version of the temptations of Jesus (Mt. 4:1–11; Lk. 4:1–13), Matthew and Luke differ as to which temptation they place second and which third – jumping off the temple to be rescued by the angels or worshipping Satan to receive all the kingdoms of the earth. But Luke has linked the three temptations only with the connecting words 'but' and 'and' (Matthew uses 'then' and 'again') and has probably placed the second temptation last so that the climax of his account would end with Jesus at the temple in Jerusalem. Both city and building are important for Luke throughout his two-volume work, so the redactional change is most likely his.[1] But without any explicit statements of chronology, it is wholly unfair to call this a contradiction with Matthew.

4 Omissions

A Omissions of entire passages or sections

Why the evangelists omitted certain stories or episodes from the life of Christ which their sources contained is almost always an impossible question to answer. Did Luke pass over all of Jesus' 'withdrawal from Galilee' (Mk. 6:45–8:26) because he was structuring his gospel along the lines of a geographical outline which covered only Jesus' ministry in Galilee, Samaria and Peraea, and Judaea, and in that order? Or did he delete it for a more practical reason, knowing that he wanted to add a lot of non-Marcan material to his gospel and that the typical size scroll could contain little more than the amount of detail which he finally did include? Both suggestions are plausible but neither is demonstrable. At any rate, one can hardly accuse a gospel writer of contradicting his sources simply because he omits some of their information.

The same is true at the level of an individual paragraph. Sometimes one can suggest plausible reasons for omission, but at best they are still educated guesses. For example, perhaps Luke left out the remarkable miracle of Jesus' cursing the fig tree (Mk. 11:12–

---

[1]Marshall, *Luke*, p.167; Carson, 'Matthew', p.111.

14, 20–25) because he had included a parable, unique to his gospel, on the same topic (Lk. 13:6–9). It is easy today to express disbelief that a particular evangelist could have passed over any of the amazing deeds of Jesus and to question their authenticity if they are found in only one of the gospels. But on anybody's reconstruction of the life of Christ, what the New Testament describes can only represent a small fraction of his marvellous activity and teaching, so omissions should occasion no surprise (*cf.* Jn. 20:31). What *is* striking is how much is repeated in more than one gospel. The unity of the Synoptists' witness to Jesus' life is much more impressive than its diversity. The fact that each evangelist remained highly selective in which details he chose to include in no way impugns the historical accuracy of the information which he did incorporate.

B Omissions of details within passages

The same principles apply to the choice of details within a given passage, which regularly vary from one gospel to the next. Still, occasionally the omission of certain information will make one writer appear more obviously to contradict another. Again there is room to look only at some of the best-known examples.

1 Presupposing information made explicit elsewhere

In Mark and Luke, Jesus seems clearly to forbid divorce and remarriage for any reason (Mk. 10:11–12; Lk. 16:18). In Matthew, on two different occasions he qualifies his remarks with the clause, 'except for adultery' (Mt. 19:9; 5:32). Some take the word translated 'adultery' (*porneia*) to mean sexual sin more generally, while others limit it to very specific types of illegal marriages between close relatives or to incest, but the problem remains that Matthew grants an exception to what seems to be an absolute prohibition in Mark and Luke. Others take Jesus' exception to be referring to grounds for separation rather than for divorce, but then he would not have answered the original question about when divorce was permissible. Not surprisingly, many scholars assume that Matthew or the early church simply added this concession, contradicting Jesus' original, absolute commandment because it was too severe or impractical. Yet although the exegesis of these passages is complicated by a number of ambiguous grammatical features, the most convincing solution still remains the one which sees Matthew as simply spelling out what Mark and Luke leave implicit. The debate about divorce in Jewish circles in Jesus' day pitted the followers of the famous teacher, Hillel, against those of his rival, Shammai. The former took a more liberal view, permitting divorce in a wide variety of circumstances; the latter, only in the case of adultery. In other words, both sides agreed on the exception which Matthew adds, so Jesus could have safely presupposed it without fear of misunderstanding.[1]

An almost exactly parallel example arises with Jesus' response to the Jewish leaders' request for a sign to legitimate his ministry. Mark states that Jesus replied emphatically, 'no sign shall be given this generation' (Mk. 8:12), while Matthew twice records Jesus' same statement with the qualification 'except the sign of Jonah' (Mt. 12:39–40; 16:4; this time paralleled by Luke in 11:29–30), which he goes on to explain refers to the Son of man being in the heart of the earth (and presumably resurrected) just as Jonah was in the belly of the fish (and then rescued). Nevertheless both Jesus' teaching elsewhere (*e.g.* Lk. 16:31) and the Jewish leaders' disbelief after the resurrection prove that this specific sign is not what Christ's opponents had in mind. They were looking for someone to liberate them from Rome; Jesus came to free them from their sins. As far as they were concerned, 'no sign except the sign of Jonah' meant exactly the same as 'no sign'. Despite a formal contradiction between the parallels the actual meaning of the two versions is identical.[2]

2 Excerpting different portions of a longer original

This idea has already been introduced in the section on paraphrase but here a few purer examples may be cited. In the same saying of Jesus which concluded with the divergent expressions 'good gifts' and 'Holy Spirit' (see above, pp.123–124), Matthew and Luke also differ in their description of Jesus' examples of good and bad gifts.

---

[1]For a thorough but concise defence of this view against the major alternatives, see Carson, 'Matthew', pp.414–418. Recently, several scholars, most notably William A. Heth and Gordon J. Wenham, *Jesus and Divorce* (London: Hodder & Stoughton; Nashville: Thomas Nelson, 1985), have made much of the fact that the early Greek church fathers interpreted these texts differently, but the tendency of this branch of Christianity to move quickly away from New Testament views of sexual relationships to a stricter, ascetic, pro-celibacy position offsets the force of much of this argument.

[2]*Cf.* James Swetnam, 'No Sign of Jonah', *Bib* 66 (1985), pp.126–130, who ties in Mark's omission of this 'exception' with his omission of the resurrection appearances at the end of his gospel, arguing that Mark deliberately avoided basing his apologetic for the identity of Jesus on this potentially unconvincing testimony. *Cf.* Vincent Mora, *Le signe de Jonas* (Paris: Cerf, 1983), p.26.

Both agree that Christ said, 'Which of you fathers having a son who asks for a fish would give him a serpent?' but Matthew precedes this with the parallel comparison of bread and a stone, whereas Luke follows it with one involving an egg and a scorpion. The best solution is that Jesus employed all three illustrations. His previous comments, which appear in identical form in both gospels (Mt. 7:7–8; Lk. 11:9–10), also divide into three parts, 'ask, seek and knock', and would nicely balance a tripartite illustration in the verses which follow.[1] Moreover, significant manuscript evidence favours the inclusion of the 'bread-stone' example in Luke's account, even if some of the oldest texts omit it (thus explaining its exclusion from modern translations, *contra* the AV).[2] It is easy to argue that the longer version is simply a later, scribal harmonization, but such corrections to the earliest texts are usually not this lengthy or well attested. But even if it were not in Luke's original manuscript it may at least reflect recognition that Jesus did use all three comparisons in his original saying. An alternative would be to classify the variations in imagery as representational changes (see pp.122–123).

In the case of Jesus' 'words of institution' at the Last Supper, textual criticism again comes into play. In Luke 22:15–20 Jesus blesses a cup first and then the bread, unlike Matthew and Mark who have it the other way around (Mk. 14:22–25; Mt. 26:26–29). This reversal is especially clear if Luke 22:19b–20 are omitted (they are missing from some manuscripts), since they complicate the picture by referring to a second cup. But here the textual evidence almost certainly favours inclusion of these verses,[3] so that what Luke really presents is the sequence 'cup-bread-cup'. When one realizes that the Passover ritual which the Jews even today still celebrate involved four cups of wine, then it is clear that Luke has described what actually happened by referring to an

---

[1]*Cf.* Kenneth E. Bailey, *Poet and Peasant: A Literary-Cultural Approach to the Parables in Luke* (Grand Rapids: Eerdmans, 1976), pp.136–137; A. H. McNeile, *The Gospel according to St. Matthew* (London: Macmillan, 1915; Grand Rapids: Baker, 1980), p.92.

[2]Bruce M. Metzger, *A Textual Commentary on the Greek New Testament* (London and New York: UBS, 1971), p.157, admits that 'it is difficult to decide' whether Luke's original had two or three pairs but notes that a majority of the five-person committee which produced the UBS Greek New Testament opted for the shorter text.

[3]I. H. Marshall, *Last Supper – Lord's Supper* (Exeter: Paternoster; Grand Rapids: Eerdmans, 1980), pp.36–38, 179. *Cf.* esp. Heinz Schürmann, *Traditionsgeschichtliche Untersuchungen zu den synoptischen Evangelien* (Düsseldorf: Patmos, 1968), pp.159–192; J. H. Petzer, 'Luke 22:19b–20 and the Structure of the Passage', *NovT* 26 (1984), pp.249–252. The longer version is read by all but one of the ancient Greek manuscripts (Codex Bezae).

earlier cup which Mark and Matthew failed to mention.

3 Following conventional standards of popular speech

Every language and culture has many conventional expressions which do not mean what they literally seem to say. One of these common to modern Western and ancient Eastern cultures is the habit of speaking about someone acting for himself even when he uses an intermediary. A news reporter may state flatly, 'the President of the United States today said . . .' when in fact it was his press secretary who spoke on his behalf, yet no one accuses the commentator of inaccurate reporting. Similarly, Matthew and Mark can speak of Pilate scourging Jesus (Mk. 15:15; Mt. 27:26) even though no governor himself would ever have lifted the whip but would have left that task to his soldiers.[1] This type of linguistic convention undoubtedly explains the differences between Matthew's and Luke's narratives of the Capernaum centurion (Mt. 8:5–13; Lk. 7:1–10); in the former the centurion himself comes to Jesus, while in the latter he sends emissaries to summon the Lord. Luke's account is more literally accurate, but Matthew's way of phrasing it would have been considered no less acceptable.

The same variation occurs again when Matthew and Mark differ as to who requested the seats of honour for James and John when Jesus would come into his kingdom. Was it the sons of Zebedee themselves or their mother (Mt. 20:20–21; Mk. 10:35–37)? Little imagination is required to picture the mother coming and kneeling, with her sons acting as spokesmen. The fact that even in Matthew's account Jesus replies to the mother in the second person plural, 'you (pl.) do not know what you ask' (Mt. 20:22), shows that he knew the sons were involved as well and were probably quite happy to comply with their mother's request. It is also easy, though perhaps not quite as natural, to envisage the disciples asking their mother to plead on their behalf so as to avoid appearance of immodesty. But either way, the two accounts are scarcely contradictory.

4 Compressing or telescoping a narrative

Perhaps the most perplexing differences between parallels occur

---

[1] *Cf.* further Plutarch, *Life of Alexander* 73:1, with Arrian, *Anabasis* 7:16.5, on Alexander 'meeting' the Chaldaean seers, when he actually spoke only second-hand with Nearchus; and

when one gospel writer has condensed the account of an event which took place in two or more stages into one concise paragraph which seems to describe the action taking place all at once. Yet this type of literary abridgement was quite common among ancient writers (*cf.* Lucian, *How to Write History* 56), and once again it is unfair to judge them by modern standards of precision which no one in antiquity required.[1] The two most noteworthy examples of this process among gospel parallels emerge in the stories of Jesus raising Jairus' daughter and cursing the fig tree.

In the first story, Matthew drastically abbreviates Mark's three-part account, which includes (a) the initial summons for Jesus to come to Jairus' home before the girl dies,(b) the intervening delay while he heals the haemorrhaging woman, and (c) his climactic arrival after the death of the daughter, and her subsequent revivification (Mk. 5:21–43; *cf.* Mt. 9:18–26, twenty-three verses compressed into nine). As a result Matthew omits the initial appeal, 'my daughter is dying', and has Jairus in stage (a) declare that she has just died. A comparison of the reactions of two evangelical scholars is instructive. On the one hand, I. H. Marshall remarks:

> We can, of course, explain the contradiction quite easily and acceptably by saying that Matthew, whose general policy was to tell stories about Jesus in fewer words than Mark, has abbreviated the story and given the general sense of what happened without going into details. But the fact still remains that Matthew has attributed to Jairus words which he did not actually say at the time stated.[2]

This is one of the key passages which makes Marshall feel that 'inerrancy' is an inappropriate category for analyzing the gospel data. On the other hand, Robert Stein assesses the situation differently:

---

2 Ki: 21:10 with 2 Ch. 33:10 on the Lord speaking to Manasseh, when actually it was by means of his prophets.

[1]*Cf.* Martin Hengel, *Acts and the History of Earliest Christianity* (London: SCM; Philadelphia: Fortress, 1979), pp.11–20.

[2]I. H. Marshall, *Biblical Inspiration* (London: Hodder & Stoughton, 1982; Grand Rapids: Eerdmans, 1983), p.61.

In light of Matthew's tendency toward abbreviation we can better understand what has happened in Matthew 9:18–19, 23–25. Matthew summarized the story of Jesus' raising of Jairus's daughter . . . What he omits are various interesting but unnecessary details such as that when Jairus first arrives his daughter is not yet dead . . .

Matthew's account is an inerrant summary of Jesus' raising of Jairus's daughter. Difficulties are encountered if the details of this summary are pressed in a way that Matthew never intended.[1]

A synthesis of these two opinions might state that Matthew's account seems to have a minor 'error' according to certain modern definitions of the term but not according to most ancient ones. But surely it is the latter that counts; even the most ardent defenders of biblical inerrancy admit that the original intention of Scripture must be the final arbiter, so Stein's verdict seems slightly fairer.

The same type of problem arises when Matthew telescopes the two-day sequence of events in the cursing of the fig tree into one uninterrupted paragraph which seems to refer only to the second day's events (Mk. 11:12–14, 20–25; Mt. 21:18–22). But there is no necessary contradiction unless one reads more into the account than is actually present. Matthew's introduction, 'now in the early morning', does not specify which day is in view, and there is no reason to exclude an interval of time between verses 19 and 20. Mark does not deny that the fig tree withered immediately, only that the disciples did not see it until the next day. To reject this type of harmonization as special pleading is to ignore the fact that virtually every passage in the gospels leaves out a plethora of detail which could make it much more complex; it is only when formal inconsistencies between parallels appear that one is reminded of this fact in such a vivid fashion.

A final example of compressing a two-stage event into one surfaces in the trial narratives of the Synoptics, though exactly what happened in each of the two stages of that event is impossible to determine with certainty. Matthew and Mark agree that Jesus was brought before an informal gathering of the Sanhedrin in the

---

[1]Stein, *Difficult Passages,* pp.33–34. By way of contrast, Stein notes the absurd position in which Osiander's sixteenth-century harmonization landed him – that Jesus raised Jairus' daughter twice (p.12)!

middle of the night of his arrest, interrogated, and convicted of blasphemy (Mk. 14:53–65; Mt. 26:57–68). Then 'early in the morning' the court held a consultation and reached the decision to go to Pilate to request Jesus' execution (Mk. 15:1; Mt. 27:1–2). It is not clear whether this second stage in the proceedings was a more formal trial, since the Sanhedrin could not have legally sat in judgment during night-time hours, or whether, having already broken the law in their haste to do away with Jesus, they dispensed with even the pretense of legality when daylight came and simply concluded their discussion without giving the defendant further opportunity to speak. Either way, Luke has condensed the two stages into one and prefaced his account with the time-indicator, 'and as day came' (Lk. 22:66–71). Once again no contradiction emerges here unless one presses the texts beyond their intended meaning. That the Jewish authorities did not question Jesus almost immediately upon his arrest in the middle of the night is inconceivable in view of their zeal to destroy him, and it is quite probable that they repeated their questions to make at least some kind of show of legality when daylight first dawned.[1] In the conventions of historical reporting of the day, Luke would thus have been entirely justified to narrate his account as he has, even if it meant assimilating some of the language of the earlier proceedings to that of the later.[2] On the other hand, as Marshall points out, 'Mark's account of the "trial" itself contains no time-reference,' and

> the appearance of a night-time meeting in Mk. results from the juxtaposition of the trial with Peter's denial (which certainly took place by night) and from the fact that business began extremely early in the morning. It is, therefore, probable that Mark and Luke are reporting the same incident from different points of view, namely an enquiry by the sanhedrin which took place at dawn . . .[3]

---

[1]On the accuracy of Mark's version, see A. N. Sherwin-White, 'The Trial of Christ', in *Historicity and Chronology in the New Testament* (London: SPCK, 1965), pp.97–116; and for Luke, see Catchpole, *Trial*, pp.153–203. Unfortunately neither acknowledges the force of the other's position!

[2]*Cf.* George A. Kennedy, 'Classical and Christian Source Criticism', in *The Relationships among the Gospels,* ed. William O. Walker, Jr. (San Antonio: Trinity University, 1978), p.142: 'slightly different versions of essentially the same pericope may result from varying reports of what was said about the same subject on different occasions.'

[3]Marshall, *Gospel of Luke*, p.847. So also J. A. Fitzmyer, *The Gospel according to Luke X–XXIV* (Garden City: Doubleday, 1985), p.1466.

So perhaps the council proceeded more legally than many critics have given them credit for. In either event it is certainly inappropriate to demean the evangelists' historical credibility on account of these minor variations.

5 Composite speeches

A General considerations

Matthew punctuates his narrative of the life of Christ with five major 'sermons' of Jesus (chs. 5–7, 10, 13, 18, 24–25) which are largely unparalleled in Mark and have partial parallels scattered throughout Luke's gospel, often in entirely different contexts from those to which Matthew assigns them. As a result, the vast majority of contemporary scholars believe that these 'sermons' are artificial, composite creations of Matthew, who collected together individual sayings from Q (thus the parallels in Luke) and supplemented them with material peculiar to his gospel. This additional material is variously described as Matthew's own creative invention, the sayings of early Christian prophets, or authentic teaching of Jesus acquired from other sources and given a new context. Similar assessments are then made of other shorter 'speeches' of Jesus in the Synoptics, with the result that the old form-critical axiom of discrete sayings of Jesus all being preserved in isolation from each other still prevails.

This axiom, though, proves highly improbable. Jewish teachers in the first century were not like Oriental gurus, pronouncing one pithy pearl of wisdom at a time and leaving their disciples to search their inner selves to determine its significance. They did utter memorable proverbial sayings, but they also regularly spoke, not unlike modern Christian preachers, in coherent, organized, discursive form.[1] That Jesus delivered detailed messages on discipleship

---

[1]To be sure, the organization of longer discourses was often quite different from the structure of modern preaching. Jewish midrash (see pp.43–53), *e.g.*, tended to link one theme or teaching to the next by association of similar words or concepts more than by strictly logical progression of thought. For a possible outline of the Sermon on the Mount utilizing such connections, see J. W. Doeve, *Jewish Hermeneutics in the Synoptic Gospels and Acts* (Assen: Van Gorcum, 1954), pp.191–200. Doeve notes that by itself this formal structure could represent either Jesus' own homiletical outline or one created for a collection of his teachings by later tradition. On other grounds he opts for the latter, but he self-consciously distances himself from the extreme dissection of the sermon into small, independent units typical of most form criticism.

(Mt. 5–7) or on mission (10) or on the destruction of the temple and the end of the world (24–25) is entirely likely, and the probability of such sermons having been summarized and preserved by word of mouth is equally great in view of the nature of oral tradition in antiquity (see pp.25–31). Even if Jesus is considered to be sufficiently distinct from his Jewish contemporaries so as to limit the value of analogies to other teachers of his day, it is inconceivable that he should have had large throngs assembled to hear him and only have taught for as brief a period of time as it would have taken to utter even as 'long' a message as the Sermon on the Mount. At the outset, it makes much more sense to view the Synoptic 'sermons' as substantially abbreviated accounts of much longer messages of Jesus than to imagine them as built up from small, individual bits of 'free-floating' tradition.[1]

Two problems nevertheless remain insuperable for many critics. If Matthew's five sermons are selections from longer originals, why then has Luke broken them up and scattered his parallels about in such seemingly random fashion? The beatitudes form part of Luke's sermon on the plain (6:20b–23), the Lord's prayer appears towards the beginning of his travel narrative (11:1–4), and the passage about not laying up treasure on earth is found later still (12:33–34), even though in Matthew they are all part of one unified sermon (on the mount) from earlier in Christ's ministry. Second, Jewish and Graeco-Roman writers regularly composed 'artificial' speeches of this kind, so why should the gospel writers be viewed any differently?

It is difficult, however, to find in composite discourses elsewhere a close parallel to the conclusions which Matthew gives his sermons, which in all but one case refer to Jesus 'having ended *these* sayings' (7:28–29; 13:53; 19:1; 26:1; 11:1 is the partial exception which speaks simply of his finishing his instruction). If the critical consensus is correct, then at the very least Matthew has used a quite awkward expression which easily misleads his readers into assuming that he has narrated unified sermons of material already spoken by Jesus. Granted that ancient writers did create composite speeches without any intention to mislead, they also reported genuine speeches left intact (*cf.* Thucydides, *History* 1:22.1).

---

[1]*Cf.* esp. George A. Kennedy, *New Testament Interpretation through Rhetorical Criticism* (Chapel Hill: University of North Carolina, 1984), pp.67–69, who defends a similar view in the light of the practices of ancient rhetoricians.

Since Matthew could easily have omitted or rephrased his concluding formulas, it is hard to avoid their natural implication, which leaves Matthew claiming the latter practice as the one he adopted, however abbreviated his accounts may have been.[1] At the same time, since only 26:1 refers to '*all* these sayings', Matthew may well have constructed his sermons out of shorter, connected discourses by adding or interspersing authentic teaching of Jesus on related topics.[2] A similar process lay behind the composition of the targums (see p.30) and would have been accepted as very natural. Either way, the fact that other New Testament writings which predate the Synoptics seem to know connected blocks of tradition from Matthew's sermons confirms the view that the tradition contained much more than isolated sayings of Jesus (see pp.229–230).[3]

As for the problem of the Lucan parallels, it seems that Luke rather than Matthew is the evangelist who has most frequently arranged his sayings of Jesus in topical sequence.[4] Most of the material from one of Matthew's sermons which appears in a different context in Luke falls into his central section or travel narrative (9:51–18:14), which is strikingly void of details about chronology and location of events. Luke has few transitional words which require a given passage to be describing teaching of Jesus that occurred in the same context as the preceding passage, whereas thematic parallels readily suggest a topical outline for this portion of his gospel. Luke 11:1–3, for example, combines the Lord's prayer, the parable of the friend at midnight, and the command to 'ask, seek and knock'. The first and third of these passages are paralleled in different chapters of Matthew's Sermon on the Mount, while the parable is unique to Luke. Presumably Luke has gathered the three together because they all deal with the topic of prayer.[5] The section concludes with no summary

---

[1]Carson, 'Matthew', p.123.

[2]*Cf.* R. T. France, *The Gospel according to Matthew* (Leicester: IVP; Grand Rapids: Eerdmans, 1985), p.60; Mounce, *Matthew*, p.34. On the juxtaposition of one authentic teaching of Jesus to interpret another, see Joachim Wanke, *'Bezugs- und Kommentarworte' in den synoptischen Evangelien* (Leipzig: St. Benno, 1981).

[3]*Cf.* Richard Bauckham, 'The Study of Gospel Traditions Outside the Canonical Gospels: Problems and Prospects', in *GP*,5, pp.378–379.

[4]So already V. C. MacMunn, 'Who Compiled the Sermon on the Mount?' *ExpT* 35 (1923–24), pp.221–225.

[5]For a detailed display of this topical kind of outline for all of Luke's central section, see Craig L. Blomberg, 'Midrash, Chiasmus, and the Outline of Luke's Central Section', in *GP*,3, pp.244–246.

statement suggesting that Jesus spoke them all at once, but instead shifts abruptly to a different topic, opposition to Jesus, beginning with the debate over the source of his power to exorcise (11:14–23). Moreover, for many of the shorter sayings of Jesus, one must never forget the possibility that parallels in multiple contexts in the gospels reflect Jesus' own repetition of the same teaching on different occasions. This type of solution can be the 'easy way out' at times, but it is irresponsible not to consider it at all, even when the wording is similar enough from one gospel to the next to suggest the use of a common source. As Carson comments, 'the pithier the saying the more likely it was to be repeated word-perfect,'[1] and this would be true when Jesus' teaching was translated into Greek as well. More importantly,

> there are few methodologically reliable tools for distinguishing between, say, two forms of one aphoristic saying, two reports of the same saying uttered on two occasions, or one report of one such saying often repeated in various forms but preserved in the tradition in one form.[2]

In other words if one evangelist knew that Jesus said something similar on several different occasions but only had a written account of his words from one of them, he would have felt free (and been completely justified in doing so) to follow that wording in his description of any of those occasions.

All these reflections, however, merely embody general principles. Can a view of the gospel sermons as connected messages from Jesus, however selectively condensed, be substantiated with any evidence from the texts apart from the evangelist's concluding statements? David Wenham has attempted to do this in minute detail for Jesus' eschatological discourse (Mk. 13; Mt. 24–25; Lk. 21:5–36, with partial parallels scattered elsewhere); if he is at all on target in his approach, the critical consensus will need seriously to be modified.[3] His position will therefore be discussed in some detail and then some much briefer remarks on the other Matthaean sermons offered.

---

[1]Carson, 'Matthew', p.123.

[2]Ibid., p.243. *Cf.* J. W. Wenham, 'Synoptic Independence and the Origin of Luke's Travel Narrative', *NTS* 27 (1981), p.513.

[3]David Wenham, *The Rediscovery of Jesus' Eschatological Discourse* (Sheffield: JSOT Press, 1984 [*GP*,4]).

B A test case: the eschatological discourse

Wenham argues that a version of Jesus' sermon about the last days, longer than that preserved in any of the three Synoptics, lies behind the gospel accounts of that discourse of Christ, and that all have excerpted and rearranged that account in various ways. Wenham suspects that this pre-Synoptic version was written but allows that it could have been only oral. He builds his case by beginning with the parable of the watchman, which forms the conclusion to Mark's version of the discourse (Mk. 13:33–37). Luke has relocated this parable by inserting it into his travel narrative (Lk. 12:35–38), but in a context which has parallels to Matthew's version of the eschatological discourse. The two parables of the thief and the faithful servants (Lk. 12:39–46) reappear in Matthew 24:42–51 but have no Marcan counterparts. Wenham therefore suggests that all three of these parables about faithful stewardship originally stood together near the end of Jesus' sermon. Further, the introduction to Luke's parable of the watchman ('let your loins be girded and your lamps burning' – Lk. 12:35), absent from Mark's version, sounds like the perfect conclusion or summary of Matthew's parable of the ten virgins (Mt. 25:1–12); perhaps that parable originally preceded the other three. On the other hand, Mark's parable of the watchman includes a unique statement which sounds like a reminiscence of the parable of the talents ('giving to his servants authority, to each his work' – Mk. 13:34a; *cf.* Mt. 25:14–30), so perhaps the parable of the talents originally followed this series of passages. It only requires the addition of Matthew's final parable of the judgment of the nations (Mt. 25:31–46) to this series, and all the major sections of this part of Jesus' sermon on the last days fall into line as a collection of parables which Jesus spoke, one after the other. The following chart shows how all three Synoptics preserve traces of this sequence of the original discourse's conclusion:

parable of ten virgins	Matthew 25:1–12		Luke 12:35
parable of watchman		Mark 13:34b–36	Luke 12:36–38
parable of thief	Matthew 24:43–44		Luke 12:39–40
Peter's question			Luke 12:41
Jesus' answer		Mark 13:37	
parable of faithful stewardship	Matthew 24:45–51		Luke 12:42–46
parable of talents	Matthew 25:13–30	Mark 13:33–34a	
parable of sheep and goats	Matthew 25:31–46		

142

The second section of Wenham's book applies a like strategy with similar results to the less divergent accounts of the main body of Jesus' discourse. This section, common to all three of the Synoptics, contains Jesus' less parabolic teaching about the signs accompanying the end (Mk. 13:5–32; Mt. 24:4–41; Lk. 21:8–36). Here also the pre-Synoptic version may have been longer than any of the current forms. A passage such as Luke 17:22–37 on the coming of the Son of man would then not be an isolated fragment which Matthew and Mark have joined with other sayings in order to construct a longer, composite discourse (*cf.* the parallels in Mt. 24:17–18, 23, 26–28, 37–41; Mk. 13:14–16, 19–23) but would be an account of what Jesus originally said in his sermon, which Matthew and Mark have condensed and which Luke has relocated in his travel narrative as part of Jesus' teaching about when and how the kingdom will appear (*cf.* the subsequent parable of the unjust judge in Luke 18:1–8). By the end of Wenham's study, every passage has a logical place in a reconstructed eschatological discourse which contains more detail than is found in any single gospel. The evidence for the dozens of careful, exegetical decisions that Wenham has to make to support his case varies from one instance to the next, and some of the pieces in his jigsaw should perhaps be put together differently.[1] But even if every facet of his reconstruction is not equally convincing, scholars must still face up to its significance. In all probability, Jesus originally uttered one connected, coherent eschatological discourse from which the three Synoptists have chosen to reproduce different portions in different places. They did not invent the idea of such a discourse by combining together a large number of short, isolated sayings from unconnected contexts in Jesus' life, even though they may have used a few such sayings to provide authoritative commentary on controversial details.

C The other sermons in Matthew

If Wenham's approach to the eschatological discourse is at all valid, then the likelihood of Matthew having excerpted similar, lengthy accounts of Jesus' teaching for his other four sermons increases. The Sermon on the Mount and the sermon in parables (5–7 and 13) have shorter parallels in Luke 6:20–49 and Mark

---

[1]See my review of Wenham in *Trin J* n.s. 6 (1985), pp.115–118.

4:1–34 respectively. Once again it is usually assumed that the shorter accounts are more authentic, though even they are generally supposed to be somewhat composite, while unparalleled information in Matthew is taken as his own redactional invention. But why, for example, must Jesus have spoken only four beatitudes (Lk. 6:20–22), which then inspired Matthew on the one hand to add four more of his own (Mt. 5:3–10) and Luke on the other to append four woes to balance them (Lk. 6:24–26)?[1] Is it not more natural to imagine him speaking all eight beatitudes followed perhaps by eight woes, with Matthew and Luke each choosing different ways of abbreviating? Nevertheless one must freely admit that the idea of composite speeches is not the creation of post-Enlightenment, sceptical higher-criticism; centuries ago John Calvin could write:

> Both Evangelists had the intention of gathering into one single passage the chief headings of Christ's teaching, that had regard to the rule of godly and holy living . . . It should be enough for reverent and humble readers that here, before their eyes, they have set a short summary of the teaching of Christ, gathered from his many and various discourses, of which this was the first, where He spoke to his disciples on the true blessedness.[2]

When it comes to explaining Matthew 7:28 about Jesus' finishing 'these sayings', Calvin suggests that Matthew means that 'there was a like impression over His address when He came down from the mount, as with the rest of His teaching, which had by now reached a number of the people. So the sense is that in all the various places, where He had given the people a taste of His teaching, astonishment had affected them . . .'[3] This interpretation is conceivable but it is certainly hard to derive from the particular words Matthew uses.

It has already been noted that Matthew's summary statement (Mt. 11:1) following Jesus' sermon on mission (10:5–42) is not quite so exact, and here the case for a composite discourse is more

---

[1]C. M. Tuckett, 'The Beatitudes: A Source-Critical Study', *NovT* 25 (1983), p.195. Even some relatively conservative commentators seem locked into this position. *Cf. e.g.* Guelich, *Sermon on Mount,* p.113; Jacques Dupont, *Les Béatitudes,* vol. 1 (Paris: Gabalda, 1969), pp.251–264, 299–342. Guelich finds the additions traditional in origin; Dupont, redactional. But neither is willing to affirm them as authentic sayings of Jesus.

[2]Calvin, *Harmony,* I, trans. A. W. Morrison, p.168.   [3]Ibid., p.242.

compelling. In fact it is precisely when one accepts that Matthew has combined at least two different speeches of Jesus into one that one of the most notable inconsistencies among all the Synoptic parallels can be cleared up. The sermon on mission begins with Jesus preparing the twelve for their first 'solo' expedition preaching about the kingdom of heaven to their fellow Israelites (10:5–16). The urgency of their mission is to be visibly highlighted by their travelling unencumbered by unnecessary clothing or baggage; not even 'sandals' or a 'staff' for walking is permitted (verse 10). Luke agrees with the prohibition of the staff, omits all reference to footwear and otherwise greatly curtails his parallel (Lk. 9:1–6). Mark's account is slightly longer than Luke's but not nearly as elaborate as Matthew's (Mk. 6:6b–13). Yet in Mark, Jesus does permit both staff and sandals (verses 8–9). Surely, if ever there were an unassailable contradiction in the gospels, this would be it.[1]

Nevertheless, it is hard to imagine Matthew or Luke editing Mark and rescinding Jesus' permission to take at least shoes and walking stick; a change from a more severe restriction to a lesser one would be the natural development. Moreover, Luke 10:1–24 describes a very similar commission – this time of seventy-two[2] disciples – which Matthew's account of the charge to the twelve (9:37–10:16) often echoes. These echoes sometimes create greater parallelism between Matthew's sermon to the twelve and Luke's commission to the seventy-two than between Matthew's sermon to the twelve and Luke's version of the same sermon. The most obvious illustration of this parallelism is the famous saying about the plentiful harvest with few labourers (Mt. 9:37–38; Lk. 10:2; no parallel in Mk. 6 or Lk. 9). Since the seventy-two most likely included the twelve (*cf.* Lk. 10:17 and 23), an attractive hypothesis suggests that Matthew has combined some of Jesus' instructions to the twelve with some of those to the seventy-two. On the one occasion staff and shoes were permitted; on the other they were forbidden. Since all Matthew implies is that these are commands given by Jesus to the twelve

---

[1]*E.g.* the avowedly evangelical philosopher Stephen T. Davis lists this as one of only six errors he can find in Scripture, yet declares, 'I know of no way to reconcile this inconsistency' (*The Debate about the Bible* [Philadelphia: Westminster, 1977], p.106).

[2]Some manuscripts speak only of seventy, but the overall textual evidence seems to favour the number seventy-two.

145

in preparation for mission, one can hardly accuse him of error, even if he does not spell out the two stages of that mission in the same way that Luke does. Previous examples of this kind of 'telescoping' in Matthew have already appeared (see above, pp.134–138), so a further illustration should cause little surprise. Luke has then apparently edited his ninth chapter much as he did his trial narrative; assimilating some of the wording from the second commissioning speech into the first.[1] Such practices scarcely discredited the historical reputation of ancient writers in the eyes of their contemporaries (*cf.* above, p.135), so it is unfair to malign them today by applying anachronistic standards of historiography.

6 Apparent doublets

This category can apply to differences among the gospels or to repetition within one gospel itself. It is one thing to argue that Jesus often said much the same thing in more than one setting, but it is usually much more difficult to believe that two entire incidents which seem strikingly parallel could be referring to separate events. Hence scholars frequently speak of doublets – passages created by the evangelists or the early church on the basis of a genuine incident in Jesus' life which depict him doing much the same thing all over again in a new context. Thus Mark and Matthew describe Jesus miraculously feeding both 5,000 and 4,000 (Mk. 6:32–44; 8:1–10; Mt. 14:13–21; 15:32–39; unlike Luke who includes only the former [9:10b-17], since the latter forms part of Jesus' 'withdrawal from Galilee', a section which Luke omits altogether – see above, p.130). Matthew also 'doubles' the story of Jesus' healing of the blind men (Mt. 9:27–31; 20:29–34) and the account of the Pharisees' request for a sign (Mt. 12:38–42; 16:1–4). In an example which does not involve repetition within any one of the Synoptics, Luke has apparently transformed Mark's and Matthew's story of the anointing of Jesus. Instead of describing one of

---

[1]See esp. Osborne, 'Redaction Criticism', p.314. For the same basic solution, *cf.* Carson, 'Matthew', pp.241–247, who, however, addresses the problem of Luke 9:3 by assuming that 'take' means 'acquire'. For a survey of several other proposals, *cf.* B. Ahern, 'Staff or No Staff', *CBQ* 5 (1943), pp.332–337. For additional signs of conflation in Matthew 10, see esp. Robert E. Morosco, 'Matthew's Formation of a Commissioning Type-Scene out of the Story of Jesus' Commissioning of the Twelve', *JBL* 103 (1984), pp.539–556.

the women who accompanied the disciples as attending to Jesus in the home of Simon the leper in Bethany (Mk. 14:3–9; Mt. 26:6–13), he relates a story about the profuse display of affection for Jesus by a local prostitute who entered uninvited at a dinner given by a Pharisee named Simon (Lk. 7:36–50).

In every one of these instances, however, enough details differ from the one account to the next to place the theory of fictitious 'doubling' in jeopardy. In the last example of the two 'anointings' the only unusual features which Luke and Mark have in common are the name of the man whose home provided the setting (Simon) and the use of an 'alabaster flask of ointment'. But Simon was an extremely common Jewish name (Jesus himself had two disciples and a brother so called), and the phrase describing the perfume was a stereotyped one, so neither of these parallels proves decisive.[1] Otherwise the passages are quite different and should be seen as separate events from different periods in the ministry of Christ.[2]

Support for the other three examples of potential doublets is more slender still, since in each case the parallel events occur in the same gospel. That Jesus should have healed a number of blind men with much the same dialogue and in much the same fashion, or that he repeatedly had to respond to requests for spectacular signs, is entirely in keeping with the thoroughly supernatural nature of his miracle-working ministry, on which fact all the gospels agree. The repetition of the feeding of the multitudes is more surprising, but it is quite probable that the 5,000 were mostly Israelites and the 4,000 Gentiles, so that Jesus was foreshadowing the extension of the kingdom to the non-Jewish world by the duplication of the miracle. The feeding of the 4,000 is grouped with passages in which Jesus is outside Galilee and ministering to Gentiles (*cf.* Mk. 7:24–37), and the words for the 'baskets' that were used to collect the leftovers differ in the two accounts – the one referring to a container more commonly used in Palestine (*kophinos*) and the other to one more prevalent elsewhere (*spuris*).[3] Matthew 15:32 appears to presuppose this interpretation, with the crowd seemingly the same as the

---

[1]Plummer, *Luke*, p.209; Marshall, *Luke*, p.308.

[2]*Cf.* the list of supporters of this view given by Robert Holst, 'The Anointing of Jesus: Another Application of the Form-Critical Method', *JBL* 95 (1976), p.435, n. 2, though Holst himself is not among them.

[3]N. A. Beck, 'Reclaiming a Biblical Text: The Mark 8:14–21 Discussion about Bread in the Boat', *CBQ* 43 (1981), p.52, n. 15; S. Masuda, 'The Good News of the Miracle of the Bread: The Tradition and Its Markan Redaction', *NTS* 28 (1982), pp.211–212.

Gentiles of verse 31 who had 'glorified the God of Israel'.[1] The only real obstacle to belief in the two accounts as depicting separate events is the difficulty of picturing the disciples replying to Jesus a second time by asking how it would be possible to feed such a crowd (Mk. 8:4). But in Matthew's version, the emphatic position of the Greek pronoun *hēmeis* suggests that they were only protesting their inability to feed the multitude *on their own* apart from Jesus' intervention: 'Where could *we* get such bread in the wilderness so as to satisfy such a crowd?' (Mt. 15:33).[2] Carson concurs, adding that the new Gentile audience, Jesus' rebukes to the disciples elsewhere for their little faith, and the 'vast capacity for unbelief' inherent in humanity, all ensure that the disciples' response here fails to prove this passage a doublet.[3]

In general, there is little evidence for the wholesale creation of fictitious narratives in historical writing from Jesus' day; at the very least a historical core of genuine information is usually present, even when expanded by legendary embellishment. Critics have offered no convincing reasons for viewing the gospels with any less respect, and much evidence favours treating them as even more historically reliable. As most modern synopses of the gospels now stand, at least a few of the allegedly parallel passages printed in adjacent columns really represent independent traditions from different occasions in Jesus' ministry. The shorter the passage, the more plausible this becomes. A few of the most noteworthy longer examples not treated here are certain pairs of Jesus' parables – *e.g.* the marriage feast and the great banquet (Mt. 22:1–14; Lk. 14:16–24) or the talents and the pounds (Mt. 25:14–30; Lk. 19:11–27).[4]

7 Variation in names and numbers

The last category of apparent discrepancies between gospel paral-

---

[1]France, *Matthew*, pp.248–249, Mounce, *Matthew*, p.155, finds the point of the feeding of the 5,000 to be the need for 'utter dependence on God', while the feeding of the 4,000 contrasts with the general 'lack of sympathy for the gentile world'.

[2]J. Knackstedt, 'Die beiden Brotvermehrungen im Evangelium', *NTS* 10 (1963–64), pp.315–316.

[3]Carson, 'Matthew', p.358. *Cf.* Lamar Williamson, *Mark* (Atlanta: John Knox, 1983), p.142: 'The incredible dullness of the disciples is precisely the point the feeding of the four thousand intends to make in its present context.'

[4]For details, see Craig L. Blomberg, 'When Is a Parallel Really a Parallel? A Test Case: The Lucan Parables', *WTJ* 46 (1984), pp.78–103.

lels to be examined involves the seeming confusion of names and numbers. These are often compounded by textual variants, since names were frequently translated with variant spellings, while letters and symbols very similar in appearance to each other were often used to represent different numerals.

A Personal and place names

Some of the seeming inconsistencies between parallels can be resolved fairly easily. Did Jesus follow his departure from Capernaum with a preaching tour of Galilee or Judaea (Mk. 1:39; Lk. 4:44)? Probably only Galilee; Luke in several places uses the term Judaea to refer to all of Israel as the 'land of Jews' (*cf.* Lk. 6:17; 7:17; 23:5; Acts 2:9; 10:37).[1] Did Jesus preach his first great sermon on a mount or a plain (Mt. 5:1; Lk. 6:17)? Most likely he gathered the crowds on a level place in the Galilean foothills. Luke agrees that Jesus had already been higher up in mountainous terrain (Lk. 6:12), while Matthew can scarcely have envisioned the throng of people balanced on a steep incline! Since the Greek word for 'plain' can also mean 'plateau' this harmonization is a perfectly plausible one.[2]

In other cases, the problems are more complex. According to the best textual evidence, in Mark 5:1 and Luke 8:26 Jesus went to the region of the Gerasenes when he healed the demoniac called 'Legion', whereas Matthew 8:28 identifies the location as the region of the Gadarenes. Some manuscripts however supply the opposite reading in each case, while still others refer to the Gergesenes. The cities of Gerasa and Gadara both lay east of Galilee, but too far from the lake for this narrative – thirty and five miles away, respectively. The territory of Gadara seems to have included the city of Khersa, however, which lay on the eastern shore. Khersa, in Greek, could easily have been spelled the same way as Gerasa, leading to the ambiguity. Matthew, as usual, tries to clarify the ambiguity by substituting 'Gadarenes'. He presumably did not suspect that later scribes less familiar with the geography of Palestine would find this place name equally ambigu-

---

[1]Marshall, *Luke*, p.199; Fitzmyer, *Luke I–IX*, p.555.
[2]Heinz Schürmann, *Das Lukasevangelium,* vol. 1 (Freiburg: Herder, 1969), p.320. Gundry, *Matthew*, p.66, protests that large numbers of diseased people (Matt. 4:24) would hardly have been able to climb the mountain, but he overlooks the lengths to which the sick consistently went throughout Jesus' ministry in order to try to see him and be healed.

ous, so the various textual variants developed in an attempt to sort out the problem. As modern Bible translations stand, then, Mark is simply giving a Grecised spelling of the name of the city and Matthew the name of the province.[1]

By far the most complicated divergence under this heading is the seemingly hopelessly muddled genealogies of Jesus as recorded by Matthew and Luke (Mt. 1:2–17; Lk 3:23–38). Space prohibits a treatment of all the detail.[2] Suffice it to say that the two main attempts at resolution have involved viewing (a) Matthew's list as supplying Joseph's ancestry and Luke's referring to Mary's, or (b) Matthew's giving the legal succession-list for Joseph by which he was a legitimate heir to the throne of David and Luke's mentioning Joseph's actual human parents and their family tree. Jacques Masson has recently completed an extremely detailed study of the genealogies and cleverly suggests a reconstruction which combines elements of both (a) and (b), with Mary's great-great-grandfather being the same as Joseph's great-grandfather. But although most of his study convincingly explains the differences between the two lists of names involving Jesus' earlier ancestors, this final stroke relies solely on the eighth-century testimony of St. John the Damascene.[3] It is more likely that something more along the lines of (b) is the correct solution, as Gresham Machen clearly delineated a generation and a half ago.[4]

B Numbers

In several cases, one gospel refers to two characters where the parallels only mention one (two blind men in Matthew 20:30 versus one in Mark 10:46, two demoniacs in Matthew 8:28 versus one in Mark 5:2, and two angels at the tomb in Luke 24:4 versus one in Mark 16:5). Yet this phenomenon does not recur often enough to enable one to speak of a tendency in the oral tradition

---

[1]*Cf.* esp. Franz Annen, *Heil für die Heiden* (Frankfurt a. M.: Josef Knecht, 1976), pp.201–206; Cranfield, *Mark*, p.176.

[2]Again Carson is a model of clarity and conciseness in sifting through all the intricacies ('Matthew', pp.62–70).

[3]Jacques Masson, *Jésus fils de David dans les généalogies de saint Matthieu et de saint Luc* (Paris: Tequi, 1981).

[4]J. Gresham Machen, *The Virgin Birth of Christ* (New York: Harper; London: Marshall, Morgan & Scott, 1930), pp.202–209. The strongest evidence in favour of (a) involves references in the Jewish Talmud to the father of someone named Mary being Eli (*cf.* Ernst Lerle, 'Die Ahnenverzeichnisse Jesu', *ZNW* 72 [1981], pp.112–117), and to apocryphal Christian traditions who name him as Joachim (a Hebrew variant of Eliachim from which Luke's 'Heli' could have been derived).

to add characters or of a redactional concern to provide two witnesses to an event, as some have tried to do. It is more natural to suggest that there really were two characters present in each case, but that one acted as spokesman for the two and dominated the scene in a way that left the other easily ignored in narratives which so regularly omitted non-essential details.[1] In another example, ambiguous grammar is the culprit. From one point of view, Matthew 21:7 seems to be saying that Jesus straddled two donkeys (*cf.* Mk. 11:7 and Lk. 19:35 which mention only one) during his triumphal entry into Jerusalem! But common sense dictates that the second occurrence of the pronoun 'them' in the sentence which reads, 'they led the donkey and her colt and placed upon them garments and he sat upon them', refers back to the garments, not to the donkeys (and to more than one garment on one particular donkey). Perhaps the strangest difference in enumeration among the Synoptic parallels is Luke's altered description of the chronology of the transfiguration. Instead of Mark's 'after six days' (Mk. 9:2), Luke reads, 'about eight days later' (Lk. 9:28). His insertion of the word 'about' prevents this from creating a contradiction, but the reason for the difference is very difficult to pinpoint.[2]

8 Conclusion

By now the most striking dissimilarities between the various Synoptic parallels have been surveyed in some detail. Others could be mentioned but they usually admit of easier solution. It is strange how often the reliability of the gospels is impugned by scholars who believe them to be hopelessly contradictory yet who have never seriously interacted with the types of solutions proposed here. Most of these proposals readily concede that the evangelists freely reworded and rearranged the traditions they inherited, but

---

[1]Carson, 'Matthew', p.217; Gleason L. Archer, *Encyclopedia of Bible Difficulties* (Grand Rapids: Zondervan, 1982), p.325; Vern S. Poythress, 'Adequacy of Language and Accommodation', in *Hermeneutics, Inerrancy and the Bible,* ed. Earl D. Radmacher and Robert D. Preus (Grand Rapids: Zondervan, 1984), p.373.

[2]Marshall, *Gospel of Luke,* p.382, notes several possible explanations but understandably finds it difficult to endorse any with enthusiasm. Perhaps the two most likely are that Luke has abandoned a subtle Old Testament typology (Moses received the Law on Mt. Sinai after six days' preparation) or that he is simply using a more common Greek idiom for 'one week later' (using inclusive reckoning).

not to the extent that their gospels should be considered historically unreliable. The solutions suggested here may not carry equal conviction; scholars have often put forward different reconciliations for many of them. In a few cases, better solutions may still await future research. Yet unconvincing harmonization does not discredit the method itself, if more convincing alternatives are available. When one realizes that historical research regularly seeks to harmonize apparently conflicting testimonies, it becomes clear that it is wrong to disparage this method in the way which so many today do when it is applied to the gospels.[1] And even if a few of the apparent contradictions are regarded as errors (though none discussed here has seemed to merit that label), the general trustworthiness of the gospels could remain untarnished. The student who takes the time to read any three reliable historians' accounts of other ancient figures or events will frequently find much more variation among them than he encounters in the Synoptics. All these observations add up to a strong case for the historical accuracy of the first three gospels. Those who disagree may be invited to reconsider their methodology and to reflect on the possibility that they are treating the biblical documents more harshly than is warranted.

---

[1]For a detailed defence of this rather strong criticism, see Blomberg, 'Harmonization'.

Problems in the Gospel of John

A careful comparison of the first three gospels demonstrates that the similarities between them far outweigh the differences. When one turns to the Fourth Gospel, however, one seems to be in a different world altogether. The person who reads the four gospels straight through from start to finish notices this most clearly; after having read many of the same stories three times over, he or she is amazed at how different John is. As a result, a viable case for the historical reliability of the Synoptics does not automatically apply to the Gospel of John as well. As with the study of the parallels between Matthew, Mark and Luke, one must look very closely at the differences between John and the Synoptics to see whether or not they reflect genuine contradictions which discredit John's value as a record of historical fact.[1]

1 The distinctives of John's Gospel

Even a relatively superficial comparison of John with the three Synoptics reveals at least five main categories of distinctives. Probably the most obvious involves John's selection of material. Numerous features of the life of Christ, found in all three of the Synoptics, find no place in John. Some of the most noteworthy include Jesus' baptism, the calling of twelve disciples, the exorcisms, the transfiguration, the parables, and the institution of the Lord's Supper. Instead, John includes narratives and teachings found nowhere in Matthew, Mark, or Luke: the miracle of water

---

[1]The most sceptical of the major commentators on John of the last half-century is Rudolf Bultmann, *The Gospel of John* (Oxford: Blackwell; Philadelphia: Westminster, 1971 [German orig. 1941]). Most subsequent discussion has proved less sceptical but still ranks the Fourth Gospel well below the Synoptics in historical accuracy.

turned into wine, the reanimation of Lazarus, Jesus' early ministry in Judaea and Samaria, his regular visits to Jerusalem, and extended discourses in the temple and synagogues as well as in private meetings with both his disciples and his opponents.

Almost as striking are John's theological distinctives. He is the only evangelist directly to identify Jesus as fully divine (1:1; 10:30; 20:28). Whereas the Synoptics suggest to some a gradual unfolding of Jesus' own awareness about his Messianic identity, along with his disciples' blindness on this issue until Peter's climactic confession on the road to Caesarea Philippi (Mk. 8:27–30), John's opening chapter portrays John the Baptist, Andrew, Philip and Nathanael all confessing Jesus to be the Christ. Throughout John's Gospel Jesus reinforces this conclusion by referring to himself as the bread of life, the living water, the good shepherd, the vine, the resurrection and the life, the way, the truth, and the life, and even, apparently, the absolute 'I am' of the Old Testament, the name by which God the Father makes himself known. Other differences emerge in John's view of eternal life and judgment, which he sees to be already present in Christ's ministry (*e.g.* 3:18; 5:24) rather than primarily future; his presentation of John the Baptist, who denies that he is Elijah (1:21) even though the Jesus of the Synoptics said he was (Mk. 9:11–13); and his description of the time and nature of the Holy Spirit's arrival – before the ascension privately (Jn. 20:22) rather than afterwards, publicly, at Pentecost.

A third category involves apparent contradictions of chronology. The Synoptics record Jesus' attendance only at the Passover feast which immediately preceded his death, and they give no clear indication that he had ever been in Jerusalem as an adult prior to that occasion. John, however, recounts three Passovers and other lesser festivals with extensive teaching ministries of Jesus in the Jewish capital. Specific events seem to have been mislocated too. Jesus' dramatic cleansing of the temple occurs in John not as a prelude to his execution but in the earliest days of his ministry (2:14–22; *cf.* Mk. 11:15–17), his anointing by Mary of Bethany occurs not one but six days before his death (12:1; *cf.* Mk. 14:3), and the call of Andrew and Simon to be disciples takes place in Judaea prior to his return to the north instead of along the banks of the Sea of Galilee at a later date (1:35–42; *cf.* Mk. 1:16–20). John's account of the last twenty-four hours before Christ's death is brimming with apparent discrepancies. It seems to disagree with the Synoptics concerning the day on which he died (Passover rather than the day after), the number and nature of the various hearings or trials (*e.g.* before Annas, the ex-high priest, and at length before Pilate, rather than before Caiaphas and the Sanhedrin with Pilate acting to rubber-stamp their actions), and the hour of the crucifixion (sixth rather than third).

Fourth, various other ostensible historical discrepancies emerge. John shows no knowledge of Christ's birth in Bethlehem but tells how the Jews rejected Jesus since they knew that no prophet would come from Nazareth (7:52). It seems that the temple cleansing cannot be the catalyst for Jesus' arrest as in the Synoptics, since John has moved it to the start of Jesus' ministry, and he attributes Jesus' final demise to the reanimation of Lazarus instead (11:45–53). Most notably, John's reference to Jews who believed in Jesus being 'put out of the synagogue' (9:22) is widely believed to be a gross anachronism, reflecting not the historical circumstances of Jesus' life but a policy only established at the end of the first century when John's gospel was finally compiled.

Fifth, and finally, the style of John's writing differs markedly from that of the Synoptics. Jesus' language is indistinguishable from John's. Both refer regularly to such themes as light, life, witness, truth, glory, election, knowledge, abiding, the word, and the world, topics which are relatively uncommon in the first three gospels. In the discussion with Nicodemus, for example, one cannot even be sure at what point Jesus' words end and John's narrative resumes (3:10–21; probably the break occurs between verses 15–16). Further, John's Jesus regularly speaks in extended discourses rather than the short, proverbial sayings so well-known to readers of the Synoptics. And in several instances, John's narratives seem out of sequence. In Jesus' farewell discourse, the time to leave the upper room appears to have arrived with Jesus' conclusion, 'Rise, let us go hence' (14:31), but he then continues talking for another three chapters! So also John 21 reads like an afterthought appended to the original conclusion of the gospel in 20:30–31.[1]

---

[1] The Scots New Testament goes so far as to delete chap. 21 from its text, relegating it to an appendix following its translation of the book of Revelation. Yet there is no manuscript evidence to suggest that copies of the Fourth Gospel ever circulated without this chapter, so this editorial decision is wholly unjustified and misleading.

Before examining these Johannine distinctives in more detail, the features which John and the Synoptics share should also be identified. Too often discussions of John's Gospel have failed to do this, leaving the impression that it is only the divergences which are noteworthy. In fact, there are numerous correspondences of detail, many even more remarkable because they appear in passages which otherwise seem quite independent of each other. This survey will not include the stories of Jesus' arrest, trials, crucifixion, and resurrection, because there many scholars agree that John and the Synoptics shared some common sources of information. But even limiting the analysis to the rest of the gospel, where most today would see John as independent of the other evangelists, a remarkable list of parallels of various types emerges. The apparent independence of this testimony gives it added weight, since multiple attestation is an important criterion in determining historical authenticity (see p.247).

2 Similarities between John and the Synoptics

John and the Synoptics do refer to a few of the same incidents from Jesus' pre-passion ministry. Usually these are recounted with enough variation of detail to suggest that John was not relying on any of the other gospels or on a common source. Often minor details seem to conflict with their Synoptic counterparts, but closer study suggests that in fact they do not. The most important parallels include: (a) the description of John the Baptist as the fulfilment of Isaiah 40:3 ('the voice of one crying in the wilderness . . .') and the forerunner of the Messiah (Jn. 1:23/Mk. 1:2–3 pars.), (b) the contrast between John's baptism with water and the Messiah's coming baptism with the Spirit (Jn. 1:26–27, 33/Mk. 1:7–8 pars.), (c) the Spirit's anointing of Jesus as testified by the Baptist (Jn. 1:32/Mk. 1:10 pars.),[1] (d) the feeding of the 5,000 (Jn. 6:1–15/Mk. 6:32–44 pars.),[2] and (e) the walking on the water (Jn. 6:16–21/Mk. 6:45–52 par.).

---

[1] J. Ramsey Michaels, *Servant and Son: Jesus in Parable and Gospel* (Atlanta: John Knox, 1981), p.36, argues that Mark's account implies that only Jesus saw the dove, so that John's account contradicts Mark when he involves John the Baptist in the 'vision' as well. But this reads much more into the text of Mark than is actually there.

[2] If ever John is directly dependent on Mark (or on any of the Synoptics), outside of the Passion Narrative, it would be in the story of the feeding of the 5,000, where numerous correspondences of detail appear. But P. W. Barnett, 'The Feeding of the Multitude in Mark

A second category of similarities involves stories which narrate incidents unparalleled in the Synoptics but wholly in keeping with the type of thing which regularly happens in the first three gospels. Thus in both John and the Synoptics, Jesus heals the paralysed and the crippled, even using the identical words, 'Take up your bed and walk' (Jn. 5:8; Mk. 2:11). In both, Jesus gives sight to the blind, raises the dead, and cures an official's son at a distance (Jn. 4:46b–54; Lk. 7:1–10 par.) In both, Jesus defies the traditional interpretations of the Sabbath law, even to the extent of going out of his way to do unnecessary 'work' such as mixing mud and saliva in performing a healing (Jn. 9:6–7; Mk. 8:23–25), or commanding those he cured to carry their beds. Both John and the Synoptists tell of Jesus refusing to work miracles simply to satisfy his opponents (Jn. 6:30–34; Mk. 8:11–13 pars.),[1] both know of attempts to arrest Jesus prematurely which fail due to his mysterious disappearances (Jn. 8:59; 10:39; Lk. 4:29–30), both describe his friendship with Mary and Martha and characterize the two women quite similarly (Jn. 11:20; 12:2–3; Lk. 10:38–42), and both relate how some in his audiences accused him of being possessed by demons (Jn. 10:19–21; Mk. 3:22 pars.).

So too John records specific teachings of Jesus which closely resemble those found in the Synoptics, even if the contexts and important details vary. One must be born again (or become like a little child) to enter the kingdom of God (Jn. 3:3; Mk. 10:15 pars.). An abundant harvest awaits the labourers (Jn. 4:35; Mt. 9:37–38 par.). A prophet is without honour in his homeland (Jn. 4:44; Mk. 6:4 pars.). Judgment of unbelievers will be according to their works (Jn. 5:29; Mt. 25:46). The Father reveals the Son; no one knows the Father but the Son (Jn. 10:14–15; 13:3; 17:2, 25; Mt. 11:25–27 par.). Jesus and, derivatively, his disciples are the light of the world (Jn. 8:12; Mt. 5:14 par.). Part of the purpose of Jesus' teaching is to harden the hearts of those already opposed to him, with Isaiah 6:9 cited in defence of this (Jn. 9:39;

6/John 6', in *GP*,6, pp.273–297, has made a strong case for independence. Barnett examines in minute detail the linguistic parallels and divergences and concludes that the similarities occur only in those places where an accurate account of the event could be told in no other way, but that wherever the narratives can vary they do.

[1]The often made claim that, in John, Jesus works signs to prove he is the Messiah (*contra* the Synoptics) is a one-sided view of the evidence, since John elsewhere plays down the value of signs (see esp. 20:29). For a more balanced treatment of the Fourth Gospel's ambivalent view on the value of signs, see Robert Kysar, *John: The Maverick Gospel* (Richmond: John Knox, 1976), pp.65–83.

12:39–40; Mk. 4:12 pars.; 8:17–18 pars.). Jesus identifies himself metaphorically with the good shepherd who seeks to rescue the errant members of his flock (Jn. 10:1–16; Mt. 18:12–14; Lk. 15:3–7). True discipleship means servanthood as illustrated in the Last Supper (Jn. 13:4–5, 12–17; Lk. 22:24–27). Jesus faces and resists the temptation to abandon the way of the cross (Jn. 12:27; Mk. 14:35–36 pars.). Receiving Jesus means receiving the one who sent him (Jn. 12:44–45; Mk. 9:37; Mt. 10:40; Lk. 10:16). The disciple is not greater than his master (Jn. 13:16; Mt. 10:24; Lk. 6:40). The Holy Spirit will tell the apostles what to say in the future (Jn. 14:26; 15:26; Mk. 13:11; Mt. 10:19–20 par.). The disciples will be expelled from the synagogues (Jn. 16:1–4; Mk. 13:9; Mt. 10:17–18 par.), scattered throughout various parts of the world (Jn. 16:32; Mk. 14:27 pars.), and given the authority to retain or forgive the sins of their brothers (Jn. 20:23; Mt. 18:18).[1]

Other similarities are less specific but equally worthy of mention. Granted John contains no clear narrative parables like those found so often in the Synoptics, he nevertheless presents a picture of a Jesus who is equally fond of metaphors and figurative or proverbial comparisons. In addition to those mentioned above, one may consider the vine and vinedresser (15:1–6), the son's apprenticeship (5:19–20a), working and walking in the daylight (9:4; 11:9–10), the thief, the gatekeeper, and the sheepfold (10:1–3a), sowing versus reaping (4:37), slavery versus sonship (8:35), the growth of a grain of wheat (12:24), or the pain of a woman in labour (16:21).[2] In both John and the other gospels the crowds regularly marvel at the authority with which Jesus teaches, surpassing that of the Jewish leaders.[3] Both disclose the persistent misunderstanding of Jesus' audiences, including the disciples, con-

---

[1] Barnabas Lindars, *The Gospel of John* (London: Marshall, Morgan & Scott, 1972; Grand Rapids: Eerdmans, 1981), *passim,* argues that these Synoptic-like sayings in John are authentic teachings of Jesus embedded in new contexts which the fourth evangelist has created for them. *Cf.* his 'Discourse and Tradition: The Use of the Sayings of Jesus in the Discourses of the Fourth Gospel', *JSNT* 13 (1981), pp.83–101. This is a significant advance over older scepticism even if still a fair distance from the position of historical trustworthiness for which this chapter argues.

[2] *Cf.* further C. H. Dodd, *Historical Tradition in the Fourth Gospel* (Cambridge: University Press, 1963), pp.366–387; A. M. Hunter, *According to John* (London: SCM; Philadelphia: Westminster, 1968), pp.78–89; Kim E. Dewey, '*Paroimiai* in the Gospel of John', *Semeia* 17 (1980), pp. 81–99.

[3] See esp. John W. Wenham, *Christ and the Bible* (Leicester and Downers Grove: IVP, 1984), pp.43–61.

cerning the nature of his Messiahship.[1] Both reveal that Jesus' favourite title for referring to himself was the somewhat ambiguous phrase 'Son of man', and in none of the gospels is this title used by anyone other than Jesus to describe himself.[2] Mark and John explicitly relate that the two titles most crucial to their understanding of Jesus' nature are 'the Christ' and 'the Son of God' (Mk. 1:1; Jn. 20:31). One of the most characteristic introductions to Jesus' sayings in the Synoptics is the Hebrew 'Amen' ('verily' or 'truly'); Jesus uses this equally often in John, though it always appears in doubled form ('Amen, amen, I say to you . . .').[3] In all four gospels, finally, Jesus reveals a uniquely intimate relationship with his Father as characterized by the Aramaic word 'Abba' (almost but not quite 'Daddy'), which would have horrified the Jews accustomed to approaching God with greater sense of distance and respect.[4]

Most of the above parallels match details of John with details in Mark. Many of the distinctives of John's passion narrative have striking parallels to features found elsewhere only in Luke. Gerhard Maier, however, notes additional distinctive links between John and Matthew. Perhaps the five most significant are: (a) the extensive use of Old Testament quotations and the announcement of their fulfilment, (b) the frequency, extent, location, and instructional nature of extended sermons of Jesus, (c) elaborate farewell speeches (the Upper Room and Olivet Discourses), (d) an emphasis on private instruction for the disciples, and (e) an evangelistic purpose which sees the Christian gospel as being offered first to the Jew and then to all the Gentiles. Maier concludes that John and Matthew, usually viewed as the least similar of any pair of the four gospels, are in fact much more complementary than is normally admitted.[5]

---

[1]See esp. J. Coutts, 'The Messianic Secret in St. John's Gospel', *TU* 88 (1964), pp. 45–57.

[2]John 12:34 is no exception, since the crowd is simply asking Jesus about his use of the title. 'Son of man' thus occurs thirteen times in John, compared with twelve uses by Jesus of the unqualified title 'Son', and three by him of 'Son of God' as a title. But even then the statistics are deceptive, since the Son of man references are well scattered about John's Gospel, while over half of Jesus' use of 'Son' by itself occur in 5:19–26.

[3]Lindars, *John, passim,* rightly recognizes this formula as the sign of an authentic saying of Jesus. The doubling may reflect liturgical use or recognition of the term as an indicator of emphasis.

[4]The Aramaic word appears in Greek transliteration in the gospels only in Mark 14:36 but is assumed widely to underlie Jesus' numerous uses of the standard Greek *patēr* – 'father' in all four gospels.

[5]Gerhard Maier, 'Johannes und Matthäus – Zweispalt oder Viergestalt des Evangeliums?' in *GP*,2, pp.267–291.

3 Authorship and date

Before returning to the problem of the apparent contradictions between John and the Synoptics, a few other introductory remarks are in order. Those who would defend John's historicity have regularly appealed to the privileged position of the apostle John – Jesus' 'beloved disciple', one of an intimate circle of three (with Peter and James) who experienced events which the other nine disciples did not (*e.g.* the transfiguration or the agony in Gethsemane). Even though early church tradition claimed that the Fourth Gospel was the last to be written, just before the beginning of the second century when John was a very old man, it was argued that the events and teachings of the two to three years he spent with Jesus would have been indelibly impressed upon his memory and thus reliably preserved.

Today, for a variety of reasons, not all of equal weight, all but the most conservative of scholars no longer believe that John the apostle was the author of the Fourth Gospel. The strongest of these reasons stems from the data of the gospel itself. The 'beloved disciple' (and it is never clear that this disciple must be John since he remains unnamed) is referred to in the third person, not as an 'I' or a 'we' who is writing the book, while the work concludes with a reference to a 'we' who 'know that his testimony is true' (21:24). Moreover, the last episode in the book seems designed to correct the erroneous belief that had spread around the churches that the beloved disciple would stay alive until Jesus' second coming (21:20–23). The most natural way of explaining why the gospel writer should have included these verses is that the disciple had just died, and certain Christians were having trouble reconciling his death with the fact that Christ had not yet returned.[1] Many scholars go so far as to postulate several editors who continually expanded an original core of the Fourth Gospel, so that only a small historical nucleus need be linked with eyewitness testimony.[2]

---

[1]Stephen S. Smalley, *John: Evangelist and Interpreter* (Exeter: Paternoster; Grand Rapids: Zondervan, 1978); p.81.

[2]Two of the most widely-cited representatives of this position are Raymond E. Brown, *The Gospel according to John,* 2 vols. (Garden City: Doubleday, 1966–70; London: Geoffrey

In fact a strong case for the apostle John's having written a substantial portion of the Fourth Gospel – perhaps even all but the closing verses – can still be credibly defended.[1] But the question of John's historical reliability depends surprisingly little on the viability of such a case. Recent Johannine scholarship has gone a long way to undermine earlier scepticism simply by pointing out evidence for the bulk of the gospel relying on sources with highly accurate details about Palestinian geography, topography and religious custom.[2] The Dead Sea Scrolls have provided parallels to theological concepts once associated exclusively with Greek thought. Archaeological digs have unearthed the probable remains of the pool of Bethesda (Jn. 5:2) and the Pavement (19:13), which were previously unknown (and unmentioned in the Synoptics). That John's Gospel relies heavily on early, Palestinian sources with reliable historical information, regardless of its final date and author(s), has been demonstrated in massive detail by the writings of C. H. Dodd.[3] But Dodd stops well short of arguing that all of John's information is accurate, largely due to the differences with the Synoptics already surveyed.[4] So as with the study of those three gospels, analysis must proceed

---

Chapman, 1971), who argues for five stages of composition; and J. Louis Martyn, *History and Theology in the Fourth Gospel* (Nashville: Abingdon, 1979), who reads the events of John's narrative as ciphers for the controversies plaguing the Johannine community at the end of the first century. For a survey of Johannine source criticism see D. A. Carson, 'Current Source Criticism of the Fourth Gospel: Some Methodological Questions', *JBL* 97 (1978), pp.411–429. The approach of Bultmann and earlier commentators which involved actually rearranging the order of various chapters and verses in John to try to reconstruct an original, smoother 'first edition' has now for the most part been rightly abandoned. *Cf.* C. K. Barrett, *The Gospel according to St. John* (London: SPCK; Philadelphia: Westminster, 1978), p.26. For this reason questions of alleged inconsistencies between one part of John and another will be laid to one side.

[1] See esp. in brief, F. F. Bruce, *The Gospel of John* (Grand Rapids: Eerdmans, 1983; Basingstoke: Pickering & Inglis, 1984), pp.1–6; and in detail, B. F. Westcott, *The Gospel according to St. John* (London: John Murray, 1908; Grand Rapids: Baker, 1980) vol. 1, ix–lxvii; and Leon Morris, *Studies in the Fourth Gospel* (Exeter: Paternoster; Grand Rapids: Eerdmans, 1969), pp.215–292.

[2] See esp. Smalley, *John,* pp.9–40. *Cf.* R. D. Potter, 'Topography and Archaeology in the Fourth Gospel', *TU* 73 (1959), pp.329–337; Hunter, *John,* pp.42–43.

[3] C. H. Dodd, *Historical Tradition in the Fourth Gospel* (Cambridge: University Press, 1963); also *The Interpretation of the Fourth Gospel* (Cambridge: University Press, 1953), pp.444–453. The use of sources is not incompatible with apostolic authorship. Historians of any age who were eyewitnesses of the events they report are often glad to consult other sources which enable them to double-check and to supplement their memories.

[4] As amply documented by D. A. Carson, 'Historical Tradition in the Fourth Gospel: After Dodd, What?' in *GP,*2, pp.83–145. *Cf.* the subsequent debate in J. S. King, 'Has D. A. Carson

beyond general considerations of the circumstances in which the gospel was written to face squarely the alleged contradictions.

4 The alleged contradictions reconsidered

A Omissions and singly attested material

John's omission of so much of what the Synoptics contain and his inclusion of much of what they leave out should cause little surprise. On any theory of the gospel's composition, he had much material from which to choose. If John had already read the Synoptics and was writing later, then he undoubtedly assumed that much of what they emphasized needed no further repetition. Instead he focused on information they omitted in order to supplement them. If John wrote independently of the first three gospels, then the variation is due simply to the large body of information from which he could select. John 20:30 and 21:25 plainly allow this possibility ('Jesus did many other signs . . . which are not written in this book'; 'there are also many other things which Jesus did . . .'). Any two ancient historians' accounts of a given person or period of history differ from each other at least as much as John does from the Synoptics, when they do not rely on common sources for their information.[1]

Some would argue, though, that if certain events found only in John or only in the Synoptics really happened, then they could hardly have been omitted from any fair presentation of the gospel. Yet in fact many of the omissions or singly attested events *are* broadly paralleled elsewhere. Jesus works spectacular miracles in the first three gospels, including raising the dead, even if the miracles of changing water into wine and raising Lazarus are missing. The latter did not occur in Galilee, which is the main focus of the Synoptists, and the disciples on which the first three evangelists rely for their information may not have been present for this miracle.[2] John may omit Christ's baptism and the first

---

Been Fair to C. H. Dodd?' *JSNT* 17 (1983), pp.97–102; and D. A. Carson, 'Historical Tradition in the Fourth Gospel: A Response to J. S. King', *JSNT* 23 (1985), pp.73–81.

[1]*Cf. e.g.* the emphasis on the selective nature of ancient historians' writings in Martin Hengel, *Acts and the History of Earliest Christianity* (London: SCM; Philadelphia: Fortress, 1979), pp.3–34.

[2]Murray J. Harris, 'The Dead Are Restored to Life: Miracles of Revivification in the Gospels', in *GP*,6, p.312.

'eucharist', but he alone includes Jesus' discourse with Nicodemus about the need to be born of water as well as the Spirit (3:3–21; see verse 5) and the sermon in the Capernaum synagogue on eating his flesh and drinking his blood (6:26–59; see esp. verses 53, 56).[1] In many cases the motives for the inclusion or omission of a particular detail may be irrecoverable, but that is no valid reason for rejecting its genuineness.[2]

B Theological differences

Much more serious are the apparently divergent theologies which John and the Synoptics offer. By far the most striking themes on which they seem to differ are their views of who Christ was and how he understood his own identity and mission. This theme will be dealt with first and the other themes more summarily.

1 Christology

Certainly John is the only evangelist to make such direct statements as 'In the beginning was the Word, and the Word was with God, and the Word was God' (1:1). Yet John fails to report the virgin birth, which reflects 'high' Synoptic Christology, although his prologue may be his substitute. Nor should it be thought that John stresses only the deity of Christ, for his humanity remains equally in the forefront. The starting point of John's prologue is the unity of the Father and the Son, but its culmination is the incarnation: 'the Word became flesh and lived among us' (1:14). Jesus may declare that he and his Father are one in a sense which the Jews interpret as a blasphemous equation with God (10:30), but overall his discourses dwell much more on his subordinate role in doing nothing but what the Father commands (*cf.* esp. 14:28: 'the Father is greater than I').[3] In the case of the Synoptics, Matthew and Luke could hardly have believed that Jesus was

---

[1]For a well-balanced presentation of John's 'sacramental' and 'non-sacramental' tendencies, see R. Wade Paschal, 'Sacramental Symbolism and Physical Imagery in the Gospel of John', *TynB* 32 (1981), pp.151–176. Of course, John 3 and 6 have both been interpreted so as not to refer to baptism or the eucharist at any level.

[2]*Cf.* Brown, *John*, I, xlii–xliii. Paul Doncoeur's view ('Des silences de l'évangile de saint Jean', *RSR* 22 (1934), pp.606–609) that much of what John omits paints the disciples, and especially John, in a better light than his humility permitted him to recount, also deserves further exploration.

[3]For a balanced presentation of Jesus' deity and humanity in John, with special reference to chs. 13–17, see D. A. Carson, *The Farewell Discourse and Final Prayer of Jesus* (Grand Rapids:

merely a man like all others, however exalted or honoured by God, when they include the accounts of his conception by the Holy Spirit and only one human parent (Mt. 1:18; Lk. 1:35). As I. H. Marshall emphasizes, 'the evidence in the Synoptic Gospels not only fits an incarnational understanding of Jesus but positively cries out for it'.[1]

If the evangelists' assessments of Jesus are not incompatible, what then of Jesus' own self-understanding in the various gospels? For example, how can the Jesus of the Synoptics, who is constantly telling those who confess him to be the Messiah to tell no one about it, be the same Jesus who in John responds to the Samaritan woman's statement about the coming of the Christ with the plain affirmation, 'I am he' (4:26)? What of all the other so-called 'I am' sayings? In the case of the Samaritan woman, it was no doubt precisely her identity which enabled Jesus to speak plainly. The Samaritans for the most part were not expecting the Messiah to be a nationalistic, militaristic ruler as were many in first-century Judaism; instead they were looking for a teacher and a lawgiver much more consistent with the role that Jesus envisaged for himself.[2]

The other 'I am' statements are in fact much more ambiguous and metaphorical than is generally realized, because modern readers are so influenced by the history of their interpretation. A first-century Jewish audience hearing a rabbi refer to himself as, say, the bread of life would probably not have known what to make of it, and that is precisely the response which John records (6:60). Jesus is described as using the formula 'I am' much more often in the Fourth Gospel than in the Synoptics but it is not clear that these revelations make his claims for himself that much more explicit. Jesus' apparently ungrammatical proclamation, 'Before Abraham was I am' (8:58), may refer back to the divine name revealed in Exodus 3:14, 'I am what I am', but it is not obvious that in the rigidly monotheistic context of Judaism this would be the only conclusion drawn. The fact that the Jews immediately tried to stone him does not mean they understood his statement as

---

Baker, 1980 [= *Jesus and His Friends* (Leicester: IVP, 1986)]); on these themes in the gospel more generally, *cf.* P. Pokorny, 'Der irdische Jesus im Johannesevangelium', *NTS* 30 (1984), pp.217–228.

[1]I. Howard Marshall, 'Incarnational Christology in the New Testament', in *Christ the Lord*, ed. H. H. Rowdon (Leicester: IVP, 1982), p.15.

[2]Brown, *John,* I, pp.172–173.

a direct equation of himself with God. Claiming that Abraham had seen his day (verse 56) itself bordered on blasphemy, and the Jews had already tried to kill him for much lesser 'crimes' such as healing on the Sabbath (Mk. 3:6) and speaking of God's love for the Gentiles (Lk. 4:29)!

The accuracy of John's perspectives on the self-understanding of Jesus may be defended by at least four further arguments.[1] First, whatever the precise implications of Jesus' 'I am' statements, they follow a format virtually unparalleled in the first-century world. No other known religious leaders used first person metaphors quite like 'I am the vine' or 'I am the resurrection and the life', and so forth. The nearest parallels are in papyri and inscriptions describing the claims of the mythical Egyptian goddess Isis, who was popular throughout the ancient Greek-speaking world. But these 'I am' statements tend to be more straightforward ('I am the one who discovered fruit for men'; 'I am the one who is called goddess among women') and for the most part date from a period too late to have influenced the composition of John's gospel.[2] The much more natural background for Jesus' 'I am' statements is the Old Testament name for God,[3] even if Jesus sufficiently veiled it so that his claims were not always thought blasphemous.

Second, when the Jews directly confront Jesus with the question of his identity, he replies as cryptically in John as in any of the other gospels. In John 8:25 they ask, 'who are you?' and Jesus responds, 'even what I have told you from the beginning', while in 10:25 he answers their plea to 'tell us plainly' merely with the retort, 'I told you, and you do not believe.' Even his disciples do not think he is speaking clearly to them until he has almost finished his farewell discourse on the night of his arrest (16:29).[4] Third, on

---

[1]For a vigorous defence of the authenticity of these sayings, see E. Stauffer, *Jesus and His Story* (London: SCM; New York: Knopf, 1960), pp.142–159. *Cf.* Calvin T. Stevens, 'The "I AM" Formula in the Gospel of John', *Studia Biblica et Theologica* 7.2 (1977), pp.19–30.

[2]The inscription from which these two examples of 'I am' statements are taken is the earliest of its kind so far discovered and does date from the first half of the first century. See G. H. R. Horsley, *New Documents Illustrating Early Christianity,* vol. 1 (North Ryde: Macquarie, 1981), pp.10–21. But the closer, metaphorical parallels in the Mandaean, Hermetic and Gnostic literature are at least one to two centuries later.

[3]Brown, *John,* I, pp.533–538; Philip B. Harner, *The 'I Am' of the Fourth Gospel* (Philadelphia: Fortress, 1970), who both find the most immediate background in Isaiah's use of 'I am' as a name for God (*cf. e.g.* Is. 47:8, 10).

[4]*Cf.* D. A. Carson, 'Understanding Misunderstandings in the Fourth Gospel', *TynB* 33 (1982), p.84: 'no evangelist surpasses John in preserving the sense of *confusion* surrounding Jesus' identity.'

at least two occasions, the Synoptics also utilize the 'I am' form of address, with overtones somewhat reminiscent of the divine name. When Jesus appears walking on the water, his words, 'Do not fear, it is I' (Mk. 6:50), could equally be translated, 'Do not fear, I am', and when he speaks of false Christs who will come claiming 'I am he' (Mk. 13:6), the words again literally read 'I am'.

Finally, and most importantly, however exalted John's view of Jesus may seem, it contains nothing which is not implicit in the picture painted by Matthew, Mark and Luke of a man who would sovereignly overrule Jewish interpretations of the Law, claim that his words would last forever, pronounce the forgiveness of sins, describe humanity's eternal destiny as dependent on its reaction to him, demand absolute loyalty from his disciples, offer rest for the weary and salvation for the lost, promise to be with his followers always, and guarantee that God would grant them any prayers requested in his name.[1] Even if one analyses only those few Synoptic sayings of Jesus which are regarded as authentic by almost all scholars, by virtue of their distinctiveness over against the teachings of both Judaism and the early church (the so-called 'criterion of dissimilarity' – see below, p.247), one finds included many of the above-mentioned claims which require one to assume that Jesus viewed himself as more than a man. Royce Gruenler has examined these in great detail and comes to a conclusion which is highly unusual in today's scholarly climate but worthy of serious consideration: 'I honestly cannot say that I find a single explicit christological utterance of Jesus in the Gospels, including the Gospel of John, that is generically inappropriate to his implicit claims arrived at by the criterion of dissimilarity.'[2]

2 Other themes

It is increasingly being recognized that alleged tensions between John and the Synoptics on the other theological topics noted at the outset of this chapter have been overstated.[3] John actually

---

[1]For these and similar characteristics, see R. T. France, 'The Worship of Jesus: A Neglected Factor in Christological Debate?' in Rowdon, *Christ the Lord*, p.28. *Cf.* also Westcott, *John*, I, clxix–clxx.

[2]Royce G. Gruenler, *New Approaches to Jesus and the Gospels* (Grand Rapids: Baker, 1982), p.15. For a broader overview of John's Christology as complementary to that of the Synoptics, see George E. Ladd, *A Theology of the New Testament* (Grand Rapids: Eerdmans, 1974; Guildford: Lutterworth, 1975), pp.237–253.

[3]See esp. Smalley, *John*, pp.191–242.

presents eternal life and judgment as both present and future, even if he tends to emphasize the former more than the Synoptics do.[1] Thus he can juxtapose in consecutive verses such teachings of Jesus as 'Truly, truly, I say to you that he who hears my word and believes in the one who sent me has eternal life and is not coming into judgment, but has passed out of death into life' (5:24), and 'Truly, truly, I say to you that an hour is coming, and now is, when the dead will hear the voice of the Son of God and those who hear will live . . . for an hour is coming in which all who are in their graves will hear his voice and will go out, those having done good to the resurrection of life but those having practised evil to the resurrection of judgment' (5:25, 28–29). Or, on the issue of John's view of his namesake, the Baptist may have denied being Elijah because he assumed the Pharisees were asking about a literal heavenly Elijah returning to earth, as some Jews thought he would.[2]

The so-called Johannine Pentecost is more puzzling; it certainly seems as if Jesus dispenses the Spirit before his ascension when he gives the disciples authority to lead his church in fulfilment of all the promises regarding the Paraclete, whom he had said he would bestow. Attempts to reduce Jesus' 'breathing out' the Spirit on the disciples to a symbolic gesture or enacted parable portending a still future event leave John's narrative inexplicably incomplete. Why would he bother to foreshadow an event which he never describes? Allegations that John has transformed the account of Acts 2 into this entirely different scenario overlook the fact that not all the disciples are present (Thomas is missing) and that the rest of the gospel does not at all depict the disciples as fully empowered for service. At the beginning of chapter 21, Peter simply returns to his fishing without having been reinstated as a disciple in good standing.[3] More importantly, John 20:19–23 functions quite differently from Acts 2. Luke's Pentecost narrative focuses almost exclusively on the disciples' preaching to others; here all attention centres on

---

[1]Ibid., pp.235–241.

[2]M. de Jonge, 'Jewish Expectations about the "Messiah" according to the Fourth Gospel', *NTS* 19 (1972–73), pp.246–270, who also notes that many Jews believed in a 'hidden Messiah' who would not know who he was or have any power until Elijah came and revealed him; perhaps John wanted to deny for himself this role as well.

[3]Both ch. 21 and the references to Thomas in ch. 20 have been dismissed as secondary additions, in which case these objections would lose their force. But, on ch. 21, *cf.* pp.187–188. 20:24–29 is much more difficult to separate from 20:19–23 because of its continuity with preceding material in style and content.

Jesus' commissioning the disciples. If a Lucan analogy must be found, Luke 24:49 would be a more viable candidate. There, as in John 20:21, Jesus is speaking to the disciples on the evening after his resurrection and is specifically sending them forth in a context which refers to the empowering of the Holy Spirit ('the promise of the Father').[1]

A very attractive explanation therefore views John's and Luke's narratives as describing separate events, both equally real and significant. The resurrection of Jesus was the climactic vindication of his sinless life and unjust death, yet his ascension to the right hand of the Father was needed to complete the process and to make public to the universe his triumph and sovereignty. So also Jesus' breathing out the Spirit gave the disciples the authority to lead the company of his followers, even though the full, public and permanent manifestation of this gift would arrive only at Pentecost.[2] To put it almost simplistically, in John 20 the disciples receive the Spirit; in Acts 2 they are filled with the Spirit, who empowers them to preach the gospel boldly. Luke consistently associates the filling or fulness of the Holy Spirit with special occasions in which the disciples fearlessly witness for Christ (*e.g.* Acts 4:8; 7:55; 13:9), even though the Spirit remains more generally with believers at all times. Nothing in Luke or Acts demands that Pentecost be seen as the first occasion in which the disciples had any experience of the Spirit; the reference to their coming 'baptism' in the Spirit in Acts 1:5 is best taken as referring to the immersion or filling which occurred at Pentecost, and not just to an initiatory experience. The reason for the gap between the reception and the filling of the Spirit, then, is that at the time of John 20:22 Christ was not yet ascended (*cf.* Jn. 7:39).[3]

---

[1]*Cf.* J. Ramsey Michaels, *John* (San Francisco: Harper & Row, 1984), p.335: 'Historically, there are hints in Luke and Acts that *even before Pentecost* the Spirit indeed played a role in the ministry of the risen Jesus to his disciples.' After citing Acts 1:2; Luke 24:25, 49a as examples, Michaels adds, 'Clearly something is given and something is still expected. Luke's emphasis is largely on what is still expected, whereas John's emphasis is exclusively on what is already given.'

[2]*Cf.* Bruce, *John*, p.397, n. 18. Good, detailed treatments of this problem are hard to find. M. M. B. Turner, 'The Concept of Receiving the Spirit in John's Gospel', *Vox Evangelica* 10 (1977), pp.24–42, has the best survey of previous scholarship, but the position which he adopts is not clearly explained. *Cf.* also Max-Alain Chevallier, ' "Pentecôtes" lucaniennes et "Pentecôtes" johanniques', *RSR* 69 (1981), pp.301–313; and E. C. Hoskyns and F. N. Davey, *The Fourth Gospel* (London: Faber & Faber, 1954), p.653.

[3]John 20:17b's 'I am ascending' must be a future-referring present tense, even without Luke's mention of a forty-day interval between the resurrection and ascension (Acts 1:3), since Jesus continues to appear to the disciples in the rest of John chs. 20–21 and John gives no indication

C Chronological problems

1 The overall outline of John

How long did Jesus' ministry last? Interestingly, those who find John and the Synoptics irreconcilable here usually argue that John's information is right and the Synoptics' wrong. For a number of reasons a two-to-three year ministry, which John's three Passovers demand, stands up much better to scholarly scrutiny than a one-year ministry.[1] But there is nothing in the Synoptics which *limits* Jesus' ministry to a year, so it would seem that this problem has been exaggerated. In fact, the Synoptics contain remarkably few references to time, place, or sequence of events, whereas John is replete with chronological and geographical details. Although it stands much traditional commentary of both conservative and liberal persuasion on its head, a strong case can be made for the view that John describes the ministry of Jesus almost entirely in chronological order (though omitting numerous episodes), whereas the Synoptics are more topical in their structure, especially for Jesus' Galilean and Peraean ministries.

All this of course depends on taking the gospel data at face value. Many would argue that John's references to time and place were not meant to be taken literally but symbolically. But no convincing scheme has been proposed for interpreting his wealth of references in a consistently non-historical fashion; whatever symbolism may be present seems to be in addition to the historical data rather than instead of them. Thus when John notes that the wedding at Cana happened on the third day (2:1), it may be due to a parallel he sees with the resurrection on the third day, and the joy of Jesus' restoration to his bride, the church. But whether or not this additional symbolism is present, the wedding most likely did actually happen two days after Jesus first called Peter and Andrew, since there are no particular symbolic overtones to suggest that the events of the previous day (the calling of Philip and Nathanael – 1:43–51) did not take place at that exact time.[2] If the

---

that these are different types of appearances from the one Mary experienced (as if *e.g.* he was now appearing from heaven after his ascension, as to Paul on the Damascus road).

[1]For details see J. A. T. Robinson, *The Priority of John* (London: SCM, 1985; Philadelphia: Westminster, 1986), pp.123–157, with a chart on p.157. *Cf.* R. Schnackenburg, *The Gospel according to St. John,* vol. 1 (London: Burns & Oates, 1968; New York: Crossroad, 1980), p.345.

[2]For a balanced view of history and symbolism in John's references to time and place, see R. Kieffer, 'L'espace et le temps dans l'évangile de Jean', *NTS* 31 (1985), pp.393–409. Kieffer

'second day' literally followed the first, then the 'third day' should be interpreted similarly.

Further support for John's overall outline of Jesus' ministry surfaces when one considers that even within the space of one year, faithful Jews would have tried to go to Jerusalem for several of the annual festivals held there. Whatever else Jesus may have challenged in Judaism, there is no evidence for his despising these holy days, so it is entirely appropriate that he should have made more trips to Jerusalem than just the one described in the Synoptics. More positively, the stories of the first three gospels contain specific hints that his trip to Jerusalem immediately before his crucifixion was not his first. How was he able to command his disciples to make provisions for the Last Supper just by meeting a man with a water jar (Mk. 14:13–16) or to gain a donkei and her colt for his triumphal procession just by going to a certain village and saying, 'The master needs them' (Mk. 11:1–6)? Where had he met Mary and Martha (Lk. 10:38–42), with whom he presumably lodged in Bethany during the last week before his death (Mt. 21:17)? To what occasions was he referring when he lamented over Jerusalem 'how often I would have gathered your children together as a hen gathers her chicks under her wings, and you would not' (Mt. 23:37)? Why were there Judaeans present in Galilee already stirring up trouble for Jesus at the start of his ministry there (Mk. 3:8)? All these questions find a ready answer if one accepts John's outline of Christ visiting Jerusalem frequently over a period of two or more years. Finally, one must not misread John either; he like the Synoptics knows that a large part of Jesus' ministry took place in Galilee (7:3) even if he has not chosen to emphasize this fact.[1]

2 Specific dislocations?

For many commentators, one of the divergences between John and the Synoptics which most clearly illustrates John's lack of interest in historical sequence involves the various accounts of the cleansing of the temple. In the Synoptics, Jesus re-enters Jeru-

---

notes that most of the details which have a fairly clear double meaning are not the specific references to date or location but more general expressions such as 'being lifted up' (referring both to the crucifixion and subsequent glorification in heaven) or 'it is finished' (referring both to the drink offered Jesus on the cross and his life with its atoning significance).

[1]A. C. Headlam, *The Fourth Gospel as History* (Oxford: Blackwell, 1948), p.8.

salem the morning after 'Palm Sunday', ejects the merchants, overturns their tables, forbids further commerce, and supports his stance by citing Scripture ('My house shall be called a house of prayer for all the nations, but you have made it a den of thieves' – Mk. 11:17; *cf.* Is. 56:7, Je. 7:11). In John the cleansing occurs at the very outset of Jesus' ministry. This time Jesus uses a rope for a whip to drive out the animals, again upsets the furniture and forces the merchants to leave, but objects to their actions on different grounds: 'stop making my father's house a house of commerce' (2:16). John then notes that the disciples later associated this action with the Old Testament text, 'zeal for your house will devour me' (Ps. 69:9). He also appends a subsequent dialogue in which Jesus replies to the authorities' demand for a sign to justify his action by prophesying, 'Destroy this temple and in three days I will raise it up,' a prophecy which was not understood until after the resurrection. Which version is the accurate one, or are both somewhat distorted? Or can both be 'right' at the same time?

It is tempting to suggest that both John and the Synoptics have excerpted different segments from a larger whole and to assume that, as they so often do elsewhere, one or the other has relocated this event according to a topical rather than a chronological outline. The Synoptists make it clear that Jesus' cleansing the temple proved to be 'the last straw' for the Jewish authorities, sealing his imminent doom (Mk. 11:18), so a convincing harmonization would require John to be the evangelist who has relocated the passage. The strongest evidence in support of this suggestion is twofold. First, John 2:13–25 is the only passage in the opening four chapters of John which is not linked to what precedes or follows it by an explicit reference to chronological sequence. Second, most commentators recognize a major division in John's Gospel between chapters 11–12, and chapter 12 introduces the second 'half' of the gospel with a chronologically dislocated passage (see p.173). One could therefore assume that the cleansing of the temple introduces the first 'half' in the same way, with the six-day sequence of 1:1–2:12 as an introduction.[1]

On the other hand, it is at least possible that Jesus cleansed the

---

[1]On these two points, with important variations, *cf.* R. T. France, 'Chronological Aspects of Gospel Harmony', *Vox Evangelica* 16 (1986), pp.40–43; Michaels, *John*, xxvi–xxvii.

temple twice.[1] Although this option is seldom taken seriously today except in a few conservative circles, at least six factors support it. (1) Except for the bare minimum of content required to narrate a temple cleansing, all the details differ from the one account to the other. (2) If Jesus felt strongly enough about the temple corruption to purify it once at the outset of his ministry, it would be only natural for him to do it again at the end. (3) He could probably have done the deed once with impunity, since it was an overtly Messianic act which at least some of the Jews would have approved. But once it became clear that his concept of Messiahship was not what most of the Jews were looking for, a repetition would almost certainly have sealed his fate. This danger explains why he offered no objections during his intermediate visits to Jerusalem, although the Jewish traders may well have gone back to their practices soon after the initial confrontation. (4) In the Synoptics, Jesus is accused at the end of his life of having threatened to destroy the Jewish temple and in three days build another 'not made by (human) hands' (Mk. 14:58 pars.), an apparent reference to the type of thing he explicitly says only in John 2:19. But the garbled detail of this accusation, coupled with Mark's observation that the witnesses could not agree (Mk. 14:59), makes more sense as a confused recollection of something said two or three years earlier, not just a few days ago. (5) The difference in the severity of Jesus' remarks is appropriate to each of the two contexts; only at the end of his ministry does he call the Jews thieves and incite racist outrage by referring to the Gentiles' need to pray in the temple court originally reserved for them (Mk. 11:17). (6) In John's account the Jews reply with a reference to the rebuilding of the temple having begun 46 years ago (Jn. 2:20), a figure which places this event in AD 27 or 28.[2] But Jesus was probably not crucified until at least AD 30, and John would not have invented such an incidental confirmation of chronology if he

---

[1]Unlike some of the discrepancies among the gospels which were hotly debated in the early church, this one seems to have been explained quite uniformly in this way until recent centuries. See the detailed documentation in F. Braun, 'L'expulsion des vendeurs du temple', RB 38 (1929), p.178. But recall the approach of Tatian (p.3).

[2]Herod's reign effectively began in 37 BC. Josephus, *Antiquities* 15:380, states that the rebuilding began in Herod's eighteenth year, i.e. 20 or 19 BC. The seemingly conflicting testimony of *Jewish War* 1:401 places the beginning of the rebuilding three years earlier. Either this refers to preliminary work or is a mistake, since it does not fit in with other ancient chronological data. And it would yield a date of AD 24–25 for the temple cleansing, which is even further removed from possible dates of the crucifixion (*cf.* p.178). *Cf.* further Robinson, *Priority*, pp.130–131.

were freely reshaping the Synoptic version with little concern for keeping the facts straight.[1]

The position in the gospels of Jesus' anointing by Mary may be dealt with more briefly. Again John gives a precise reference to time – six days before the Passover (12:1). But Mark's account is less specific. Mark 14:1–2 states that it was two days before the Passover when the Jews finalized their plans to kill Jesus. But 14:3 seems to start a new unit of thought, and Mark does not say that these events happened after those of the previous verses. When one sees how 14:10 resumes the account of the plot to do away with Christ, verses 3–9 (the story of the anointing) stand out as intrusive in their present context. Most probably Mark has relocated them here, without saying when they actually happened, to bring the incident into closer connection with the events that led to Jesus' death. On the one hand, Jesus himself justifies Mary's lavish 'waste' of expensive perfume on the grounds that she is preparing his body for burial; on the other hand, Mark's juxtaposition of passages provides a sharp contrast between Mary's devotion and Judas' treachery.[2] Some have made heavy weather of the fact that in John, Mary anoints Jesus' feet; but in Mark and Matthew, his head. They have thus argued from this difference, coupled with the variation in context, for two separate anointings. Nevertheless, both versions describe Jesus explaining Mary's actions as a preparation for burial, and bodies were usually covered with scented oils from head to foot. The half-litre of ointment (Jn. 12:3) poured over Jesus could easily have covered much of his body. Hypotheses about separate events seem unnecessary here. Luke's apparent parallel, however, as noted a chapter ago (above, p.147), probably does refer to a different event altogether. The principle applied here is that one must avoid assuming that a little variation in detail automatically makes separate events of apparent parallels, whereas one must be willing to

---

[1]For similar arguments, see Leon Morris, *The Gospel according to John* (Grand Rapids: Eerdmans, 1971; London: Marshall, Morgan & Scott, 1974), pp.189–191; Westcott, *John*, I, pp.96–97; William Milligan and William F. Moulton, *Commentary on the Gospel of St. John* (Edinburgh: T & T Clark, 1898), p.27; E. H. Askwith, *The Historical Value of the Fourth Gospel* (London: Hodder & Stoughton, 1910), p.195; A. Plummer, *The Gospel according to S. John* (Cambridge: University Press, 1891; Grand Rapids: Baker, 1981), p.89; D. A. Carson, 'Matthew', in *The Expositor's Bible Commentary*, ed. Frank E. Gaebelein, vol. 8 (Grand Rapids: Zondervan, 1984), p.441.

[2]William L. Lane, *The Gospel according to Mark* (Grand Rapids: Eerdmans, 1974; London: Marshall, Morgan & Scott, 1975), pp.491–492; Morris, *John*, p.573.

move in that direction when the differences greatly outweigh the similarities.

Harmonizing the various accounts of the call of Simon Peter and his brother Andrew provides a final example of this principle. John 1 only speaks of four disciples, apparently because this is an initial call to identify and travel with Jesus, not the more formal beginning of his Galilean ministry, as in Mark 1:16–20.[1] Strictly speaking, in John only Philip was specifically called by Jesus. Peter, Andrew, and Nathanael associated themselves with him voluntarily, and John gives no indication to what extent they intended to continue following him. Again the two different gospels each give the other greater credibility. The unexplained suddenness of the Synoptic callings makes more sense if some of the twelve had associated with Jesus previously and begun to tell others about him, while the continued association of the disciples with Jesus in John is explained by their more formal selection in the Synoptics. C. K. Barrett's claim that John's narrative leaves no room for a subsequent call, since the disciples never go back to their fishing practice, ignores the highly selective nature of the Fourth Gospel which Barrett otherwise rightly stresses.[2]

The initial enthusiasm of the first disciples, along with that of John the Baptist, is not inconsistent with the progression of Messianic understanding outlined in the Synoptics. Messianic fervour was rampant in Israel; no doubt many 'charismatic' leaders were hailed as prophetic figures by over-eager adherents.[3] Jesus deserved at least equal enthusiasm and no doubt received it. But when John the Baptist was languishing in prison, and the other disciples were trying to cope with Jesus' reinterpretation of the Messiah in terms of the suffering servant, they would only naturally begin to question their initial zeal. Even at the end of chapter 1, John depicts Jesus as refocusing Nathanael's attention away from his Messianic confession of the 'Son of God' and 'King of Israel' to 'the Son of man' on whom angels would ascend and descend[4] (most probably a reference to the crucifixion and resur-

---

[1]Brown, *John,* I, p.77; A. J. B. Higgins, *The Historicity of the Fourth Gospel* (London: Lutterworth, 1960), p.42; Hunter, *John,* pp.43,59; J. N. Sanders and B. A. Mastin, *The Gospel according to St. John* (London: A & C Black; New York: Harper, 1968), p.99.

[2]Barrett, *John,* p.79.

[3]*Cf.* P. W. Barnett, 'The Jewish Sign Prophets AD 40–70: Their Intentions and Origin', *NTS* 27 (1981), pp.679–697.

[4]*Cf.* Schnackenburg, *John,* I, p.319.

rection).[1] Significantly, no one again confesses Jesus as the Messiah in John's Gospel until many have left off following him. Only then does Simon Peter reply to Jesus' question to the twelve, 'Do you also want to go away?' with the confession, 'Lord, to whom shall we go? You have the words of eternal life; and we have believed and come to know that you are the Holy One of God' (6:66–69). This interchange, in turn, functions much like the confession of Peter on the road to Caesarea Philippi in the Synoptics (Mk. 8:27–30 pars.), as Christology becomes increasingly explicit in the remaining portions of the gospel narratives. As it turns out, John and the Synoptics are not at all incompatible in their portraits of the disciples' progression of commitment.[2]

3 The passion narrative

In one respect there are fewer historical problems with the closing chapters of John's Gospel because they describe essentially the same sequence of events as the Synoptic narratives. If John is independent of the first three gospels, then his text offers valuable corroboration of many of the details which they report concerning Jesus' death and resurrection. But when the texts run closely parallel, there is also a greater possibility for allegations of contradiction when minor divergences occur. The three most troublesome involve the day of Jesus' death, the events surrounding his arrest and trials, and the hour of the crucifixion.

Despite the Synoptics' clear references to the Last Supper as a Passover meal (Mk. 14:12, 14, 16; Mt. 26:17, 19; Lk. 22:7–8), John seems to believe that Passover fell on the Friday of Jesus' execution, rather than the Thursday preceding it (Jn. 13:1; 18:28; 19:14, 31). Most scholars therefore argue that one of the accounts altered the date for theological purposes; either the Synoptists wanted to turn Jesus' last meal into a Passover celebration or John wanted to link Jesus' death with the slaughter of the sacrificial lambs. Either way, one of the versions' dates would be incorrect. Those who have held out for the possibility of harmonizing the two have usually appealed to some kind of theory by which not all Jews celebrated the Passover at the same time. Some evidence suggests

---

[1]Bruce, *John*, pp.62–63. The exegesis of John 1:51 is hotly disputed, though, and the point being made here still holds even if this interpretation is incorrect.

[2]*Cf*. Lindars, *John*, p.113; Sanders and Mastin, *John*, pp.14–15; de Jonge, 'Jewish Expectations', p.252.

that the Essenes in Qumran, the community south-east of Jerusalem famous for the Dead Sea Scrolls, celebrated the Passover
earlier in the week than others did. Others suggest that Galilean
Jews differed from their Judaean brethren or that Pharisees disputed with Sadducees over the correct date. Similar, less widely
held approaches also compete for acceptance.[1] A few argue that
Jesus himself simply decided to celebrate the meal a day early,
perhaps knowing that he would not live long enough to do it the
following night.

That debates over the correct day for the Passover occurred in
ancient Judaism is quite probable. Later references in Jewish
tradition point to such debates, and the fact that the Passover
lambs were to be slaughtered on the afternoon of the fourteenth
day of the month, calculated from the first sighting of the new
moon, left room for dispute on the basis of changing weather
conditions. But there is no evidence that such disputes ever led
the Jews *in Jerusalem* to permit two consecutive days of Passover
meals to accommodate conflicting positions; whichever group
won out at a given point in history fixed the date as long as it held
power. Jerusalem would have experienced virtual chaos if different groups of Jews had tried to observe all the holy day rituals
and taboos during conflicting twenty-four hour periods. Nor is
there much to suggest that Jesus would have so identified with
any particular Jewish subgroup as to be forced to follow its customs over against the majority. And how would any reader of the
gospels ever know which method of dating the evangelists were
following? In any event Mark 14:12 seems to prevent any type of
early celebration of the Passover; Jesus and his disciples ate the
meal on the day the lambs were slaughtered.[2] Like the proposal
that postulates two Jerichos to solve the problem of where Jesus
healed Bartimaeus (see above, p.128), the recourse to two
different calendars or days for celebrating Passover founders on
the lack of any hint of such a distinction in the gospels them-

---

[1]For a good survey of the various theories see I. H. Marshall, *Last Supper and Lord's Supper*
(Exeter: Paternoster; Grand Rapids: Eerdmans, 1980), pp.71–75. *Cf.* also Harold Hoehner,
Chronological Aspects of the Life of Christ (Grand Rapids: Zondervan, 1976), pp.81–90.

[2]France, 'Harmony', pp.50–54, reinterprets Mark 14:12 differently, since technically the
Passover meal began a new day (Jewish days being reckoned from sundown to sundown). But
by his own admission, usage of terminology was loose, and the rest of his defence is less
persuasive than the interpretations defended above, which he dismisses without feeling their
full force (pp.47–49).

selves.[1]

The most plausible harmonization of John and the Synoptics therefore requires a closer look at the specific terms which John uses in his apparently contradictory verses and the contexts in which they are found. In 13:1 John maintains that it was 'before the feast of the Passover when Jesus knew that his hour had come'; in verse 2, that they were now eating dinner. One could assume that this dinner refers to his last evening meal prior to the night of the Passover, but it seems natural to take it to refer to the meal just announced in verse 1. Verses 1–2 would thus describe the depth of the love Jesus had for his disciples already before the Passover. Such love led him to see his mission through to the end, culminating in the Last Supper, with all the rich symbolism which he invests in it (be it the foot-washing ceremony of John's Gospel or the 'first communion' of the Synoptics). In 13:29, then, when some of the disciples think that Judas left in order to buy provisions for 'the feast', the word that is used would refer to the week-long festival. Which particular meal during those seven days the provisions were required for is left unspecified. If the meal in progress were the first night's banquet, then 'the feast' would quite naturally refer to part or all of the remaining six days.[2]

This explanation makes equally good sense of 18:28, where the Jewish leaders wish to avoid defilement which would prevent them from eating the Passover. In fact, defilement incurred during the daylight hours would expire at sundown and would not prevent their celebration of an evening dinner, so it is more likely that John has in mind the lunchtime meal known as the *chagigah*, celebrated during midday after the first evening of Passover. 19:14 and 31 do not contradict this by their labelling the day of Jesus' death 'the day of Preparation of the Passover' since the Greek word *Paraskeuē* translated 'day of Preparation', was (and still is)

---

[1]The most detailed discussion of these issues and of the harmonization proposed here is Norval Geldenhuys, *The Gospel of Luke* (London: Marshall, Morgan & Scott, 1950; Grand Rapids: Eerdmans, 1951), pp.649–670. *Cf.*, more briefly, Carson, 'Matthew', pp.530–532; Lewis A. Foster, 'The Chronology of the New Testament', in *Expositor's Bible Commentary*, ed. Gaebelein, vol. 1 (Grand Rapids: Zondervan; Glasgow: Pickering & Inglis, 1976), p.599.

[2]Both Hoehner (*Chronological Aspects*, p.81) and Marshall (*Last Supper*, p.70) have rejected this interpretation by citing Morris (*John*, pp.778–779) who points out that while the term Passover can refer to the entire week-long feast it cannot refer to the last six days of the feast *apart* from the initial meal. But the argument here is not that the word itself means only the six remaining days; the word refers to the whole week. Yet when used at some point in the middle of that week in reference to some upcoming part of *the whole festival* it can, logically, mean only that which is yet to come. *Cf.* Carson, 'Matthew', p.531.

the standard name for Friday in Greek. Since Friday was always Preparation Day for the Sabbath (Saturday), it came to be called by that name. John's language is thus a natural shorthand for saying 'the day of preparation for the Sabbath during Passover week' or simply 'Friday in Passover week'. Mark 15:42 confirms the appropriateness of this interpretation, since Mark also calls the day of Jesus' death 'the day of Preparation' but then immediately explains, 'that is, the day before the Sabbath'.

A final, incidental corroboration of this solution comes from recent computer-assisted astronomical calculations. If Jesus was crucified on the fifteenth day of the Jewish month Nisan as this reconstruction requires, rather than on the fourteenth day, before the Passover had been eaten by most of the Jews, as the other proposed harmonizations require, then the only year close to the time of Christ's ministry in which he could have been crucified would have been AD 30. In all other years immediately before and after, 15 Nisan did not fall on a Friday.[1] But AD 30 turns out to be the very year that many scholars have accepted as the year of Christ's death, for other reasons.[2] Once again the gospels prove to be more accurate than many critics give them credit for.

F. F. Bruce concisely summarizes the problems in the Fourth Gospel surrounding the legal action taken against Jesus and points out plausible solutions.[3] To begin with, many have questioned John's reference to Roman troops superintending Jesus' arrest (the 'soldiers' in 18:3 are more literally an imperial 'cohort'), since the Jews had the right and responsibility to arrest those they suspected of crimes. But the volatile political climate of Jerusalem at feast time makes their involvement quite natural, and since John's redactional emphasis focuses on the guilt of the Jews in

---

[1]Herman H. Goldstine, *New and Full Moons, 1001 BC to AD 1651* (Philadelphia: American Philosophical Society, 1973), p.86. Colin J. Humphreys and W. G. Waddington, 'Dating the Crucifixion', *Nature* 306 (1983), pp.743–746, note that 15 Nisan AD 30 fell either on a Friday or a Saturday, depending on the atmospheric conditions at the time of the previous new moon. They proceed to defend an AD 33 date for the crucifixion, in which 15 Nisan definitely fell on a Saturday, primarily by assuming that Peter's mention at Pentecost of the moon turning to blood (Acts 2:20) referred back to a lunar eclipse at the time of the crucifixion (3 April 33). This is an unlikely interpretation of a clearly prophetic and apocalyptic passage (Peter is citing Joel 2:31), which is included in the Pentecost sermon because of the more relevant verses which surround it. If, however, the astronomical evidence conclusively pointed to AD 33 as the year of the crucifixion, then the preferable solution would be France's (see above, p.176 n.2).

[2]For an excellent summary of details, see G. B. Caird, 'The Chronology of the New Testament', in *IDB*, I, pp.599–603.

[3]F. F. Bruce, 'The Trial of Jesus in the Fourth Gospel', in *GP*,1, pp.7–20.

condemning Jesus it is unlikely that he invented this detail which implicates the Romans as well. Second, only John includes a reference to an informal hearing for Jesus before the ex-high priest Annas (18:13; *cf.* Lk. 3:2). But again this is perfectly believable, since Annas' continuing influence even in his 'retirement' would have been quite natural. In Jewish thinking the priesthood was conferred for life, irrespective of Roman action in deposing a given priest and replacing him with another. Also, simple deference and respect for one's elders would have made this hearing an appropriate courtesy even if modern customs make it seem unnecessary. Third, the claim that the Romans retained the sole right of capital punishment (18:31) has often been termed a Johannine error, especially in view of the counter-example in the stoning of Stephen (Acts 7:58). But this right is strikingly confirmed by a passage in the Talmud, which says that capital punishment had been taken from the Jews forty years before the destruction of the temple in AD 70 (pSanh. 1:1, 7:2). Stephen's stoning reads more like mob action which defied technical legalities. Finally, John greatly elaborates on Jesus' audience with Pilate, but does so in a way that dovetails remarkably with Roman judicial procedure. Far from undermining confidence in John, his unique additions to the passion narrative – the formal charge and condemnation, the reference to Pilate as 'Caesar's friend' (*i.e.* legal representative), and the use of the tribunal seat – all serve only to strengthen it.[1]

Perhaps the most puzzling of all the differences between John and the Synoptics comes with the simple little variation between Mark 15:25 and John 19:14. Was Jesus crucified at the third or the sixth hour of the day? The former time has no symbolic significance; the latter has often been taken to point to the noon hour when Passover lambs were slaughtered, counting, as was normally done, from 6 a.m. onward. But if the above solution concerning the day of Jesus' death is correct, then this cannot be the meaning of the hour, even for John, since the Passover sacrifice would have occurred the day before. There is even less evidence for the view that John was adopting the practice of later Roman civil reckoning whereby hours were counted from midnight on. This would permit John to end the trial before Pilate at 6 a.m. and to begin the crucifixion (as in Mark) at 9 a.m. But it would also force one to

---

[1]*Cf.* also A. E. Harvey, *Jesus on Trial* (London: SPCK, 1976), pp.61–65.

imagine the culmination of the Sanhedrin's deliberations, the audience with Pilate, the subsequent hearing before Herod (found only in Luke 23:6–12), Jesus' return to Pilate and the final dialogue with the Jews all occurring in the space of less than half an hour. For the other gospels assert that all these events occurred after dawn, and dawn at that time of year in Jerusalem could have been no earlier than 5:30 a.m.

A better suggestion equates Mark's references to time with quarters of a day. In his gospel, indeed in every case save one in all the Synoptic Gospels and Acts (Mt. 20:9; in the context of a parable which requires this specificity), the only hours of the day ever mentioned are 'third', 'sixth', and 'ninth' (Mt. 20:3, 5; 27:45, 46; Mk 15:33, 34; Lk. 23:44; Acts 2:15; 3:1; 10:3, 9, 30; 23:23). When one recognizes that the widespread lack of precise time-keeping devices in the ancient world led to the practice of dividing the day into fourths so that people often did not worry about speaking any more specifically than this, it becomes plausible to interpret Mark's 'third hour' to mean any time between 9 a.m. and noon. John's 'about the sixth hour' would also then refer to sometime before midday, perhaps within an hour or so.[1] John does refer to the in-between hours elsewhere in his gospel (1:39; 4:52), so that, as generally in a study of his chronology, he seems to be somewhat more precise than the Synoptics. But neither account contradicts the other.

D Alleged historical discrepancies

Is John unaware that Jesus was born in Bethlehem rather than Nazareth? In fact, John knows the birthplace, but apparently some in Jesus' audiences did not. Their ignorance is not surprising since Jesus had grown up and lived in Galilee for all but the earliest years of his life. That John lets this mistaken impression stand without comment testifies only to his skilful use of irony. Not only do these Jews not realize where Jesus was born (7:42), but they even challenge Jesus' admirers to cite any Scripture supporting the rise of a prophet from Galilee (7:52), overlooking the clear Messianic prophecy of Is. 9:1–2 about the people of the regions later known as Galilee who had walked in darkness but saw a great light

---

[1]See esp. Johnny V. Miller, 'The Time of the Crucifixion', *JETS* 26 (1983), pp.157–166. *Cf.* William M. Ramsay, 'About the Sixth Hour', *Expositor* 7 (4th series; 1893), pp.216–223; H. J. Cadbury, 'Some Lukan Expressions of Time', *JBL* 82 (1963), pp.277–278.

(*cf*. Mt. 4:14–16).[1]

As for the problem of the cause of his arrest – the reanimation of Lazarus or the second cleansing of the temple – it is entirely plausible to accept both incidents as causes.[2] Neither John nor the Synoptics maintain that only one factor brought on the hostilities; both even specifically mention other motives as well. In Mark, Jesus' transgression of the Sabbath laws causes the Jews to plot his destruction from early on (Mk. 3:6), while in John his problems are compounded by his claims of oneness with God (Jn. 5:18; 7:32). His power over death paradoxically sealed his fate in the minds of the chief priests, and his revolutionary ministry in the temple undoubtedly alienated a large segment of the middle and upper class, who stood to benefit most from the business transacted there. But even after both of these events, it was not until Judas volunteered to betray Christ that the officials could conveniently arrest him. Had this scheme not presented itself so quickly, the gospel writers might well have told of still other reasons for the provocation of the authorities.

The most blatant of the alleged historical errors or anachronisms in the Fourth Gospel involves John's reference to the Jewish edict to excommunicate followers of Jesus from the synagogue (9:22). Commentators of virtually every theological stripe admit that at least here John has too quickly read the circumstances of his own time at the end of the first century back into his account of what happened a half-century or so earlier. The widespread policy of banning Christians and other dissidents from the synagogue, known as the *birkath ha-minim* (a curse on the heretics), only emerged about AD 90 after a long and painful process of growing separation between Christians and Jews. Yet Reuven Kimelman's recent study has placed a large question mark in front of this typical reconstruction of events. In a symposium of Jews and Christians on the early history of their co-existence, Kimelman, and to a lesser extent other participants, argued for three key points. First, nothing in the context of John 9:22, or of 12:42 and 16:2 where similar references occur, suggests that this policy of excluding Jesus' supporters from the synagogue extended outside

[1]*Cf.* Lindars, *John*, p.305; Bruce, *John*, pp.183–184.
[2]See esp. J. P. Martin, 'History and Eschatology in the Lazarus Narrative – John 11:1–44', *SJT* 17 (1964), p.332; J. Armitage Robinson, *The Historical Character of St. John's Gospel* (London and New York: Longmans, Green & Co, 1908), pp.40–41.

Jerusalem. Second, the word used in each of these passages for being put 'out of the synagogue' (*aposynagōgos*) occurs nowhere else in early Jewish or Christian discussions of the later, more universal ban, so it is doubtful if that is what John had in mind here. Most important of all, a re-examination of the ancient sources makes it likely that the *birkath ha-minim* was never a watershed in finally dividing Jews from Christians, nor a single edict uniformly enforced, nor even a policy extending beyond Jewish sectarians to include Gentile Christians as well.[1] A perusal of older commentators on John's Gospel quickly reveals that this whole problem is in fact the creation of recent scholarship; unlike most of the issues discussed in this chapter, this one seems to have gone wholly unnoticed in past generations.

E Johannine style

1 Jesus' extended discourses

Jesus' last recorded reply to Nicodemus' questions begins, 'Are you a teacher of Israel and do you not understand these things? Truly, truly, I say to you, we speak of what we know and testify to what we have seen . . .' (Jn. 3:10–11). In the next two verses, the dialogue shifts from first person speech to third person, yet apparently Jesus is still speaking: 'how will you believe if I tell you heavenly things? And no one has ascended into heaven except . . . the Son of man' (verses 12–13). All four gospels depict Jesus referring to himself in this indirect way as the Son of man, so the shift from first to third person is not that surprising. But after a second reference to the Son of man in verses 14–15 as having to be 'lifted up, so that all who believe in him may have eternal life', John continues for six more verses in language which repeatedly refers to Jesus as the 'Son', the 'only Son', and the 'only Son of God'. This paragraph sounds exactly like the way John writes elsewhere (*e.g.* 1:14–18) and not like Jesus' own teaching. This is all the more noteworthy since this paragraph begins with the well-known verse, 'for God so loved the world . . .' (verse 16), which closes by echoing Jesus' final words of verse 15 ('. . . may

---

[1]Reuven Kimelman, '*Birkat Ha-Minim* and the Lack of Evidence for an Anti-Christian Jewish Prayer in Late Antiquity', in *Jewish and Christian Self-Definition*, vol. 2, ed. E. P. Sanders, A. J. Baumgarten, and Alan Mendelson (Philadelphia: Fortress; London: SCM, 1981), pp.226–244. For additional literature supporting these conclusions, see Robinson, *Priority*, pp.72–81; Carson, 'After Dodd, What?' pp.123–125.

have eternal life'). Many modern scholars therefore punctuate the text so as to indicate that Jesus' words ended at verse 15, with verse 16 resuming John's commentary. A similar phenomenon recurs later in the chapter when John the Baptist's words (3:27–30) seem to flow directly into John the evangelist's comments (3:31–36) without a distinct break.

The modern translations are no doubt correct in this analysis. But even if one were to assume that Jesus and John the Baptist spoke all this material, the question of why the style and language of the writer of the Fourth Gospel is so similar to that of the discourses would remain. Also unsolved would be the problem of why Jesus speaks in frequent, prolonged and unparalleled sermons seemingly unlike anything found in the Synoptics. Of course the previously discussed considerations about the significance of omission and singly-attested material (see pp.162–163) apply here too. At least eight additional points, however, help to counterbalance the claim that John has simply invented speeches for his characters in language no different from that of his narrative elsewhere.

(1) As noted in the discussion of the Synoptic parallels in the last chapter (p.118), one does not need to claim that the long sermons in John represent Jesus' *ipsissima verba* (actual words) but only that they give a faithful summary and interpretative paraphrase of what he said (the *ipsissima vox*, or 'actual voice'), however much they may have been couched in distinctively Johannine style.

(2) It is not true that the discourses of Jesus in John are wholly indistinguishable from John's narrative style elsewhere. H. R. Reynolds' much-neglected commentary lists over 145 words spoken by Jesus in John which are never used by the evangelist elsewhere, and many of these are general enough that they would have been appropriate in narrative as well as discourse.[1]

(3) Some of John's style may have been directly or indirectly inspired by Jesus' own manner of speech. In at least one famous passage from Q (Mt. 11:25–27; Lk. 10:21–22), Jesus uses language almost identical to that which characterizes his speeches in John, when he thanks his Father for having revealed himself to babes rather than to wise men, adding, 'all things have been given to me

---

[1]H. R. Reynolds, *The Gospel of St. John*, vol. 1 (London and New York: Funk & Wagnalls, 1906) cxxiii–cxxv.

by my Father, and no one knows the Son except the Father, nor the Father except the Son and the one to whom the Son wishes to reveal him.'

(4) Much of John's homiletic or sermonic style for Jesus' teaching may reflect the use of that teaching in preaching or liturgical contexts in the early church. As with point (1) above, the form may have been changed without necessarily altering the content.

(5) John's unique emphasis on the role of the Holy Spirit in helping the disciples to remember everything which Jesus taught them as well as leading them into new truth (Jn. 14:26; 15:26; 16:12–13) must not be neglected. On the one hand, these verses suggest that the writer of this gospel believed that the Spirit had superintended the process by which the traditions about Jesus and the memories of the eyewitnesses of his life were preserved so as to safeguard their accuracy. On the other hand, they claim that what was unintelligible or unacceptable to the disciples during Jesus' earthly life would become clear and credible later. If the Synoptics come closer than John to preserving Jesus' actual words in many places, John may well believe that he has better expounded their significance in the light of what the Spirit has taught the church since Jesus ascended to his Father.[1] At the same time, John is the only evangelist who repeatedly stresses that the disciples later came to recognize the significance of certain teachings which they failed to understand during Jesus' lifetime (*e.g.* 2:18–22; 7:37–39; 12:16; 16:25). The very fact that he takes pains to preserve what Jesus said even when it was not fully understood strongly suggests that he has not blurred the lines between the earthly Jesus and the risen Lord. And whenever a theological insight arose after Christ's resurrection, however Spirit-inspired it may have been, John does not seem to confuse that insight with a saying of the historical Jesus.[2]

(6) Some of the differences between John and the Synoptics probably stem from the different contexts in which Jesus found himself. Privately, with his disciples, he was likely to explore the depths of theological perplexities more readily than in his public addresses to the crowds. This observation, for example, goes a long way to account for John 13–17, Jesus' upper room discourse,

---

[1]*Cf.* Herman Ridderbos, 'The Christology of the Fourth Gospel', in *Saved by Hope,* ed. James I. Cook (Grand Rapids: Eerdmans, 1978), pp.19–21.
[2]See esp. Carson, 'After Dodd, What?', pp.121–122.

especially since this was the last time he would be with the twelve before his death. Other differences derive from the Fourth Gospel's regular accounts of Jesus' more formal teaching in the synagogues and the temple rather than his informal addresses to crowds in the open air as in the Synoptics.[1]

(7) Pitting the brief sayings of Jesus characteristic of the Synoptics over against the longer discourses in John also overlooks the fact that both types of speech occur in all four gospels, even if the emphasis differs. Even in Mark, an entire chapter is devoted to the eschatological discourse (Mk. 13), while Matthew contains five extended sermons (Mt. 5–7, 10, 13, 18, 24–25). If the arguments are correct in chapter four concerning the probable unity of at least some of these sermons, then the likelihood of John also having preserved the outlines of longer discourses increases.

(8) Further evidence that the sermons in John are not composite mosaics of a few historical sayings of Jesus glued together with creative additions by the evangelist comes from various recent studies pointing to their tightly knit unity. The 'bread of life' discourse in John 6:26–59 is a carefully constructed exposition of parts of Exodus 16 dealing with the manna God provided for the Israelites, in the style of typical rabbinic commentary of the day.[2] John 10:1–16 may be a similar 'midrash' (*cf.* pp.43–44) on the good shepherd of Ezekiel 34.[3] Jesus' discourse on the relationship between the Father and the Son in 5:19–30 is an intricately wrought chiasmus (inverted parallelism) with close verbal correspondences between verses 19 and 30, 20 and 28–29, 21 and 26, 22 and 27 and 24 and 25.[4] The implications of such patterns for unity and authenticity have already been noted (pp.61–62). Jesus' conversation with Nicodemus, finally, follows the interesting pattern of Nicodemus' questions becoming progressively shorter and Jesus' answers growing ever longer, exactly as modern studies of the psychology of persuasion would lead one to expect. The rever-

---

[1]*Cf.* Oscar Cullmann, *The Johannine Circle* (London: SCM; Philadelphia: Westminster, 1976), p.24; Leon Morris, *Studies in the Fourth Gospel* (Exeter: Paternoster; Grand Rapids: Eerdmans, 1969), p.134.

[2]Peder Borgen, *Bread from Heaven* (Leiden: Brill, 1965); Hunter, *John*, pp.97–98. Borgen argues for the unity of the discourse but does not attribute it to Jesus; Hunter recognizes that, granted the unity, nothing prevents one from seeing the sermon as authentic.

[3]Birger Gerhardsson, *The Good Samaritan – The Good Shepherd?* (Lund: Gleerup, 1958), p.13.

[4]A. Vanhoye, 'La composition de Jn 5:19–30', in *Mélanges Bibliques,* ed.A. Descamps and A. de Halleux (Gembloux: Duculot, 1970), pp.259–274.

sal occurs as Jesus ignores Nicodemus' opening gambit ('we know you are a teacher sent from God' – 3:2) and little by little successfully redirects attention away from who he is to who Nicodemus is and ought to be.[1] This discussion, like the more formal addresses in John, is more credible as it stands than is usually admitted. What often seem like abrupt transitions more likely reflect Jesus' characteristic freedom in moving from one topic to the next without always indicating his transitions. Because he perceived people's unspoken thoughts and recognized questions intended to trap or distract him, he often bypassed customary amenities and spoke directly to the heart of the matter at hand. One perhaps needs to question the plausibility of the elaborate source- and redaction-critical reconstructions of modern scholars rather than charging John with widespread distortion of the facts. To be sure, sources and redactors can create tightly knit unities too, but if they do then they cover the very tracks – the seams and inconsistencies – which otherwise enable them to be detected.

2 Other redactional seams?

Surely the most awkward transition in the discourses in John occurs in 14:31 when Jesus encourages his disciples to rise and leave the upper room but then proceeds to preach to them for another three chapters. Even relatively conservative commentators often admit that here John has confused the order of things. A few take Jesus' words more metaphorically to mean something like 'let us be prepared for spiritual warfare', but this seems rather forced. D. A. Carson suggests a more helpful approach:

> Far from indicating a seam, 14:31–15:1 evidences a momentous recollection of detail. Jesus and his disciples leave the room in response to his quiet Ἐγείρεσθε, ἄγωμεν ἐντεῦθεν [Rise, let us go hence]. They leave the city, walking in several clumps: twelve men can scarcely walk in one group in the narrow streets of Old Jerusalem and along the narrow path across the Kidron and up the Mount of Olives. This circumstance explains the description surrounding the dialogue in 16:17–19. Moreover, as

---

[1] F. P. Cotterell, 'The Nicodemus Conversation: A Fresh Appraisal', *ExpT* 96 (1985), pp.237–242; also his 'Sociolinguistics and Biblical Interpretation', *Vox Evangelica* 16 (1986), pp.61–76.

they pass by vineyards, Jesus finds in them another metaphor to use on this most awesome of nights; and he begins, 'I am the true vine . . .' (15:1).[1]

That this view is not the desperate expedient of an uncritical conservatism is proved by its endorsement by Ernst Haenchen in a commentary which is otherwise one of the most sceptical of current works on John.[2]

Similarly, Paul Minear argues that chapter 21 was planned from the outset to deal with the unfinished business of Peter's reinstatement and the future of his and the beloved disciple's ministries, even though 20:31 reads like the conclusion of a gospel.[3] In both his discussion and Carson's one may wonder whether or not full weight has been given to the undeniable abruptness of John's narrative, but even if their solutions are questioned, it is at least important to stress that the apparent lack of smoothness in these parts of John does not support theories of additional stages of redaction. Why, if John's gospel was reworked as many as five times (so Brown), should these 'seams' still be here at all? Lack of fluency in writing points more to the *omission* of a final stage of editorial proofreading and revision than to additional editors who still could not smooth things out! In any event, the number of revisions of a document has no necessary relationship to its historical accuracy.

Grant Osborne notes several additional features of chapter 21 which support its historicity, although he believes it was added by the writer of the first twenty chapters as something of an afterthought. The most important of these are: (a) the apparent aimlessness of the disciples upon their return to Galilee, which would hardly have been invented by the early church, since it consistently sought to portray the apostles in a good light; (b) the similarity of the miracle of the great catch of fish to Luke 5:1–11, coupled with enough difference in detail to discount the theory that the stories are mere doublets; (c) the apparent allusion in 1 Peter 5:2 to Peter's commissioning by Jesus to 'tend his sheep'; and (d) the ambiguity of the prophecies about the fates of Peter and John (verses 20–23), which would have been made much plainer if John

[1]Carson, 'After Dodd, What?', p.123.
[2]Ernst Haenchen, *John 2* (Philadelphia: Fortress, 1984), p.128.
[3]Paul S. Minear, 'The Original Functions of John 21', *JBL* 102 (1983), pp.85–98.

were simply inventing material to satisfy the curiosity of late first-century Christians.[1]

5 Conclusion

One of the most prolific of modern British New Testament scholars, James D. G. Dunn, issues a strenuous appeal in a recent article to 'let John be John'.[2] By this he means that one must not assume that John intended to write the same kind of history as the Synoptics. The Fourth Gospel must be seen, so Dunn argues (following the consensus of modern scholarship), to be a highly developed theological interpretation of the meaning of Jesus, quite unlike a factual selection of the things he did and said. One should heartily agree that the interpreter of any document must be faithful to the purposes and intentions of its original author, and that John delves into theological issues more deeply than the Synoptics do. But the survey undertaken here of the apparent problems involved in affirming historicity in the Fourth Gospel leaves one wholly unconvinced that John was not also trying to record accurate information about Jesus' life. In fact, in terms of detail of chronology and geography, John supplies much more information than Matthew, Mark, or Luke. And the alleged contradictions between John and the Synoptics begin to disappear upon closer scrutiny.

A remarkable witness who would agree with much of what this chapter has defended is the late Bishop John Robinson. Robinson's last book, edited posthumously, draws together a lifetime of research on the Gospel of John and defends its historical accuracy with an enthusiasm and rigour not otherwise found among recent scholars.[3] Robinson still needlessly pits John against the Synoptics

---

[1] Grant R. Osborne, 'John 21: Test Case for History and Redaction in the Resurrection Narratives', in *GP*,2, pp.293–328.

[2] J. D. G. Dunn, 'Let John be John', in *Das Evangelium und die Evangelien*, ed. Peter Stuhlmacher (Tübingen: Mohr, 1983), pp.309–339.

[3] Robinson, *Priority*. The best of his earlier work appears in *Twelve New Testament Studies* (London: SCM; Naperville: Allenson, 1962); *Twelve More New Testament Studies* (London: SCM, 1984); and *Redating the New Testament* (London: SCM; Philadelphia: Westminster, 1976), pp.254–311. There is a danger that Robinson's most recent work will be quickly dismissed by critics who find his views so different from their own, but this would be a pity. Unlike portions of his *Redating*, the *Priority* consistently depends on arguments based on positive evidence rather than on silence.

from time to time, but when he does so he always sides with John's account of events, unlike the majority of scholars, who prefer the Synoptics. Robinson also dubiously alleges that traditional inter-pretations of John's Christology have read the idea of Christ's deity into John's texts when it is not really there. Notwithstanding these criticisms, one cannot help but admire the meticulous scholarship which leads a theologian of liberal persuasion to put forward a powerful case for John's historical trustworthiness.

It is difficult, finally, to reconcile John's insistence on the eyewit-ness nature and truth of his narrative with views which would claim he is not trying to write reliable history, however theologically interpreted it may be.[1] Claims like 19:35 ('he who has seen it [the crucifixion] has testified, and his testimony is true, and he knows that he speaks the truth, in order that you also may believe') are not easily explained away.[2] F. F. Bruce's conclusion to his study of John's trial narrative provides a fitting summary for this investiga-tion of the entire gospel:

> John presents the trial and execution of Jesus, as he presents everything else in his record, in such a way as to enforce his theological *Leitmotiv* [leading motif]: Jesus is the incarnate Word, in whom the glory of God is revealed. But the events which he presents in this way, and pre-eminently the events of the passion, are real, historical events. It could not be otherwise, for the Word became flesh – the revelation became history.[3]

---

[1]Leon Morris, 'The Fourth Gospel and History', in *Jesus of Nazareth: Saviour and Lord,* ed. Carl F. H. Henry (London: Tyndale; Grand Rapids: Eerdmans, 1966), pp.129–30.

[2]*Cf.* Frank Kermode's attempt to do so (*The Genesis of Secrecy* [Cambridge, MA and London: Harvard, 1979], pp.101–123), which utterly fails to convince.

[3]Bruce, 'Trial of Jesus', p.18.

The Jesus tradition outside the gospels

From a modern perspective, the life and teachings of Jesus seem so significant an influence on the last twenty centuries of world history that it is hard to imagine them escaping the attention of ancient historians. It is surprising to hear scholars claim that in fact there is very little corroborating evidence outside the gospels for the life of Christ. F. F. Bruce uses this claim as the springboard for his survey of *Jesus and Christian Origins Outside the New Testament*.[1] In this book, Bruce discusses the testimony of Graeco-Roman historians, ancient Jewish sources and non-canonical Christian testimony to the actions and sayings of Jesus concluding on the one hand that the amount of evidence confirming the gospel portraits of Jesus has been underestimated and on the other hand that there are good reasons for many of the extra-biblical sources not to say much about Jesus. Approximately half of R. T. France's new study of *The Evidence for Jesus* covers much the same territory.[2]

This chapter does not propose to duplicate Bruce's and France's very readable studies. It will merely survey very briefly the areas which they touch upon, focusing on some of the recent scholarly debate not treated in their discussions. It will also go into some detail on a topic which Bruce does not treat and which France only mentions in passing – the seeming shortage of references to the details of Jesus' earthly life *in the other New Testament writings*. This chapter may be divided into four parts, therefore, involving discussion of (a) apparent historical errors in the gospels when compared with other ancient sources, both biblical and secular, (b) references to Jesus' life by non-Christian writers at the

---

[1](London: Hodder & Stoughton; Grand Rapids: Eerdmans, 1974).
[2](London: Hodder & Stoughton; Downers Grove: IVP, 1986), pp.19–85, 140–157.

beginning of the Christian era, (c) the pictures of Jesus painted by non-canonical Christian writers during the earliest stages of church history, and (d) the corroborative testimony of Acts, the epistles, and Revelation to the words and works of Jesus' ministry.

1 Apparent historical errors

Compared with the number of apparent discrepancies among the four gospels themselves, the problems created by seeming conflict with evidence from other sources are very few. This is largely due, of course, to the sheer lack of any information in those sources either to corroborate or to contradict the details of the accounts of Matthew, Mark, Luke and John. Here is a discussion of four especially well-known problems which indicate the sort of difficulties that do arise and how they may be treated. One seems to pit Matthew against Acts, two involve the evangelists appearing to contradict the Old Testament, and one questions the accuracy of Luke, in the light of the evidence of ancient, secular historians.

A The death of Judas

The only portion of the gospels longer than a sentence or two to be paralleled elsewhere in the New Testament is the description in the first chapter of Acts of Jesus' resurrection appearances and ascension and the disciples' return to Jerusalem (Acts 1:1–26; *cf.* Lk. 24:36–53). In this context, Luke adds a description of Judas' death (1:16–20) which is paralleled only by Matthew (Mt. 27:3–10). Still, the details of the two accounts diverge. According to Luke, Judas bought the field in which he died (subsequently nicknamed the 'Field of Blood'), and he took his life by 'falling headlong' (another possible translation is 'swelling up') and bursting open in his midsection. In Matthew, Judas hanged himself, while the chief priests used the money he returned to buy the 'Field of Blood' as a cemetery for foreigners. Taken by itself, Luke's account is the more puzzling of the two. What kind of fall would have killed Judas and caused his bowels to spill out? And why would he have bought a field in the first place just in order to kill himself in it? If the information Matthew supplies is accepted as the background required to make sense of Luke, then the two accounts may be combined in a fairly natural way. I. H. Marshall, who consistently resists all but the most plausible of harmonizations among gospel parallels, explains:

> the following possibilities arise: (1) Judas hanged himself (Mt.), but the rope broke and his body was ruptured by the fall (possibly after he was already dead and beginning to decompose); (2) What the priests bought with Judas's money (Mt.) could be regarded as his purchase by their agency (Acts); (3) The field bought by the priests (Mt.) was the one where Judas died (Acts).[1]

Marshall prefaces this harmonization by cautioning that 'it is quite possible that Matthew or Luke is simply reporting what was commonly said in Jerusalem, and that we are not meant to harmonize the two accounts'. But since both evangelists elsewhere distinguish popular but unreliable reports from trustworthy ones (*e.g.* Mt. 28:11–15; Acts 9:11–14), this seems less likely. Alasdair Gordon's conclusions are also worth quoting in full:

> There is no doubt that there are difficulties in this question but none of these seems irreconcilable. One could agree with the great Princeton scholar, J. A. Alexander, when he points out that Matthew wrote 'for a wide circle of readers, many of whom had no previous knowledge of the case; he therefore states the main fact, and according to his usual custom passes over the minute details. Peter, orally addressing those who knew the facts as fully as himself and less than six weeks after their occurrence . . . assumes the main fact as already known, and naturally dwells upon those very circumstances which the Evangelist, many years later . . . leaves out altogether'. In magisterial tones Alexander concludes: 'there is scarcely an American or English jury that would scruple to receive the two accounts as perfectly consistent, if the witnesses were credible, and any cause could be assigned for their relating two distinct parts of the same tradition.'[2]

---

[1] I. H. Marshall, *Acts* (Leicester: IVP; Grand Rapids: Eerdmans, 1980), p.65. *Cf.* F. F. Bruce, *The Book of the Acts* (London: Marshall, Morgan & Scott, 1954; Grand Rapids: Eerdmans, 1956), p.49, who notes that elements of this harmonization date at least as far back as the time of St. Augustine.

[2] Alasdair B. Gordon, 'The Fate of Judas according to Acts 1:18', *EQ* 43 (1971), pp.99–100, citing J. A. Alexander, *The Acts of the Apostles* [orig. 1857], pp.27–28. If Acts 1:18–19 be taken

B Abiathar or Ahimelech?

In Mark 2:25–26 pars., Jesus defends his disciples' 'working' on the Sabbath (by plucking ears of grain) with an appeal to the Old Testament example of David disobeying the Jewish law when he ate the sacred showbread reserved exclusively for priests (*cf.* 1 Sa. 21:1–6). Mark alone includes the detail that the incident with David occurred 'when Abiathar was high priest'. Yet 1 Samuel clearly states that Ahimelech, Abiathar's father, held that office then. The best solution to this problem arises from the recognition of the unusual meaning of a prepositional phrase found in Mark 2:26, *epi Abiathar archiereōs*. The preposition *epi* usually means 'upon', but in this context it makes no sense to translate 'upon Abiathar the high priest'. Nevertheless, since in eighteen of the twenty-one places Mark uses this preposition with the genitive case it does refer to location rather than time, the translation 'when' is not very likely. John Wenham notices a close parallel in Mark 12:26 where Jesus cites the story of God appearing to Moses at the burning bush, in which he translates *epi tou batou* with the explanatory paraphrase 'in the passage of Scripture concerning (or, entitled) the Bush'. Similarly, Mark 2:26 makes good sense if translated 'at the passage of Scripture concerning (or, entitled) Abiathar the High Priest', for the passage referred to comes in the chapter (1 Sam. 21) which immediately precedes the record of the first exploits of Abiathar.[1] Since Abiathar is the more noteworthy of the two priests throughout the larger context of 1 Samuel, as the man who first brought the priesthood to David's side in his struggle against Saul, it would not be unnatural to refer to several chapters under his name. Wenham's translation thus preserves the more common use of the preposition *epi* as referring to location, even if the specific location in view is a passage of Scripture rather than a place on the globe.

C Zechariah son of Berachiah

In the middle of his woes on the hypocritical scribes and Phar-

---

as Luke's and not Peter's words, a reminiscence of Luke 12:46, where the wicked servant is punished by being 'cut in the middle' (*dichotomeō*), may be intended, in order to hint at the nature of Judas' eternal punishment (Otto Betz, 'The Dichotomized Servant and the End of Judas Iscariot', *RevQ* 5 [1964], pp.50–51).

[1] J. W. Wenham, 'Mark 2:26', *JTS* n.s. 1 (1950), p.156.

isees, Jesus refers to the sins of their forefathers 'from the blood of Abel the righteous to the blood of Zechariah, son of Berachiah, whom you murdered between the sanctuary and the altar' (Mt. 23:35). Zechariah the son of Berachiah was the prophet whose book now stands second from the end of the Old Testament. But the Old Testament says nothing about this Zechariah being murdered, and the location of this murder – in the temple court – calls to mind the account of the death of the priest, Zechariah son of Jehoiada, in 2 Ch. 24:20–22. Has Jesus (or Matthew) simply confused the two Zechariahs? Several alternatives have been suggested[1] and it is hard to know which is best. The fact that some rabbinic traditions (*e.g.* the Targum to La. 2:20 and the Midrash Rabbah on Ec. 3:16) also refer to Zechariah the prophet as being killed in the temple make the suggestion very attractive that Jesus is following extra-biblical tradition here. The coincidence of having two Zechariahs killed in a similar way leads many Jewish commentators to reject their traditions as also confused or in error, but the coincidence is certainly not that impossible. After all, there are thirty Zechariahs in the Old Testament, prophets and priests were not infrequently murdered by their rivals, and it is not clear that the locations within the temple complex referred to by Matthew and Chronicles are identical.[2] One might object that the traditions for the murder of Zechariah the prophet are not well attested, but Matthew's account of Jesus' belief must be considered as attestation too. There is an unfortunate tendency in modern scholarship to prefer any ancient testimony to that of the gospels when it seems to conflict with them, while refusing potential corroboration from extra-biblical sources unless they pass the most stringent tests of historicity. But it is hard to imagine that

---

[1]See Robert H. Gundry, *The Use of the Old Testament in St. Matthew's Gospel* (Leiden: Brill, 1967), pp.86–88. Most prominent are hypotheses about (1) a primitive textual error, (2) Berachiah as the unnamed father of Jehoiada, (3) an otherwise unknown martyrdom of the father of John the Baptist, and (4) a murdered Zechariah *after* the time of Christ of whom Josephus speaks. (1) is unlikely since virtually all the textual evidence weighs against it. (4) would be anachronistic on the lips of Jesus. (2) and (3) have no evidence for or against them but require taking 'Zechariah son of Berachiah' to refer to someone other than the one person Scripture positively identifies in that way.

[2]*Cf.* Walter L. Liefeld, 'Luke', in *Expositor's Bible Commentary,* vol. 8, ed. Frank E. Gaebelein (Grand Rapids: Zondervan, 1984), pp.957–958. For the various Jewish traditions, see Sheldon H. Blank, 'The Death of Zechariah in Rabbinic Literature', *HUCA* 12–13 (1937–38), pp.327–346.

Jesus, the Jewish teacher, would not have known reliable traditions about Jewish history which have been preserved in few, if any, other sources.

D Quirinius

When Joseph and Mary headed for Bethlehem to be registered in the empire-wide census, Luke tells us that Quirinius was governor of Syria, under whose jurisdiction Israel would have fallen (Lk. 2:2). Unfortunately, the information which can be pieced together from the ancient Jewish and Roman historians lists other men as governors of Syria in the years leading up to Christ's birth and dates Quirinius' term of office from AD 6–9. However, some ancient sources also speak of Quirinius leading military expeditions in the eastern provinces of the Roman empire a decade earlier in a manner most naturally explained if he held some official post in Syria (Tacitus, *Annals* 3:48; Florus, *Roman History* 2:31). Since various forms of 'joint rule' were common in the ancient world, it is quite possible that Quirinius was some type of 'governor' (the word Luke uses [*hēgemoneuō*] is a very general term meaning 'to rule' or 'to lead') before his more formal, later term of office. Two fragmentary Latin inscriptions which have been discovered give greater credence to this hypothesis. Uncertainties in dating and translation make it difficult to appeal to these inscriptions as decisive, but recent 'micrographic' analysis (*i.e.* examinations of microscopic writing discovered on these inscriptions) seems to point to their corroborating an earlier term of office for Quirinius before Christ's birth. The details of this analysis have yet to be published, however, so it is too soon to be sure. There is not enough evidence yet to prove that Luke was right, but there is certainly enough to make it very presumptuous to argue that Luke must have been wrong.[1] And since the evidence for Quirinius' activities recoverable from other sources is not always consistent, one must also allow for the possibility that the extra-biblical

---

[1]For more detail, see Craig L. Blomberg, 'Quirinius', in the revised *ISBE*, vol. 4 (Grand Rapids: Eerdmans, forthcoming). On the micrographic analysis, see the preliminary report by E. J. Vardaman, *Archaeology and the Living Word* (Starkville, MS: Sherwood, 1981), p.138. Vardaman's earlier, unpublished work was endorsed, notably, by Jack Finegan, 'Chronology of the NT', in *ISBE*, rev., I, p.687.

historians have got some of their information wrong.[1]

2 The testimony of non-Christian writers

A Graeco-Roman sources

None of the Graeco-Roman historians of the first generations of the Christian era has much to say about the life of Jesus. But there are several important passages which provide brief, independent testimony to Jesus' existence. The early third-century historian, Julius Africanus, cites an interesting statement from the historian Thallus who wrote a chronicle of world history in Greek in the first century, in which the author refers to the darkness which occurred at the time of the crucifixion.[2] Pliny the Younger, the Roman legate of Bithynia-Pontus (what is now part of north-central Turkey) in the early second century, wrote to the emperor Trajan, requesting advice on how to deal with Christians who refused to reverence Caesar's image. Pliny noted that these Christians met regularly and sang hymns 'to Christ as if to a god' (*Letters* 10:96.7). The phrase 'as if to a god' suggests that Pliny knew Jesus had been a person who had lived on earth but was reluctant to call him divine.

A third source of evidence for Jesus' human career is the Roman historian Tacitus who wrote early in the second century. He describes Christians as those who had received their name from 'Christ who had been executed by sentence of the procurator Pontius Pilate in the reign of Tiberius' (*Annals* 15:44). These details mesh perfectly with the information found in the New Testament. Writing about five years later than Tacitus, another Roman historian of the day, Suetonius, refers to the expulsion of Jews from Rome in the time of the emperor Claudius (AD 41–54). The cause for this imperial edict he attributes to rioting 'at the instigation of Chrestus' (*Claudius* 25:4). Many scholars view this as a variant or mistaken spelling of the

---

[1]Colin Hemer, 'Luke the Historian', *BJRL* 60 (1977), p.50, makes this point more generally, with respect to the frequent scholarly comparisons of Luke and Josephus. In many cases Josephus seems somewhat less credible.

[2]For all eight extant fragments of Thallus, see F. Jacoby, *Die Fragmente der griechischen Historiker IIB* (Berlin: Weidmann, 1929), pp.1156–1158 (not accessible to me).

Latin *Christus* (Christ) and believe that it was turmoil among Jews and Christians in Rome to which Suetonius refers – mistakenly thinking that Christ himself was present to instigate it. The reference nevertheless 'points to Jesus as the leader of a band of dissident Jews, if not the founder of Christianity'.[1]

Combining the evidence of Thallus, Pliny, Tacitus and Suetonius, one can accumulate enough data to refute the fanciful notion that Jesus never existed,[2] without even appealing to the testimony of Jewish or Christian sources. But apart from these references to his crucifixion and the movement which outlived him, one discovers nothing else from Graeco-Roman sources. This should not be too surprising though, in light of the humble beginnings of Christianity, the remote location of Palestine on the eastern frontiers of the Roman empire, the small percentage of the works of ancient Graeco-Roman historians which have survived, and the lack of attention paid by those which are extant to Jewish figures in general.

B Jewish sources

When one considers how quickly Christianity became a predominantly Gentile religion and how relationships between Christians and Jews deteriorated, it is not quite as surprising that the Jewish traditions should also make little mention of Jesus. But they do supply more data than the Graeco-Roman sources offer. And the references that remain have regularly been censored, with later copies or parallel accounts omitting Jesus' name. So it is entirely likely that the Jewish tradition knew much more about Jesus' earthly life than what is recorded in the documents that have survived. The significance of that which does remain, however, is shrouded with uncertainties.[3]

---

[1]Murray J. Harris,'References to Jesus in Early Classical Authors', in *GP*,5, p.356. The rest of Harris's article (pp.343–368) gives a more detailed discussion of the passages noted in this section and provides the translations which are adopted here.

[2]*Contra* G. A. Wells, *The Jesus of the Early Christians* (London: Pemberton, 1971); also his *Did Jesus Exist?* (London: Pemberton; New York: Prometheus, 1975); and *The Historical Evidence for Jesus* (New York: Prometheus, 1982). France, *Evidence,* repeatedly exposes the fallacies in Wells' works but agrees with him that the Graeco-Roman historians were merely parroting Christianity's own account of its origins rather than supplying independent historical testimony. The opposite view is more cogently defended by Harris, 'References'.

[3]For many of the following details, see Graham H. Twelftree, 'Jesus in Jewish Traditions', in *GP*,5, pp.289–341, from which the translations given here are also adopted.

1 The rabbinic traditions

None of the testimony of the ancient rabbis perfectly matches the information recorded in the four gospels about Jesus, but most of it becomes intelligible when viewed as developments and distortions of the historical facts. Several traditions do not specifically mention Jesus' name, even though he is clearly in view. For example, in the Palestinian Talmud, the third-century Rabbi Abbahu says, 'If a man says to you "I am (a) God", he is a liar; "I am (a) Son of Man", he will regret it; "I go up to heaven", he has said it but he will not be able to do it' (P. Ta'an. 65b). This tradition reflects no first-hand acquaintance with Jesus' life, only a knowledge of the Christian claims for him. Yet the interesting feature of this and similar rabbinic traditions is that these claims are never disputed as inventions of his followers; they are merely rejected as in error. Unlike modern sceptics, the rabbis apparently never denied that Jesus made such claims for himself; instead they called one who makes such claims a liar. Surely if Jesus had been a simple teacher whose self-understanding was greatly distorted by Christians of subsequent generations, some recollection of this fact would have remained for those opposed to Christianity to exploit.[1]

Other rabbinic traditions refer to Jesus more directly. In the fifth-century Babylonian Talmud a rebellious disciple is compared to one 'who publicly burns his food like Jesus of Nazareth', using a metaphor which refers to the distortion of Jewish teaching (b. Sanh. 103a). A few columns further on, the claim is made that 'Jesus the Nazarene practised magic and led Israel astray' (b. Sanh. 107b). Both of these traditions reflect Jesus' disputes with the prevailing Jewish interpretations of the Law, and the second one seems to admit that he worked some kind of miracles or wonders as well, even if it explains them differently than do most Christians. Again the Christian claims are not denied but simply given a different interpretation.

In several places Jesus is called 'Jesus ben (=son of) Pandera', and the second-century Christian writer Origen explains that the Jews believed that Jesus was the child of Mary by an adulterous relationship with a Roman soldier by that name (*Contra Celsum* 1:32). The name and hence the legend could come from a

---

[1]*Cf.* E. Stauffer, *Jesus and His Story* (London: SCM; New York: Knopf, 1960), pp.155–156.

198

corruption of the Greek word *parthenos* for 'virgin' and reflect knowledge of the Christian doctrine of the virgin birth. It is impossible to know how old this Jewish allegation is, but charges that Jesus was born out of wedlock are apparently alluded to already in John's Gospel (Jn. 8:41). Both the Christian and the Jewish traditions, however, seem to imply that Joseph was not Jesus' natural father.

The two items in the rabbinic traditions which are most widely believed to contain a core of independent testimony to genuine, historical information about Jesus refer to his death and his disciples. In b. Sanh. 43a, Jesus is said to have been hanged on the eve of the Passover. On the assumption that crucifixion could be termed 'hanging', this tradition would provide powerful support for John's account of Christ's death, in which the Jews seem not to have begun celebrating the Passover when Jesus was crucified, and would fly in the face of the reconstruction of the last day of Jesus' life adopted above (see pp.177–178), in which Jesus died on the day following the evening of the main Passover meal. This rabbinic tradition goes on, though, to claim that 'for forty days before the execution took place, a herald went forth and cried, "He is going forth to be stoned because he has practised sorcery and enticed Israel to apostasy".' Since the Jews generally hanged the dead bodies of criminals whom they stoned, as a public deterrent and disgrace, it is more natural to interpret this passage as a reference to a true hanging, which would then not apply to Jesus. Moreover the notion of a forty-day period of heralding an execution contradicts Jewish criminal procedure, so this whole tradition is historically suspect.

In the same section of the Talmud, the rabbis go on to teach that 'Jesus had five disciples, Mattha, Naqai, Neẓer, Buni and Todah'. Scholars have conjectured that Mattha, Naqai, and Todah are alternate or corrupt spellings of the Hebrew for Matthew, Nicodemus, and Thaddaeus, and that Neẓer refers to a Nazarene or follower of Jesus more generally. Buni might just conceivably be a corruption of the Hebrew for John. Still, all of this is guess-work. At the end of the day, one must admit that the rabbinic traditions offer precious little independent testimony to the ministry of Jesus.[1]

---

[1]For a book-length treatment of these and related texts, see Johann Maier, *Jesus von*

2 *Josephus*

At first glance, the Jewish historian Josephus, who wrote during the second half of the first century AD, would seem to offer much more promising material. In his *Jewish Antiquities*, he makes passing mention of 'James, the brother of Jesus who was called the Christ', who he claims was delivered up to the Sanhedrin to be stoned sometime in the decade of the 60s (*Ant.* 20:200). Josephus also tells of John the Baptist, whom Herod killed even 'though he was a good man and had exhorted the Jews to lead righteous lives, to practise justice towards their fellows and piety towards God, and so doing to join in baptism' (18:117). But the most striking and significant passage occurs in 18:63–64:

> About this time there lived Jesus, a wise man, if indeed one ought to call him a man. For he was one who wrought surprising feats and was a teacher of such people as accept the truth gladly. He won over many Jews and many of the Greeks. He was the Messiah. When Pilate, upon hearing him accused by men of the highest standing amongst us, had condemned him to be crucified, those who had in the first place come to love him did not give up their affection for him. On the third day he appeared to them restored to life, for the prophets of God had prophesied these and countless other marvellous things about him. And the tribe of the Christians, so called after him, has still to this day not disappeared.

If this passage, in its entirety, were an authentic part of the original text of Josephus' *Antiquities*, it would provide dramatic corroboration of the main contours of the gospel testimony about Jesus by one who otherwise shows no signs of biasing his history in favour of Christianity. But it is precisely because Josephus was not a Christian that it is hard to attribute all these words to him. Some scholars have therefore rejected the whole passage as a later interpolation by a Christian scribe copying Josephus' work. Many recent studies of Josephus, however, agree that much of the passage closely resembles Josephus' style of writing elsewhere, so that

---

Nazareth in der talmudischen Überlieferung (Darmstadt: Wissenschaftliche Buchgesellschaft, 1978). Maier concludes that none of the rabbinic traditions about Jesus can be dated with any probability to the first two centuries of the Christian era.

if it were tampered with, probably only the details about Christ's dubious humanity, his Messiahship and his resurrection were added.[1] A few are willing to leave the passage almost entirely intact, supposing that the original varied only by including phrases something like 'the so-called Christ' (as in the passage about James) and 'some said he appeared . . .'[2] The fact that later quotations and versions of Josephus do vary on some of these details makes the hypothesis of minor interpolations of some kind fairly probable, although scholars will continue to dispute their exact nature. But most of the passage seems to be authentic and is certainly the most important ancient non-Christian testimony to the life of Jesus which has been preserved.

3 Extra-biblical Christian traditions

The earliest non-canonical Christian literature which has survived falls into three main collections. First are the 'apostolic fathers' – a group of second- or very late first-century writings, largely epistolary in nature, which stem from individuals or communities that saw themselves as faithfully preserving and transmitting the public teachings of Jesus' twelve apostles but without claiming the type of inspiration or infallible authority which they ascribed to their predecessors.[3] Second is the Nag Hammadi library – an extensive collection of writings discovered in Egypt shortly after World War 2, most of them Gnostic[4] in origin, a few possibly contemporary with or even predating the birth of Christianity but most stemming from the second, third and fourth centuries. These works usually

---

[1]Louis H. Feldman gives a wide-ranging survey of recent research in 'The *Testimonium Flavianum:* The State of the Question', in *Christological Perspectives,* ed. Robert F. Berkey and Sarah A. Edwards (New York: Pilgrim, 1982), pp.179–199. Less comprehensively, *cf.* J. Neville Birdsall, 'The Continuing Enigma of Josephus's Testimony about Jesus', *BJRL* 67 (1985), pp.609–622, who is more sceptical about the authenticity of this passage.

[2]See esp. A.-M. Dubarle, 'Le témoignage de Josèphe sur Jésus d'après la tradition indirecte', *RB* 80 (1973), pp.481–513; also his 'Le témoignage de Josèphe sur Jésus d'après des publications récentes', *RB* 84 (1977), pp.38–58.

[3]The standard Greek-English edition of J. B. Lightfoot and J. Harmer (*The Apostolic Fathers* [London: Macmillan, 1891]) has now been reprinted (Grand Rapids: Baker, 1984).

[4]Gnosticism embraces so many diverse movements that it is impossible to summarize it adequately in a sentence. The word comes from the Greek *gnōsis* ('knowledge') and refers to various sects which often combined elements of pagan, Jewish and Christian belief, believing that they had received some secret revelation about the nature of true religion and that salvation was achieved through that knowledge. The modern-day legacy of Gnosticism is perhaps best seen in such groups as the Christian Science or Theosophist churches.

presented themselves as Christian but came to be rejected by the early church as heretical. They include gospels, epistles, apocalypses, diatribes and various other genres. Where the teachings of Jesus are cited, they are usually described as private or secret revelations given only to certain disciples, thus explaining why they were not known by the church at large.[1] The third category of literature is the New Testament apocrypha – works which also imitate all the biblical genres but which have been known for much longer than the Nag Hammadi library. This is the most diverse collection of the three, but like the Gnostic writings, these other apocrypha generally claim to be as reliable or authoritative as their canonical counterparts even if they were rejected by the majority of Christians as unreliable.[2]

A The apostolic fathers

The seven most important of the Greek works which comprise the collection known as the apostolic fathers, and which include references to the gospel traditions about Jesus, are: (1-2) two epistles ascribed to Clement, bishop of Rome – one to the Corinthians, and one of a more general, homiletic nature, probably written by someone else in Clement's name; (3) a group of short epistles by Ignatius to churches and individuals as he passed on his way from Antioch to Rome *en route* to his martyrdom there; (4) an epistle of Polycarp, the disciple of the apostle John, to the Philippians; (5) the Didache, or The Teaching of the Apostles, an early handbook on practical matters in Christian ethics and church order; (6) a general epistle attributed to Barnabas, probably wrongly, with harsh polemic against those who would not radically reinterpret the Jewish Law in light of its fulfilment in Christ; and (7) the Shepherd of Hermas, named after its main character who receives a series of visions, commands and parables of Christian doctrine from an angel of the Lord. 1 Clement, the Didache, and Barnabas probably come from the end of the first century, Ignatius and Polycarp from the early second century, and 2 Clement and Her-

---

[1]The standard English translation is *The Nag Hammadi Library in English*, ed. James M. Robinson (Leiden: Brill, 1977). Quotations of Nag Hammadi documents throughout this chapter follow this translation.

[2]The standard English translation is that of R. McL.Wilson in E. Hennecke & W. Schneemelcher, *The New Testament Apocrypha*, 2 vols. (London: Lutterworth; Philadelphia: Westminster, 1963–65).

mas from the middle of the second century.[1]

The apostolic fathers all quote the Old Testament as authoritative Scripture, often in great detail. They also include frequent references to the teachings of the New Testament, though only rarely with a specific introduction labelling them as Scripture. In the case of passages which parallel the gospels, it is usually very difficult to know whether the fathers were citing or paraphrasing written, canonical texts, or whether they had access to earlier written sources or oral tradition which preceded the final composition of the gospels. A third possibility is that they relied on oral tradition as it developed or was rephrased after the gospels had been written. Although the written documents of the New Testament quickly began to assume an authoritative position in the early church, even in the first half of the second century, Papias, the bishop of Hierapolis, could claim that he trusted the oral tradition delivered to him by the successors of Christ's apostles more than any written texts (Eusebius, *Eccl. Hist.* 3:39.3–4).[2] In most cases where the wording of a gospel tradition in the apostolic fathers very closely parallels that of the written texts of Matthew, Mark, Luke or John, the natural assumption is that the fathers knew the canonical form of the passages they cite. The best case for this procedure can be made for 2 Clement, which quotes teachings of Jesus in at least twelve of its twenty paragraphs, and explicitly introduces its first quotation, 'I did not come to call the righteous but sinners', with the words, 'another Scripture says' (2 Clem. 2:4; *cf.* Mk. 2:17 for the identical Greek wording). Yet the author of this homily also knew of sayings attributed to Jesus which are not found in the gospels. The most famous of these, which recurs in several Gnostic writings, speaks of the kingdom coming 'when the two shall be one, and the outside as the inside, and the male with the female' (2 Clem. 12:2; also found in Gosp. Thos. 23 and ascribed by early Christian writers to the lost Gospels of the Egyptians and of the Ebionites). So it is possible that

---

[1]All these dates are debated. For details see Donald A. Hagner, 'The Sayings of Jesus in the Apostolic Fathers and Justin Martyr', in *GP*,5, pp.233–268, and the literature there cited. This article also informs much of the rest of this chapter's discussion of the apostolic fathers. The fullest study of this topic is Helmut Köster, *Synoptische Überlieferung bei den apostolischen Vätern* (Berlin: Akademie-Verlag, 1957). Köster consistently discounts the possibility that the same traditions underlay both the gospels and the apostolic fathers, but more recent research has proved less sceptical.

[2]For the view that Papias' apparent disparagement of written texts applies only to non-apostolic sources, see A. F. Walls, 'Papias and Oral Tradition', *VC* 21 (1967), pp.137–140.

2 Clement also relied on non-canonical sources for some or all of the traditions paralleled in the canonical gospels.[1]

For the rest of the apostolic fathers, conscious quotation of the canonical New Testament, however probable in theory, is even harder to prove in practice. The question here, though, does not concern how reliably the New Testament was cited by later Christian authors but is about the reliability of the Jesus tradition *before* the written gospels took their final form. So attention should focus on those passages in which it seems most probable that the apostolic fathers depended on oral or written traditions which predated the composition of the four gospels. The most objective method for identifying such passages involves a careful analysis of the quotations in the fathers in the light of New Testament source criticism (see pp.12–18). Three possible applications of this method will be considered.

1 The Didache and Q

The Didache begins with a detailed contrast between the 'way of life' and the 'way of death' (§§1–6). The description of the way of life contains numerous parallels to Jesus' Sermon on the Mount/ Plain. The lengthiest such passage reads as follows:

> First, you shall love the God that made you; second, your neighbour as yourself. And all that you do not want to happen to you, do not you also do to another . . . Bless those who curse you and pray for your enemies and fast for those who persecute you. For what credit is it if you love those who love you? Do not even the Gentiles do the same? But you shall love those who hate you, and you shall have no enemy. Put away fleshly and bodily lusts. If someone gives you a blow on the right cheek, turn to him the other also, and you will be perfect; if someone forces you to go with him one mile, go with him two; if someone takes away your outer garment, give him your tunic also . . . (Did. 1:2–5).

The rest of the book deals with instructions on baptism, fasting, prayer, the eucharist, church leadership and teaching, and the

---

[1]The most detailed defence of this thesis is K. P. Donfried, *The Setting of Second Clement in Early Christianity* (Leiden: Brill, 1974), pp.56–81. The same ambiguity characterizes the rather infrequent allusions to the Jesus tradition in Hermas.

return of Christ. In these contexts occur parts of the great commission (Mt. 28:19), the Lord's prayer (Mt. 6:9–13; with only a few words varying from Matthew's Greek text), the command not to give what is holy to dogs, the principle that a workman is worthy of his food, and the warning to be ready with lamps not quenched and loins not ungirded, since one does not know the hour in which the Lord will come.

Except for this final reference, which appears to come only from Luke 12:35, every quotation or allusion to Jesus' teaching in the Didache is paralleled in Matthew. Not surprisingly, older commentators generally held that the Didache had simply cited selections from Matthew's gospel.[1] Thirty years ago, Richard Glover challenged this consensus by pointing out that only certain portions of Matthew's information about Jesus appear in the Didache. Specifically, the Didache never includes traditions which are also found in Mark, but only those which Matthew acquired from other sources. Several of these passages are paralleled in Luke (the so-called Q material) and some are peculiar to Matthew. Glover therefore suggested that the Didache did not depend on canonical Matthew but on a source which Matthew and Luke shared, perhaps Q itself.[2] Glover's conclusions have not gone unchallenged[3] but they have for the most part prevailed, especially in recent research by Jonathan Draper.[4] But if the Didache's quotations predate the canonical gospels, then they provide powerful testimony in support of the reliability of the gospel tradition at that early date, since the details of those quotations are very close to their canonical counterparts. The words of Jesus are excerpted, rearranged, joined with other exhortations, and applied to new situations. But, as Draper concludes, the Didache 'largely supports the evidence of Matthew and Luke concerning the teaching of Jesus', and 'the differences are rather a matter of wording than

---

[1]See esp. E. Massaux, 'L'influence littéraire de l'évangile de saint Matthieu sur la Didachè', *ETL* 25 (1949), pp.5–41.

[2]Richard Glover, 'The Didache's Quotations and the Synoptic Gospels', *NTS* 5 (1958–59), pp.12–29. The Epistle of Barnabas contains a shorter version of the teaching on the ways of life and death, which most scholars believe predates the Didache. So the Didache may have relied on more than one pre-Synoptic source or it may have depended in part on Barnabas' form of the tradition as well.

[3]See esp. B. C. Butler, 'The Literary Relations of Didache, Ch. XVI', *JTS* 11 (1960), pp.265–283, who argues that the Didache depended on canonical Luke and a Greek source of Matthew's non-Marcan material indistinguishable from the canonical form.

[4]Jonathan Draper, 'A Commentary on the Didache in the Light of the Dead Sea Scrolls and Related Documents' (Cambridge: PhD. Thesis, 1983. Unpublished).

of substance, and the same authentic, challenging voice of Jesus rings through the sayings'.[1]

2 Ignatius and M

In the epistles of Ignatius, only brief excerpts of the gospel tradition are either alluded to or quoted. Three examples are: 'A tree is known by its fruit' (Ign. Eph. 14:2; *cf*. Mt. 12:33b), 'In everything be as shrewd as the serpents and forever as innocent as the dove' (Ign. Polyc. 2:2; *cf*. Mt. 10:16b), and 'for there is (only) one teacher' (Ign. Eph. 15:1, *cf*. Mt. 23:8). Virtually all of the excerpts again find parallels in Matthew's Gospel. This is not surprising since Matthew was the most popular gospel from early on in the history of the church (*cf*. below, p.219). What is surprising is that nearly three-quarters of the references in Ignatius are found in M material, that is, in passages peculiar to Matthew, even though such material comprises only about one quarter of the gospel. Smit Sibinga has examined these passages in detail and concludes that there is no convincing explanation for this phenomenon if Ignatius were depending on the entire Gospel of Matthew. Instead he must have been following different sources, including those distinctive traditions on which Matthew alone, of the four evangelists, relied.[2]

The significance of this conclusion, if correct, is even greater than that of the Didache's use of a Q-like source. Many scholars doubt whether Matthew relied on actual sources for his canonically unparalleled sections, whereas here is strong evidence that he did. What is more, some of Ignatius' quotations of Matthew excerpt material which is almost universally attributed to Matthew's editorial modification of his sources. For example, in the story of Jesus' baptism, only Matthew quotes Jesus as saying to John, 'Let it be so for now, for thus it is fitting for us to fulfil all righteousness' (Mt. 3:15). Most redaction critics assume this statement to be Matthew's own unhistorical addition to Mark's version of the baptism (Mk. 1:9–11). But Ignatius also knows this saying of Jesus; in his epistle to Smyrna he writes

---

[1] Jonathan Draper,'The Jesus Tradition in the Didache', in *GP*,5, pp.284, 287, n.48.
[2] J. Smit Sibinga, 'Ignatius and Matthew', *NovT* 8 (1966), pp.263–283. *Cf*. Christine Trevett, 'Approaching Matthew from the Second Century: The Under-Used Ignatian Correspondence', *JSNT* 20 (1984), pp.59–67.

that Jesus was 'baptised by John in order that all righteousness might be fulfilled by him' (Ign. Smyr. 1:1). So if Ignatius did not know the final form of Matthew's gospel, then Matthew could not have invented this saying. It must have come from an earlier source to which both Matthew and Ignatius had access, and the earlier its pedigree the more confident one can be of its authenticity.[1]

3 1 Clement, Polycarp and early catechesis

1 Clement contains only two clear passages with gospel excerpts of at least a sentence in length. One of these combines in a very stylized pattern a number of teachings reminiscent of the Sermon on the Mount/Plain, along with some unparalleled exhortation:

> Be merciful in order that you may receive mercy. Forgive in order that it may be forgiven you. As you do, so shall it be done to you. As you give, so shall it be given to you. As you judge, so shall you be judged. As you show kindness, so shall kindness be shown to you. With what measure you measure out, it shall be measured to you. (1 Clem. 13:2)

A shorter, rearranged version of this passage occurs in Polycarp's letter to the Philippians (2:3) in conjunction with the beatitude, 'Blessed are the poor and those who are persecuted for righteousness' sake, for theirs is the kingdom of God' (*cf.* Mt. 5:10). Since there is no evidence that Clement or Polycarp knew each other's work, it is unlikely that both would independently create such similar pastiches of Jesus' teachings. The parallel, rhythmic form of the passage suggests that in the oral tradition the teaching was deliberately phrased this way for easy memorization and accurate preservation. The New Testament epistles (especially Ephesians, Colossians and 1 Peter) also share hortatory material which they probably acquired from a common source, perhaps from the early church's instruction for new converts, possibly at baptismal services, or from a simple liturgy of worship. All this adds up to a plausible case for Clement and Polycarp depending

---

[1]*Cf.* Richard Bauckham, 'The Study of the Gospel Traditions Outside the Canonical Gospels: Problems and Prospects', in *GP*,5, p.395. Bauckham endorses Sibinga's general approach but concludes that the differences between Ignatius and M suggest that M was the oral tradition on which Matthew drew and hence somewhat flexible in its wording.

not on Matthew or Luke, or even on Q, but on an oral tradition of the teachings of Jesus which goes back to a very early stage of the gospel tradition.[1]

As with Ignatius and the Didache, one's confidence in the reliability of the tradition can only be strengthened by these findings. Donald Hagner's conclusions apply to a broad spectrum of gospel traditions in the apostolic fathers:

> although the sayings of Jesus are reproduced freely and adapted to special purposes, the amount of significant variation between the same sayings in our sources is relatively small.
>
> . . . if the tenacity and relative stability of oral tradition in the first half of the second century was as impressive as we have seen it to be, the trustworthiness of that oral tradition in the middle decades of the first century was, if anything, even more substantial.[2]

Moreover, although occasionally sayings of Jesus are presented which are without canonical parallel, such 'agrapha' (unwritten sayings) are few and far between. The testimony of the apostolic fathers speaks strongly against the notion that the early church felt free to invent teachings which Jesus never really uttered.

B The Nag Hammadi library

Most of the Nag Hammadi documents, predominantly Gnostic in nature, make no pretense of overlapping with the gospel traditions of Jesus' earthly life. A number claim to record conversations of the resurrected Jesus with various disciples, but this setting is usually little more than an artificial framework for imparting Gnostic doctrine. The major exception is the so-called Gospel of Thomas, preserved in a fourth-century Coptic manuscript, but originally written in Greek probably in the mid-second century. Smaller numbers of gospel parallels and agrapha occur in the Apocryphon of James, the Gospel of Philip and the Gospel of Truth. Other documents only occasionally contain information about Jesus' earthly life and teaching, so attention will be limited to these four. Several of the scholars who have devoted themselves

---

[1]For the most detail, see D. A. Hagner, *The Use of the Old and New Testaments in Clement of Rome* (Leiden: Brill, 1973), pp.135–178.

[2]Hagner, 'Apostolic Fathers', pp.256, 259.

to the translation and critical analysis of these texts argue that they deserve to be considered at least as seriously as the canonical gospels as sources of genuine information about Jesus. Perhaps no one has campaigned as vigorously on behalf of the apocryphal gospels as the distinguished Harvard divinity professor, Helmut Koester. In a recent article, Koester maintains that 'at least four apocryphal gospels belong to a very early stage in the development of gospel literature – a stage that is comparable to the sources which were used by the gospels of the NT'.[1] These four include the Gospel of Thomas and the Apocryphon of James along with two documents not found at Nag Hammadi, the Gospel of Peter and the Unknown Gospel of Papyrus Egerton 2 (on which see pp.217–218).

1 The Gospel of Thomas
The Gospel of Thomas is not a connected narrative of the events of Jesus' life, but a collection of 114 sayings attributed to Jesus, most of them introduced simply with the words, 'Jesus said'. These were allegedly revealed in secret to the apostle Thomas, but no one today believes this claim. Many of the sayings have a patently Gnostic flavour, and little can be said in support of their authenticity. One of the most striking of these is the final one (Thos. 114), which forms a brief dialogue:

> Simon Peter said to them, 'Let Mary leave us, for women are not worthy of Life.' Jesus said, 'I myself shall lead her in order to make her male, so that she too may become a living spirit resembling you males. For every woman who will make herself male will enter the Kingdom of Heaven.'

This saying resembles the passage quoted from 2 Clement earlier in this chapter (p.203) and issues from an ascetic milieu in which expressions of sexuality were discouraged and an asexual or androgynous human being was looked upon as ideal. Clearly there is no support from the New Testament gospels for such a doctrine.

However, over half of the sayings in the Gospel of Thomas

---

[1]Helmut Koester, 'Apocryphal and Canonical Gospels', *HTR* 73 (1980), p.112. *Cf.* Elaine Pagels, *The Gnostic Gospels* (New York: Random House, 1979; London: Weidenfeld & Nicolson, 1980); J. D. Crossan, *Four Other Gospels* (Minneapolis: Winston, 1985).

resemble teachings of Jesus found in the canonical gospels, though they seldom appear in identical form. A representative example is one of the longer sayings on the kingdom (Thos. 3):

> Jesus said, 'If those who lead you say to you, "See, the Kingdom is in the sky," then the birds of the sky will precede you. If they say to you, "It is in the sea," then the fish will precede you. Rather, the Kingdom is inside of you, and it is outside of you. When you come to know yourselves, then you will become known, and you will realize that it is you who are the sons of the living Father. But if you will not know yourselves, you dwell in poverty and it is you who are that poverty.'

The middle section of this passage resembles Luke 17:20b-21, in which Jesus says, 'The kingdom of God is not coming with observable signs; nor will they say, "Behold, here it is!" or "There!" for behold, the kingdom of God is in your midst, or, 'within you'. Both passages can be interpreted to mean that Jesus did not believe that the kingdom of God would arrive with the Messiah's spectacular display of power but with humble beginnings in the more ordinary events of his ministry and the ministry of his disciples. This saying in the Gospel of Thomas *may* have preserved within it an otherwise unknown, authentic saying of Jesus. On the other hand, the sentence about coming to know oneself can very easily be seen as a later creation, in view of Gnosticism's emphasis on salvation by knowledge, so at least part of the passage seems inauthentic. But if it were thoroughly Gnostic, then one would not have expected it to declare that the kingdom was external as well as internal to the individual. What is perhaps most likely is that the passage is a combination of authentic and inauthentic segments.[1]

It is probably impossible to determine with any confidence which of the previously unknown sayings of the Gospel of Thomas, if any, are authentic. Two that are widely cited as strong candidates, because of their similarity to the memorable form and contents of the gospel traditions, are Thos. 82, 'He who is near Me is near the fire, and he who is far from Me is far from the Kingdom', and 77b, 'Split a piece of wood, and I am there. Lift up

---

[1]For further discussion of this and other 'kingdom' passages in the Gospel of Thomas, see Bruce Chilton, 'The Gospel according to Thomas as a Source of Jesus' Teaching', in *GP*,5, pp.155–175.

the stone, and you will find me there'.[1] But where Thomas parallels the four gospels it is unlikely that any of the distinctive elements in Thomas predate the canonical versions. In a number of cases these distinctives reappear in the Coptic translation of the New Testament, which no one would claim reflects independent sources of information about Jesus. Others are paralleled by late textual variants of the Greek New Testament or by Tatian's late second-century harmony of the gospels, the *Diatessaron* (see pp.2–3). When one realizes that parallels also appear to every source-critical layer of the Synoptic tradition (*i.e.* Mark, Q, M and L), and even to the parable of the seed growing secretly (Thos. 21; Mk. 4:29), one of the rare examples of a tradition found only in Mark, it is hard to avoid the conclusion that the author of the Gospel of Thomas knew the New Testament gospels as they now stand, even if he may have quoted them fairly loosely.[2]

Given this premise, one important further observation emerges. The parable is the one type of passage in Thomas which recurs frequently enough and which contains sufficient detail to enable patterns of modification to be detected. Thomas recounts thirteen narrative parables of Jesus, eleven of which are paralleled in the Synoptics. Of these eleven, nine are noticeably abbreviated and less detailed than their biblical counterparts. The most dramatic example is the parable of the wheat and the tares (Thos. 57; *cf.* Mt. 13:24–30) which reads,

> The Kingdom of the Father is like a man who had [good] seed. His enemy came by night and sowed weeds among the good

---

[1]These are two in a list of eighteen sayings of Jesus found in various sources other than the canonical gospels which J. Jeremias (*Unknown Sayings of Jesus* [London: SPCK, 1958]) thinks may be authentic. For a critical analysis of these agrapha by one who thinks that only three or four are probably authentic, see O. Hofius, ' "Unbekannte Jesusworte" ', in *Das Evangelium und die Evangelien,* ed. P. Stuhlmacher (Tübingen: Mohr, 1983), pp.355–382. *Cf.* also William L. Lane, 'A Critique of Purportedly Authentic Agrapha', *JETS* 18 (1975), pp.29–35.

[2]For further evidence and relevant literature, see Craig L. Blomberg, 'Tradition and Redaction in the Parables of the Gospel of Thomas', in *GP*,5, pp.177–205, of which the following paragraph is also a summary. The dependence of Thomas on the canonical gospels is hotly disputed, but it is held by a majority of recent studies devoted specifically to the question, despite assertions to the contrary. The latter include a recent, book-length attempt to place Thomas on a par with Q as a gospel source, by Stevan Davies (*The Gospel of Thomas and Christian Wisdom* [New York: Seabury, 1983]). William G. Morrice's review of *GP*,5, in *Themelios* 11 (1986), pp.100–101, offers no reasons for his dissent from the view defended in detail in my article. He apparently adds two shorter metaphors to his count of parables (see next paragraph), which have no bearing on the tendencies noted, so the point of his 'correction' is unclear.

seed. The man did not allow them to pull up the weeds; he said to them, 'I am afraid that you will go intending to pull up the weeds and pull up the wheat along with them.' For on the day of the harvest the weeds will be plainly visible, and they will be pulled up and burned.

Far from displaying a tendency to elaborate, embellish, or allegorize the parables, in the way in which so many scholars believe the gospel tradition developed, the tendency in Thomas is to eliminate and to streamline. Where details not found in the Synoptics do appear, they can almost always be explained as conscious, Gnostic redaction.[1] Pheme Perkins has come to much the same conclusions for the pronouncement stories in Thomas.[2] There is thus little evidence for the theory that the oral tradition behind the canonical gospels expanded and embellished the original testimony on which it was based.

2 The Apocryphon of James

Like the Gospel of Thomas, the Apocryphon of James purports to be the secret revelation of the risen Jesus, this time to his brother, James. Unlike Thomas, this apocryphon is in the form of a dialogue between Jesus and his disciples *en route* to his ascension, with which the sixteen columns of Coptic text culminate. Nowhere does an undeniable parallel with the gospel tradition emerge, but neither is most of the document demonstrably Gnostic or unorthodox. Jesus responds to his disciples' questions by discussing the need to protect the kingdom of God, to guard against Satan and the desires of the flesh, to practise love and the other manifestations of the Spirit, and to await his glorious return. In several places, new parables and kingdom sayings appear, which a number of recent studies have claimed are mostly authentic.[3] In the three new parables Jesus compares the kingdom of heaven to a palm-shoot, a seed of wheat, and an ear of grain. The last of these, for example, reads: 'The kingdom of heaven is like an ear of grain

---

[1]*Cf.* esp. Andreas Lindemann, 'Zur Gleichnisinterpretation im Thomas-Evangelium', *ZNW* 71 (1980), pp.214–243.

[2]Pheme Perkins, 'Pronouncement Stories in the Gospel of Thomas', *Semeia* 20 (1981), pp.121–132.

[3]See esp. Charles W. Hedrick, 'Kingdom Sayings and Parables of Jesus in *The Apocryphon of James:* Tradition and Redaction', *NTS* 29 (1983), pp.1–24; Ron Cameron, *Sayings Traditions in the Apocryphon of James* (Cambridge, MA: Harvard, 1984).

after it had sprouted in a field. And when it had ripened, it scattered its fruit and again filled the field with ears for another year' (Apoc. Jas. 12:22–27). The similarity with the agricultural parables of the gospels (*e.g.* the sower, mustard seed, or wheat and tares) is inescapable.

At the same time, the Apocryphon of James also describes Jesus rebuking his disciples for not having understood earlier parables. In this context, Jesus laments that

> you have compelled me to stay with you another eighteen days for the sake of the parables. It was enough for some <to listen> to the teaching and understand 'The Shepherds' and 'The Seed' and 'The Building' and 'The Lamps of the Virgins' and 'The Wage of the Workmen' and 'The Didrachmae' and 'The Woman'. (Apoc. Jas. 8:1–10)

Not only does this chronology contradict the canonical gospels (the Apocryphon also claims that the Lord appeared for 550 days after his resurrection, compared with only 40 in the New Testament), but the references to parables by means of a short title suggest that they have already become so widely known in the church that no further detail is necessary. This suggestion, coupled with the fact that the parables cited seem to come from all strands of the Synoptic tradition, again including even the peculiarly Marcan material (assuming 'The Seed' equals 'the seed growing secretly'), makes it more probable that the Apocryphon is at least in part later than and dependent on the canonical gospels.[1] And while there is not much in this work that must be interpreted in a Gnostic fashion, there is little, including the additional parables, that does not readily yield itself to such an interpretation.[2] One can therefore deduce very little with any degree of confidence from this document about the development of the gospel tradition in more orthodox circles.

3 The Gospel of Philip

The Gospel of Philip is the most obviously Gnostic of the three texts

---

[1]J.-M. Sevrin, 'Paroles et paraboles de Jésus dans les écrits gnostiques coptes', in *Logia*, ed. J. Delobel (Leuven: University Press, 1982), p.524.

[2]D. Rouleau, 'Les paraboles du Royaume des cieux dans l'*Epître apocryphe de Jacques*', in *Colloque international sur les textes de Nag Hammadi,* ed. Bernard Barc (Quebec: Laval, 1981), pp.181–189.

so far discussed. It does not claim to be the revelation of the Lord but is merely a manual of Gnostic theology and ethics which occasionally refers to the words and works of Jesus. It is pre-occupied with the sacraments and espouses the ideal of the androgynous 'unisex' noted earlier in the Gospel of Thomas. All but one of the Gospel of Philip's allusions to the Synoptic tradition are to Matthew, including material which Matthew has acquired from Mark, Q and his distinctive source(s), as well as that which Matthew has added editorially to his sources. Some examples include: 'already the ax is laid at the root of the trees' (81:12; *cf.* Mt. 3:10; Lk. 3:9), 'let them feed from the crumbs that fall from the table, like the dogs' (82:21–23; *cf.* Mt. 15:27; Mk. 7:28), and 'go into your chamber and shut the door behind you, and pray to your Father who is in secret' (68:10–12; *cf.* Mt. 6:6). The one exception is the saying which speaks of 'the Samaritan' who 'gave nothing but wine and oil to the wounded man' (78:7–9; *cf.* Lk. 10:34). Christopher Tuckett rightly concludes that Philip is dependent primarily on Matthew's gospel for his information about Jesus and that he reveals next to nothing about the pre-Synoptic stages of the gospel tradition.[1]

4 The Gospel of Truth

The Gospel of Truth is an even more esoteric Gnostic treatise, which includes portions of the Gnostic salvation myth. In the myth, the creator God remains distant and remote from the world. Between the creator and his creation emanate a series of divine beings or 'aeons', one of which falls out of the 'fulness' or 'god-head' and brings error and darkness to the world. Another eman-ation must therefore descend to redeem the world. This redeemer imparts secret knowledge to those who discover the divine spark within them. In 'Christian' forms of Gnosticism this saviour quite naturally becomes Jesus. A feature which distinguishes the Gospel of Truth from many of the other Nag Hammadi writings which elaborate the Gnostic myth of salvation is its frequent allusion to New Testament passages and to the gospel tradition. Undoubtedly

---

[1]Christopher Tuckett, 'Synoptic Tradition in Some Nag Hammadi and Related Texts', *VC* 36 (1982), pp.173–178. E. Segelberg, 'The Gospel of Philip and the New Testament', in *The New Testament and Gnosis*, ed. A. H. B. Logan and A. J. M. Wedderburn (Edinburgh: T & T Clark, 1983), pp.204–212, believes that Philip is dependent on both Matthew and John but cannot determine whether he knew them in their canonical form.

the most striking reference is its interpretation of the parable of the lost sheep:

> He is the shepherd who left behind the ninety-nine sheep which were not lost. He went searching for the one which was lost. He rejoiced when he found it, for 99 is a number that is in the left hand which holds it. But when the one is found, the entire number passes over to the right (hand). Thus (it is with) him who lacks the one; that is, the entire right which draws what was deficient and takes it from the left-hand side and brings (it) to the right, and thus the number becomes 100. It is the sign of the one who is in their sound; it is the Father. (Gosp. Truth 31:35–32:17)

Here the Synoptic parable is reinterpreted with reference to an ancient form of counting on one's fingers, in which hands were switched when passing from 99 to 100. And since left-handedness was a sign of deficiency, the lost sheep had to be found in order to make the number complete. Similarly, the good Gnostic becomes complete or whole when he comes to know himself properly – *cf*. 32:38–39 where the text addresses its readers as 'sons of interior knowledge'. The original meaning of Jesus' parable, about God's gracious compassion for one lost individual regardless of the number already saved, has entirely disappeared from sight! Tuckett aptly sums up: 'there is no evidence for the use of sources other than the canonical gospels for synoptic material' in the Gospel of Truth, and it throws 'little light on the history of the synoptic tradition prior to its incorporation in the canonical gospels.'[1]

C Other apocryphal gospels

The Greek and Latin church fathers of the first four Christian centuries frequently refer to spurious writings, including gospels, which different individuals and sects used. Copies of some of these apocrypha were rediscovered in the nineteenth century; some have been known for much longer. A few have never been found, and only their names and selected excerpts which other ancient writers chose to quote are known. Compared with the apostolic

---

[1] C. M. Tuckett, 'Synoptic Tradition in the Gospel of Truth and the Testimony of Truth', *JTS* n.s. 35 (1984), p.145.

fathers and the Nag Hammadi library, the New Testament apocrypha is the collection of works least often appealed to in the search for authentic information about the Jesus tradition. But, as noted earlier, several recent voices have called for a reconsideration of the value of the Gospel of Peter and Papyrus Egerton 2, and at least one recent study has pleaded that the so-called infancy gospels should be taken more seriously.[1] So these various documents require a brief survey.[2]

1 The infancy gospels

Most of the New Testament apocrypha show little overlap with the information found in Matthew, Mark, Luke and John. This fact alone is significant; it means that even in those circles where early Christians apparently felt free to invent stories about Jesus, they almost never tried to deny the truth of the canonical accounts. Instead they went about 'filling in the gaps' in the historical record, imagining what Jesus' childhood was like, describing his correspondence and travels to other lands, and adding adventures of his disciples, primarily involving their later Christian ministries. Most of these stories, however, differ so radically from the portraits of Christ in the gospels and of the apostles in Acts that it is hard to believe they could rest on any secure historical foundation. Nevertheless one can often point to details in the New Testament which would have given rise to the legends, however warped they may have become. For example, in the infancy gospel attributed to Thomas (not to be confused with the Coptic Gnostic work already discussed), the child Jesus appears as a prodigy. He can fashion sparrows out of clay and breathe life into them or confound his teachers by explaining to them the true meaning of

---

[1]Clare Drury, 'Who's In, Who's Out', in *What about the New Testament?* ed. M. D. Hooker and C. J. Hickling (London: SCM, 1975), pp.223–233.

[2]Perhaps the most noteworthy omission from this survey is the so-called Secret Gospel of Mark, referred to in a fragment of a text ascribed to Clement of Alexandria, which describes a young man coming to Jesus by night, in nothing but a linen robe, for instruction in 'the mystery of the kingdom'. Morton Smith of Columbia University reported his discovery of this fragment in 1958, and his vigorous campaign on behalf of its historical credibility has won him some adherents. But the sect in which this secret gospel was allegedly circulating is that of the Gnostic Carpocratians, notorious for their sexual licence and other perversions of the gospel. Although 'Clement' believes that this gospel came from Mark and had been misinterpreted, it is more likely that it arose in Gnostic circles from the start (France, *Evidence*, p.83). The distinguished patristic scholar, Henry Chadwick, has evaluated Smith's view with the remarks: 'marvellously implausible, delightful to read; and there is not the slightest chance that it is true' (cited by J. D. G. Dunn, *The Evidence for Jesus* [London: SCM; Philadelphia: Westminster, 1985], p.52).

the letters of the alphabet. In one notorious instance, Jesus turns on a playmate who is pestering him and withers him up like a barren tree. One might think of the withered fig tree in Mark 11:14 par. as a parallel but the purpose and object of Jesus' wrath there is entirely different (see pp.95–96).

The Protevangelium of James begins with an account of the special birth of Mary, Jesus' mother. According to this apocryphal book, Anna and Joachim, Mary's parents, were unable to have children until the Lord sent his angel to promise a miraculous conception. As a result, they dedicated the child-to-be to the service of the Lord's temple. The Protevangelium (which means 'before the gospel') goes on to narrate an expanded version of Luke 1–2 combined with Matthew 1–2, including such details as Jesus' birth in a cave, the motionlessness of the nearby animals and river at the moment of birth, and Mary's subsequently unspoiled virginity. There are portions of the infancy gospels which are not objectionable in principle, but with so many obviously fanciful embellishments it is difficult to give much credence to the rest of the narratives.

2 The Gospel of Peter

Several fragmentary texts from the first few centuries of the Christian era expand the story of Jesus' arrest, trial, crucifixion and resurrection. The most famous of these is the Gospel of Peter. Most of the Gospel's additions to the canonical accounts display no apparent purpose except to fill out the story. But in some places it reveals a 'docetic' tendency – supporting the view that Christ, while fully divine, was not fully human and thus did not truly suffer during his execution. Gosp. Pet. 4:10b, for example, states that 'he was silent, as if having no pain'. In the account of Jesus' resurrection, more obviously legendary elements appear: three men emerge from the tomb, 'two sustaining the one, and a cross following them, and the heads of the two reaching to heaven, but that of him who was led by them by the hand going beyond the heavens' (10:39–40). It is conceivable that the pre-resurrection portion of Peter contains historical reminiscences even if the post-resurrection segment inspires no such confidence. But even at the outset of this 'gospel', historical inaccuracies occur. Pilate, for example, has to request Jesus' body from Herod even though the latter had no jurisdiction over legal proceedings in Judaea. So it is doubtful that any new facts about Jesus' death will emerge even in this part of the work.[1]

3 The 'Unknown Gospel'

In 1934, a fragment of an ancient Egyptian papyrus containing four passages, three with gospel parallels, was purchased and analysed by officials in the British Museum in London, where it is now on display. Known as Papyrus Egerton 2, and dating to before AD 150, the document contains portions of several accounts: a dialogue between Jesus and the Jewish rulers similar to those in John 5 and 9–10; the cleansing of a leper reminiscent of Mark 1:40–44 pars.; the question about paying taxes (*cf.* Mk. 12:13–15 pars.), introduced in a manner similar to Nicodemus' approach to Jesus (Jn. 3:2) and answered with a quotation of Isaiah 29:13 (as in Mk. 7:6–7 par.); and an apparent miracle of quickly growing seed on the bank of the Jordan which has no clear canonical counterpart. Close verbal parallels with Mark, Luke and John all occur, and the various passages seem to be linked by similarities in wording or theme. This suggests that the text's unknown author drew on the traditions of the gospels as they now exist, so that he provides no independent testimony to the earliest stages of the gospel tradition. Although certain scholars have argued that some of the papyrus' distinctives are to be preferred to its canonical parallels, the evidence is scarcely strong enough to overturn the initial presumption in favour of the New Testament accounts. More importantly, the papyrus is simply too short and mutilated to permit confident conclusions about the origin of its contents.[2]

4 Conclusion

After widely scanning a broad panorama of ancient sources outside the New Testament, little has been uncovered that impinges on the historical reliability of Matthew, Mark, Luke and John.

---

[1]*Cf.* further David F. Wright, 'Apocryphal Gospels: The "Unknown Gospel" (Papyrus Egerton 2) and the *Gospel of Peter*', in *GP*,5, pp.221–227; F. Lambiasi, 'I criteri di autenticità storica dei vangeli applicati ad un apocrifo: il vangelo di Pietro', *BeO* 18 (1976), pp.151–160. The other main 'gospel' which resembles the Gospel of Peter is the Gospel of Nicodemus, containing an account of Christ's passion and of his descent into hell. The first part of this work is also called the Acts of Pilate. On its worthlessness as a historical document, see G. W. H. Lampe, 'The Trial of Jesus in the *Acta Pilati*', in *Jesus and the Politics of His Day,* ed. E. Bammel and C. F. D. Moule (Cambridge: University Press, 1984), pp.173–182.

[2]*Cf.* further Wright, 'Apocryphal Gospels', pp.210–221; F. Neirynck, 'Papyrus Egerton 2 and the Healing of the Leper', *ETL* 61 (1985), pp.153–160.

The probability that any of the extra-biblical sources preserve accurate information, otherwise unknown, about the life and teaching of Jesus is very slight, apart from the possibility of a few unparalleled sayings surviving. Where information parallels the four gospels and where no obviously sectarian theology has intruded into the texts, one is amazed at how faithfully the wording matches that of Scripture. There are variations to be sure, often due to the flexibility of oral tradition, but the substance usually remains unchanged. Perhaps the most significant observation relates to what does not appear. There is scarcely any evidence to support the contention that anyone in the early church put forward their teachings, inspired by the risen Lord, as sayings of the pre-Easter Jesus. Even the more outlandish Gnostic sayings and dialogues are explicitly claimed to be revelations of Jesus to his disciples after his resurrection. It would seem that anyone who wished to augment or challenge the canonical traditions knew that their historicity could not be impugned; all one could hope to do was to claim additional knowledge which went beyond what the New Testament had recorded. Even then, it seems that few in the ancient world were convinced by the new claims, apart from the sects supporting them. That greater credence should be given the apocrypha today in a more sceptical age would be highly incongruous.

4 The Jesus tradition in Acts – Revelation

It has been argued that good reasons existed for non-Christian writers in the ancient world not to say more than they did about Jesus. It is not surprising that sectarian Christians, wishing to dispute the growing consensus as to what was 'orthodoxy', should play down or distort the authentic teachings of Christ. One might have expected a more evenly distributed use of the gospel traditions by the apostolic fathers, with Matthew and his sources less dominant. Yet Matthew's gospel was by far the most popular of the gospels in the early church, because it included so many of Jesus' famous sermons, his teachings about the church and its worldwide mission, and frequent quotations and links with the Old Testament.

When one turns to the final topic for consideration in this

chapter – the gospel traditions in Acts, the epistles and Revelation – a much more remarkable phenomenon occurs: the rest of the New Testament only rarely quotes an explicit teaching of Jesus or refers back to some incident in his life, apart from the complex of events surrounding his death and resurrection. Surely if all that the gospels relate is historically accurate, then the writers of the epistles, the Acts and the Apocalypse would contain more evidence to corroborate the gospels' testimony. It is little wonder then that some question the age and reliability of that testimony. On the other hand, the paucity of corroborating evidence is often overstated. If there are few direct quotations from the gospel tradition, there are numerous allusions. And there are probably very good reasons why these other New Testament documents do not refer back to Jesus' earthly life more often than they do.

A The Acts of the Apostles

In Acts, nearly every sermon of Peter, Stephen, Philip, or Paul refers to Jesus of Nazareth. But the events of his life, if mentioned at all, are summarized very briefly, with attention concentrating on his death and resurrection. This pattern of early Christian preaching provided the model followed throughout the rest of the New Testament. With the flourish of a rhetorical hyperbole, Paul can go so far as to say that in Corinth he determined to 'know nothing' among them 'except Jesus Christ and him crucified' (1 Cor. 2:2). The reason for this concentration is easy to discover – Christians believed that apart from his sacrificial death, Jesus' life would have no permanent significance. Yet, in at least three places in the book of Acts, Luke can refer to further details. In 13:24–25 he recounts Paul's reference to John the Baptist in his sermon in Antioch and recalls the specific teaching of John about his unworthiness even to untie the sandals of the one coming after him (*cf.* Lk. 3:16 pars.). In 20:35 Luke relates how Paul quoted to the Ephesian elders an otherwise unknown saying of Jesus: 'It is more blessed to give than to receive.' In more detail, 10:36–41 includes among the words of Peter to Cornelius and his friends this summary of Jesus' life:

> You know the word which he [God] sent to the sons of Israel, preaching good news of peace by Jesus Christ (he is Lord of all), the word which came to all Judaea, beginning from Galilee after

the baptism which John preached: Jesus of Nazareth – as God anointed him with the Holy Spirit and with power, who went about doing good and healing all who were oppressed by the devil, for God was with him. And we are witnesses of everything that he did both in the country of the Jews and in Jerusalem, who also killed him by hanging him on a tree. This man God raised up on the third day and made him manifest; not to all the people but to witnesses who were previously selected by God – to us – who ate and drank together with him after he rose from the dead.

In an influential little book, C. H. Dodd suggested that this outline of the life of Christ provided the framework for the narrative of the first gospel writer, Mark, which Luke in turn followed.[1] Whether or not the link is this close, this excerpt of early Christian preaching at the very least shows that Luke believed that the church knew and taught more about Jesus' life than his abbreviated, summary statements might otherwise suggest. More importantly, Luke also wrote a gospel. Herein lies the fatal flaw in the argument that the silence of the rest of the New Testament proves that its writers knew little about the details of Jesus' life. Whatever may be surmised about the other New Testament authors, one cannot escape the fact that the author of Acts also penned a gospel. Luke knew all manner of information about Jesus but chose not to repeat it in his history of the life of the early church. That was not his purpose. Early Christian preaching dwelt at length on topics which Acts omits or treats in barest outline form, and Luke had no need to repeat them; he had already recorded them in his first volume. The argument from the silence of Acts collapses after only momentary probing.[2]

B The epistles of Paul

Paul too undoubtedly knew much more of the Jesus tradition than his epistles reflect. All his letters address communities or individuals who had already learned about Jesus; Paul's purpose in

---

[1]C. H. Dodd, *The Apostolic Preaching and Its Developments* (London: Hodder & Stoughton, 1936; Chicago: Willett, Clark, & Co., 1937), esp. pp.54–56.

[2]For thorough discussion, *cf.* Graham N. Stanton, *Jesus of Nazareth in New Testament Preaching* (Cambridge: University Press, 1974), pp.67–85, 113. More briefly, and with respect to Paul's 'silence' as well, *cf.* Leonhard Goppelt, *Theology of the New Testament,* vol. 2 (Grand Rapids: Eerdmans; London: SPCK, 1982), pp.44–46.

writing was not to retell the gospel story but to elaborate on key theological and ethical matters and to counter opposition which he faced in various places. As Martin Hengel puts it, 'In the ancient world it was impossible to proclaim as Son of God and redeemer of the world a man who had died on the cross . . . without giving a clear account of his activity, his suffering and his death.'[1] But this had already happened; Paul was moving on to further considerations. Moreover, if Paul had been writing to those who had not heard the gospel message, it is doubtful if an epistle would have been the vehicle by which he would have conveyed detailed information about Jesus' life. The evidence already discussed in this and previous chapters suggests that this information was passed along orally in relatively fixed and memorable form. Whatever written notes or sources preceded the first complete gospel, they did not take the form of a letter.[2]

One must therefore not expect abundant quotations of Jesus in the epistles, but neither must the extent to which the Jesus tradition has permeated them be underestimated. Paul in fact displays a fairly detailed knowledge of the gospel traditions if one reads him carefully. And since most, if not all, of Paul's letters predate the composition of Matthew, Mark, Luke and John, the awareness of these details is a significant confirmation of the early existence of the traditions that went into the formation of the gospels. A summary of the biographical information about Jesus that can be pieced together from the Pauline epistles would include his descent from Abraham and David (Gal. 3:16; Rom. 1:3), his upbringing in the Jewish law (Gal. 4:4), his gathering together disciples, including Cephas (Peter) and John, and his having a brother named James (Gal. 1:19; 2:9), his impeccable character and exemplary life (*e.g.* Phil. 2:6–8; 2 Cor. 8:9; Rom. 15:3,8), his Last Supper and betrayal (1 Cor. 11:23–25), and numerous details surrounding his death and resurrection (*e.g.* Gal. 3:1; 1 Thes. 2:15; 1 Cor. 15:4–8).[3] More widespread are signs of a fairly detailed knowledge of the teachings of Jesus, especially in Romans,

---

[1]Martin Hengel, *Acts and the History of Earliest Christianity* (London: SCM; Philadelphia: Fortress, 1979), pp.43–44. *Cf.* A. M. Hunter, *Paul and His Predecessors* (London: SCM; Philadelphia: Westminster, 1961), p.12.

[2]*Cf.* Peter Stuhlmacher, 'Zum Thema: Das Evangelium und die Evangelien', in *Das Evangelium und die Evangelien*, pp.18–19.

[3]*Cf.* F. F. Bruce, *Paul: Apostle of the Free Spirit* (Exeter: Paternoster [= *Paul: Apostle of the Heart Set Free* (Grand Rapids: Eerdmans)], 1977), pp.95–96; Stanton, *Jesus*, pp.99–110.

1 Corinthians, and 1 Thessalonians.

1 Romans

After a systematic presentation of the theology of the Christian gospel in chapters 1–11 of his epistle to the Romans, Paul turns his attention to the ethical implications of that theology. Chapters 12–16 thus contain numerous commands, several of which are similar enough to passages in the gospels to allow one to conclude that they probably come from the traditions or sources which supplied the evangelists with their material as well. Romans 12:14 commands one to 'bless those who persecute you; bless and do not curse' (*cf.* Lk. 6:27b–28a par.); 12:17, to 'repay no one evil for evil' (*cf.* Mt. 5:39); and 13:7, to pay 'tribute to whom tribute is due, tax to whom tax is due, reverence to whom reverence is due, honour to whom honour is due' (*cf.* Mk. 12:17 pars.). In 13:8–9 Paul sums up the whole of the Law in the commandment to love one's neighbour (*cf.* Gal. 5:14; Mk. 12:31 pars.); in 14:10 he condemns judging one's brother since all will be judged (*cf.* Mt. 7:1–2a par.); and in 14:14 he declares, 'I am persuaded in the Lord Jesus that nothing is unclean by itself' (*cf.* Lk. 11:41; Mk. 7:19b). Finally, in 16:19 he encourages wisdom concerning the good and innocence as to evil, an apparent allusion to Matthew 10:16b.

Commentators disagree as to which of these allusions most probably derive directly from the gospel tradition rather than from sayings of other ancient Christian and non-Christian teachers, a disagreement which recurs in studies of the rest of the epistles and Revelation. But nearly all agree that at least some of these allusions disclose Paul's dependence on the tradition, and some would make the list noticeably longer.[1] And even where apparent parallels occur in other religious literature, including the Old Testament, it is still *a priori* likely that Christian writers would have derived their information from Christ's teachings. Paul's vigorous exposition of his independence from the Jerusalem apostles during the earliest stages of his Christian life (Gal. 1–2) makes him no exception, since he elsewhere makes explicit his indebtedness to the tradition (1 Cor. 15:3–7).[2]

---

[1]See esp. Peter Stuhlmacher, 'Jesustradition im Römerbrief?' *TheolBeitr* 14 (1983), pp.240–250.

[2]Galatians 1–2 in fact implies a fundamental agreement between Peter and Paul, since their dispute was not over the contents of the gospel tradition but over its application. This provides,

It is possible to say even more about the allusions in Romans. David Wenham has noted that Romans 12:17–20 actually contains several phrases reminiscent of the teaching of Jesus – all from the Sermon on the Mount/Plain and in the order in which they occur in Matthew 5:38–43 – not to return evil for evil, to live at peace with all, to take no revenge and to feed/love one's enemy. The command in 12:14 to bless one's persecutors, however, more closely parallels Luke's version of the sermon (Lk. 6:27b–28a). Wenham therefore suggests that Paul knew of at least this portion of Jesus' sermon as a connected account, which formed one of the sources for Matthew's and Luke's later gospel-writing. That source could even have been Q. This evidence would then call into question the view that the individual verses of the sermon all 'floated' in the oral tradition independent of each other and were only artificially assembled by the evangelists at a later date.[1]

2 1 Corinthians

Three of the four explicit quotations of Jesus by Paul occur in this epistle, perhaps because it devotes more attention to issues of practical theology and to ethical disputes than do the rest of his letters. In 1 Corinthians 7:10, Paul supports his views on marriage and divorce by giving the charge, 'not I but the Lord [says] that the wife must not separate from her husband (but if she does separate she must remain unmarried or be reconciled to her husband) and that the husband must not divorce his wife.' Later in the same chapter he gives commands to partners in mixed marriages, speaking as 'I, not the Lord' (7:12), while nevertheless affirming that what he says comes from the Spirit of God (7:40). Although some have tried to distinguish between different levels of inspiration or forms of revelation,[2] the most natural way of interpreting this passage is to understand Paul to be quoting a teaching of the historical Jesus when he refers to 'the Lord'. On some issues Paul knows no tradition on the topic and so must depend on less

---

according to Herman Ridderbos (*Paul and Jesus* [Philadelphia: Presbyterian and Reformed, 1957], p.52), 'one of the most powerful counter arguments against the opinion that Paul introduced an entirely new proclamation of Jesus as the Christ'.

[1]David Wenham, 'Paul's Use of the Jesus Tradition: Three Samples', in *GP*,5, pp.15–24.

[2]One of the most innovative and well-reasoned of these approaches is found in Peter Richardson, ' "I say, not the Lord": Personal Opinion, Apostolic Authority and the Development of Early Christian *Halakah*', *TynB* 31 (1980), pp. 65–86, who sees the word of 'the Lord' as referring to established Christian practice and Paul's 'I' as his own principles developed from that practice.

mediated guidance. Since there are several Synoptic passages which contain instructions closely paralleled by 1 Corinthians 7:10 (Mk. 10:10–12 pars.), but none which mirrors verse 12, this interpretation seems preferable.[1] In that event, there once again emerges powerful confirmation of the care with which the first Christians distinguished the words of the historical Jesus from later instructions inspired by his Spirit.[2]

In 1 Corinthians 9:14, Paul refers to another saying of Jesus as part of his argument that the full-time Christian minister should receive pay for his services: 'Thus also the Lord commanded those who proclaim the gospel to get their living by the gospel'. The past tense, 'commanded', points even more clearly than the present tense verbs of chapter 7 to a word from the gospel tradition: 'the worker is worthy of his wage' (Lk. 10:7; *cf.* Mt. 10:10). Paul at times refuses to avail himself of this privilege of receiving financial support, since Jesus' original saying is not phrased as an absolute imperative but as a matter-of-fact statement of what the ministry of the gospel is worth.[3] But Paul charitably insists on it with respect to others. Of great interest is the recurrence of Luke 10:7 in 1 Timothy 5:18 where it is cited along with an Old Testament text (Dt. 25:4). The two quotations are introduced with the formula, 'for the Scripture says . . .' In view of the reluctance of the apostolic fathers even in the second century to refer explicitly to New Testament quotations as Scripture, this juxtaposition is astonishing, all the more so if, as seems quite possible, Paul himself wrote 1 Timothy.[4] In that case, the letter would have been written in the early or mid-60s of the first century, just a few years

---

[1] For a detailed consideration of how the pre-Synoptic traditions may have been phrased, see Wenham, 'Paul's Use', pp.7–15. *Cf.* D. R. Catchpole, 'The Synoptic Divorce Material as a Traditio-Historical Problem', *BJRL* 57 (1974), pp.92–127.

[2] David L. Dungan, *The Sayings of Jesus in the Churches of Paul* (Philadelphia: Fortress; Oxford: Blackwell, 1971), p.92, argues that while Paul relied on a traditional saying of Jesus, he felt free to disregard it, since he added the more lenient, unparalleled clause, 'but if she does [divorce]. . .' This entirely misunderstands Paul's remarks. He is not granting permission to divorce, but dealing with what should happen if someone disregards, or has already disregarded, his first command. It is possible too that he is thinking of the legitimate exception by which Christ permits divorce in the case of adultery (Mt. 19:9, 5:32), and this would further confirm his knowledge of the details of Jesus' teaching.

[3] Dungan, *Sayings*, p.25, again argues, without warrant, that Paul feels free to set aside a direct command of the Lord.

[4] Pauline authorship of the Pastoral Epistles (1 & 2 Timothy and Titus) is widely disputed. But see the detailed defences of C. Spicq, *Les epîtres pastorales* (Paris: Gabalda, 1969), pp.157–214; J. N. D. Kelly, *A Commentary on the Pastoral Epistles* (London: Black; New York: Harper, 1963), pp.1–34; and Donald Guthrie, *New Testament Introduction* (London: Tyndale; Downers Grove: IVP, 1970), pp.584–622.

after the completion of the Gospel of Luke.[1] Not surprisingly, most commentators of all theological persuasions offer alternate explanations: perhaps 'Scripture' (*graphē*) should be translated simply as 'writing', perhaps it refers only to the Old Testament quotation, or perhaps a Q-like source gained an authority equal to that of the Old Testament in certain early Christian circles. But serious problems beset each of these alternatives and none is easily deduced from the text itself. If Paul and Luke were close companions, why might Paul not have known of his friend's gospel and recognized its inspired nature quite soon after it appeared, even if the church as a whole did not embrace this view as quickly? Regardless of the explanation chosen, one is a long way from the view that the rest of the New Testament does not know of or substantiate the gospel traditions.

The third quotation of a Synoptic-like passage in 1 Corinthians is clearest of all. In his discussion of the Corinthian abuses of the Lord's Supper, Paul enunciates what have become known in Christian liturgy as the 'words of institution' (1 Cor. 11:23–25). They read:

> For I received from the Lord what I also delivered to you, that the Lord Jesus on the night in which he was betrayed took bread, and after he had given thanks, he broke it and said, 'This is my body which is for you. Keep on doing this in my remembrance.' Likewise also the cup, after eating supper, saying, 'This cup is the new covenant in my blood. Keep on doing this, as often as you drink, in my remembrance.'

These words are almost entirely paralleled in the Synoptic accounts of the Last Supper (Mk. 14:22–24; Mt. 26:26–28; Lk. 22:19–20), and a number of expressions parallel Luke where he differs from Matthew and Mark, for example, 'which is for you', 'keep on doing this in my remembrance', 'after eating supper', 'cup', and 'in my blood'. This demonstrates that Luke's variations do not stem from his own creative modification of the tradition but

---

[1]Luke and Acts fit together so well that most scholars assume they were composed within a short time of each other. But Acts covers events up to approximately 62 AD, so Luke was probably not written much before then. Many scholars hold that both Luke and Acts were written much later, in which case 1 Timothy could not be citing Luke, unless it too was written later. But in that case Paul could not have written 1 Timothy, since he died in the mid-60s. These latter alternatives are less convincing.

from older sources to which Paul also had access. Confidence in their authenticity is thus similarly strengthened.[1]

In addition to these explicit quotations, 1 Corinthians contains a number of apparent allusions to teachings of Jesus,[2] but none are as clear-cut as the allusions in Romans. 1 Corinthians 13:2, on faith moving mountains, might well hark back to the tradition behind Mark 11:23 pars. A number of Paul's metaphors – the stumbling block, the faithful steward, the good foundation, the sower, and the leaven – could easily have originated from Jesus' own use of such imagery, especially in his parables,[3] but none are certain. What is certain is that there were plenty of controversies which Paul would doubtless have liked to have been able to settle by means of an authoritative teaching of Jesus but did not – the correct use of spiritual gifts, the role of women in the church, or the problem of meat sacrificed to idols. Apparently the church knew of no Jesus traditions on these topics and did not feel free to invent any.

3 1 Thessalonians

While Romans and 1 Corinthians were written in the mid to late 50s, the Thessalonian epistles probably stem from the first year or two of that decade. Depending on when Galatians is dated, 1 Thessalonians is either the oldest or second oldest of the Pauline epistles. Paul's knowledge of the words of Jesus this early in his literary career therefore reflects the state of the gospel tradition only twenty years after Christ's death. Interestingly, 1 Thessalonians contains several apparent references to that tradition.

In 1 Thessalonians 2:14–16 Paul compares the persecution the Thessalonian Christians endured to that of the Judaean Christians at the hands of their countrymen who executed Christ. These verses contain numerous echoes of Matthew 23:29–38, Jesus' woeful invective against the Jewish leaders shortly before his execution. Most noteworthy are the parallel phrases about persecuting and killing the prophets in times past, about filling up the

---

[1] For more detail, including a discussion of the important textual variants in the Lukan passage, see I. H. Marshall, *Last Supper and Lord's Supper* (Exeter: Paternoster; Grand Rapids: Eerdmans, 1980), pp.30–56.

[2] For a survey of their relative merits, see Peter Richardson and Peter Gooch, 'Logia of Jesus in 1 Corinthians', in *GP*,5, pp.39–62.

[3] *Cf.* D. M. Stanley, 'Pauline Allusions to the Sayings of Jesus', *CBQ* 23 (1961), pp.34–38; Harald Riesenfeld, *The Gospel Tradition* (Philadelphia: Fortress, 1970), pp.190–191, 199–204.

measure of Israel's sins, and about the wrath which has come upon her at last. Strictly speaking, these details are unnecessary elaborations of the point Paul is making, but they would make good sense if he were simply rounding off a reference to the teaching of Jesus which he knew.[1]

In 4:15–5:4 even clearer parallels emerge. Paul introduces his description of the return of Christ in 4:16–17 as 'the word of the Lord' (verse 15). No single connected passage in the gospels parallels all this teaching, so some commentators attribute it to later Christian prophecy or revelation. But most of the details find a parallel of some sort in Jesus' eschatological discourse (Mk. 13 par.), so it is possible that Paul derived his imagery from that source. In 5:2–4, the double reference to the day of the Lord coming like a thief in the night almost certainly harks back to Jesus' parable of the thief (Mt. 24:43; Lk. 12:39) since this imagery appears nowhere else in earlier sources. Numerous other passages in both letters to the Thessalonians also contain reminiscences of the Synoptic apocalypse.[2] David Wenham notes how these parallels appear not only in that part of the discourse which all three Synoptics share but also in sections peculiar to Matthew. Wenham consequently employs this observation in his larger argument that Paul must have known a unified, pre-Synoptic version of this sermon of Jesus, which included more detail than is found in any one of the gospels as they now appear (see pp.142–143).[3] As with the parallels in Romans to the Sermon on the Mount, this evidence seems to contradict the pure form-critical hypothesis of disconnected teachings of Jesus circulating for a long time before being artificially grouped together by the later church.

4 Conclusion

The evidence from the rest of Paul's letters proves more ambiguous. Does the language of Paul's description of his conversion ('not by flesh and blood') and of his dispute with Peter (whom he

---

[1]*Cf.* further David Wenham, 'Paul and the Synoptic Apocalypse', in *GP*,2, pp.361–363; R. Schippers, 'The Pre-Synoptic Tradition in 1 Thessalonians II, 13–16', *NovT* 8 (1966), pp.223–234. P. Nepper-Christensen, 'Das verborgene Herrnwort: Eine Untersuchung über 1 Thess. 4:13–18', *ST* 19 (1965), pp.136–154, argues, less convincingly, that the parallels with John 11:25–26 are even closer.

[2]See esp. J. Bernard Orchard, 'Thessalonians and the Synoptic Gospels', *Bib* 19 (1938), pp.19–42.

[3]Wenham, 'Paul and the Synoptic Apocalypse', pp.345–375; *cf.* also his *The Rediscovery of Jesus' Eschatological Discourse* (= *GP*,4), pp.54–55, 176–180, 295–296, 351–352.

otherwise calls Cephas) in Galatians 1–2 reflect a knowledge of Peter's apostolic commission in Matthew 16:17–18?[1] Does the 'law of Christ' (Gal. 6:2) refer to a collection of Jesus' teachings which had become authoritative for the early church?[2] Do the frequent references in 2 Corinthians to the poor and to humility, almsgiving and forgiveness betray familiarity with the details of Christ's human concern for the outcasts of his society?[3] These and many other suggested allusions are all plausible, but none is demonstrable. Victor Furnish displays needless pessimism when he labels the search for parallels between Paul and the gospels altogether fruitless,[4] but there is no question that the amount of similarity can be exaggerated.[5] Helpful lists of the most probable allusions have been given by Heinz Schürmann, A. M. Hunter and W. D. Davies, who identify 12, 24 and 31 such references, respectively.[6]

Whatever the precise number of Pauline parallels to the gospels, one may heartily endorse the conclusion of a recent systematic survey of the problem by Dale Allison: 'the persistent conviction that Paul knew next to nothing of the teaching of Jesus must be rejected.'[7] What is more, as Allison also argues, it is likely that Paul knew connected blocks of Jesus' teaching, including most probably the traditions behind Jesus' great sermon (esp. Lk.

---

[1]J. Chapman, 'St. Paul and the Revelation to St. Peter, Matt. XVI, 17', *Revue Bénédictine* 29 (1912), pp.133–147, endorsed by Wenham, 'Paul's Use', pp.24–28.

[2]See esp. the influential article of C. H. Dodd, "Ἔννομος Χριστοῦ', in *More New Testament Studies* (Manchester: University Press, 1968), pp.134–148. *Cf.* Bernard H. Brinsmead, *Galatians – Dialogical Response to Opponents* (Chico: Scholars, 1982), pp.174–175, who develops the view that Gal. 5–6 is an exposition of the law of Christ with reference to the traditions behind Mt. 22:34–40; 18:15–20 and 11:28–30.

[3]R. V. G. Tasker, 'St. Paul and the Earthly Life of Jesus', *ExpT* 46 (1934–35), pp.557–562.

[4]Victor P. Furnish, 'The Jesus-Paul Debate', *BJRL* 47 (1965), p.374.

[5]*Cf. e.g.* R.J. Knowling, *The Testimony of St. Paul to Christ* (New York: Chas. Scribner's Sons, 1905; London: Hodder & Stoughton, 1906), pp.200–350; A Resch, *Der Paulinismus und die Logia Jesu* (Leipzig: J. C. Hinrichs, 1904).

[6]Heinz Schürmann, ' "Das Gesetz des Christus" (Gal 6,2)', in *Neues Testament und Kirche*, ed. J. Gnilka (Freiburg: Herder, 1974), pp.282–300; Hunter, *Paul*, pp.47–51, 126–127; W. D. Davies, *Paul and Rabbinic Judaism* (Philadelphia: Fortress, 1980), pp.138–140.

[7]Dale C. Allison, Jr., 'The Pauline Epistles and the Synoptic Gospels: The Pattern of the Parallels', *NTS* 28 (1982), p.25. D. M. Stanley, 'Significance for Paul of Jesus' Earthly History', in *Sin, Salvation and the Spirit,* ed. Daniel Durken (Collegeville, MN: Liturgical Press, 1979), pp.279–288, argues that the more one admits the validity of form- and redaction-critical findings about the flexibility of the wording of the gospel traditions in the early church, the more likely Paul's terminology reflects those traditions even when it does not verbally parallel the gospels. *Cf.* also Murray J. Harris, *Raised Immortal: Resurrection and Immortality in the New Testament* (London: Marshall, Morgan & Scott, 1983; Grand Rapids: Eerdmans, 1985), p.41: 'We should not imagine that we can convert our ignorance of the extent of Paul's knowledge into a knowledge of the extent of his ignorance.'

6:27–38), his missionary instructions (Mk. 6:6b–13 pars.), the teaching on discipleship (Mk. 9:33–50 pars.), and portions of the narrative of the last week of Jesus' life.[1] The gospel narratives were already beginning to take shape and become widely known when Paul was writing. They were scarcely the product of well-meaning Christians too far removed from the original events to know what Jesus actually said and did.

C The rest of the New Testament

Of the remaining New Testament writings, the three which have been most often searched in hopes of gleaning allusions to the gospel tradition are James, 1 Peter, and Revelation.

1 The Epistle of James

Of all the New Testament epistles, none contains as many passages which verbally resemble the teaching of Jesus as does James. One need look no further than the first main paragraph of his letter to observe a pattern of allusions which remains constant throughout the work. 'Consider it all joy, my brothers, whenever you encounter various trials' (1:2; *cf.* Mt. 5:11–12 – 'Blessed are you when men reproach you . . . rejoice and be glad' – and Lk. 6:23); 'that you may be perfect and complete' (1:4; *cf.* Mt. 5:48 – 'be perfect as your heavenly father is perfect'); 'let him ask God, who gives to all generously and . . . it shall be given to him' (1:5; *cf.* Mt. 7:7 – 'ask and it shall be given to you' – and Lk. 11:9); 'but let him ask in faith, doubting nothing' (1:6; *cf.* Mt. 21:21 – 'if you have faith and do not doubt . . .' – and Mk. 11:23). These allusions embrace all three of Matthew's main sources, Mark, Q and M, and three of the four come from the Sermon on the Mount/Plain. Both of these features continue throughout the rest of the epistle. As a result, many scholars have argued that James must have known the canonical gospels, or at least Matthew. But there are good reasons for dating James very early, perhaps in the 40s, making it the earliest of all the New Testament writings.[2] If this dating is correct, then the allusions to Jesus' teaching afford the most abundant and convincing evidence so far considered that the gospel traditions were known and applied very soon and very widely in fledgeling

---

[1] Allison, 'Pauline Epistles', pp.10–17.
[2] See esp. Peter H. Davids, *The Epistle of James* (Exeter: Paternoster; Grand Rapids: Eerdmans, 1982), pp.2–22.

Christianity. The oral transmission was fluid enough to permit variations in phraseology but the meaning was not distorted. Moreover, Peter Davids argues persuasively that the allusions to Jesus' teaching form the backbone around which all of James' epistle is structured. Thus Jesus' words were not only carefully preserved but commanded great respect, playing a central and authoritative role in the life of the early church.[1]

2 1 Peter

Echoes of the gospel tradition in 1 Peter are not nearly as clear as in James, but there is no lack of candidates for the label 'allusion'. Robert Gundry, Merrill Tenney and Ceslaus Spicq have all produced impressive lists.[2] Ernest Best, on the other hand, has challenged the significance of such lists, arguing that almost all the proposed allusions could be accounted for in other ways – for example, as ethical traditions which Christians shared with Jewish or Graeco-Roman sources, early catechisms or creeds, or liturgy used in worship.[3] Gerhard Maier has catalogued this debate and favours Peter's more direct dependence on the Jesus tradition. For Maier, what is most significant is that several of the apparent allusions refer back to John's Gospel as well as to the Synoptics – *e.g.* being born anew in 1 Peter 1:2 (*cf.* Jn. 3:3); loving Jesus without having seen him in 1:8 (*cf.* Jn. 20:29); or being called out of darkness into light in 2:9 (*cf.* Jn. 8:12).[4] But many of the allusions Maier perceives reappear regularly in ancient writings, so it would be wise in this instance not to make too much of the similarities.

3 The book of Revelation

That Revelation relies heavily on Old Testament imagery for its many visions and symbols is universally accepted. Not as widely

---

[1]Peter H. Davids, 'James and Jesus', in *GP*,5, pp.63–84. For a chart of parallels, see pp.66–67. A more exhaustive but probably exaggerated list appears in J. B. Mayor, *The Epistle of St. James* (London and New York: Macmillan, 1910), lxxxv–xc.

[2]Robert H. Gundry, ' "Verba Christi" in 1 Peter: Their Implications Concerning the Authorship of 1 Peter and the Authenticity of the Gospel Tradition', *NTS* 13 (1966–67), pp.336–350; also his 'Further Verba on Verba Christi in First Peter', *Bib* 55 (1974), pp.211–232. M. C. Tenney, 'Some Possible Parallels Between 1 Peter and John', in *New Dimensions in New Testament Study,* ed. R. N. Longenecker & M. C. Tenney (Grand Rapids: Zondervan, 1974), pp.370–377; C. Spicq, 'La la Petri et le témoignage évangélique de saint Pierre', *ST* 20 (1966), pp.37–61.

[3]Ernest Best, '1 Peter and the Gospel Tradition', *NTS* 16 (1969–70), pp.95–113.

[4]Gerhard Maier, 'Jesustradition im 1. Petrusbrief?' in *GP*,5, pp.85–128.

noticed are its parallels to New Testament books, including the gospels. Louis A. Vos, in *The Synoptic Traditions in the Apocalypse*, identifies 25 passages in Revelation which he believes demonstrate knowledge of the traditions incorporated into Matthew, Mark and Luke.[1] G. K. Beale argues that Revelation's use of the famous 'Son of man' passage in Daniel 7 is more extensive than is usually recognized and was inspired by Jesus' own use of that Scripture in his eschatological discourse.[2] Regardless of the date of the composition of Revelation, which might well be late enough to allow its author to know of the Synoptic Gospels in their final form, Vos and Beale believe that the wording of the gospel traditions in Revelation betrays a pre-Synoptic origin. As with the debate on the Jesus tradition in 1 Peter, the arguments on both sides seem too evenly balanced to yield a confident verdict one way or the other.

5 Conclusion

A vast terrain has been covered in surveying the whole of the New Testament outside the gospels, the most relevant of the other earliest Christian writings, and Jewish and Graeco-Roman traditions about Jesus as well. Each of the issues introduced poses unsolved questions for further investigation; the data of the gospels themselves, on which the rest of the book has focused, have been much more carefully scrutinized than all the collateral areas covered in this chapter. One may well wonder, even after this whirlwind tour of the evidence for the Jesus tradition outside the gospels, why more was not recorded about the details of Christ's earthly life. Imagining the influence of that tradition where it does not exist will not help. But many genuine references do exist and their significance must not be minimized. In the words of the French scholar F. Prat, 'C'est peu et c'est beaucoup.' It is, at one and the same time, little and much.[3] The external evidence for the

---

[1](Kampen: Kok, 1965).

[2]G. K. Beale, 'The Use of Daniel in the Synoptic Eschatological Discourse and in the Book of Revelation', in *GP*,5, pp.129–153; *cf*. also his *The Use of Daniel in Jewish Apocalyptic Literature and in the Revelation of St. John* (Washington, DC: University Press of America, 1984).

[3]Cited, endorsed, and elaborated by Harris, 'References to Jesus', pp.343, 356–360.

gospel traditions reinforces the confidence in their historical reliability which the internal evidence has been building in previous chapters.

Final questions on historical method

Many readers assume that the gospels narrate historical events simply because they read as if their authors are attempting to recount things which actually happened. The narratives are vivid but uncluttered, full of incidental details, ordinary people and psychological realism, which set them apart from most ancient fiction and tendentious history.[1] Luke endorses this impression by explicitly claiming to have followed all things closely for a considerable time in order to produce an accurate narrative (Lk. 1:1–4). Some students of Scripture would prefer to take these impressions and claims at face value and bypass all the careful, critical analysis which previous chapters have surveyed. This preference, however well motivated, is both naïve and dangerous, since some fictitious narratives are couched in the guise of history, and many careful historians fail to achieve their objectives of complete accuracy.

In this chapter, however, it is proper to return to the gospels' *prima facie* appearance. A wide variety of charges have been examined which would call into question the gospels' reliability – allegations concerning the instability of the oral tradition which preceded the gospel writers' editorial activity, the redactional intentions of the evangelists, the early church's lack of interest in preserving the details of Jesus' life, the apparent contradictions among the Synoptics, the distinctive nature of John's Gospel over against the Synoptics, the seeming lack of sufficient corroboration for the Jesus tradition in other ancient writings both within and outside the New Testament, and the peculiar problems associated with miracles. In every case it has been concluded that an even-

---

[1]See esp. Erich Auerbach, *Mimesis* (Princeton: University Press, 1953), pp.40–49. *Cf.* E. M. Blaiklock, *Jesus Christ: Man or Myth* (Homebush West, NSW: Anzea; Nashville: Thomas Nelson, 1984), pp.38–47, 68–78.

handed treatment of the data does not lead to a distrust of the accuracy of the gospels in what they choose to report, even though many might wish they had reported more or related what they did in more precise or systematic fashion. Do any reasons remain, then, for rejecting an equation of the gospels with some kind of accurate, historical writing? How does one assess the historicity of all their details which have not been discussed, and for which there may be no other testimony to provide a comparison?

The final task of this study must therefore involve some concluding reflections about the genre of the gospels and about a methodology for assessing the reliability of particular details within them. If one may presume that the gospels represent genuine attempts at recording historical information, however selective that record may have been, then the standard procedures of historical research may be applied in evaluating the successfulness of those attempts. Historians freely admit that they are often unable to find corroborating or conflicting data for many of the events related in ancient narratives, but this does not prevent them from arriving at judicious assessments of the reliability of those data. They begin by forming a general presumption about the trustworthiness of a given document, deciding where the burden of proof is to be placed – whether on the person who would claim a certain detail to be factual or on the one who would claim it to be in error. Next they apply criteria of authenticity or inauthenticity to determine where the exceptions to their general presumption lie, that is, where errors have crept in to otherwise reliable narratives or where truth has been preserved in otherwise dubious texts. Some sample applications of this methodology will illustrate how it should be applied to the gospels.

1 The genre of the gospels

The mere identification of a few errors in the writings of a given historian does not lead to the conclusion that his work belongs to an unhistorical genre,[1] such as a legend, novel, or historical

---

[1]Genre has traditionally been defined as a category of literary composition characterized by a particular style, form, or content, although the whole question of whether or not literature can be so categorized is one of increasing debate. A balanced survey and assessment of the debate

fiction. So too with the gospels; even if some of the apparent contradictions proved to be genuine this would not necessarily discredit the rest of the narratives. The view held by some Bible students that admission of one error in a book makes all the rest of it equally suspect presupposes a method which no reputable historian would adopt.[1] If one is going to label the gospels as something other than history one must do more than point to seeming inaccuracies; an entirely different genre of writing into which the gospels fit must be proposed. To this end, recent scholarship has proposed no less than seven such genres, but in each case the parallels with the gospels sooner or later break down.[2] Several of these categories will be mentioned only briefly since they have been dealt with previously; others require a more detailed examination.

(1) A few scholars have compared the Gospel of Mark to an apocalypse[3] – an account of the events surrounding the end of the age in symbolic and usually unhistorical form – like the canonical book of Revelation or the second half of Daniel, as well as numerous intertestamental documents. But while much of the gospels' teaching deals with apocalyptic themes, the gospels themselves are not characterized by the bizarre visions and symbols, the glimpses of heaven and profusion of angelic beings, or the dualistic pessimism about the future of humanity so common in many apocalypses. Not surprisingly, this option has gained few adherents.

(2) A second suggestion classifies the gospels as aretalogies – accounts of episodes from the life of a 'divine man', usually embellishing and exaggerating the feats of some famous hero or warrior of the past.[4] But the viability of this classification depends heavily on the pre-Christian use of a clearly defined category of 'divine

---

appears in Grant R. Osborne, 'Genre Criticism – Sensus Literalis', *TrinJ* n.s. 4 (1983), pp.1–27.

[1]*Cf.* Maurice Mandelbaum, *The Anatomy of Historical Knowledge* (Baltimore and London: Johns Hopkins, 1977), p.172: where contradictions arise in presumably historical texts, 'they do not usually undermine the basic structure of the account that has been building; they often contradict only specific items that a historian has previously accepted, and do not force a change in the general outline of the account'.

[2]The most complete survey of the topic is Robert Guelich, 'The Gospel Genre', in *Das Evangelium und die Evangelien,* ed. Peter Stuhlmacher (Tübingen: Mohr, 1983), pp.183–219.

[3]Most notably Norman Perrin, 'Historical Criticism, Literary Criticism and Hermeneutics: The Interpretation of the Parables of Jesus and the Gospel of Mark Today', *JR* 52 (1972), pp.365–366; *cf.* the more nuanced assessment of Howard C. Kee, *Community of the New Age* (London: SCM; Philadelphia: Westminster, 1977), esp. p.76.

[4]See esp. Morton Smith, 'Prolegomena to a Discussion of Aretalogies, Divine Men, the Gospels and Jesus', *JBL* 90 (1971), pp.174–199.

man', which probably did not exist (see p.86). The popularity of this view seems also on the wane.

(3) A few scholars apply to the gospels the literary categories of 'tragedy' or 'comedy', well-known from the study of various play-wrights, depending on whether the events of the passion and crucifixion of Jesus are most emphasized or whether the resurrection narratives are seen to give the gospels a more triumphant ending.[1] More detailed formal and structural parallels may also be identified, but it is important to note that neither classification directly impinges on the question of historicity. Drama, both comic and tragic, can recount either historical or fictitious events.

(4) The popular view which equates the gospels with midrash has already been discussed (see pp.44–49). There it was concluded that this term might apply, given careful definition, to component elements within the gospels, but that it was not helpful as a way of classifying their overall genre (p.53).

(5) More historically reliable Jewish precedents have often seemed attractive, however. Some have argued that the longer sections of the Old Testament dealing with one key figure or period of time offer the closest analogies to the gospels – *e.g.* the Exodus narrative focusing on Moses, or the lives and sufferings of some of the prophets.[2] This is a more promising approach than the others so far noted, although it does not automatically enhance the case for the gospels' historicity, since many of the same types of doubts as those surrounding the gospels emerge afresh in Old Testament criticism. More to the point, the Old Testament historical narratives never seem to describe the events or teachings of God's spokesmen with an eye to focusing specifically on the nature of those prophets or leaders, as the gospels do with Jesus. Instead, attention is diverted beyond the individual to God's dealings with his covenant people more generally, whereas in the gospels all the material seems constantly designed to raise the questions of Jesus' identity (recall *e.g.* Mk. 1:1; Jn. 20:31) and of allegiance to him.

(6) As noted in the discussion of the new literary criticism, some analysts attempt to extrapolate from the form of the parable to

---

[1]For comedy see esp. Dan O. Via, Jr., *Kerygma and Comedy in the New Testament* (Philadelphia: Fortress, 1975); for tragedy, Gilbert Bilezikian, *The Liberated Gospel: A Comparison of the Gospel of Mark and Greek Tragedy* (Grand Rapids: Baker, 1977).

[2]For the former, see Meredith G. Kline, 'The Old Testament Origins of the Gospel Genre', *WTJ* 38 (1975) pp.1–27; for the latter, Heinrich Kraft, 'Die Evangelien und die Geschichte Jesu', *TZ* 37 (1981), pp.321–341.

conclude that the entire gospel narratives are parabolic – stories designed to teach theological truth without reference to whether or not the events depicted within them actually happened (see p.57).[1] In addition to the criticisms of this view mentioned already, one should take notice of James Williams's recent critique of this theory, entitled *Gospel against Parable*. While agreeing with many of the insights of the new literary methods, Williams argues that the gospel genre came about by the combination or juxtaposition of two somewhat opposite fields of meaning: the parable ('realistic fiction based on the extension of a metaphor') and biography (a more historical structuring of 'the virtuous deeds and teachings of the hero').[2] Thus the gospels are significantly different from parables both in form and historical trustworthiness.

(7) This leads to the broadest and most widely proposed genre for the gospels–biography.[3] To modern readers, this categorization might immediately seem to reinforce belief in the gospels' historical reliability, but the matter is not so simple. In the ancient world, biographers often felt much freer than historians did to manipulate and elaborate their sources with speculative details which they believed would help to convey the character or personality of their subjects. By far the best known recent attempt to link the gospels with a relatively unhistorical type of biography is the work of C. H. Talbert.[4] Talbert finds three key elements which the gospels share with many ancient Graeco-Roman biographies – a mythical structure, an origin in the legends of the 'cult' or ritual of a religious community devoted to the traditions of its founder, and an optimistic 'world-affirming' perspective in spite of the many pessimistic philosophies of the day. The last of these three features seems valid and weighs against the identification of the gospels with apocalyptic as under (1) above. But the first two claims, if valid, would diminish the gospels' historicity. In fact, however, Talbert has misrepresented both the gospels and numerous Graeco-Roman biographies by lumping too many disparate texts into one broad category. Like those who see the gospels as are-

---

[1] See esp. Werner Kelber, *The Oral and the Written Gospel* (Philadelphia: Fortress, 1983), esp. pp.117–129.

[2] James G. Williams, *Gospel against Parable* (Sheffield: Almond, 1985), p.213.

[3] *E.g.* C. H. Votaw, *The Gospels and Contemporary Biographies in the Greco-Roman World* (Fortress: Philadelphia, 1970 [orig. 1915]); Philip L. Shuler, *A Genre for the Gospels: The Biographical Character of Matthew* (Philadelphia: Fortress, 1982).

[4] C. H. Talbert, *What is a Gospel?* (Philadelphia: Fortress, 1977; London: SPCK, 1978).

talogies, he relies too heavily on the notion of a fixed category of divine or immortal men in antiquity, into which he would place Jesus. He also bases too much on an older version of form criticism, which emphasized the origin of various gospel forms in the ritual and worship of the early church, at the expense of the findings of more recent redaction criticism which play down this element.[1]

Current research has therefore not overturned the consensus which W. G. Kümmel's standard New Testament introduction summarized over a decade ago:

> Viewed as a literary form, the Gospels are a new creation. They are in no way lives after the manner of Hellenistic biographies, since they lack the sense of internal and external history (as in lives of heroes), of character formation, of temporal sequence, and of the contemporary setting. Neither do the Gospels belong to the genre, memoirs, in which the collected stories and sayings from the lives of great men are simply strung together. Nor do they belong to the genus, miracle stories, in which the great deeds of ancient wonder-workers are glorified in a more or less stylized manner.[2]

Nevertheless, the question of the closest analogy to the gospels remains a valid one, even if none of the analogies is close enough for one to speak of identical genres. Here Martin Hengel's discussion proves instructive. Hengel maintains that the gospels should be compared to that form of ancient biography which supplied a 'relatively trustworthy historical report'.[3] As Hengel sees it, the three main reasons this comparison is often rejected are that (1) the gospels are too selective in what they report, (2) similarities with unhistorical writings of antiquity suggest themselves, and (3) early Christianity showed little interest in preserving historical information apart from the gospels and Acts. Hengel replies that

---

[1]For these and other criticisms in the most discerning analysis of Talbert's work to date, see D. E. Aune, 'The Problem of the Genre of the Gospels: A Critique of C. H. Talbert's *What is a Gospel?*', in *GP,2*, pp.9–60.

[2]W. G. Kümmel, *Introduction to the New Testament* (Nashville: Abingdon; London: SCM, 1975), p.37. More recently, *cf.* A. Dihle, 'Die Evangelien und die griechische Biographie', in *Das Evangelium und die Evangelien*, pp.383–411.

[3]Martin Hengel, *Acts and the History of Earliest Christianity* (London: SCM; Philadelphia: Fortress, 1979), p.16.

(1) is a problem besetting almost all ancient sources but it does not prevent one from labelling other texts as historical, (2) is exaggerated (as noted above, pp.236–238), and (3) underestimates the amount of corroborating evidence for the life of Jesus which does exist (much as chapter six pointed out).[1] The gospels may well differ from every other piece of literature in the history of writing but that does not permit one to treat them as unhistorical accounts of the events and people they choose to describe. Scholars may proceed by applying the valid canons of historical investigation to them.[2]

2 The burden of proof

A The theory[3]

Once one accepts that the gospels reflect attempts to write reliable history or biography, however theological or stylized its presentation may be, then one must immediately recognize an important presupposition which guides most historians in their work. Unless there is good reason for believing otherwise one will assume that a given detail in the work of a particular historian is factual. This method places the burden of proof squarely on the person who would doubt the reliability of a given portion of the text. The alternative is to presume the text unreliable unless convincing evidence can be brought forward in support of it. While many critical scholars of the gospels adopt this latter method, it is wholly unjustified by the normal canons of historiography. Scholars who would consistently implement such a method when studying other ancient historical writing would find the corroborative data so insufficient that the vast majority of accepted history would have to be jettisoned.[4] In the words of the historian G. J. Renier,

---

[1]Ibid., pp.3–34.

[2]F. Gerald Downing, 'Contemporary Analogies to the Gospels and Acts: "Genres" or "Motifs"?' in *Synoptic Studies,* ed. C. M. Tuckett (Sheffield: JSOT Press, 1984), pp.51–65, argues that one should look for common motifs rather than genres, in which case numerous parallels with other biographies and histories emerge.

[3]For further details on this section, see Stewart C. Goetz and Craig L. Blomberg, 'The Burden of Proof', *JSNT* 11 (1981), pp.39–63. *Cf.* esp. R. T. France, *Jesus and the Old Testament* (London: Tyndale, 1971; Grand Rapids: Baker, 1982), pp.15–24.

[4]As Neil J. McEleney, 'Authenticating Criteria and Mark 7: 1–23', *CBQ* 34 (1972), p.446, puts it, this is 'a presumption which one exercises in the reading of all history. Without it no historiography, ancient or modern, would win acceptance. Briefly, it is this, that one accepts a statement upon the word of the reporter unless he has reason not to do so.' The application of this presupposition to the gospels has been vigorously argued by conservative scholars but, as

We may find ... an event is known to us solely through an authority based entirely upon the statements of witnesses who are no longer available. Most of the works of Livy, the first books of the history of the Franks by Gregory of Tours, belong to this category. Since there is no other way of knowing the story they tell us, we must provisionally accept their version. This brings us back full sail to accepted history as the starting point of all historical investigation.[1]

Of course, 'revisionist' historians in fields other than biblical research often adopt needlessly sceptical stances too, but this quotation describes the way most historians normally operate.[2]

Some scholars attempt to adopt a mediating position between the 'extremes' of systematically doubting or trusting all unparalleled testimony. At first glance the position of M. D. Hooker, speaking of the gospel records of the teachings of Jesus, might seem fairest of all:

a debate about 'the burden of proof' is not very profitable, and is appropriate only if one takes the extreme position that the gospels represent historical reports of the words of Jesus, or the equally extreme view that Jesus himself said nothing sufficiently memorable to have come down to us ... It is perhaps more appropriate to suggest that the 'burden of proof' lies upon each scholar who offers a judgement upon any part of the material, to give a reasonable explanation for the existence of that saying, and to suggest a suitable *Sitz im Leben* [life-situation] for every saying or pericope.[3]

While undoubtedly well intentioned, this approach is unwork-

McEleney's endorsement demonstrates, it is by no means limited to them. *Cf.* also D. Lührmann, 'Die Frage nach Kriterien für ursprüngliche Jesusworte – eine Problemskizze', in *Jésus aux origines de la Christologie,* ed. J. Dupont (Gembloux: Duculot, 1975), p.70; Fritzleo Lentzen-Deis, 'Kriterien für die Beurteilung der Jesusüberlieferung in den Evangelien', in *Rückfrage nach Jesus,* ed. Karl Kertelge (Freiburg: Herder, 1974), p.96; Edward Schillebeeckx, *Jesus: An Experiment in Christology* (London: Collins; New York: Crossroad, 1979), pp.83, 87; and Jan Vansina, *Oral Tradition: A Study in Historical Methodology* (London: Routledge & Kegan Paul; Chicago: Aldine, 1965), pp.95–112.

[1]G. J. Renier, *History: Its Purpose and Method* (London: George Allen & Unwin, 1950), pp.90–91.

[2]For an incisive critique of revisionist tendencies among recent historians, see Oscar Handlin, *Truth in History* (Cambridge, MA and London: Harvard, 1979).

[3]Morna D. Hooker, 'Christology and Methodology', *NTS* 17 (1970–71), p.485. *Cf.* R. S. Barbour, *Traditio-Historical Criticism of the Gospels* (London: SPCK, 1972), p.46.

able in practice. It might prevent one from too hastily assuming as factual that which is not, but it would also leave one powerless to reject the obviously legendary, since frequently the rationale for the existence or use of fictitious material is too obscure to be recovered.[1] Moreover, as E. P. Sanders candidly admits, when one writes about Jesus this seemingly neutral attitude 'has the effect of shifting the burden of proof to the shoulders of those who affirm the authenticity of a saying or group of sayings'. Sanders goes on to explain, 'I find that I am not neutrally canvassing the material, assigning it as best I can to an appropriate place. I am . . . looking with a somewhat sceptical eye; I want to be *convinced* that a given saying is at least probably by Jesus before employing it.'[2] General presumptions about the trustworthiness or untrustworthiness of a document are crucial when one comes to evaluate its details which have no clear confirmation or contradiction elsewhere. Sanders' thorough study of the historical Jesus tellingly neglects virtually all the evidence which this book has surveyed in favour of the gospels' reliability and therefore eliminates a large percentage of the gospel material as inauthentic. In fact, the evidence which he neglects actually creates an overall presumption of the gospels' reliability, so that the proper approach should be to accept the specific details unless there is good reason for rejecting them.

Of course, many scholars believe there are good reasons for rejecting the authenticity of various passages and themes in the gospels. Legitimate criticism must then proceed to evaluate the validity of each objection. Many studies could be cited which employ this method but two excellent illustrations in recent articles will have to suffice. The one deals with Jesus' view of his death as an atonement for sin (Mk. 10:45), and the other examines his interpretation of the parable of the sower (Mk. 4:13–20).[3] The former passage supports one of the cardinal tenets of the Christian faith, while the latter influences the way

---

[1]*Cf.* Gilbert J. Garraghan, *A Guide to Historical Method* (Westport, CT and London: Greenwood, 1973 [orig. 1946]), p.262: 'to prove a tradition untrustworthy it is not by any means required that its origin be satisfactorily accounted for'.

[2]E. P. Sanders, *Jesus and Judaism* (London: SCM; Philadelphia: Fortress, 1985), p.13. For an incisive critique of Sanders' important study, see Scot McKnight's review in *TrinJ* n.s. 6 (1985), pp.219–225.

[3]Sydney H. T. Page, 'The Authenticity of the Ransom Logion (Mark 10:45b)', in *GP*,1, pp.137–161; Philip B. Payne, 'The Authenticity of the Parable of the Sower and Its Interpretation', in ibid., pp.163–207.

one interprets the rest of Jesus' parables, which comprise a large percentage of his teaching in the Synoptics. Clearly both issues merit attention.

B Sample applications

1 Mark 10:45

Sydney Page lists four main reasons why many scholars do not think that Jesus ever enunciated the doctrine of his death as a substitutionary sacrifice for sin, as found in Mark 10:45 – 'For the Son of man also came not to be served but to serve, and to give his life as a ransom for many.' (1) The two clauses do not fit well together; the first speaks only of service rather than atonement. (2) The past tense 'came' is not appropriate for a pre-crucifixion saying, since it refers to an event which has not yet occurred. (3) The word and concept of 'ransom' is found nowhere else in the teaching of Jesus. (4) Luke's parallel to this verse – 'I am among you as one who serves' (Lk. 22:27) – shows no knowledge of the second clause concerning Jesus' death.

None of these four objections proves very weighty. The concepts of servanthood and sacrifice are surely more similar than dissimilar, so a transition from the one to the other is quite natural. The very same combination appears in Isaiah's description of God's suffering servant (Is. 53:10), which has often been seen as the background for Jesus' remarks here.[1] The Greek past tense (the aorist) employed in the clause, 'The Son of man . . . came' refers to the overall purpose of Jesus' entire life. The gospels frequently uses this word 'came' (*ēlthon*) to describe Jesus' mission, even before it is complete (as *e.g.* in Lk. 12:49 – 'I came to cast fire on the earth and how I wish it were already kindled'), so it is scarcely inappropriate here. Jesus' lack of reference elsewhere to a 'ransom' is a particularly weak objection; if speakers had to say everything at least twice before historians would believe they had spoken on a topic, history books would have to be drastically rewritten. But in fact, Jesus does broach the topic elsewhere, if not in identical language, with his 'words of institution' at the Last Supper: 'this cup is the new covenant in my blood which is poured out for you' (Lk. 22:20b –

---

[1]This background has been strongly challenged. But see Martin Hengel, *The Atonement* (London: SCM; Philadelphia: Fortress, 1981), esp. pp.59–60; William J. Moulder, 'The Old Testament Background and the Interpretation of Mark x. 45', *NTS* 24 (1977–78), pp.120–127.

on the authenticity of these words, see p.133). Finally, it is not clear that Luke 22:27 refers to the same saying of Jesus as Mark 10:45. The contexts are different and Jesus makes similar statements about his role as servant elsewhere (*e.g.* Mk. 9:33–37; Mt. 23:11). So it seems to have been a topic with which he dealt more than once, without repeating the identical information on each occasion. Even if the two verses were genuinely parallel, the priority of Mark would create the presumption that Luke had deliberately omitted the missing clause instead of Mark's having invented it.

2 Mark 4:13–20

Very few scholars accept the authenticity of the interpretation of the parable of the sower. Yet Mark 4:13 claims that the interpretation of this parable supplies the key to interpreting all the parables of Jesus. Philip Payne itemizes no less than nine major reasons why Mark 4:13–20 has been labelled inauthentic, but they may be combined under three headings: (1) As a master of the art of telling parables, Jesus would not have had to explain them, any more than a good joke teller explains his punch lines. Even if he did occasionally add a brief conclusion, he would hardly have allegorized a parable point-for-point as appears here. (2) This particular interpretation, by focusing equally on each of the four kinds of soil, misses the main point of the parable which emphasizes the amazing harvest of the seed that fell in good soil. (3) The language of the interpretation shows a high percentage of words not regularly found on the lips of Jesus, not easily derived from an Aramaic original, and strikingly similar to the later vocabulary of a Hellenistic church.

The most forceful of these objections is the first. Current parable research, however, while rightly rejecting the arbitrary explanations and allegorizations so often given to the parables in the past, is coming to recognize that the parables often do require some interpretation in order to be intelligible. Almost all the ancient Rabbinic parables were given brief explanations and many ended with fairly elaborate allegorizations. The danger of misinterpreting Jesus' parables does not lie simply in perceiving detailed symbolism behind the key people and objects which they describe but in making equations which no one in Jesus' first-century Galilean peasant audience could have imagined.[1] Equating different types of seed, soil and fruit with the reception of a message and the results it produces would have been as natural among ancient Jewish farmers as it is today for those who have heard the parable explained so often. Other details which seem foreign today may have been less so then; for example, birds are not commonly linked with the devil (verse 15) in modern Western thought, but Old Testament and inter-testamental symbolism regularly used birds as harbingers of evil (*e.g.* 1 Ki. 14:11; Jubilees 11:5–24; Apocalypse of Abraham 13).

The fact that commentators cannot agree on what the main point of the parable is does not inspire much confidence in the claim that the interpretation is faulty as it stands. Probably most parables should be seen as making a cluster of two or three related points rather than being reducible to one brief summary statement. As for the linguistic distinctives, some have been exaggerated while others are only to be expected as the Jesus tradition was translated and applied. As Payne puts it, 'it is natural that the translation of Jesus' teaching into Greek in the church community would use "church vocabulary" where that vocabulary faithfully expressed Jesus' teaching. *Greek* vocabulary statistics cannot determine the authenticity of Jesus' *Aramaic* sayings.'[2]

When one examines the objections that have been raised over the authenticity of the ransom saying and the interpretation of the parable of the sower, one can see that they fall into two broad categories. Some are based on the lack of a certain type of evidence expected – the language does not reflect a Semitic substratum or the concept does not reappear elsewhere – while others stem from apparent contradictions with parallel testimony or forms. Usually, only the latter type of objection merits close examination. As David Fischer explains in his excellent guide to *Historians' Fallacies*, 'the nonexistence of an object is established not by nonexistent evidence but by affirmative evidence of the fact that it did not, or could not exist.'[3] More simply, arguments from silence usually prove little.[4] And since

---

[1] On the details of this paragraph and the next, see further Craig L. Blomberg, *Interpreting the Parables* (forthcoming) ch. six.

[2] Payne, 'Parable of the Sower', p.178.

[3] (New York: Harper & Row, 1970; London: Routledge and Kegan Paul, 1971), pp.62–63.

[4] *Cf.* John Lange, 'The Argument from Silence', *Hist & Th* 5 (1966), pp.288–301.

the most difficult cases of apparently contradictory testimony in the gospels have already been examined, it is unlikely that further detailed consideration of objections to particular passages would undermine the evidence which has been accumulating for the gospels' reliability. Virtually every portion of the gospels has been analysed many times over by scholars of all theological perspectives, and coherent responses are available in the scholarly literature to almost every sceptical objection.

3 Criteria of authenticity

A Theory

The proper procedure for evaluating the historicity of any portion of the gospels is thus to assume from the outset that its testimony is reliable and then to consider the force of various objections which might cause a person to change his or her mind. Much critical scholarship, however, inverts this process altogether by assuming the gospels to be unreliable unless powerful evidence can be brought forward in defence of specific passages or themes. The type of evidence which is accepted in this latter enterprise is that which passes stringent 'criteria of authenticity'. Not surprisingly, many scholars who adopt this method accept a much smaller percentage of the gospel material as authentic. Clearly much depends on one's starting point.

Nevertheless, even if for the sake of argument one adopts this more sceptical methodology, one should soon discover that critical scholarship is often *too* sceptical. With each passing decade since a group of German scholars, discontented with the wholesale historical scepticism of a previous era, embarked on 'the new quest for the historical Jesus',[1] more and more of the gospel tradition has been acknowledged as authentic. Some even view miracles and a high Christology as possible in principle. German scholarship, so often criticized as promoting extremely radical theories, has actually produced several of the

---

[1]The title derives from James M. Robinson's *A New Quest of the Historical Jesus* (London: SCM; Naperville: Allenson, 1959), although this work had important predecessors beginning with Ernst Käsemann's Marburg address in 1954, later translated as 'The Problem of the Historical Jesus', in *Essays on New Testament Themes* (London: SCM, 1964), pp.15–47.

chief proponents of this new openness to the trustworthiness of the gospel records.[1]

The four criteria of authenticity most commonly employed in the search for authentic gospel material are the criteria of multiple attestation or forms, of Palestinian environment or language, of dissimilarity and of coherence.[2] According to the first criterion, information or teaching which appears in more than one of the gospel sources or in several of the different categories of passages identified by form critics may be accepted as authentic. The more independent testimony one has to an event, the more confident one may be of its accuracy. Second, if the Greek text of a portion of the gospels seems to reflect a fairly literal translation of a Semitic original or if it describes events or concepts distinctive to early first-century Palestine, then one need not look to the later, more Hellenistic church for its origin. Third, the criterion of dissimilarity maintains that where the gospels' portrait of Jesus differs from the typical perspectives both of ancient Jewish belief and of early Christianity, then one may be sure of having authentic Jesus tradition. Because Jesus seemed to stand out so much from his contemporaries and because his first followers so easily deviated from his very demanding requirements, this criterion has appealed to many as the most helpful. Yet it can point only to what was distinctive about Jesus, and many critics make the grave mistake of arguing that wherever the gospels do not depict Jesus as noticeably different from both his predecessors and his followers then they must be rejected as inauthentic. They fail to realize that this use of the dissimilarity criterion brings it into flat contradiction with the criterion of Palestinian environment, which assumes that

---

[1]Ben F. Meyer, *The Aims of Jesus* (London: SCM, 1979), p.54, describes the recent stages of this growing conservatism as a shift from the new quest to the 'newest questioning'. Meyer lists the following distinguished German advocates of this new movement: Wolfhart Pannenberg, Peter Stuhlmacher, Jürgen Roloff, Martin Hengel, Heinz Schürmann, and Leonhard Goppelt. Of course, scholars continue to write books about Jesus, describing him in widely diverse ways, and some of Bultmann's students have become even more liberal than their teacher. A good introduction to the various perspectives is John Ziesler, *The Jesus Question* (Guildford: Lutterworth, 1980). For a comprehensive bibliography, see Warren S. Kissinger, *The Lives of Jesus: A History and Bibliography* (New York and London: Garland, 1985).

[2]For an elaboration of these criteria under eleven headings, see Robert H. Stein, 'The "Criteria" for Authenticity', in *GP*,1, pp.225–263. The most detailed study of these criteria and their application to the gospel tradition, with very positive conclusions about its reliability, is F. Lambiasi, *L'autenticità storica dei Vangeli: Studio di criteriologia* (Bologna: Dehoniane, 1976). It deserves translation into English.

Jesus was in part a product of his time. Finally, the criterion of coherence argues that whatever fits well with material authenticated by one of the other three criteria may also be accepted.

B Application

Using these criteria, even the person who is suspicious of the gospel tradition may come to accept a large percentage of it as historically accurate. A fairly widespread consensus of scholars would accept most of the parables as authentic. They appear in all the gospel sources and are based on a well-known Semitic form of speech. Yet Jesus' parables differ from those of the ancient rabbis by focusing primarily on the elucidation of the kingdom of God rather than the explanation of Jewish law. Virtually no subsequent Christian teaching took the form of parables, so it is impossible to accept the notion that some anonymous church member invented these rhetorical gems and successfully passed them off as having come from Jesus.[1] Many of the sayings about God's kingdom are received with equal enthusiasm. Jesus' teaching delicately balances belief in the arrival of God's reign or rule in the mission and message of Jesus himself with promises about events still in the future which will consummate that kingdom in all its fulness. This 'inaugurated eschatology' marks Jesus off as different from other Jews, who saw the kingdom as still primarily future, and from the church, which from its inception has more often than not neglected the doctrine of the second coming in practice if not in theory. Some scholars believe that the future and present aspects of Jesus' teaching on the kingdom of God create an irresolvable tension so that one or the other must be jettisoned as inauthentic. The more tension one perceives between the two, however, the less likely it is that the first Christians would have invented either, thereby creating a problem where it had not previously existed.[2]

---

[1] For more detail, see Philip B. Payne, 'The Authenticity of the Parables of Jesus', in *GP*,2, pp.329–344. One of the few who dissent on this issue is John Drury, *The Parables in the Gospels* (London: SPCK; New York: Crossroad, 1985). Drury convincingly argues that almost all the parables are allegories and that they fit their contexts in the gospels, but he wrongly deduces from these two points that they must be the redactional inventions of the evangelists. *Cf.* further, Blomberg, *Parables,* passim.

[2] The most comprehensive study of the kingdom of God in the teaching of Jesus is now G.R. Beasley-Murray, *Jesus and the Kingdom of God* (Exeter: Paternoster; Grand Rapids: Eerdmans, 1986). Beasley-Murray uses all the tools of critical scholarship and interacts with a large

Together the parables and other teachings on the kingdom comprise a sizeable majority of Christ's words in the gospels, so criticism has already gone a long way towards reaffirming the authenticity of the sayings tradition.

Equally widely attested, Semitic in language and content, and distinctive of the life and teaching of Jesus were the following: his concern for those rejected or looked down on by the various Jewish sects – the poor, the 'sinners and tax-collectors', women, lepers, Samaritans, and even Gentiles;[1] his frequent conflicts with the various Jewish authorities over the interpretation and application of the Law, especially the Sabbath regulations;[2] and his stringent demands for discipleship, involving total commitment to himself, with his enigmatic sayings about 'letting the dead bury the dead' (Mt. 8:21–22), 'hating father and mother' (Lk. 14:26), or 'selling everything' to follow him (Mk. 10:21 pars.).[3] In each of these three areas Jesus' beliefs and practices were much more radical than that which most of his contemporaries could tolerate. And the history of the church in all ages has demonstrated that it is much easier to revert to prejudice, legalism and half-hearted discipleship than to follow in Christ's steps.

Another substantial portion of the gospel tradition widely accepted as authentic, at least in part, is the collection of sayings in which Jesus refers to himself as the Son of man. This expression is never used elsewhere in the earliest Christian literature except on the lips of Stephen just before he is stoned (Acts 7:56). It occurs in the Old Testament as a messianic title only in Daniel 7:13,[4] and its meaning in intertestamental documents varies greatly – being applied for example both to Enoch and Melchizedek. As a result, while most scholars are ready to admit that some or all of the Son of man sayings in the gospels are

body of secondary literature, yet concludes that the vast majority of the gospel traditions relating to the kingdom of God are authentic.

[1]Jesus' 'manifesto' for the liberation of several of these oppressed groups appears in Luke 4:16–21; on the authenticity of which see Bruce Chilton, 'Announcement in *Nazara*: An Analysis of Luke 4:16–21', in *GP*,2, pp.147–172.

[2]See esp. Robert Banks, *Jesus and the Law in the Synoptic Tradition* (Cambridge: University Press, 1975); Stephen Westerholm, *Jesus and Scribal Authority* (Lund: Gleerup, 1978).

[3]*Cf.* Martin Hengel, *The Charismatic Leader and His Followers* (Edinburgh: T & T Clark; New York: Crossroad, 1981).

[4]Some would dispute its use as a messianic title even here, but see Robert D. Rowe, 'Is Daniel's "Son of Man" Messianic?' in *Christ the Lord,* ed. H. H. Rowdon (Leicester: IVP, 1982), pp.71–96.

authentic, they differ sharply over the meaning of that title. An important school of thought today holds that 'Son of man' was not messianic, but merely a Semitic figure of speech meaning 'a man' or 'a man in my situation' or even simply 'I'.[1] So for example when Jesus says that 'foxes have holes and the birds of the air have nests but the Son of man has nowhere to lay his head' (Mt. 8:20; Lk. 9:58), he means merely that someone in his situation, as an itinerant preacher, has no regular place to sleep from one day to the next. Sayings which use the title Son of man to refer to a heavenly being going to or coming from the presence of God (*e.g.* Lk. 12:8 – 'whoever confesses me before men, the Son of man will also confess him before the angels of God') are then often rejected as later developments of Christian theology.

Several considerations challenge this non-messianic interpretation of 'Son of man'. First, the evidence for the pre-Christian use of this expression, and even of just the word 'man', as a messianic title, is more widespread than many recognize.[2] Second, it is not as easy as many think to partition the Son of man sayings in the gospels into messianic and non-messianic categories. Even those passages which make sense when 'a man like me' is substituted for 'Son of man' usually involve claims by Jesus which imply an authority transcending that of his contemporaries. Third, the non-messianic interpretation requires the belief that the gospel writers universally mistranslated the Aramaic expression into Greek, since they use the definite article 'the' as if it were a title applicable to one person alone.[3] The best explanation for Jesus' use of this title, to the virtual exclusion of all other titles, is that the more common expressions for the Messiah were often linked in contemporary Jewish

---

[1]*Cf.*, with varying nuances, G. Vermes, *Jesus the Jew* (London: Collins; Philadelphia: Fortress, 1973), pp.160–191; Maurice Casey, *Son of Man: The Interpretation and Influence of Daniel 7* (London: SPCK, 1979); Barnabas Lindars, *Jesus Son of Man* (London: SPCK, 1983; Grand Rapids: Eerdmans, 1984). Dogmatic theology often arrives at similar conclusions by assuming that Son of man and Son of God must be opposites – the one referring to Jesus' true humanity and the other to his true deity. But there is no exegetical warrant for this opposition of the titles.

[2]See esp. William Horbury, 'The Messianic Associations of "The Son of Man" ', *JTS* 36 (1985), pp.34–55, who notes the following usually overlooked references: 11Q Melchizedek 1. 18 (from Qumran), Ezekiel the Tragedian (quoted by Eusebius), the fifth Sibylline oracle, the Targum to Psalm 80, and the Septuagint's rendering of Numbers 24:7.

[3]For these last two points, see esp. Seyoon Kim, *'The "Son of Man" ' as the Son of God* (Tübingen: Mohr, 1983).

thinking with a nationalistic, militaristic figure. Jesus eschewed this role and so preferred to use a form of self-reference which pointed to the prophesied heavenly representative of his people but which was sufficiently ambiguous to allow him to invest it with his own distinctive understanding of his mission.[1]

When scholars turn to more explicit titles for Jesus' unique origin and identity, they often balk at acknowledging their appropriateness. Yet a fair application of the criteria of authenticity should lead to their acceptance as well. For example, the 'Son of God' is a title applied to Jesus by the gospel writers to highlight his messianic and divine origin as the fulfilment of such Old Testament prophecies as Psalm 2:7 and 2 Samuel 7:14.[2] All but the most conservative commentators refuse to accept the idea that Jesus could have understood himself to have such a supernatural origin and relegate this title to the creativity of the later church in its desire to exalt Jesus and embellish the traditions about his life.

Nevertheless, the same commentators will often quickly admit, utilizing the criterion of dissimilarity, that one of the most authentic data about Jesus' self-understanding was his unparalleled use of the intimate word for Father, *Abba*, in his prayers to God. By the criterion of coherence, however, it is only a short step from here to accepting the view that Jesus saw himself as the Son of God. Richard Bauckham traces the logical progression of reasoning which should be followed: if Jesus' use of Abba is authentic, then his language about sonship in Matthew 11:27 par. should also be accepted ('All things were delivered to me by my Father, and no one knows the Son except the Father, nor does anyone know the Father except the Son and those to whom the Son desires to reveal him'). This passage, which has been often called a 'Johannine thunderbolt' in the Synoptic tradition, because of its remarkable similarity to many of John's otherwise distinctive discourses of Jesus, in turn permits one to accept much of the Fourth Gospel's teaching about Jesus' sonship, where he is most frequently referred to as the Son of God, despite the special scepticism often reserved for

---

[1]Similarly, *e.g.,* F. F. Bruce, 'The Background to the Son of Man Sayings', in *Christ the Lord,* pp.50–70.

[2]See esp. Martin Hengel, *The Son of God* (London: SCM; Philadelphia: Fortress, 1976).

John's traditions (see chapter five).[1] Or, in A. E. Harvey's words,

> Jesus had indeed shown that absolute obedience to God, had spoken of God with that intimate authority, and had acted with the unique authorisation which belonged to God's representative and agent on earth, which would be characteristic of one who was (in the sense usually ascribed to 'sonship' in antiquity) in very truth 'Son of God'; and the reversal of the world's judgment upon him, which was implied by the event his followers called the Resurrection, enabled them to describe Jesus with absolute confidence as 'the Son', a title which would certainly have been correct in his lifetime, and was presumably acknowledged by supernatural beings, but was too momentous to be openly acknowledged even by those of his followers who had found their way to faith in him.[2]

Illustrations could be multiplied. A chapter has already been devoted to the authenticity of the miracle stories and it was noted how well they cohere with Jesus' authentic teaching about the kingdom of God (see pp.92–96). One of the most doubted portions of Jesus' teachings in the Synoptic gospels is his use of the word 'church' (*ekklēsia*). Jesus' three references to founding a church, all in Matthew (Mt. 16:18; 18:17 [2X]), seem to put him at odds with his other teaching, which appears anti-institutional and which envisages the near demise of this age. Thus plans for organizing a community of his followers into settled patterns of worship would be superfluous. Still, both the Greek and underlying Semitic words for church need mean nothing more than an 'assembly', and the mere fact that Jesus appointed twelve disciples, apparently corresponding to the twelve tribes of Israel, suggests that he intended that some kind of organization of people carry on his work after him. The question of the imminence of the end is bound up with the faulty notion that Christ was convinced he would return within the lifetime of his disciples (see above, pp.33–34). A criterion of 'necessary

---

[1]Richard Bauckham, 'The Sonship of the Historical Jesus in Christology', *SJT* 31 (1978), pp.245–260.

[2]A. E. Harvey, *Jesus and the Constraints of History* (London: Duckworth; Philadelphia: Westminster, 1982), pp.167–168. In Harvey's understanding of 'the sense usually ascribed to "sonship" in antiquity', there are of course no metaphysical overtones of equation with deity.

explanation' can be invoked here too. Some historical event must lie behind the rise of Peter to prominence as leader of the early church; Peter's record of unfaithfulness in discipleship would have otherwise disqualified him rather than promoting him. Without some commissioning from Jesus such as that found in the famous 'keys to the kingdom' passage, which includes the statement 'on this rock I will build my church' (Mt. 16:18), one is hard pressed to explain how the man who denied Jesus three times gained a position of such prominence in the church so soon afterwards.[1]

In fact, patient application of the criteria of authenticity can itself eventually lead one to accept virtually all the gospel tradition. I. H. Marshall's *I Believe in the Historical Jesus* well illustrates the confident spirit with which one can approach the testimony of the Synoptics while utilizing the standard critical methodology, although Marshall does not attempt to canvass all the data.[2] René Latourelle displays even greater optimism and provides a long list of details in the gospels which have been accepted as genuine by authors of major critical studies employing the criteria of authenticity. These include the linguistic, social, political, economic, cultural and religious environments depicted; the great events of Jesus' life–baptism, temptation, transfiguration, teaching on the kingdom, call to repentance, parables, beatitudes, teaching on God as Father, the miracles and exorcisms as signs of the kingdom, the betrayal, agony, trial, crucifixion, burial and resurrection; the controversies with the scribes and Pharisees; Jesus' attitudes of simplicity and authority, of purity and compassion; the Christology implied by the sign of Jonah, the sign of the temple and the 'Son of man' title; the rejection of a space- or time-bound kingdom; and the calling and mission of the apostles, coupled with their initial enthusiasm, subsequent lack of understanding and final betrayal and desertion. Latourelle sums up: 'On each of the subjects enumerated, we can invoke the testimony of many exegetes. To the extent that researches [*sic*] go on, the material acknowledged as authentic grows ceaselessly until it

---

[1] For a full discussion of the arguments in favour of the authenticity of the 'church' passages, see Ben F. Meyer, *The Aims of Jesus* (London: SCM, 1979), pp.185–197; Gerhard Maier, 'The Church in the Gospel of Matthew: Hermeneutical Analysis of the Current Debate', in *Biblical Interpretation and the Church: Text and Context,* ed. D. A. Carson (Exeter: Paternoster, 1984; Nashville: Thomas Nelson, 1985), pp.45–63.

[2] (London: Hodder & Stoughton; Grand Rapids: Eerdmans, 1977).

covers the whole Gospel.'[1] Royce Gruenler studies in detail the one area noticeably absent from Latourelle's otherwise comprehensive list – the 'high' or explicit Christology which portrays Jesus as more than a man. Gruenler shows how even the small handful of sayings accepted as authentic by more radical critics contain within them claims for authority and power which make no sense for a merely human teacher to put forward. The criterion of coherence thus permits one to accept those portions of the gospels which elucidate more explicitly Jesus' divine origin.[2]

Whichever perspective is adopted at the outset, then, an identical conclusion may be reached. Whether by giving the gospels the benefit of the doubt which all narratives of purportedly historical events merit or by approaching them with an initial suspicion in which every detail must satisfy the criteria of authenticity, the verdict should remain the same. The gospels may be accepted as trustworthy accounts of what Jesus did and said. One cannot hope to prove the accuracy of every detail on purely historical grounds alone; there is simply not enough data available for that. But as investigation proceeds, the evidence becomes sufficient for one to declare that what can be checked is accurate, so that it is entirely proper to believe that what cannot be checked is probably accurate as well.[3] Other conclusions, widespread though they are, seem not to stem from even-handed historical analysis but from religious or philosophical prejudice. As the Roman historian, A. N. Sherwin-White, once marvelled, 'it is astonishing that while Graeco-Roman historians have been growing in confidence, the twentieth-century study of the Gospel narratives, *starting from no less promising material*, has taken so gloomy a turn.'[4] Such gloom should be replaced by a radiant endorsement of the historical reliability of the four gospels, and there are some encouraging signs that in places this is in fact beginning to occur.

---

[1]René Latourelle, *Finding Jesus through the Gospels* (New York: Alba, 1979), pp.238–239.

[2]Royce G. Gruenler, *New Approaches to Jesus and the Gospels* (Grand Rapids: Baker, 1982), pp.19–131.

[3]*Cf.* Humphrey Palmer, *The Logic of Gospel Criticism* (London: Macmillan; New York: St. Martin's, 1968), p.34.

[4]A. N. Sherwin-White, *Roman Society and Roman Law in the New Testament* (Oxford: Clarendon, 1963), p.187. *Cf.* the similar, more recent verdict of another classicist, Blaiklock, *Jesus*, p.34.

Postscript

Are the gospels historically reliable? Some conservative readers would reply affirmatively simply because they believe their doctrine of the inspiration of Scripture requires them to. This overlooks the fact that God can communicate truth through a wide variety of literary forms; in fact over half of Scripture is written in literary genres other than historical ones – poetry, proverbs, prophecy, epistles, and apocalypses. Even within the gospels, Jesus' teaching in parables highlights how narrative prose can communicate theological truth by means of realistic but fictitious stories. A superficial appearance of history therefore proves little. There is no short-cut to valid biblical interpretation; detailed historical analysis with all its uncertainties must be employed. And although Christians understandably emphasize the role of the Spirit in illuminating the interpreter, objective standards must be maintained against which apparent illumination may be measured (1 Jn. 4:1–3; 1 Cor. 14:29). At the other end of the confessional spectrum, many radical critics would answer the question negatively, thinking that proper historical method requires them to disbelieve any narratives as thoroughly permeated by supernatural events, theological interpretation, and minor variations among parallels as are the four gospels. This approach misunderstands the role and methods of historical enquiry and often stems from a faulty view of the findings of philosophy and natural science as well (see chapter three).

Against both of these extreme positions, it has been argued here that the gospels must be subjected to the same type of historical scrutiny given to other writings of antiquity but that they can stand up to such scrutiny admirably. Admittedly, this conclusion represents a 'minority report' among biblical scholars worldwide, but the minority is not nearly as small as it was a generation ago. The *Gospel Perspectives* series, on which this study has so heavily drawn, would command widespread approval among the five hundred or so members of two international societies of biblical and theological scholars – the British-based Tyndale Fellowship and its

North American counterpart, the Institute for Biblical Research. Most of the series' contributors belong to one of these societies.

If the trustworthiness of the gospels represents a verdict which careful historical analysis can yield regardless of the confessional perspectives of its practitioners, why do so many still resist this conclusion? The answers vary from one person to the next. Anti-supernaturalism is still deeply entrenched in many circles, even where it is not explicitly affirmed. Others, more aware of the proper use of historical criticism, nevertheless implement that criticism inconsistently. Some seem merely to bow to the pressure of consensus, reiterating what is most academically respectable without ever seriously grappling with unfashionable alternatives. Still others may simply be unaware of many of the studies surveyed in this volume. In many cases, however, scholars appear genuinely convinced that the historical evidence points to different conclusions. One must sincerely respect their right to this opinion, but this book is offered in the hope of illustrating the types of arguments which would have to be countered successfully if such opinion is to be objectively supported. More often than not, it seems that the full weight of the case for the gospels' trustworthiness has not been felt.

The question of presuppositions is equally crucial. Too often conservatives summarily dismiss sceptical studies as merely developing the logical inferences of invalid assumptions. To be sure, this allegation has some force, but few works are so consistently deductive that they contain no discussion of hard data for others to take the time to sift through. Similarly, more radical critics regularly charge conservatives with concluding only what their beliefs about Jesus and the Bible already permit. This charge is also occasionally valid. Perhaps some will try to apply it to this book; the series on which it is based represents the research of committed evangelicals so it surprises no one that its conclusions are conservative. The crucial difference, however, is that this research has self-consciously tried to avoid presupposing the infallibility of Scripture or the deity of Christ, but has merely attempted to follow the standard methods of historical enquiry. It derives from a willingness to consider the possibility that these traditional beliefs might have to be abandoned if historical investigation were to demonstrate them to be unwarranted. No such demonstration has yet appeared. On the other hand, the critical scholarship which has abandoned these beliefs virtually never considers where its investigations might lead if it questioned *its* starting-point and took seriously the possibility of the divine origin of Scripture and of Jesus.

In the introduction to this volume, it was argued that C. S. Lewis's famous 'trilemma' overlooked an important fourth possibility. If Jesus was not the Lord as the gospels claimed he was, he need not have been a liar or a lunatic; the stories themselves could have been legendary (see p.xx). Although the difficulty of trying to summarize so much detail in short compass has become obvious, an attempt has been made to look at all the main reasons why parts of the gospels have been viewed as legendary or unhistorical. Those reasons all seem unconvincing. The gospels may therefore be trusted as historically reliable. Now Lewis's conclusion follows with relentless logic:

> I am trying here to prevent anyone saying the really foolish thing that people often say about Him: 'I'm ready to accept Jesus as a great moral teacher, but I don't accept his claim to be God.' That is the one thing we must not say. A man who was merely a man and said the sort of things Jesus said would not be a great moral teacher. He would either be a lunatic – on a level with the man who says he is a poached egg – or else he would be the Devil of Hell. You must make your choice. Either this man was, and is, the Son of God: or else a madman or something worse. You can shut Him up for a fool, you can spit at Him and kill Him as a demon; or you can fall at His feet and call Him Lord and God. But let us not come with any patronising nonsense about His being a great human teacher. He has not left that open to us. He did not intend to.[1]

Yet that is one thing biblical critics too often continue to say. If it is unfair to begin historical enquiry by superimposing a theological interpretation over it, it is equally unfair to ignore the theological implications that arise from it. It is thus the earnest desire of all of the contributors to the *Gospel Perspectives* series, and of many other recent researchers, that the growing openness to the reliability of the gospel tradition in many scholarly circles will

---

[1] C. S. Lewis, *Mere Christianity* (London: Collins; New York: Macmillan, 1955), p.52.

continue to increase and that the invitation to discipleship which the historical Jesus extended to those who heard him will be heeded within the walls of academie. It is the aim of this book to bring the academic debate to a wider readership and to introduce its audience to the substantial body of literature which supports the historicity of Matthew, Mark, Luke and John. Readers ought not to stop with the conclusion of this book but to be encouraged to immerse themselves in the rich resources of modern gospel scholarship surveyed here.

SCRIPTURE·INDEX

263

A U T H O R · I N D E X

267